ONE LIFE

CHRISTIAAN BARNARD

ONE LIFE

by CHRISTIAAN BARNARD
and CURTIS BILL PEPPER

THE MACMILLAN COMPANY

Library of Congress Catalog Card Number: 78-99020

FIRST AMERICAN EDITION 1970

The Macmillan Company
Collier-Macmillan Canada Ltd., Toronto, Ontario

Printed in the United States of America

*For Louis Washkansky
and Denise Darvall*

CONTENTS

PART I
THE GREAT KAROO

CHAPTER 1

PERHAPS THE FIRST TIME I doubted God could handle all the accidents of mankind occurred while attending a church service on New Year's Eve in Beaufort West, South Africa, where I grew up as a boy.

My mother was there to play the organ and I stood next to her. She was slightly deaf and a quick nudge was needed to start her off at the correct moment. I was expected also to fill the bellows of the organ, keeping the air pressure at a level marked by a little weight on a cord. This was done by pumping a hand lever, and often all my force—I was twelve then—was needed to keep the weight at its proper level.

Success depended largely upon what music was played. Light trills and runs did not affect the weight much. But deep notes and chords—especially in numbers such as "Many a Brave Heart Is Asleep in the Deep"—sent it soaring upward toward disaster. When this occurred, I pumped wildly to catch up, desperately aware that I could never provide sufficient wind for everyone to shout their love of the Lord—at least not long enough for it to count much or be heard very far.

Yet this evening had not gone too badly. Dominie Rabie, the minister, had dropped one hymn to pick up extra time for his New Year's sermon, saving me a lot of work. So I imagined the service would end with the weight down low and my spirits on high.

The minister began by standing erect and wordless in his circular pulpit, until the congregation fell into obedient silence. Once I had entered the church at night and seen the devil in that same pulpit. He had long donkey ears, a tail crawling about like a snake, and a pitchfork long enough to skewer anybody, even in the back row. Now in the same spot stood Dominie Rabie—his little gray beard jumping up and down over the Bible as though it, too, was pointing the way—while behind him, beyond the organ pipes, lay dark shadows. The devil could be lurking there, hiding from the bright light which fell on a cloth draped over the lectern, bearing the golden words *Die Waarheid*—meaning in Afrikaans, The Truth.

Perhaps it was this and the late hour—the bells were soon to toll midnight—that caused me to remember this entire night so vividly, including the minister's first startling words,

"Add up all your sins for this past year and put them in a pile before you! [pause] Which one of us, I repeat which one of *you* can lift up his awful load? [pause] Or who among us can walk out of here without his back bent under his own terrible burden?"

I tried to figure out how big was my burden and if I could pick it up. But it was no use and I soon gave up. For how was it possible to put into one pile such differing events as cheating the city on dead mice, eating stolen candy, killing a cat, robbing an orchard, or touching a girl's leg under a wild apple bush? Besides, all of these happenings involved other people— some of them grownups. So whose pile did they belong in?

Take the mice, for example. The city paid one penny for every mouse. We caught them in traps and then, mouse in hand, ran down to the health department to receive a piece of paper worth one penny when presented at the City Hall. In order to get the paper, it was necessary to show the mouse to Tom, the caretaker, then raise the lid off a big drum full of corrosive Jeyes Fluid and drop it in.

That was theoretically the end of the mouse—but not always. If old Tom was not looking, we would drop the mouse behind the drum, bang down the lid, and take the receipt. Afterwards, we would sneak back, grab the mouse and stuff it into a pocket—showing up again later in the day with the same old mouse for another penny.

Fanie Bekker claimed the largest mouse tally of four pence, but I came close to him with a little brown number that brought me a tickey, or three pennies, before its tail broke off. You had to work fast on them before something like that happened, or they got suspiciously stiff and too dangerous to handle.

Even so, I suspected Tom knew what was going on and was either kind to us or perhaps figured that a little extra money for one mouse would only drive us into catching many more in the long run. So he was either a partner in our crime or simply moved by good Christian charity. Whatever it was, the mice did not all belong in my pile.

Most certainly, Conradie, the fat policeman, was as guilty as we were in stealing fruit. This was really fun and always a success. It began by sneaking into the orchards on the south side of town, to gather pomegranates, apricots, quince, and lemons—big, thick ones you could eat without sugar. We would pick for a while, until Conradie came—announcing himself from a distance by shouting. This gave us a good headstart, which we needed since he had a bicycle and we were running it barefoot, our shirts bulging with fruit.

The usual escape route was through a blue gum grove, then past Gold-enboom's shop, and so down to the river bank. Conradie followed, huffing and puffing and yelling at us—but always at a safe distance. Once at the riverside, we would sit down to eat the fruit and give Conradie his share when he eventually caught up with us, crying, "Naughty boys!"—laughing until he choked on fruit pits.

That sin certainly belonged more in his pile than in my own or in that of Fanie Bekker or Michel Rossouw or Piet Theron.

From the pulpit on high, Dominie Rabie was now reading Psalm 141:

> Set a watch, O Lord, before my mouth;
> Keep the door of my lips.
> Incline not my heart to any evil thing,
> To practise wicked words with men
> That work iniquity:
> And let me not eat of their dainties.

By not eating dainties did he mean the food we stole from Mortimer & Hill? Michel Rossouw did it and he was always very successful since his father was general manager. He simply walked in and helped himself to sardines, condensed milk, Vienna sausages, peppermint crisps, and choco-lates. Loaded with these delights, we would ride on his bike out to the dam at the edge of town. Or we would go next door to my backyard and climb up into the little house in the walnut tree. This feast was a regular weekly event.

> Let the righteous smite me; it shall be
> a kindness . . .

Nobody was smiting Michel for all that food. Nor were they after us for stealing the feed sacks. These were kept in a rear shed by old Jaap, the storekeeper, who used them for sugar and corn meal. Empty sacks were worth two pennies each. Translated into more practical terms, a sack was thus worth one Billy Bunter magazine for boys and one red Nestlé choco-late from the slot machine at the railway station. Or five sacks were equal to a movie ticket. Michel used to crawl into the shed on Wednesday after-noon, when the store was closed, and throw them over the fence into my backyard. He worked fast and hard, and the sacks would come sailing over like kites, settling on the woodpile, on top of the outhouse, and even in the pear tree.

Later we would sell them back to old Jaap, who said, *"Ya, ya"* and paid us twopence each without any questions asked.

> When their judges are overthrown in stony places,
> They shall hear my words;
> For they are sweet.

So were the words of Michel, for he was very kindhearted and would share everything he had with me. If I lacked money for a movie, he would obtain enough for both of us. If he had a sweet, half of it would be mine. It went like that in all things. I could not remember how he entered my life or how I met him. He was just there. He came in the afternoons and he had a special call, a sort of yodel. Then I knew Michel was there and we would go out together.

His family was rich and they lived up on a hill in a house named "Petra"—rock. They had a radio set, a Frigidaire and a pantry filled with food. In the backyard they had an extra large reservoir for rainwater—used especially for ladies to wash their hair—where we swam naked at night when everyone was in bed. I slept there sometimes, ate there often, and I loved Michel and his family.

His father was always very neat and well dressed, even when we went hunting springbok. I called him Mister Rossouw and liked the way he threw back his head and laughed at a good joke. His wife, Aunt Connie, was short and fat, but a very lovable sort of woman. I don't think she ever beat Michel or his brother, Laurie.

I felt secure and safe in their house—as though I was on a vacation. The return to my own home late at night, or the next morning if my father allowed me to sleep over, was the end of fun and laughter—a return to household chores, school work, and to the mystery of my own self before my three brothers, my mother—and my father.

> Our bones are scattered at the grave's mouth,
> As when one cutteth and cleaveth wood upon the
> earth.

Yes, I killed the cat—but that cat killed six little bantam chicks. They were my chicks and they had just been hatched. I could see them from my window where I was studying—moving about in the sunlight. After a bit, I went into the kitchen for a drink of water and suddenly heard the mother bantam making a big racket. I ran outside, but it was too late. Yellow feathers and tiny heads lay scattered over the gravel, separate from four motionless chicks. Two of them had been carried away or just gobbled up.

Back in my room, I tried to study. Then I saw the cat sitting on top of the wall cleaning itself in the sun. That did it for me. I took down my eighteen-gauge and killed it with one shot through the window. When I told my father about it he was sad—but he saw my grief and did not scold me.

> Keep me from the snares which they
> Have laid for me . . .

Jessie Grimbeeck did not put out a snare for me, nor did I lay one for her. It just happened without any plans at all during a game at the school social when we both hid under a kei-apple bush. I was there first when she popped in after me. There were flowers on the bush like yellow stars and when she wiggled close to hide better, her leg touched my hand. I did nothing at all except stay there, but afterwards I felt unclean and sorry because she was such a nice girl. I knew it was wicked and something I should not do again. Yet merely thinking about it made me excited and very worried about what would happen if Jessie and I ever ended up under another bush.

Dominie Rabie closed his service with a benediction for everyone. All that remained was for my mother to play a hymn while the congregation filed out. She sat there, her rich auburn hair up in a bun, her head tilted toward the ceiling as though waiting for a sign from on high. I gave it to her from nearer at hand, using two fingers to indicate people walking from the church. She got the message and plunged into a spirited "Onward Christian Soldiers"—obviously convinced this had the proper spirit to send everyone with his bundle of sin from the House of the Lord into the waiting New Year.

Earlier, I had looked for Jessie but not seen her. Now I looked again— with a mixed sense of joy and guilt—only to discover that a group of people had gathered around the front pew where a woman had fainted. She was old and dressed in black, and they had stretched her out on the bench as though she were dead and ready for Dominie Rabie to make a funeral oration.

Oh Lord, I thought, if that happens I'll never be able to pump the whole thing—unless there is very little music.

Gradually everyone left, except the small group gathered around the old lady on the front bench. One woman removed her shoes and began massaging her feet. Another put a hymnbook under her head, causing a yellow, pie-shaped hat to spring away like a departing halo.

I leaned forward, wondering how this could happen in church. You could faint in a closed car or in a crowd, or you could even go to sleep and never wake up. But while singing the praises of the Lord—wasn't this the safest, most glorious moment of the whole week? Had the old woman been so wicked she could not pick up her bundle? If so, then church was a dangerous place for those suffering from great sin. It did not seem right, and I decided to ask my father about it.

In the excitement, I forgot to tell my mother to stop playing. As a result, her music urging Christian soldiers onward boomed out over an empty church, bouncing off the vaulting brown ceiling and onto the little group huddled below.

Finally, one of the elders called up to me, "Son, every Christian soldier who can do so has gone home. So your mother can let up now, thank you."

On the way out, the church door was flung against us by a man who seemed very frightened. He was out of breath and he rushed down the aisle toward the old lady. I wanted to follow for a closer look—maybe the woman was really dead—but my mother was in a hurry. It was after midnight and we had to be up at 4 A.M. to begin the drive to the seacoast for our summer vacation.

"I still have to get the food ready," she said.

"I'll be along in a minute."

"No—you come now."

On the sidewalk, a little girl ran toward us. I had never seen her before but obviously she was in trouble. Her blonde hair was a mess from running, and she was sobbing so much she could hardly run anymore. I watched her turn into the church and decided she was the daughter of the man we had seen. Her father had gone ahead, leaving her to follow, all alone and frightened. This made me quite sad and I wanted more than ever to go back into the church.

"Please, Mother, I'll come soon."

"No."

Once, many years ago, that had happened to me. I must have been six at the time—about the same age as that little blond girl—and it was linked to the first memories of my father. I was lying with him in bed, as a young boy lies with his father, when a doctor came to examine him. Upon seeing us, the doctor said: "My boy, your father is too ill for you to lie with him in the bed."

They took him to the hospital with double pneumonia and my mother began to send me across the town each day with something for him to eat—a little soup, or some jelly or custard in a bowl.

One night they sent word my father was dying and my mother hurried to the hospital. After some time, she came home and made some hot soup— telling me to take it to my father. It might, she said, help save his life.

I ran alone through the dark streets, afraid I would not get there in time. As I ran, the soup spilled on my legs, burning them. It began to rain and I was frightened, realizing for the first time that someday I would be alone in the world.

I remember the red polished cement floor of the hospital, the smell of disinfectants and medicines—and then my father. He had almost suffocated from parotitis, until the doctors slit his throat. When I arrived, the throat was bandaged, yet blood continued to seep through and my father was gasping for air. He seemed to be dying and I could only think of how often he had spoken of God and the angels—and now he was going to see them in Heaven.

Sometime later, I returned to find him in the garden, walking between two nursing sisters with long white veils. They appeared beautiful—luminous and white, with the sun shining through their veils. My father was walking for the first time, his arms around their shoulders, and both sisters were smiling as though they shared with him a secret too deep to tell anyone.

"It looks as if your father hasn't finished yet," said my mother.

We had walked across Church Street, passed the Town Hall, and were standing in front of a smaller church—my father's. It had not yet let out, which was unusual since both churches generally finished at the same time. Yet from inside we could hear my father was still engaged with his sermon. After that was over, he normally met with the church elders. My mother was concerned that this might keep him too long.

"Go in and let him know after he's finished that he's needed to help us get ready for the trip."

I nodded and ducked into the church—glad not to be sent to bed.

> And Jesus said unto him:
> "Foxes have holes,
> And birds of the air have nests—
> But the son of man hath not where to lay his head . . ."

It was my father in the pulpit. He had white hair and a white mustache and hazel-green eyes, and, standing in the box above us, he looked like an old eagle peering from his nest into a distant valley. Over the pulpit hung a white plaster canopy and from below it was supported by curving arms of wrought iron. The Bible lay open on a flatboard and below it in front hung a black velvet cloth with golden tassels and five golden words: THE HOUSE OF THE LORD. My father stood as always, his arms extended, hands grasping the rim of the pulpit as though he continued to peer into the valley and relate what happened to Jesus on his way to Jerusalem—how it happened that a man came up and said he would also go along, but first needed to go home and say good-by to everyone. Jesus, however, did not want that:

> No man, having put his hand to the plow,
> And then looking back,
> Is fit for the kingdom of God.

The assembly nodded approval, and I wondered if this applied to my mother. She wanted my father home to help pack as soon as he finished the sermon, while he was in the pulpit saying anyone who took his hand off the Lord's plow was not fit for the kingdom of God. That certainly meant talking to the elders for as long as they needed him. It was an impossible situation, and I tried to decide what to do. Finally I gave up and began to look around the church. One of the Morkels saw me and nodded. Every member of that family could sing beautifully, and I hoped my father would finish soon so that we could hear them sing the final hymn. This was a different church than the other one. I felt more at home here. It was my father's church, of course, but there was something else which I came to recognize when I grew older.

The other church, the *Boerekerk,* or Farmer's Church, had a great white steeple that rose up over the town—so high that when you looked at it from Donkin Street it seemed to be taller than the Nuweveld Mountains. It shot up into the sky in a most startling manner, helped along the way by thrusting gothic arches and stone ramparts. In its race to heaven, the tower paused briefly at a black-faced clock with white, bold Roman numerals. Then it shot upward into a white steeple, topped by a black weather-vane rooster that turned about haughtily—often refusing to move unless the wind shook every tree in town.

Our church, on the other hand, had a plain red roof like a big barn and no steeple in the sky. There was a black one, shaped as though made for a church in Russia, on top of the Town Hall next door. It was this white mansion topped by a Russian steeple that stood between us and the great Farmer's Church—two houses of worship separated by the seat of civic power. Nor did we have a church bell. The bell which hung on a frame in the yard of the big church also summoned us.

The two churches were also different inside. Being of Dutch Reformed faith and thus of Calvinist descent, they were both severe and lacked any art suggesting the children of God could sweat and love and—alas—sin. Yet they differed in the substance of their simplicity. The other church had a vast interior, made of natural wood that pleased the eye with beautiful planes and joints. They rose with the ease of a soaring hymn into a vaulted ceiling that surely touched a corner of heaven. Our church more clearly touched a corner of the earth where man had come to sing and pray. It was made of broad beam planks and painted blue and white. It had little gothic arches shaped from pine wood and patches of red and blue glass in its windows. Less than a reach for heaven, it resembled more a shelter on earth and was as warm and comfortable as a manger.

Yet something else separated the two churches—beyond their different appearance or the walls of the Town Hall. The barrier was immediately evident in the faces of men and women, as they often sang the same hymn at the same moment under separate roofs. For the people of the big church were white, and those who came to my father were colored.

The main difference was there—in the color of the skin. For just as they shared the same God, the two people also shared a common ancestry more recent than the parenthood of Adam and Eve. The whites were a mixture of Dutch, French Huguenot, German, and British—and called themselves Europeans. The nonwhites were a mixture of European, Malayan and Hottentot—an indigenous, pre-Negroid South African people, today almost extinct. As such, they were called non-Europeans, or, more commonly, "coloreds."

So the two people shared some common ancestors, yet sat in different, untouching churches. Similarly, the two ministers shared a common faith, yet stood in separate, untouching pulpits. Both were ordained pastors of the Dutch Reformed Church. Yet their different assignments in the same town gave them different titles. Mr. Rabie was a Dominie, or minister to the Europeans. My father was Eerwaarde, or Reverend, and a missionary to the coloreds. There were 7,000 of them, against 3,400 whites, living in primitive conditions—suffering from sickness, hunger, and all the inherited ills of social outcasts. My father's mission was therefore immensely more difficult. For this, and for occasionally standing in as minister to the Europeans, he received each month twenty pounds, or about fifty dollars—one-third of the sum paid to Dominie Rabie. Besides this, the minister of the European church socially had little to do with my father, his brother in Christ.

To help relieve our poverty—on Christmas morning my brothers and I would find our hung stockings empty, except for a few pitiful pieces of toffee candy—my mother played the organ in the European church when they had no one else. My father also got one pound ten shillings, or about four dollars, a month for preaching to prisoners in the jail. Every Sunday he would rise early and walk two miles through town to be at the jail by seven o'clock.

He wore a black suit and waistcoat, with a white strikkie, or bowstring tie. He carried his Bible and hymn book and people in town seeing him would say: *"Goeie môre, Meneer,"*—Good morning, sir. There were some, however, who said little more than that and avoided further contact with him because of his close association with coloreds. Years later, at Beaufort West, a lawyer confessed to me: "I am ashamed to say this, but I avoided shaking your father's hand whenever possible. I knew he shook the hand of thirty or more coloreds every day and I didn't want any of it to rub off on me."

As a boy, however, I was not acutely aware of this. I played freely with other children my age and was accepted in their homes—including that of Eric Louw who later became Minister of Foreign Affairs. Yet I was set apart in many ways which could not be hidden. There were no presents on Christmas morning. At the yearly sports show I ran the mile in my bare feet. There was no steeple with a fat cock on my father's church. The people who prayed with him were colored. And when the day came for me to be confirmed in the Dutch Reformed Church, I would make my vows to God before a minister in a pulpit who would be Dominie Rabie—and not my father whom I loved and admired above all other men.

> Behold I give unto you power
> To tread on serpents and scorpions,
> And over all the power of the enemy;
> And nothing shall by any means hurt you.

My father had given me that—and more. He had shown me scorpions under rocks. He had taught me the names of the trees, the wildflowers, and the succulent plants. He had brought me to the birds, to the animals, and even to the lizards—especially the rare, blue-headed koggelmander which stares to the north when rain is on the way.

But above all else, he taught me to hunt on the Great Karoo—the vast and wonderful plain of semidesert where we lived. He was a good shot and an excellent hunter, and walking in the veld he seemed more than ever to have the eyes of an eagle, often seeing game long before anyone else.

We hunted an antelope called springbok and the desert hare—hasie in Afrikaans. Most of the time we went after hare, my father and I with three of his friends, walking in a row fifty yards apart until we jumped one. The men used twelve-bore guns while I had a smaller eighteen-gauge one.

We used to make a fire in the veld at midday, roasting chops and sausages, then washing it down with hot, black coffee. After that, we would put the bags again on our backs and continue to hunt until evening. I learned to love the Karoo then—the flat plains with distant mountains, blue in the morning, pink and purple and gold at sunset. Sometimes on the way home the sun would be a red ball sinking over the horizon. But often it was after nightfall and in the darkness the day's companionship would be gone, leaving me with a deep, almost painful loneliness.

> All things are delivered to me of my father
> And no man knoweth who the son is, but the father;
> And who the father is, but the son . . .

Whenever we were ill, my father got up at night to doctor us. My brothers and I went constantly barefoot and often during the winter our feet would toughen up and crack open. This was quite painful, especially when we washed them at night. Our father helped us to soften them by rubbing in a mixture of paraffin and candle wax. Besides this, I suffered from festering toenails that pained so much that I would cry in bed. My mother, who helped us greatly with schoolwork during the day, did not hear us calling at night. My father came instead, with a *wildeblare* home remedy, wrapping it around my toe in a bandage. He also used to draw out the fester with a poultice made of milk and bread crumbs, or Sunlight soap and sugar. And when I had a cold, he would rub my chest with Vicks and cover it with a red flannel cloth.

Sunday afternoons we walked together to the top of the hill by the dam. Once there, we would sit on a rock and look at the town below us, and across the valley at the distant Nuweveld Mountains. Sometimes one of my brothers came along, but usually it was only the two of us. Then I would tell my problems to my father, and he would speak of his to me.

One day I asked him to explain death and the soul leaving the body. I did not know how important this would be to me some day, and I asked it as would any boy of his father.

"How do you know it happens? You can't see it."

"Do you see that train?"

Far across the valley, a freight train pulled around Lemoenfontein Mountain. We watched it approach the bridge and saw a white puff of steam come from the whistle. Ten seconds later, its sound came to us on the hilltop—who! whooo!

"You saw the steam?"

"Yes."

"And the sound?"

"The steam and sound—they became separated."

"How do you know—did you see it happen?"

Another time I wanted to know about dancing with girls. Was it all right—or was it wrong?

"By dancing do you mean placing your two bodies in contact with one another and vibrating to music?"

"Yes."

I had not yet begun to take out girls, and did not even know how to dance. Yet, other older boys were doing it, and I knew the main purpose was to do just that—vibrate together in harmony with music.

"I don't think it's wise to be that close to a girl," said my father. "You're throwing yourself into the arms of temptation."

I said nothing. We were cracking almonds on a rock and eating them with raisins.

"On the other hand," he said, "Paul says we can trust God to always provide us with an escape from temptation. And Peter says to be joyful when tempted, since you are blessed when you resist it."

"You can trust me," I replied, with the confidence of a boy who had never held a girl.

So my father helped me. He did not, however, have easy answers for all his own problems—especially financial ones. We owed five hundred pounds on our house at the seaside, and there were other expenses too. My eldest brother, Johannes, whom we called Barney, had failed twice at the university. Besides this, there were three other sons to put through school.

One day on the hilltop he revealed his secret solution for all our troubles: a lottery ticket. I stared at it in amazement. The church was opposed to gambling and I could not believe what I saw.

"It's a lottery ticket," he said.

I nodded. A strong wind was blowing and it whipped the ticket in his hand. It also tugged at his mustache and it flapped our pants about our legs.

"If I win first prize," he said, "it will pay a fortune."

"And take care of the mortage on the house," I said, trying to be helpful.

"And Johannes' university bills," he said. "Then a thousand for your schooling, plus two more for Dodsley and Marius. We can even get an electrical hearing aid for your mother so she can hear something in church."

With a stick he wrote our names on the ground and next to them he put how much was needed. Obviously, this was not gambling. It was more in the nature of a family investment—even a municipal one.

"We'll have enough left over," he said finally, "to build an extension on the colored school and maybe even dig a well for them."

> He answered, saying:
> Thou shalt love the Lord thy God,
> With all thy heart,
> And with all thy soul,
> And with all thy strength,
> And with all thy mind;
> And thy neighbor as thyself.

In the pulpit, my father paused. The congregation waited in silence. Finally he spoke:

"That is the great commandment. I did not say two commandments because it is not two. It is one, since you cannot love God unless you love man. And you cannot love man unless you love God. It's all one piece—like an open-ended pipe . . ."

"AAAAA-MENNNNN!"

I looked at the men and women before me, packed between the blue and white walls and crammed onto the balcony where some had carved their names into the wooden benches.

I remember now the ladies' hats—was it actually that night or was it years later or maybe really a composite of all my boyhood? They were of many colors, each tilted differently as though a great wind had blown through a flower garden. It was these, the hats, which suggested the women were the brightest and most intense. Yet their eyes told you otherwise, shifting eventually to their men who sat there, each one very much alone, with gnarled hands on old, dog-eared psalm books, hands beaten and shaped like worn tools. Above all else, there was something in the triangle of jaw, mouth, and eyes that seemed to ask: "How can *you* explain it?"

At that age I did not know what "it" was, although I sensed there was an unexplored area, an untouched field where they stood alone, waiting for someone to come and write their names with ours on the earth.

So the unasked question was always there, becoming most intense after the service when there was contact with them, their hands pressed into my father's—and so into mine—before they took leave to go back to the Location, their ghetto on the edge of town where their dogs bit white men, and children behind walls made of mud asked their parents the unasked question.

It went that way this same night, with the deacons and elders pressing around my father. After wishing him well on the New Year, and safe return from his vacation, they spoke their fears. There was a move underway to deconsecrate our church and so force the coloreds to worship in a church away from the center of town. Would it happen while my father was away?

"It will never happen while I am alive," he replied.

"May God spare you until you die," said one.

"Reverend, don't go too far out into the sea," said another.

I whispered my mother's message to come as soon as possible and left, going through the vestry that was attached to our home. On the way I found my father's office open, with a lamp lit. Normally no lights were allowed after nine o'clock. Electricity was too expensive, and late studies had to be done by oil lamp or candlelight. Yet this was New Year's Eve, the family were packing, the lights were on—and my father's study was open.

I sat down at his big roll-top desk where often he let me study. I knew every drawer, including the one on the upper left, which I pulled out to discover, as always, the little tin candy box. Inside the box was an old envelope, tied with a red ribbon, which I opened quickly to find my father's two most precious treasures: a little brown Marie biscuit and a sharpened matchstick—all that remained of the touch of my dead brother.

One corner of the biscuit had been bitten off, leaving marks of little teeth, and the matchstick was bent slightly at its sharpened point. I touched them both gently, wondering what he would be like if he had lived. They had called him Abraham, but he had not lived long enough to hear it with pride. Perhaps he did not even know it belonged to him. He could speak, they said, but he died before he was four—dying of a heart disease while my father sat beside his bed, trying to be of help, giving him a little biscuit to eat, then cleaning his tiny fingernails with the matchstick.

It was not the first death in the family. Barney had come with a twin sister, but she had died at birth—too soon to have a name or to be kissed or to leave her mark on a biscuit or a matchstick. I looked at them again, wondering if Abraham would have been a good friend like Michel. My brothers were too old or too young to be close to me. Barney was ten years ahead of me, Dodsley was five, and Marius was four years younger.

In later years, I learned Abraham had a congenital defect of the heart that modern surgery could have corrected. But as a boy, I did not know this and could only wonder why there was no way to stop death, to somehow send it away. Why did it come so suddenly—snatching little boys from the bedside of their fathers, grabbing old ladies while praying in church, yet leaving others to sit and stare at a biscuit, a matchstick, or an old photograph?

There was a photo of him in the living room, hanging on the wall. It showed a baby sitting in a chair on a velvet cushion staring out at the world with mixed wonder and fright. Yet this was more a record of grief than joy, for next to it hung another one of my mother, dressed in black with a white handkerchief in her hand, standing beside a fresh grave with a jar of flowers tilted against a white cross. A third photo in the line-up was of a little angel in a cloud, its hand raised as though waving good-bye.

I had never seen my mother cry, or even with tears in her eyes. But once Barney had found her weeping before these photos, my father standing beside her with his arm around her waist, saying her name over and over—her true name and not just Mommy—"Maria, Maria . . ."

"Christiaan!"

It was my mother in the doorway holding a wrinkled mosquito net and an old pair of Dodsley's pants. Her hair had come loose and hung down over one ear.

"What are you doing here?"

"Waiting for Daddy."

I rose quickly, hoping she would not see the opened candy box. She could get very angry. When we did something terribly wrong, she would even beat us with a hairbrush.

"Did you tell him to hurry up?"

"Yes, I did that, Mother."

I nodded as I spoke to make certain she understood. Without her ear-horn, she did not always hear everything. Sometimes this led to misunderstanding and trouble.

"Come to bed immediately. I want you to try on these pants for the summer."

"I have to go outside first."

"What?"

"I have to go to the toilet!"

"Be quick about it," she said, turning down the corridor.

I closed the tin and put it back into the top drawer. Then I went out into the back garden where the toilet was in a corrugated iron shed, separate from the house. I always dreaded making this trip at night, fearing ghosts would leap upon me. Everybody in Beaufort West knew about the man who went into the graveyard one night, only to be jumped by a spook who slapped him in the face, leaving a hideous burn caused by five flaming fingers.

Worse than that was the dreaded *oog,* or eye, a fiery and awful will-o'-the-wisp, larger than a new moon. Most often it was seen moving up and down the river bank—the demented spirit of a woman with a lantern looking for her drowned daughter. Everyone had seen it. Even horses began to sweat and panic as it approached, vanishing at the last minute—but not always. Once, a man charged at it with a carriage and became a raving lunatic. After that, everyone stayed away. Michel and I had seen it when driving with his father to Jeffrey's Bay. It came along the top of a little hill and suddenly headed toward us. We raced away in the car as Michel was screaming, "Daddy, the *oog*, the OOG IS COMING AT US!"

The black form of the outhouse loomed before me, and with it came the familiar feel of the door handle. At that moment, there was a clank-clanking, coming through the garden gate. Hearing it, I leaped inside the privy and slammed the door shut—just in time, for the clanking came nearer and nearer, until it struck the back of the outhouse with a terrible groan. Trembling with fear, I leaned against the door and held my head, certain I was about to be seized by the throat.

Then I heard the latrine bucket under the toilet seat being pulled out through a back trap door, with another one slid into its place. No ghosts, these were the coloreds on their nightly round to empty latrines. I waited for them to leave, then hastened to finish and hurry back toward the safety of lights in our home.

In the kitchen there was the odor of freshly baked *soetkoekies*. It made me immediately hungry and I began to sniff around looking for some. My mother was a wonderful cook. When she won prizes at the annual domestic show, we went around proudly looking at the red cards on her cakes and cookies. Our wood stove had no thermometer, but she could judge the heat by simply putting her hand into the oven. On these special baking days we were not even allowed to tiptoe through the kitchen, for fear the cake would fall. Our reward came afterward, when we helped beat the egg whites for frosting and could lick the pan.

In the kitchen, the longer I looked for the cookies the hungrier I became. There was nothing in the cupboard or the pantry. Everything had been put away and packed for the trip. Finally, in the breakfast room I found a picnic basket. The cookies were in it—and within two seconds I had one in my mouth and a spare in my pocket.

The family trunk and some other bags were in the hall, ready to be loaded into the car. The linoleum floor had lost its polish, but I could forget about that for a month or until we came home. Then it would begin again—the weekly chore of polishing the hall floor that ran through the center of the house. It had an orange and green pattern and my mother wanted it to shine like a mirror. To achieve this, I had to go over it three times on my knees, first with wax and a rag, then with a brush and another rag, and finally with a clean rag to obtain a bright finish. The hall ran from the front door, past the living room and the room we rented out to boarders—for many years, a beloved teacher, Miss Dodsley-Flamstead—continuing alongside other bedrooms to the dining room we never used except for special dinners, ending finally at the cramped breakfast room where we ate all the time.

After that, I would polish the furniture, or stamp the washing with my feet, or haul firewood by wheelbarrow from the front to the rear of the house. Sometimes I also helped make soap in the big iron pot filled with sheep fat, caustic soda, and a lye obtained from a special bush growing in the veld. The round of chores was always the same, but the long hall was worst of all. It collected dust from the street all week long and no matter how hard I tried, I could never please my mother. She would always find a corner or a little spot that did not shine like the rest, saying, "You haven't done this properly."

This hurt because I had tried so hard, only to have her knock everything down. She was a strongly determined woman—insisting everything be perfect, that we boys be first in school, and that we never admit defeat. I was afraid of my mother, of displeasing her, and of making her angry.

Marius and I shared a bedroom next to my parents with a door in between. When I entered he was already asleep. Dodsley's pants were laid out on my bed, and I tried them on. They were the usual khaki shorts we all wore, but a little big around the waist.

"You'll fill it out during the summer," said my mother in her room when I showed them to her. She was in her nightgown, and knelt on the floor to inspect the fit.

"If you made them a little tighter, they wouldn't fall off when I run— like this."

I sucked in my stomach and wiggled and the pants fell to the floor around my ankles.

"All right," she said, giving me a pat on the rear, "I think you're going to be skinny all your life, just like your father."

My father was sitting on the bed, taking off his shoes. They were high ones, above the ankles, and he was opening the laces.

"Daddy, a woman fainted tonight in the church while she was praying."

"A woman what?"

"Fainted, in the big church."

"Who was she?"

I looked toward my mother who was now seated before her dressing mirror, letting down her hair.

"Mommy, the woman who fainted—who was she?"

"It looked like one of the Stroebel relatives."

"Which one?" asked my father.

"I don't know."

"The cousin from Knysna?"

"I don't know—why must you feel responsible for everybody?"

My father peeled off his socks and said nothing.

"Everybody," said my mother, "everybody from everywhere and all colors—he worries about them."

Daddy wiggled his toes and winked at me.

"Yes?"

"What I wanted to know is how can it happen there, I mean in church, while you're praying?"

"Son, if people believed they could not die while praying in church, we'd never be able to close our doors. The Lord knows this and asks only that we keep ready to go at any time—even while praying to him, which is rather beautiful when you think about it."

It did not seem beautiful at all. In fact, it made me decide to say my prayers as fast as possible. As though aware of this, my father pulled a big watch from his waistcoat pocket and flipped open the lid.

"It's after one o'clock, Chris. You'd better go to bed."

"Yes, Daddy."

The watch was silver and it had a silver chain. Leaving the lid open, he always put it on the stand next to the bed. Then he took off his waistcoat and began unbuttoning his shirt. On the other side of the bed my mother was brushing her hair. She had never cut it and it came down to her waist. Against the pink nightgown it was like a dark waterfall and was lovely to look at. She combed it with the same brush with which she beat me, pulling it slowly. In the oval mirror, her face was framed by the dark hair, her brown eyes were soft and sleepy, and I thought she looked beautiful.

My father had asked her to marry him one day when they were walking together. He had picked a pomegranate from a tree and had broken it apart, saying: "Maria, so is my heart open to you."

We all knew these blushing words of love, given with the two red halves of the fruit in his long, delicate hands. But none of us ever knew how Maria Elizabeth de Swart, the young school teacher from George, said her first "yes" to our father. I had my own version of her reaction to his romantic proposal: She took one half of the split pomegranate, and then nodded—her eyes downcast.

Even when older, I never imagined either of them kissing with their eyes open or actually making love, other than in the dark. In fact, I had never seen them kiss with the heat of lovers. They were for us two ends of a house, fixed and untouching as different doors—one with an arch, the other with pillars, one who came to you at night, the other who drove you on by day with a hairbrush. One whom you loved, the other whom you loved and feared.

I looked at the double bed where they slept every night together—its black iron frame topped by bright bronze balls and a bronze headpiece. Everything had happened there—or most everything. I was born in that bed, and so were all my brothers, except Barney. He was nearby, however, the night of my birth—apparently dying of double pneumonia in an adjacent room where my father knelt praying at his bedside while I came into the world, November 8, 1922. At the same moment, Barney passed his crisis—to live and not to die as had Abraham before him.

All of that, and more, had happened in the bed of bright bronze. It was there my mother and father said their *huisgodsdiens,* or prayers, each day before rising. Often I awakened to hear my father already underway, in soft, peaceful prayer. Then my mother would pray. She was more excited about it and more definite in what she asked from God. After that they would sing together in bed. They did not do this in bed at night because we always said *huisgodsdiens* at the evening dinner table, kneeling by our chairs after my father read from the family Bible, then all singing together. Most often, it was my father's favorite, "Rock of Ages."

Before retiring, however, my parents always knelt at the side of their bed, doing it separately as soon as one or the other got into night clothes. My father wore pyjamas that consisted of pants and shirt with a white vest, and he prayed in silence on his knees. My mother did not always pray in silence, because of her deafness, and you could often hear what she said.

". . . and please dear Lord help us on the road tomorrow, preserve us against accidents or trouble with those awful tires, and keep our loved ones forever in your care, Amen."

Back in my bedroom I recalled my father as saying we should be ready to be snatched away by God's hand, especially during prayer. So I raced through mine in record time. Then I hopped into bed and tried to sleep. The trip to the seaside was always exciting and many things happened along the way.

There was the far-off cry of a train going across the Karoo plain. I thought of my father in the pulpit, saying only a father could know his son, and only a son would know his father. I remembered once seeing him in the garden trimming roses. Thorns pricked his hands, and as he came toward me in the evening light I saw blood on them, and I feared for him.

CHAPTER 2

"CHRIS! MARIUS! GET uuuuUUUPPP!"

Barney stood over us, pulling off the sheets, then stomping out as we sat up, dazed with lack of sleep. It was dawn, and from the kitchen there came the wonderful odor of fresh coffee. Excitement mounting, I began to get dressed. The sooner I got out into the car, the more certain I would be to have an outside seat and not find myself stuck in the middle between my brothers.

The first car we owned was a big event in the family, beginning with the first day. It happened in 1923, when I was hardly one year old, but everyone recalled the event for years. My father had purchased the car without telling anyone, until he called my mother and Barney and Dodsley out to stand in a little group before the red garage doors. Then, with a dramatic gesture, he flung them open.

"Look what's happened!" he exclaimed.

Everyone gaped in amazement at the happening—a dark brown Willys Overland touring car, with convertible top, wooden spoke wheels, and a spare tire sunk into the left fender. Standing alongside the battered Model-T Ford, which belonged to the parish, it looked beautiful. My mother was speechless, my father bursting with pride, and my brothers delirious with joy. Barney, who already knew something about cars, suggested we immediately go for a trial spin. My father hesitated, then nodded agreement.

"Do you know how to drive it?" asked Barney.

"Yes," replied my father.

He said it with his eyes shut, however, indicating there might be some doubt about it.

My mother saw this, or intuitively knew better, and headed for the house. Dodsley piled into the back, my father climbed in behind the wheel and Barney cranked her up. The motor caught suddenly with a cough and a roar and sent up a cloud of smoke. Barney leaped aboard, there was a grinding of gears, and they started out.

The garage drive ran between the church and the Town Hall and along the way there were cement buttments. They got past the first one, but backed into the second. This so startled my father that he put his foot on the gas and banged it again. Luckily, that stalled the motor—or he would probably have done it a third time.

Barney hopped out to look at the fender.

"It isn't too bad," he said. "But we have to go forward now."

He tried to crank it, but the car was still in reverse. After putting it in neutral, it caught again with a wild roar from too much petrol. Barney leaped onto the running board, shouting instructions: "Go ahead a bit— then back up again!"

My father nodded and they took off with a lurch, quickly gathering speed and going ever faster until it seemed certain they were going back into the garage and out through the rear wall.

"Hold it, Dad!" cried Barney from the running board.

"Whoa!" yelled my father, pulling back on the wheel as though driving a team of horses.

"Put on the brake!" yelled Barney, ducking his head as they approached the garage entrance.

My father closed his eyes and jammed his foot on the brake—throwing Barney off the running board and dumping Dodsley up against the front seat. They had stopped just in time.

But they were back where they started from with a dented left rear fender. The motor had also stalled again, though it made sounds indicating it was hot and ready to go in any direction with the slightest turn of the crank. Barney prepared to do this, but before turning the handle he made certain it was in neutral and not going to run over him. Then he gave one last minute instruction before starting the motor:

"Stay clear of the church this time, Dad, and go nearer the Town Hall."

My father nodded—and backed out into the church wall.

"Whoa!" he cried again, pulling up on the wheel.

After this second collision, he got out with his sons to survey the damage in respectful silence. Both rear fenders were bent, and there was a scratch on the right front one. It seemed fairly obvious that my father was not very good at backing up. He admitted it with a sigh.

"They gave me lessons," he said, "but always going forward—not backing."

That explanation seemed sufficient, and everyone assumed a little more practice would quickly make him an expert at reversing. But it never did. Getting out of the drive was always a risky venture, even in later years when I rode with him. If he made it in one straight shoot, without scraping a fender or having to start over, we considered it a visible miracle.

His major trouble, however, stemmed from the gearshift, which he could never master. It worked on the H-pattern, first and second being lower left and upper right, with third in lower right and reverse in upper left. My father's problem was to get from first to second without putting it into reverse—causing a terrible grinding of gears. When that happened, he would look down to see what he was doing—and so go off the road.

This led him to avoid changing gears unless forced into it. Such tactics inevitably got him into further trouble—mainly in passing and in making turns. One day, climbing a hill in second gear, we approached a farmer on a horsecart with a little boy sitting alongside him. My father hooted his horn for horse and cart to move over, but the farmer stayed in the middle of the road. This forced my father to slow down to the point where he would soon have to shift from second to first gear. Seeking to avoid this, he began to honk at the farmer until there was a small opening which allowed him to squeeze by. Upset by the farmer, my father leaned out to yell: "Your back wheels are turning!"

The farmer yelled back: "If you had washed your face this morning you'd see the front wheels are turning, too!"

At first stunned, my father slowly began to smile. Then he broke into laughter.

"With both his wheels turning—and at the speed he wants them to go—he's better off than I am!"

Sharp turns also caused endless trouble, since he tried to do them without shifting or slowing down. We would be going along at regular clip when suddenly he would go into the turn—generally too soon or too late. This sent him crashing through gates, onto lawns, across sidewalks—and once up onto the steps of the church. It was too much for my mother.

"Look, Adam," she said, "You don't have to go to church with the car. You can go without it."

Most likely, it was this incident that caused my father to give up driving whenever possible. It was just too complex. He could comprehend God's evolving, over-all plan for mankind, but the fixed pattern of a gear box remained a mystery. So Barney, when he was home from the university, drove the car. And since he was studying to become a mechanical engineer, this made sense.

"If you drive," said my father, "it'll be a form of homework."

As a result, Barney drove us to The Wilderness, the seaside village where we spent our summer holidays. The trip was always an event of many miracles. The first miracle was that the car—we now had a blue Chev sedan—could even move under its load of bags and people. A big *trommel,* or trunk, made of iron and tin was placed on the rear rack. Suitcases covered with Hessian sack went on top of this—all of it tied down with rope. More bags were stacked along the running board and still others were wedged in between the front fenders and the engine hood. Finally, a canvas water bag was hung from the front radiator.

Fragile and bulky items went inside, mainly on top of my brothers and myself in the back seat—the picnic basket and coffee kettle, brooms and mops, and various other items such as glassware, a lampshade, or even a dresser mirror. Buried under all this we naturally fought for outside seats like surfacing dolphins. In the middle you risked having a lampshade fall over your ears or a broom handle stuck into an armpit. The outside had only one disadvantage: the one there had to do last-minute errands—as happened on this particular morning when I was safely in an outside seat, with Marius in the middle and Dodsley on the far side. We were ready to go, my parents sitting in the front seat and Barney behind the wheel, when my mother remembered the back gate was not closed.

"Christiaan," she said, "get out and close it."

"Hurry up, Chris!" cried Barney revving up the motor.

I hopped out and ran down the garage drive into the back yard, running then through the orchard in the first light of dawn until I came to the big lemon tree that stood in the middle of the garden.

I stopped there, suddenly aware I was all alone among the trees where I had played since I could remember—the garden of my childhood. The house was boarded up, my family sitting in the car on the street, and I was alone in an orchard bathed in a strange light which cast no shadows. One by one, the trees began to appear to me as being alive and somehow aware that I was going away. Had I been sent to close a gate—or perhaps to say goodbye to something? Or was it the trees around me, the garden itself, that in some mute way was saying good-by?

Here my brothers and myself had been given shelter and secrecy, and here we had found our first taste of sweet fruit. Each tree was different and had a special meaning to us. We swung from the pepper tree in an old tire. We hid in a tree house in the limbs of the walnut. We sat under the plum tree and ate its red-blue fruit while the heavy limbs hung low upon our shoulders and my mother warned: "When you come first in your class at school, remember the plum tree and how its branches which are laden with fruit hang low to the ground. That's how you must be—low and humble."

Yet most wondrous of all was this one before me—the big lemon tree with a grape vine winding around its trunk, up into the limbs like a giant snake. This was the tree of double fruit and threatening thorns. The grapes came first—big, lush purple clusters hanging down amid the thorns. The lemons came later, but the thorns were always there.

A bird flew out of the tree without a sound, leaving me more alone than ever. At the same time, I had a sense of being still closer to all the trees, as though I was seeing them for the first time in my life. Oddly, it was happening at the moment that I was going away. Perhaps—who knew?—I would never see them this way again. Suddenly I wanted to speak, to say something—but what?

"Good-bye lemon tree."

I walked on toward the back gate. Passing the pepper tree, I said good-bye to it, too. Coming back from the gate I could hear the car hooting for me and I began to run, calling good-bye to the others as I flew past them.

"Bye pomegranate! Bye walnut! Bye pears! Bye almonds! Good-bye . . . EVERYBODY!"

This strange sense of feeling close to things and wanting to say good-bye to them continued in the car on the way out of town. So I said silent good-byes to the pear trees along Donkin Street. Beneath them, on each side of the gravel road, ran open furrows filled with cool spring water used for irrigating the orchards. It was forbidden to wade or flop around in these little streams, but, on hot days we would pretend we had slipped and then fall into them. So I said good-bye to them too. At crossroads and drive-ways, the water ran under culverts. We sailed our boats under these and also caught frogs and crabs there. To all that, I also said good-bye. There was much more, especially the dam where we played cowboys and crooks in the reeds. Above this was the reservoir where we swam out to the island with its big willow tree. Sometimes we tried to row there in boats made of bent, corrugated iron, but unless all the holes were plugged with soapy rags and unless you bailed very fast, they always sank before reaching the island.

I waved good-bye to all that and suddenly felt very sad.

"Daddy?"

"Yes, Chris?"

"We are coming back, aren't we? I mean after the vacation we will come back and it will all be the same, won't it?"

"Yes, of course. Why?"

"I don't know, I just wondered."

Once outside of town, we headed across the lower half of the Great Karoo—a broad plain of roughly 30,000 square miles inside the tip of South Africa. It is a world by itself—cut off from the Cape by mountains lost in clouds, crisscrossed by hills like table tops, and dotted with *koppies,* or cone-shaped mounds, standing like fixed sentinels. Beneath its red soil lay untouched skeletons of prehistoric dinosaurs and on top of them have been found the bones of the first men to walk upright on this earth. It is a silent, sun-scorched, wind-swept world of endless plains under a big sky, of animals and men, of hunters and the hunted, of drought and flood, of bleached bones in empty riverbeds and waving grass as high as a man, of rock with the ring of iron and desert bush that at twilight can cast a shadow thirty feet long.

I belonged to it, for here I had learned to hunt. Here I had known the taste of springbok and hare, of hot coffee with men, and the smell of rain on the land. Here I learned to build a campfire and listen to stories of our forefathers—the first *trekboers,* or pioneering farmers, who came over the mountains bringing their covered wagons in pieces on the backs of donkeys and mules.

Here they found roving herds of antelope, zebra, and lion. Here they met the leopard who could kill twenty sheep without waking a dog. And here they found the cave-dwelling Bushman who skinned his animals with sharp stone, who had believed he was the only man on earth and so painted his walls with happy scenes of dancing and hunting—free of battle or death.

The Bushman was our American Indian—though far more primitive. Every boy grew up knowing about these little men with big hearts and incredible eyesight. Before Galileo saw the satellites whirling around Jupiter, the Bushman had followed them with his naked eye. He had also followed the arrival of white trekkers, bringing guns, cattle, and brandy. And he watched them kill his game herds—then the Bushman himself.

They signaled to each other from their mountain caves with thin columns of smoke from damp grass—too faint to be seen by any but Bushmen. They prepared to defend their land and began to fight back. They fought with bow and poisoned arrow. They tore out fingernails of their victims. They scalped them and pulled out their bowels. They gave no mercy and they asked none. A Bushman shot through the arm would use his foot to draw the bow. Rather than see his children taken by the enemy he would bury them alive. So they fought and, in the last half of the eighteenth century, nearly drove out the white settler. But slowly numbers and guns had their effect. The Bushmen killed by the score—yet died by the thousand.

Their last stand at Sneeuberg is still told in the Karoo. Isolated on a mountain top, a clan of Bushmen fought a settler commando unit, throwing their dead and dying over the cliff, until one warrior remained—alone on a high rock. With a last arrow in his bow, he shouted his defiance at guns below him. Moved by such courage, the commando leader offered to spare the Bushman's life if he would surrender. In reply, the Bushman shot his poisoned arrow securely into one commando, shouting "A chief knows how to die!"—and leaped to his death.

The trip from Beaufort West to The Wilderness was only 120 miles, but it usually took twelve hours. The roads were dirt or gravel and often so corrugated that the car shook until it seemed it would fall apart and dump us all in the middle of the road. Most of the rivers had no bridges, and sometimes in fording them we would become stuck. When that happened, the whole family would get out and shove, often with the water up to our knees. Occasionally we had to use horses or donkeys from a nearby farm.

One of the most difficult stretches was the thirteen-mile pass through the Swartberg Mountains at Meiringspoort where there were thirty-two river crossings. Once beyond that, we generally reached Oudtshoorn by midday when my father bought us all meat pies from a café. We loved this and looked forward to it on every trip.

The approach to The Wilderness was always exciting. You came over the hills, and suddenly there was the sea in the distance. Then you would see the village itself, hemmed between the long white beach and the dark purple of the forest. After that we would go down the winding road to our home, finding the garden always overgrown with weeds. And as we unloaded the car, my mother invariably began to complain about the dirt inside and the weeds outside—putting us immediately to work with mops and hoes.

Once this was over, we were free to plunge into a boy's paradise. In the warm water of the Indian Ocean there were twenty-seven different kinds of fish and you could pull some of them in with a stiff bamboo pole, using a bright hook on a wire line, yanking them onto the shore, one after the other. There was also a river, running cool and clear from the higher lakes, leading to the Ebb and Flo Nature Reserve. Finally, there was a nine-hole golf course where we caddied for pocket money.

My earliest memories, however, were not of swimming or fishing, but rather of walking with my father in the forests where he taught us the names of the trees and their uses—stinkwood for furniture, yellowwood for flooring, ironwood for wagon wheels—showing us how to bring saplings of every kind from the forest and plant them around the house. He also taught us how to avoid the puff adder and the deadly green snake that dropped from trees with the speed of an arrow, killing its victims in less than one minute.

My father knew his way through the woods for he had grown up in even wilder forests around Knysna, thirty-one miles further east along the Indian Ocean front—his birthplace and where he was eventually to die. Here were some of the biggest and oldest trees on earth—such as the 2,000-year-old yellowwood known as "Big Tree," which still stands in the Tsitsikama forest. Here there was wild life and constant danger. Elephants crushed men, snakes poisoned them, and leopards leaped from behind, ripping off a scalp with one sweep of claw in midflight. From these forests my grandfather brought out giant stinkwood logs by ox team to the saw mills. He also fished, navigating the treacherous Knysna Heads with his brother, Koos Barnard, when no other man dared to go to sea.

My father told me stories about these men of his family, and I imagined them to be giants, filled with great courage. There was one, a woodsman, who failed to return from the forest. A search party found him on the trail homeward—dead, his right leg chopped off above the knee, and his little dog sitting nearby. Following the blood, they came upon a giant tree felled by the woodsman. Beneath it was pinioned his leg and next to it the bloody axe—as he had left them after hacking himself free with the hope of crawling home before his blood ran out or he was devoured by the big cats and jackals.

This had been the world of my father, but he had turned his back upon it—seeking another one. He found it, at thirty-one, with the Salvation Army, wandering as an official over South Africa and Rhodesia helping the poor and the broken. Finally he entered the Dutch Reformed Church Seminary at Wellington and, after his ordination three years later, was sent out to various mission stations. One of these was Joubertina where he opened his heart under a pomegranate tree to my mother. They married, and for a brief period my father was stationed at Graaf-Reinet where Barney was born—moving then to Beaufort West.

It was a close marriage, despite their differences. My mother was strong-willed and very ambitious for her sons. My father was gentle and proud of them. He allowed my mother to have her way—except occasionally when she claimed that God was on her side and together with Him she knew more than my father. When this happened, Reverend Adam Hendrik Barnard pulled her back to her senses with the realism of a woodsman's son.

This occurred at the end of that same summer when we began the drive back to Beaufort West. On the way, we stopped to visit an aunt at Cango

Caves. She had one of those oldtime gramophones with a large speaker and when we arrived it was playing "The Blue Danube." My father grabbed a broom and began to dance around the room, humming to himself and quite happy. My mother did not approve of such levity and immediately said so.

"Adam!"

He kept on dancing, paying her no heed. So she persisted.

"Adam—God will punish you for this."

"Nonsense," he said, and waltzed some more.

"You'll see," she said sternly. "You'll see."

It began to rain after Oudtshoorn and going over the Swartberg pass the rain came down in heavy waves.

"I knew something like this was going to happen," said my mother.

My father said nothing and we drove in silence. At the second river crossing we became stuck and my mother made another observation that her team was winning.

"God's punishment," she said, as we stepped out of the car into the rain and running stream to help shove. We got across eventually—only to bog down in a mudhole.

"We deserve it," said my mother.

This was going too far.

"We deserve nothing," said my father.

"Yes, we do and you know why."

"If you think God is punishing our entire family because I waltzed with a broom, you've got a foolish idea of His mission," he said.

"Oh no I haven't," she said, leaving no doubt now that she considered God to be constantly running the ball for her.

We eventually got out of the mud with the help of a donkey team, but other troubles followed and the trip took twenty-four hours instead of the usual twelve. It rained all the way, our clothes were wet, and the rain soaked through both trunk and suitcases, wetting everything—excepting one pair of my mother's panties.

Holding them up like a triumphant pink banner, she came into my father's study, saying, "This is the only thing that was spared."

"Give it to me," said my father, "I'll wet it my way and even up everything."

Beaufort West, upon our return, seemed quite the same. Along Donkin Street the pear trees were heavy with fruit and occasionally one of them plopped on a passer-by or clonked onto the top of a car. The street furrows were filled with running water and in our garden the muscatel grapes were turning purple in the lemon tree. Despite my fears, all seemed to be as we had left it.

Yet a change was taking place. I felt it in the first week of my last year

at grammar school. It happened on the way to class, while I was crossing the
Gamka River by jumping from one stone to the next above the water. It
was the usual way we went, when the river was low, rather than use the
bridge that was further upstream. From a large, flat rock in midstream, I
paused to look at our school, at the top of the opposite bank. Two hundred
yards away to the left was the high school. Next year this time I would leap
these same stones but take a separate path up the bank to the other
school.

When that happened everything would be different. The school had a
sports field and a stadium where the crowds cheered heroes. There were
student cadets who wore uniforms and marched in parade. There were
girls, too, in classes with boys—unlike primary school where we were separated. Somehow, the prospect of sitting next to a girl in class was disturbing. How would it be possible to concentrate on what the teacher said?

"Chris—wait for me!"

It was Michel coming across the river, carrying his books and a long
stick. He joined me on the flat rock in the middle.

"Let's fix somebody," he said.

I agreed and together we dug the stick around the base of the next rock,
loosening its balance so that it would flip if stepped on. We then hurried on
across, reaching the opposite side when Piet Theron, the policeman's son,
began to come over.

"Perfect!" cried Michel. "It's old Piet!"

Piet seemed in great form. He was jumping from one rock to the other
with high arcs, like a young klipspringer that knew every rock and spacing
—until he came to the one we had loosened. We had expected the rock to
tilt and cause him to get his feet wet. But he was leaping in such high and
fancy style that it send him skidding on his backside with a splash into the
stream. Michel and I ran up the bank laughing. Piet yelled from the river:
"You bastards! I'll get you, just wait, I'll get yooouuuuuu!"

We ran on up the slope to school—but not to escape Piet. Even mad as
a hornet, his wrath could never equal that of our geography teacher, Biggie
Viviers, who had the first class and was feared by us all. Biggie worked on
the principle of collective guilt. If anyone did not know the answer to a
question, he would hit everybody—or as many as he could before running
out of energy. This was especially terrifying since someone was sooner or
later bound to miss a question. Biggie, for his part, was always ready to let
go—especially when his eyes were bloodshot from heavy drinking, which
was often.

It must have been this same morning, or one during the first week of
school, when he thundered down upon me. We had just finished morning
prayers, when Biggie laid aside the Bible to pick up his cane and start in
my direction. He wore thick glasses which made his red eyes seem enor-

mous. He was a little man, and he was bald, and when he became angry his head would turn pink as though he was blushing. At the same time, his voice rose like a woman's.

"Barnard," he said, with his voice rising, "what's the yearly rainfall in the Transvaal?"

I looked at his cane—*a kweperlat,* or shoot from a quince tree—and hardly had time to duck before it lashed over my back, followed by rhythmic encounters with other students behind me.

"What's the . . ."

Swish!

"Transvaal!"

Swish!

Eventually somebody would yell the answer, but Biggie would keep on going, anyway. If you guessed and made a mistake, it was bad on the others because this seemed to wind him up again.

We had ways of getting even with Biggie during recess when he skipped over the bridge to the Beaufort West Hotel for a *doppie,* or double brandy. If it had been a bad day with the cane we would take it from the cupboard and break it to pieces. Or we would stick *dubbeltjie* thorns in his cap, then wait behind the bushes after school to see him clap on the cap—only to quickly pull it off with both hands, while his papers spilled onto the ground. The next morning he would be waiting for us with a new quince shoot, crying "Duffers!"

Flailing away, he would gasp his basic creed:

"You lot of . . . uncouth . . . unpolished medals . . . damn . . . I'll polish you . . . damn you . . . and God bless my soul!"

He kept his word. No one ever failed Biggie's class. As a result, our fear of him contained also some awe and respect. Besides, he was a highly educated man who spoke Latin as easily as Afrikaans or English—proving it the night he drove home drunk and ran his car through the back end of his garage wall. This also served as bathroom wall for Noa Pienaar's mother who at that moment happened to be sitting on the toilet. The sudden shower of plaster and bricks so frightened her that she stayed right in place while staring in amazement at Biggie in his car.

"*Ag* man," she said, "you're drunk again tonight."

"*Ag* Annie," he replied, "stop your jabbering *et age quod agis*"—which we all quickly learned meant "get to the business at hand."

At the end of every morning Fanie Bekker and I went across the river to fetch soup for the school. Mrs. Frances Pienaar prepared it—four gallons of bean or pea or barley soup—which we carried together in a large pail. It had a lid, but this did not prevent the soup from occasionally scorching our legs and bare feet. It was a long haul, too—about one mile from Baird Street down Union, then across the riverbed or over the bridge.

Yet Fanie and I felt it was worth it. We got an extra cup or two of soup for ourselves before leaving Mrs. Pienaar's kitchen. Then on the way we stopped at Diaz', a Portuguese who bought old bottles, rags, and bones, selling him any bones in the soup. One day the bones were Fanie's, the next day mine. As a result of this transaction, Mrs. Pienaar suffered a distorted idea of what school children expected from her soup. Fanie would come into the kitchen, taste the soup, and shake his head sadly.

"Lacks bones," he said. "All the kids are complaining about no taste from lack of bones."

"Even in the pea soup?"

"Even in the pea soup," said Fanie gravely, "needs more bones to make it stand up."

The soup run had another advantage. By the time we delivered it, to be dished out under the arcade next to the playground, we had obtained a comfortable thirty-minute break—usually from the history class.

Another way of getting out of class was to ask permission to go to the lavatory that stood outside in a field. Looking back, I marvel now that none of our teachers ever noted the mystery of nature's ways that impelled Fanie Bekker and myself to simultaneously feel its call just as the one-thirty express was rolling into the station. Once out, we would not run toward the toilet in the field, but rather across the square—two barefooted boys in short pants—to stare at the passengers in the first-class Pullman car. Here were men of money and power with beautiful ladies. Someday we would be like that. But to get there you had to be tops in everything. My mother drove this into me and my brothers, year after year: "I expect you to be first—not second or third, but first."

With this constantly behind me, I was usually first in my class. In the same spirit, I won the school tennis championship, using a racket Michel gave me and wearing old tennis shoes stuffed with pieces of cardboard. It became impossible to turn back from any challenge—including my first fight, which, like most such encounters, happened suddenly.

We were coming in from recess, when a boy jumped another one and began to bully him. I stopped it, and the bully said, "Okay, I'll see you after school."

This was unexpected and something of a shock. In class I wondered how I was going to fight the boy. I had never fought anybody and did not want to start now. Just thinking about it made me lose my breath, and all afternoon I heard nothing the teacher said. Finally, after class was over, all the boys went into a nearby field where the bully and I made little mounds of dirt and then, tight-lipped, with fists clenched, we stood before them. The bully spoke first.

"Skop my ouma," he said, meaning, "Kick my grandmother." The next move was for me to kick his mound which would be the same in the field of honor as kicking his grandmother. Yet before I could do this, he kicked my mound with a sneer and came toward me.

"There's your cash," he said, hitting me on the chest.

I hit him then. I never knew where I hit him or even how I did it because I was so excited. Suddenly I saw him on the ground, looking up at me and I was full of courage, saying "Come on, man, fight fair—get up!"

He remained there, however, unwilling to fight further. With shouts of triumph, Fanie Bekker and Michel and my friends carried me off on their shoulders. I saw the boy on the ground, then a lofty glimpse of the high school and, beyond that, the sports field. For the first time, I felt no anxiety about taking that separate path up from the river bank.

CHAPTER 3

WHEN THE DAY arrived to start high school, I did not go alone. Excepting for Michel Rossouw, who was sent away to boarding school, all my old classmates and chums were with me. This was comforting, for we came with a sense of unity before the new challenge. We had all known one another since childhood and we moved into our new world with a sense of being safe in numbers. We were also near to our old grounds. A bare two hundred yards separated the two schools. You could look out of the high school science class and see our old privy in the field where we had puffed our first cigarettes, the field where we had fought and tested our first strength.

This sense of unity was intensified during the few days before we underwent an initiation ritual from the older students. We knew we were going to be beaten and humiliated, and this drew us closer as we confided on how best to undergo the ordeal. Nor were we wrong to be worried, for the initiation was wilder and more painful than expected.

The older students stood in a double line, each with a leather belt. We had to run through this barrage to the end where our heads would be immersed into a pail of cow manure. The boys, especially the bigger ones, held their straps in a mean way, and some cracked them like whips, with wild hoots and hollers. Even more disturbing were the faces of girls who stood behind the boys, flushed with excitement and whispering as they looked us over. Three of them looked at me and laughed, and I turned away, blushing, to talk with Fanie Bekker and Piet Theron.

"In the pail, don't open your eyes," said Fanie.

"Who's going to look into cow shit?" said Piet.

"That stuff burns the eyes," said Fanie gravely.

We turned back to the waiting barrage and saw a couple of bullies had reversed their belts, with the buckle at the swinging end. This could really cut and bring blood, and I was frightened.

Fanie said he would go first and walked off into it. We were expected to run through the two lines of swinging straps, but Fanie bravely walked it, the straps flailing so hard that he was thrown forward by their blows. It was an act of bravery and defiance that made me tremble. Then a buckle caught him, tearing his shirt, and he jogged through the rest.

I went next, not running but walking as fast as I could go, plunging into a white and red and yellow tunnel of eyes and mouths shrieking: "Get him ... bust his poop! ... that Barnard kid ... wow ... look at it will you! ... ha! ... ha-HAAAH!"

After the first painful blow, I felt nothing except when a buckle cut my calf and a belt whipped across my shoulder, stinging my cheek and causing involuntary tears. At the end, another group of boys was huddled around the pail of cow manure.

"Here's the Barnard kid!"

"Give him good!"

"Have a taste of porridge, freshman!"

I was grabbed on all sides. One boy cut off part of my hair, while several others pushed my head into the pail. As I went under, I remembered to keep my eyes closed, but made the mistake of breathing out so that very quickly I had to come up or swallow some of the muck. I struggled for air, and they shoved me deeper. Desperate, I kicked back, and must have caught somebody in the groin because there was a painful groan and I was suddenly released—to find them all sneering at me.

I walked away, toward Fanie who had taken off his shirt and was using it to clean his face. There were large red welts on his back and he was bleeding from one shoulder. Two seniors were talking to him. You could tell from their voices that they had a respect for any boy who had the guts to walk through the barrage. Listening to this, I realized we had gone through something more than an initiation.

We had been passed through a sieve which broke up our unity and left each of us very much alone—some to get the nod from the seniors, others to be overlooked and forgotten. Before this, we had lived in a compact world of boys, riding wild donkeys or dumping one another into the river— yet always inside our closed group. Now we were competing to get out of it, beyond our ranks, and we were suddenly, unexpectedly, alone. Before, we had all gone to class in our bare feet—joined in common sufferance of their painful cracking in the wintertime. Now most of us were wearing shoes—some more stylish than others, indicating the owner was better equipped to go it alone, to survive outside the group.

These were signs of new strength in our new world. There was also one other, lying somewhere between a fancy pair of shoes and a nod from a senior. It was having a girl—not just any girl, but one who could cause other boys to look and whistle.

We used to hang around in front of the school when they came down the road, most of them on bikes with their lovely legs going up and down. Sometimes the wind would blow so that they had to pedal with one hand on the bike and the other holding down the skirt—until they had to brake using both hands, allowing everything to soar upward in splendid fashion. Then the boys would whistle—if the girl was somebody to look at. I was going with the van Heerden girl at that time, and the first day they whistled at her I felt very proud.

I left poems for her under a rock, and when she lingered after school I lingered too. Sometimes, when everybody had gone, we walked part of the way home together—yet always without touching, until one day in the chemistry class when I showed her how to make hydrogen sulphide. On that day she leaned close to me and I felt her breast touch my arm. This was so exciting that I kept explaining the same experiment over and over in order to feel it some more. She kept it there, too, as though hearing me for the first time. After that, we met without poems or notes under the rock. Then one day we did not meet anymore because I went wild for another girl, Sissie Grimbeeck, who was in love with another boy.

Yet we were all very innocent, especially me, and girls were only one part of our challenge at school. With studies and sports, they were the third part of a triangle—the darkest, most secret part, perhaps, but also the most untouched. They brushed against you while you made hydrogen sulphide, they watched you from the side of the rugby field, and you walked them halfway home—wondering what it would be like to go all the way.

Professor Robert Broom, the archaeologist, came to Beaufort West one day looking for fossils. The Karoo in our area is famous for this, and at school we had built a small museum. The Professor needed two young men with pick and shovel to help him. Fanie Bekker and I were chosen, and we started for the dig at six o'clock. Riding in the rumble seat of the car with picks and shovels next to us, we were bitterly cold. The Professor rode in the front with our science teacher. He had a pair of binoculars and from the car would select a *koppie,* saying it appeared to be loaded with fossils. To our amazement, he was always right. We dug all day and found a great many outcroppings that were marked for further excavation by expert teams.

In the car coming back, it was warmer and easier to talk. The day had been exciting, we were going to be paid well for our work, and Professor Broom fascinated us. We had expected a real professor to have a white beard. Instead, he was young-looking and seemed to enjoy his life.

"How'd you like to be a professor?" asked Fanie.

"Maybe," I said. "But . . ."

"But what?"

I did not know what I was going to say until I said it: "I don't want to work with old, dead bones. I want to work with live human beings."

"You mean like being a doctor?"

"Yes, maybe like a doctor."

"My old man wants me to be a missionary like your old man, but I want to be an actor."

Fanie, I decided, would be good at that. He was always putting on a show by himself—especially with the girls.

"Tell me about Friday night."

"You mean with Annatjie Krynauw?"

"Yes!"

Annatjie was more developed than any other girl our age. She had breasts like a grown woman. We all stared at them, and now Fanie claimed he had done more than that.

"Her parents weren't home and we were playing hide and seek at this party, switching off the light, when I got my chance and hid with her . . . putting my hands here and there . . ."

"Wow! . . . What did it feel like?"

"Like this, Chris . . . put your hand out."

Fanie held his hand up, cupping it against the wind.

"That's what it feels like!" he said.

I tried it, and it felt so wonderful I put both hands up. Then, to get more, I stood up in the rumble seat. This sent Fanie into wild laughter.

"Chris, don't be so greedy! Leave some of it for the rest of us!"

In the wind, I had a sense of speed and then of the flight of time. Did this shorten the amount of time you had to live—or stretch it out? I recalled the still moment that morning in the garden, before driving to the seaside, when there was no sound or shadow and time seemed to have stopped—only to be caught again as I ran among the trees saying good-bye to them. It had also been something else: a good-bye to childhood. And now this strange cupping of the hands in the wind—was it not good-bye to boyhood? So you grew older and life was measured that way—not by birthdays or by successive New Years. It was a string of good-byes. It was a race from the garden of childhood and a reach into the wind. It was a leap toward the unknown and a seizure of the untouchable. Yet why—why did we have to torture ourselves?

I did not know the answer, any more than I knew why I began to break my own heart running the mile in bare feet against Daantjie Rabie.

Neither of us realized at the beginning that it would end in such a struggle—or even that it would happen. Daantjie was four years ahead of me and already at Stellenbosch University near Cape Town where he ran the mile and was Western Province Champion. I ran the mile for my school and was unbeaten in any track meets with other high schools. During a holiday at home, Daantjie saw me run one day and suggested we practice together. After that, we saw one another often. He helped my technique and encouraged me to keep training when he was away.

I had begun to run the mile because I was not as fast as other boys on shorter distances. So I chose an event where will and endurance would have greater effect—the 880 and the mile. I ran them in bare feet because I had no track shoes or money to buy them. But I liked it, and with Daantjie's encouragement I cut my time to below five minutes. This created enough attention for the school to enter me in Beaufort West's biggest sporting event—the annual meet on Union Day.

This was always a great day. Everybody who could move came to the sports ground. People arrived from farms in cars, and others came by bus and train from distant cities. There were flags and judges, and the women of the church had a cafeteria where they sold cakes, sandwiches, coffee, and local ginger beer. There were cyclists from Cape Town, including the famous Binneman brothers, Chris and Dick. They had bikes with thin wheels that flashed in the sun. They wore bright yellow shirts with short pants slit up the sides and their huge legs gleamed from wintergreen oil. There were other athletes, mainly from Stellenbosch, and some girls were among them. They all wore track suits with varsity colors and each one began to warm up for his event—the shot put and jumping events in the middle of the rugby field, while runners jogged about on the track that circled the field.

For years I had watched this from the stands, sometimes sneaking in by hiding beneath the closed rumble seat of a car. And now suddenly I was in it—wearing white shorts and shirt, running in bare feet up and down the sidelines to make myself ready and to show off to the grandstand. Daantjie was there, too, with other runners. All of them had spikes that dug neat little holes into the dirt—holes I closed over when I ran on top of them.

I was entered in the mile against Daantjie with a 150-yard lead. This put me one-quarter of the way around the track—in the middle of the bend at the end of the field, while Daantjie took a starting position before the grandstand at the finish line. There were others running with him but I knew he would quickly outdistance them and catch me as well. My hope was to delay this until the last lap.

Daantjie crouched into starting position, and I did the same, although without blocks or spikes it made little sense. The gun went off and we were away. We went three times around the track and Daantjie caught me on the last turn, finishing with a twenty-yard lead. Everyone, including Daantjie, congratulated me for staying ahead until the last turn, and I thanked them and said nothing because already I wanted something else—to close that gap and maybe even beat him. It was a wild, crazy dream but it would not leave me. I had one more year at high school. That meant one more Union Day meet and a second crack at Daantjie.

A good miler needs endurance, speed, and strength. You can be a great half-miler with just speed. You can also be a great half-miler with a lot of endurance and little speed. But a good miler needs all of it, especially the speed with a kick coming off the last turn—where Daantjie caught me. I had the endurance and strength, but lacked this speed. So throughout the school year I practiced on 100-yard and 150-yard dashes to pick up speed.

While planning my assault, I was unexpectedly helped by Daantjie's father who took me to Cuthbert's Shoe Store and bought me a pair of track shoes. It was a touching gesture and immediately invested our contest with an extra dimension. Dominie Rabie, with his white congregation, had never been close to my father whose time was spent with problems and needs of the colored people. Now this gap between our families was being narrowed. A race around a dirt track was doing more to draw us together than our common belief in one God.

When the day finally arrived, Daantjie came up from Cape Town. He saw me practicing starts at the track, wearing the new spikes.

"How do you feel?"

"Fine," I said, "like a tiger."

"Good," he said, patting me on the shoulder and jogging off for a warm-up.

I did not feel at all like a tiger. There were giant butterflies in my stomach. I kept telling myself they would go away once we started running —but I did not believe it. The officials announced the start of the mile race, and we went to our positions. I took my old spot at the bottom of the track and was hardly in position when the gun went off.

I got away a little late and quickly decided to take the first lap at a faster clip than usual, hoping this would keep my lead and so force Daantjie to overextend himself too early in the race. Coming out of the second bend, I could see him across the field, going into the bend. He was running free and open with the easy grace of a *wildebeest,* already ahead of his rivals but more than a hundred yards behind me.

I dug in and kept my pace, saying to myself, "Go, go man, go . . . even if you drop dead on the track, drop dead with him behind you."

Later I was told they started to cheer me in the second lap and kept on cheering until the end, but I heard nothing except the sound of my feet, my breathing, the feel of the wind in my face—and then, coming into the last bend, I could hear Daantjie behind me.

Go man, go man, go.

Down the straight track I could see the finish ribbon, the judges gathered on each side, the crowd in the stand—then Daantjie alongside me, slowly pulling ahead until he crossed over and I saw his back before me. I tried to stay close behind him by locking step, but his stride was longer and he pulled away steadily. I felt my strength going, and fought to hang on.

Go man, go man go, go, go, go . . .

It was over—with no ribbon and Daantjie turning back to see me coming up. He had won by a good ten yards. I had cut the gap by half. I had run a mile, minus 150 yards, in 4.42—the best I had ever done—and Daantjie put his arm around me.

"Good going, Chris, you did great!"

"Thanks, Daantjie."

I turned away not wanting him to see my tears. I tried to stop them but they came, anyway. In the shower I told myself it was nothing—a race against a college boy and I had not done badly.

Yet it was something—an unbroken barrier. I was first in studies and chosen by my class to give our farewell address. As a cadet I held the highest student rank of sergeant-major. Outside school I had formed a popular musical trio. And, in her living room, I had finally kissed Sissie Grimbeeck.

But I had not won the race against Daantjie Rabie, and for a long time I dreamed of the ten yards separating us, crossing it in a thousand ways. I ran it with legs like wings. I leaped it with a burst of the heart. I smashed it with flailing arms. And I drank it like the wind.

So I ran the race over and over again during the weeks that followed, until it was eventually replaced by an even larger challenge. Upon graduating, I had decided to study medicine at the University of Cape Town and, after a summer at the sea, we returned to Beaufort West to prepare my departure for the distant city where there would be many races far more difficult than the mile.

It was a week of strange and disturbing emotions. Once again, I felt I had a sudden clarity of vision, an unexpected ability to see old things in a new way—a special gift of insight that was granted only when departure became inevitable.

Perhaps most acutely I sensed the naked and defenseless love of a parent for the child. No other love was so true, so committed, so unselfish, and so destined to be walked upon. For by nature of its being, the child eventually walks out, as I was now doing—yet not without looking back.

All week my mother made ready my college clothes and prepared special dishes she knew I liked. My father grew quieter, saying less and less. Once again, I knew, there were to be more good-byes—more tears like crystal beads to thread without meaning on the string of life.

I walked in the garden, looking at the trees, and felt a stabbing sadness. Here it was again—this same fear of leaving something known for the unknown, of exchanging a familiar world for one that still had to be explored and made secure. Was life always going to be like this—constantly upset by change and by fear of leaving behind what had been touched and tasted and loved? A new taste, a new love could be wonderful. Yet what if there was nothing there? Or worse, perhaps I would fail to seize it. Barney had twice failed his year-end examinations, closing himself in his room for two days after the humiliation of such a defeat. I could never face my parents if this happened to me. Their sacrifice was too great to permit such a failure. Yet it could happen. I was going to a big city where I had never lived, to compete against boys and girls who had friends who could help them while I would be a stranger and alone.

These were terrible fears, like black baboons shaking the tops of trees. Yet I knew I had to live with them. I wanted to be a doctor, maybe even a famous one. And in Cape Town I wanted to again see Ninky, a girl I had met during the summer at Wilderness. She swam in the river without clothes like a nymph, she had a laugh that was an echo of mine, and she kissed in a way I had never known. I was wildly in love with her.

So the week passed, in a shuttling of doubt and desire, until the afternoon when I kissed my mother good-bye and then, piling two bags into the car, drove with my father to the train station. We did not speak in the car, but I knew he was feeling it very deeply because he was biting his mustache.

It was Friday and as always there were people at the train station who had nothing else to do or had strolled over to get the newspapers that came in on the evening train. We got there early and sat in the sun on a bench. There were many things I wanted to say to my father, and I hoped the train would be late so there would be time to say them all. But I did not know how to begin. So we sat there for a long while without speaking. He bit his mustache and smiled at me with sad, hazel-green eyes but these did not answer all my questions.

"You will do well," he said finally.

Then he said, "But you must study hard, and I will pray for you and for God to keep you well."

I nodded.

"Give our love to Barney and Joyce, and let us hear any news about Dodsley."

I nodded again. I was to stay with my brother and his wife while going to the university. Dodsley had joined the army and been taken prisoner of war by the Germans at Tobruk.

There was a far-away hoot of the train coming around the Nuweveld Mountains, then the hollow sound of it crossing the bridge. Finally, it came into the station before us—big and black and hissing with steam. We walked up to my coach and stood for a moment before the steps. Then I kissed him on the lips, as was the custom in our family, and climbed aboard. He helped shove my second bag up and he was still there when I found my seat and looked out the window. He was dressed in a dark suit, with a little *strikkie* tie and his mustache seemed snow white.

Suddenly I realized he would have to drive the car alone, without anyone to help him.

"Dad, will you be all right with the car?"

He nodded.

"Don't try and drive it into the church."

It was supposed to be funny, but it did not sound funny.

"I'll miss you, Dad."

He nodded again and attempted a little smile, looking very small but brave and somehow strong.

With a hoot, the train began to move. For a moment I did not look at my father, but rather at everything in the station I had known as a boy. I saw the red chocolate slot machine where we put in a penny and then, with a hooked wire, pulled down three or four extra bars. Beyond this were the white steps going up to the switch house where I used to wander in a forest of long switch handles, flashing lights of many colors, and bells ringing like electric hearts. Next on the platform, I saw a pile of crates with homing pigeons—waiting to be released to fly back across the Karoo to their nests in distant towns where their owners would scan the skies for their return.

That was what they were supposed to do—fly home. Yet I was expected to do just the opposite. All my life up to this moment had been a preparation to leave home and not come back until I had made a success. That was our difference. The bird could come home as he was, lucky bird. I could not—not any longer. I had to go into the world, taking with me nothing more than what I had learned in school and the memories of my mother and father.

I looked for him then far down the platform, his hand raised in farewell—an unmoving figure in a dark suit, a little man with white hair, all of it already smaller in my vision than he was, immense and large and real, within me. Then he was no more and soon we were on the great flat plain of the Karoo at night. I thought of how we had walked that veld, hunting rabbits, sleeping there with my father and his friends around a campfire. I looked to see if someone else had built a fire tonight but saw nothing—other than the dark shapes of bush and *koppie* under the moonlight.

In the second-class compartment with me there were five other men, talking and smoking and enjoying themselves. Eventually they left to go into the salon for a drink. When they returned, they were loud and rowdy. I crawled up into one of the bunks with my clothes on and fell into a disturbed sleep.

PART II
CAPE TOWN

CHAPTER 4

LITTLE BY LITTLE, I surfaced from sleep to the sound of slowly turning train wheels. It seemed to take some time, until there was the sudden shock of recalling where I was—en route to Cape Town and the biggest challenge of my life.

I opened my eyes to peek at the edge of a pillow and a brown curtain. I was still in my clothes, but someone had kindly covered me with a blanket and pulled the curtain. Behind it, a little time still remained to be alone and unchallenged.

The train wheels went on clanking away in an unbroken monologue, as though asking someone to answer for them.

Mak-ka-das-das, mak-ka-das-das, mak-ka-das-das . . .

After a bit, they speeded up and it became clearer.

Make-a-dash, make-a-dash, make-a-dash . . .

On a train, no one dashed anywhere. You could stop a car and get out, but on a train you were a prisoner pulled across desert and mountain to the end of the line where you had to get off—or be swept out with crumbled newspapers and cigarette butts.

In the lower berth a man began to cough. He kept it up, each cough connected to another and deeper one, until it seemed that he was surely going to strangle himself. Finally it stopped.

"Oh, Lord," he said.

"Man," said another voice, "You'd better slow down."

"*Ya,* I've got to."

Make-a-dash, make-a-dash . . .

"Next month," he said, "next month I'm going to take a vacation. They keep promising me, then they send me out again."

"That's it," said the second one, "they keep moving you until you're worn out. Then they kick you out."

"Not me," said the first one, "I've got a plan. I'm getting out before it's too late . . ."

Make-a-dash, make-a-dash . . .

"The Hex River Valley—lovely place," said the second man, as though suggesting they should get off here.

"Yes, indeed."

I climbed around in my bunk to look out the window curtain. It was lovely. Green vineyards ran down the length of the valley like a rolling sea that eventually washed up onto the mountain slopes. On its surface white farmhouses bobbed up and down—sister ships of the same flotilla. Together they had harnessed their green sea with anchoring roots of the Barlinka grape.

On the trek north from the Cape into the Karoo, someone had indeed gotten off here. It could be done. You did not have to cough out your lungs on a train seat while other men cast you here and there like thrown dice. You could anchor yourself with a vineyard. Or you could become a famous doctor if you were good enough, if you remained your own self.

So I told myself as we climbed slowly over the pass, leaving behind the Karoo and the world I knew. Yet it did not lessen my anxieties, and when a crow appeared in the sky near Worcester, I anxiously looked for another one to make it safe.

> One for sorrow,
> Two for joy . . .

There it was, and then there was a whole field of them.

> Three for a letter,
> Four for a boy,
> Five for a wish,
> Six for a kiss . . .

That was enough. Ninky would have one for me in Cape Town, like all those others she had given me during our summer at the Wilderness—starting with the first night.

We had met on the golf course one afternoon. She was walking with her two sisters, and I was with Michel and Marge, Dodsley's wife, who started talking to them. We came to a green and Ninky and her sisters started singing "Boo-Hoo, You've got Me Crying For You." Then she did a little dance by herself on the green while they all sang "Begin the Beguine," and I thought, hell man, this is really a fantastic girl. That night we went to their house to do some dancing and then, outside, I held her and she came close and kissed me. That was the first time anybody had ever kissed me like that, and I fell madly in love with her.

One day we went up the river in a canoe to the Ebb and Flo where the mountains came down to the water and there are trees and birds. Her sister, Faith, was with us and there was nobody else around. We stopped at a rock and the girls began to take their clothes off.

"Come on," said Faith, "there's nobody here."

"Yes, let's!" cried Ninky.

Singing "Anchors Aweigh," she pulled off her blouse while Faith unbuttoned her trousers. I took off my shirt, but suddenly could go no further. The girls kept it up, however, and very quickly they had everything off, standing before me on the flat rock like two river nymphs, their bodies white and pink and also dark at mysterious places I hardly dared look upon. I looked anyway and recalled that everybody in that family were vegetarians. How was it possible for some turnips and lettuce to be transformed into something like that?

They giggled and began to pull me, their little breasts bobbing like separate suns. I held my knees against my chest, clinging for dear life, until they gave up and dived into the river—two little bottoms going in double arcs before splashing with all the rest of their wonderful delights into the blue water. I jumped in after them with my pants on, feeling like a fool, but unable to do anything else.

I had never slept with a girl or even seen one nude. Ninky had seen all sorts of nudes because she was an art student and already going to the university. I would see more of them now, as a medical student, but nothing would ever equal the splendor of Ninky's body. I had her phone number and could hardly wait to see her again—though my mother thought she was too old for me and was worried about this.

They have torn down the old train station at Cape Town, even though it is always sad to see such monuments disappear. This one was a creature of the Victorian age—arching spans of cast iron forming a curved canopy above alternate platforms and tracks. These berthed the great engines as they came in, steaming and hissing like spent dragons, their flanks covered with coal dust, Karoo topsoil, and—in the early days—bits of goat, chicken, and pig.

Such an arrival calls for a structure equal to the dignity of its guest. This station had all that. It was pure Railway Functional, similar in its skeletal beauty to Paddington or King's Cross—romantic monuments charged with the optimism and courage and philistinism of their ruthless creators. Built to hold the image of an era, it had outlived both Queen and Empire. Across its platforms had walked royalty and commoner, empire builder and petty crook, people with songs in their hearts and others with voiceless memories. They had been coming for a century, speaking more than sixty different languages, yet all of them looking for much the same thing: religious freedom, fresh lands, new frontiers, diamonds, gold—new lives.

It was onto such a platform that I was disgorged from my curtained berth, last physical link with Beaufort West, to land in a flood of carts, bags, and people—as though this would surely wash away any remaining links I had with my past, my home, my family. And should that fail, should the heart still murmur the names of those left behind, there was a roar of many noises strong enough to extinguish the most anguished cry of farewell.

Above all else, this deafening roar was most overwhelming. The great arched roof bellowed back the sounds that came up from below, transforming them into those of an excited and enraged jungle. Dominating all else was the lion cough of engines with iron lungs, followed by the jackal whine of electric motors, baboon grunts of angry porters, parrot squawks of peddlers, and finally, like a frightened tribe of monkeys, the babble and squeal of arriving passengers.

Through all of this I wandered, lugging one suitcase, until I fell into the arms of my brother and his wife. Above the din, we called to each other by our names, as though it were a miracle to be still alive. Holding onto one another, we walked past a café with the delicious smell of mutton pies, collected my large bag at the luggage stand, then hurried out past the police office and into Barney's Riley—starting then toward my new home.

Barney and Joyce were in the front, and I was in the back, and, as we drove alongside the buses with overhead wires on Adderley Street, my brother pointed out the sights as though the city was an outdoor museum— the park, the City Hall with palm trees, the Grand Parade with its flower and fruit stalls and finally the Castle—second building to be erected in South Africa in 1666 by Jan van Riebeeck, father of Cape Town—with its orange, white, and blue flag waving in the breeze.

I nodded and dutifully looked at each one. But in between I returned to gaze at the most inspiring monument of all—Table Mountain, rising over the city like a mammoth bastion. A mist lay about it, resembling a giant tablecloth draped over a craggy rim of granite and pine.

From the mountain's immense hulk, greater than all the elephant herds of Africa or whales of the sea, two giant arms appeared to go down toward the city, cupping it in an embrace—Devil's Peak on the right, Lion's Head and Signal Hill on the left. Bernini had extended two such arms in his colonnade which reached out from St. Peter's in Rome—so-called arms of the mother church to gather in her wandering children. Other cities, such as New York, had rivers for arms to receive the ships and sailors of the world. But these were something else—giant limbs of a creature larger than any yet conceived by man, holding a city in its grasp so that all the gales of the antarctic, all the shakes and quakes of hell, could not dislodge one stone of it.

Over it all blew a wind that seemed to be the first wind of the world, coming to us on the tip end of the African continent—a wind born some-where over the sea where the first winds are born, blowing over the tops of humpbacked waves and beneath clouds as white as whales' bellies, unfelt and untouched by man until it came upon us, removing all that was foul or worn or noxious, lifting all away except that tablecloth atop our protective bastion. If ever a mount deserved to be inhabited by gods and so wor-shiped by man below, this was it.

"I'm glad you came," said Barney. "There's a pervert on the loose."

"A what?"

"A sex maniac," said Joyce. "Barney is very worried about me."

My brother and his wife had been married only a few months and you could feel the tension that exists between two people who still like to touch each other. Joyce had auburn hair with a rather nice figure—maybe a little plump, but nice.

"I'm not worried like Barney," she said.

"Because you don't know what people like that can do," he said.

The pervert, he explained, watched a home carefully, noting when the husband left and returned. When he was sure of this, he would get inside the house, criminally assault the woman, and murder her.

"Mind you, I'm not saying I'd like that to happen to me," said Joyce.

"You bet," said Barney, squeezing the wheel.

The pervert had so far murdered five women and since my brother was away most of the time, my daily presence in his home would ensure Joyce's safety. He was a mechanical engineer and often rode steam engines to see if the company could put a larger load on them. While that was going on, I could protect his wife from a roaming pervert.

"Like I say," said Joyce, "I'm not so worried as Barney, even though each time he attacks a woman nearer to us. And last time it was less than a mile away. Except at nights, then I do worry a bit."

"It's just as well Chris stays home nights, anyway," said my brother. "He has to study hard. Nights out can come later, after the first couple of years."

First couple of years? Was he kidding? Ninky could never wait that long. Neither could I. Barney was wrong. He had failed twice at varsity because of fooling around—something I would rather die than have happen to me. But he was not going to lock me up in his house on a two-year lookout for some pervert.

"Are we near Mowbray?"

"Not yet, why?"

"Nothing, just wondered."

Ninky lived at Mowbray, but I was not going to mention her—not now.

"That's the hospital, Groote Schuur," said Barney.

It sat up on the side of the mountain—a great white honeycomb with a million worlds inside its cells. Immediately below it was the medical school.

"That's where you'll be going after one year at the university," said Barney. "You have to pass that first year to get into medical school."

In between the school and Main Road was a cemetery. The gravestones came right down to the edge of the highway.

"Not a very good advertisement for the school or hospital," I said.

"Everybody makes mistakes," said Barney. "Except we can't afford to—right, Chris?"

"Right," I said, wishing he would shut up.

A little further on, we passed a wooded hillside to the right. My brother explained this was Rondebosch, another suburb. The university was on top of the hill, beyond the woods. They lived nearby, on Rustenburg Road, in a small flat on the first floor where I found my room to be very small—barely holding a single bed and a desk, with a window facing onto a courtyard wall four feet away.

"It's not very big, I'm afraid," said Barney.

"It's quiet, though," said Joyce.

"It's fine," I said, knowing they could afford nothing better and grateful for any place to sleep and study.

I began to unpack, and Barney hung around to watch. There was little to see because I was wearing most of my important clothes—a brown plaid jacket given to me by Michel Rossouw, with a pair of beige worsted pants that had belonged to Dodsley and had been skillfully lengthened with false cuffs by my mother. In my bag there was another pair of gray flannels.

"I think those were mine," said Barney.

"No, they were Dodsley's. Everything I have was his once."

"*Ya,* but he got it from me."

When I had tried on the clothes in Beaufort, in front of my mother's dressing mirror, they had seemed wonderful. They had a special splendor. They were the pants and the jacket—used, perhaps, but made new by my mother working at nights—with which I would win my honors as a medical student. Yet now, with my brother counting out how many of us had gone through them, they seemed to lose their beauty and value. I did not like to think of wearing the same pants which Barney had worn six or seven years ago—sitting in class with them, going with girls in them, studying in them —and flunking in the same pair of gray flannels.

"Did you bring a yellow tie?"

"No."

"As a fresher, you have to wear one."

"I know, but I don't have it."

"So you'll have to buy one tomorrow. Otherwise, they'll make it rough on you."

"Life gets simpler," I said. "Last time they pushed us into cow manure."

We laughed, but it was not true. Life had become far more complex. It would be much easier to put my head in a pail of manure than spend all my money on a school tie and so have nothing left to take Ninky to a movie. Quite clearly, the odds were against us.

School opened two days later and I set out on foot to climb the mountain. At first I was alone and it was exciting. Going up Rustenburg and then turning onto Grotto Road, I walked under an arcade of trees, ushered onward by bird song and shafts of sunlight. At Lover's Walk and crossing De Waal Drive, I began to join streams of other students. They increased until I was surrounded by varying groups talking excitedly with each other —girls with boys, or boys looking at groups of girls. Some would call to one another, while others walked arm in arm, their words linked more intimately than their bodies.

I walked alone, knowing no one, conscious of pants that had been worn by my brother, my jacket that had been given to me by my dear friend, Michel, and, most important, the bright yellow tie on which I had spent nearly all my money—symbol that I was a freshman and properly dressed. This, at least, was new and part of the march up the hill.

At the edge of the rugby field, I looked back toward the valley below— at the Main Road where I had come in Barney's car two days ago, and beyond that, the Cape Flats stretching out to the distant blue mountains. This mountain, I thought, was like education: The higher you climbed, the farther you could see.

On the other side of the rugby field was a statue of Cecil John Rhodes with its inscription from Kipling:

> I dream, I dream by rock and heath and pine,
> of empires to the northward . . .

Before me lay a great flight of white steps leading up to Jameson Hall at the top. It resembled a Greek temple with six white columns and pediment. That was my north, up there lay my empires, in that temple whose massive doors opened up into the heart of the mountain.

"Hey, fresher!"

I stopped.

"Hey, you there!"

It was for me and it came from a student sitting on the side of the steps.

"Come on over here a second."

Obediently, I went. He was a well-dressed young man, with the compact body of a rugby player. I nodded and smiled but he looked back at me with dark eyes as though I had been caught sneaking through the back door of his home.

"Listen, fresher, you're all wrong."

I did not know what he meant, but I could tell he was a mean one. He had a little mouth, and his eyes did not blink. I felt I had met him before but could not recall where.

"What's the matter—did you lose your tongue?"

He spit it out, and I knew why he was familiar. He was the same type of bully I had fought at school. You ran into them all the time. They were mean, with little mouths, and they beat anyone weaker than themselves.

"Where you from, fresher?"

"Beaufort West."

"So—and in Beaufort West there's nobody to tell you the color of the tie you must wear?"

"And why not?"

"I'll tell you why, fresher. Your tie must be yellow. First years wear yellow tie, not an *orange* one. An orange tie is distinctive among the yellow ones . . . makes you stand out, hey?"

Good God, I thought, he was right. It was more orange than yellow. I had gone to the best store in Cape Town. The clerk had said this was what they all wore.

Two other students walked by with yellow ties—truly yellow. It was all wrong, and this mean bastard was right.

"Why do you want to stand out, fresher? Who do you think you are?"

He lifted himself off the wall and, standing before me, was much taller and bigger than I was.

"Get yourself a yellow tie, immediately, you hear? There's penalties for smart freshers who don't follow rules. Either do it, or else you'll find me waiting for you."

"Yes," I said, looking at my tie again, as though it might have suddenly changed color. It was still a ghastly orange.

"Yes, of course," I said again, confused and humiliated.

I climbed the rest of the steps up to Jameson Hall where I registered for classes—so acutely embarrassed by the orange tie that I signed my name twice in the wrong place—and then hurried down the hill to my brother's house. In my room, looking out the window at the wall, I wondered how I could have been so stupid. Even worse, where was I going to get the money for another tie? The answer was simple. I had no money, so the tie had to be returned.

It was from Garlick's, and the clerk remembered me and nodded in a friendly way. But when I explained what was wrong, he lost all signs of being a friend.

"I'm afraid we can't do that, sir."

He said "sir" the way butlers do before slamming the door in the face of peddlers.

"Goods bought," he said, "cannot be exchanged."

CAPE TOWN   51

This was a disaster and my head whirled.

"But you must," I said. "I mean, *please* take it back. I must have a yellow tie. I have no money for another one."

Embarrassed, I looked down at the floor. When I glanced up again, the clerk was in the corner of the shop, talking to an older man. The man glanced over at me, then nodded and the clerk returned.

"It will be all right," he said, free to smile again.

They returned my money, since they had no yellow ties, and I bought one at Stuttaford's. It looked so sharp I put it on immediately and phoned Ninky. She had begun classes at the art school in town and was always out. This time she was in, and we made a date for Saturday night. Everything was finally falling into place. Leonardo da Vinci had noted the natural gait of the free horse was a trot—and, being free, I ran most of the way home.

The free run did not last long. Almost immediately, I discovered I could barely creep through some classes. We took four subjects—botany, chemistry, physics, and zoology—which were more than mere subjects in themselves. They were designed to equip us with a language for the study of medicine. They were to be our tools, our weapons to seize and hold the knowledge to come in the next five years. Without this, it was impossible to go ahead.

Yet I quickly found I was less prepared than other students. At Beaufort West we had taken chemistry, and my father had added to our high school botany. With these two subjects I felt at home. I could read the language of the course. Yet in the other two—physics and zoology—I did not understand basic words being used to explain other words or concepts. It was like reading a dictionary where the explanation is written in an unknown language.

"What's velocity?" I asked Barney, who was a mechanical engineer and had taken the same course.

"Speed," he said.

"Here it says 'velocity is time rate of motion in a given direction and sense'."

"So?"

"So what is 'time rate of motion' and what is 'given sense'? Whose sense? What sense?"

"Don't worry," said Barney. "I'll explain it all to you after dinner."

After dinner he went to bed, and the next day he was on a steam engine heading for the Orange Free State—and I was in trouble. Besides this, he could never help me on the nervous system of a frog—first of zoology's three creatures, to be followed by the rabbit and the dogfish. This was going to be a real scramble. I would have to learn everything, even if I did not understand it, like a parrot.

Yet even this was impossible in physics, since I was repeatedly kicked out of class. Dr. Grinley, the physics lecturer, had constant trouble with his students. He would enter and say one word only, "Gentlemen . . ."—causing everyone to roar with laughter. In reply, Dr. Grinley would dismiss three rows of the class—the first three, the middle ones, or those in the rear. My problem consisted in failing to anticipate his choice of the day. Each time I moved—front, middle or rear—I ended up among those being kicked out. The one class I needed most to follow I couldn't even attend.

When I eventually told Ninky about this, she had a quick solution.

"Wait outside the classroom until he turfs out his batch, then go in saying 'Doctor, I'm innocent as a little lamb—I just arrived'."

We laughed and sipped our soft drinks. We had seen a Gary Cooper film at the Savoy and now were next door in the café. It must have been our second or third date in Cape Town because I remember knowing what to expect when I took her home. All our movie dates were alike, except this one, which led to a talk I have never forgotten.

"As for the zoology class," said Ninky, "I know nothing about frogs. But in our anatomy class, we studied the human body. When you get to that, I can help."

"I can't wait."

"For what?"

"To study the human body."

I wanted to say *your* body, but I did not have the nerve.

"It's the greatest cathedral ever built by God," she said.

We were quiet a moment thinking about that, and I recalled her on the rock without her clothes.

"Complete with arches and tunnels . . ."

"And pillars," she said with a mischievous smile. She had light gray eyes with dark pupils, and when she smiled it was like they said yes.

"Yes," I said.

"Talking of he-men," she said, "Gary Cooper is my ideal."

That required a he-man sort of reply, but I did not know what to say. The thought of her thinking of anyone else paralyzed me.

"He's the quiet type," she said. "But when needed, he always hits the mark."

I nodded. "He can pull that gun, but how good is he really?"

Ninky sucked her drink and muttered something incomprehensible.

"I mean when do they practice? We always see them knocking off hats or putting out lights or drilling the gun hand of a bad guy. But we never see them practice. They have to learn somewhere. We never see them learning."

"Instinct," she said. "They fire from instinct. Do you know what I mean?"

I nodded. She had a fantastic expression and a lovely mouth.

"I don't think you do. I think you choke up your instinct."

This probably referred to my holding onto my pants on the rock. It meant I was afraid to open up and show what was inside me. On the radio they were playing "Everybody loves somebody somehow, Everybody finds somebody somewhere." Why did Ninky think I was different from anyone else?

"I'm wild about you, Ninky."

"I like you, too, Chris . . ."

She gave me a nervous little smile and looked into her empty glass. For a moment I thought she might want another one which would be embarrassing because I had no more money. Barney gave me ten shillings a month for pocket money and I had spent it all that night—after carefully planning every detail of the evening.

I had taken a bath and shaved early in the afternoon, hoping this would hasten me toward seven o'clock. Then I had walked two miles to Ninky's house, stopping on the way to buy two tickets at the Savoy and so make sure we had seats. After chatting with her father and mother, we had walked to the movie and now, in the café, we had one soft drink each, which finished off the ten shillings.

It would be another month before I could take Ninky out again—another month without lunch money. But it was worth it because we really clicked.

"I like you," she said again, "but I'm talking about something else. You think everything in life is in school books, and I don't."

"Where is it then?"

"In people mostly."

"Yes, but you can understand people better after reading books."

"No, Chris. Living is more important. Living and using your instinct."

"I do that all the time."

"No, you've disciplined yourself like a machine. Like these dates once a month . . . why once a month? Why make a fixed routine out of it . . . or would that cause you to fail physics?"

Shortly after registering at the university, I found I did not have enough to pay for books and tuition fees. I was being aided by the Helpmekaar Fund, besides having food and shelter from my brother, but this was not enough. So I had gone to Knot Craig, University Registrar, and explained I needed help—or could not stay. He looked at my records and, after some talk, gave me a three-year scholarship. But to keep it, I had to pass every course. "Don't fail one," he warned. "If you do, it's canceled." I told him not to worry. "Nothing will come between me and my studies."

Ninky did not know about this or about my having only ten shillings a month. But she knew a lot more. She had met my parents, she had prayed on her knees beside my father's table, asking God to forgive her for her sins (while I, kneeling next to her, our bodies barely touching, wondered on the elusive nature of sin—how could making love to her be sinful at any time or in any fashion?). There, on her knees, she had seen the worn hands of my mother and my father wearing tennis shoes to save his good ones. She could sense, if only through instinct, what sacrifices were necessary to put me through school. More than anyone else in the world, she had to understand this.

"Ninky, I can't fail anything. I can't ever fail—don't you understand that?"

"Why?"

Her lovely eyes narrowed and she asked it again: "Why?"

I shook my head, unable to go on. How in the hell did we ever get from Gary Cooper to this?

"Chris, I'm trying to say that often you can learn more from defeat than from success."

"No, I can't afford to learn that way. I can't drop one subject."

"Why can't you afford it if everyone else can, and does? You just think you can't. You lost the mile to your good friend, didn't you?"

"So what?"

"So didn't that teach you more than all the victories?"

It had taught me how to cry, but at nineteen that is not considered a virtue.

"It taught me to run faster—always faster."

"Maybe too fast, maybe even the wrong way."

This hurt because it meant there was a gulf between us. Success in studies, going to the top, meant everything to me. She was talking about not getting there, yet being just as happy.

"Don't you believe in success?" I asked.

"I believe in being," she said. "Everything that helps me to be is what I believe in. Does success help you to be?"

"Yes, of course—why not? You are nothing without it. If you want to really be, as you put it, then you must really be something."

"But you're still nothing—if you're inhuman."

This hurt even more and I did not know what to say. She saw it and began to apologize.

"Chris, I don't mean you're not human. You are, and I think you're wonderful. I mean you're different somehow, like you were carrying someone else around inside you who was giving you orders all the time . . ."

She stopped. Then she said: "Do you know what I mean?"

Were the voices I obeyed my own, or someone else's? Was it my mother, or my father—or was it hidden under a bundle of sin that I would have to pick up on New Year's Eve? I did not know.

"Listen, sweetie, why don't you ask Gary Cooper that question?"

She laughed, indicating withdrawal. On the walk home, she put her arm around me, and at the door she kissed me again, in the close way she had done at The Wilderness.

"Do you forgive me?"

"Yes, yes," I said.

I wanted to go on with it, but she said no.

"Good night," she said softly.

I kissed her again, that way.

"Um," she said. "And now good night."

"You accuse me of holding in my instincts, then when I set them loose, you say good night."

"Silly," she said, kissing quickly and slipping into the house.

I walked the two miles home in a delirium of projected dreams generally associated with love, wondering how I could wait another month for it to happen again—and naïve enough to believe she would wait a month for me. And covered with such sweet victory, I gave little thought to what she had tried to tell me about the value of defeat.

Yet I had a glimpse of what Ninky meant when they posted the results of the midterm exams. With horror, I saw my mark in physics was forty-three—seven under passing. It was not the final, year-end exam, and two more tests were scheduled for those who had not passed. However, it was the first exam I had ever failed in my life and I was alarmed.

Fortunately, Barney was at home and able to help me recross once more the first pages of the text that had made no sense and so had left me without a foundation for all that followed. After a week of cramming, I walked into the second exam feeling less like a parrot. The mark showed it: sixty-five. Immediately I went to Dr. Grinley.

"Sir, I would like to take the second repeat test."

"But you passed, you got sixty-five."

"I need more."

"Why?"

"It's not good enough."

"All right," he said. "If that's the way you feel, let's see what you can do."

I did seventy-three and never again felt like a parrot in physics. Nor was botany, a six months' course, any trouble. I passed it with top marks. Chemistry was under control as well, but zoology was not. I had just gotten by in it, and the finals in this were notoriously difficult.

With some money from Barney—and my mother who followed this as though she had a son in a foreign war—I bought a scalpel, a pair of scissors, and a dissecting forceps. I also bought frogs, dogfish, and rabbits from the laboratory attendant and took them home—working until dawn dissecting them away to the skeleton. When we began on the bones of a rabbit, I put one on the stove in a pot with caustic soda and, to the horror of Joyce, digested away the flesh so that only the bones remained. "Next year," she moaned, "I can just see it—you're going to boil away people like that!"

I had dropped everything for these studies. I never went to dances: I had no dress suit or car—nor time to make friends with boys who had cars. I ducked the students' cheering section at the annual intervarsity match. Like every other fresher, I was given a tin can to shake on the street, while dressed as a sailor or pirate, to raise money for the Rag—a street procession that ended in the year's one big variety dance. But I never shook that can anywhere. Joyce's brother, who was visiting us, gave me ten shillings, saying, "Change it into coppers, stuff it into your can, and say that's what you collected." I did just that and memorized all the bones of a rabbit.

Sports went out the window, too. I had no time for them—and was not good enough. At Beaufort West, I was the best miler and played scrumhalf on the first string rugby team. But I was outclassed in fresher tryouts at Cape Town. Also it required more time than I could spare. Rugby practice started at five-thirty, which meant you were home after dark— even with a car. Later in the year, I went out for the swimming team and did three-meter diving. But that was a summer sport and came along after my subjects were more under control.

When final exams arrived, I got through chemistry and physics in good style, but zoology suddenly loomed as possible disaster. I did not do well on the written test, which meant high marks were needed in the second half. We would be tested in the laboratory on one of three subjects: frog, rabbit, or dogfish. One of these would be laid out in our trays as we entered the room—but which one?

Early on the morning of the exam, I went down to the zoology building. The windows on the ground floor, where we would be tested, were blinded against anyone looking inside. Yet nothing could prevent sniffing—and sniff I did, smelling what seemed to be dogfish. Excitedly, I sat down under a nearby pine and for one hour reviewed the cranial nerves of the dogfish. When they finally opened the doors and we entered a laboratory littered with dogfish, I could have kissed my lovely, stinky little *squalus acanthias* —cranial nerves and all.

Rather than hurry to Beaufort for the summer holiday, I waited around for my marks to be posted. They looked beautiful: first class in physics, first in chemistry, first in botany, second in zoology. I had passed with honors and now had the language, the tools, to become a doctor.

I phoned my brother, who was overjoyed, and then Ninky who was leaving for The Wilderness.

"I knew you would do it, Chris. Will you come to The Wilderness this summer? I'll wait for you."

"Yes," I said, "I'll come."

I meant it, but never arrived. My father had sold our Wilderness home to buy one for Joyce and Barney in Cape Town. So I spent the summer hunting in the Karoo, visiting friends, and occasionally looking in at the Beaufort West hospital.

All of us who had passed the first year were now anxious for the second year when we would begin the proper study of medicine. Some could hardly wait—like Percy Helman who shared a compartment with me on the train homeward. I liked Percy. He was one of the few friends I made in that first year. We used to study chemistry together in his room at the men's residence, eating wonderful Jewish cakes sent by his mother from Laingsburg.

As the train pulled into his station, Percy took out a bottle of ether and began to sprinkle himself with it. It made a terrible odor.

"Percy, are you mad—what are you doing?"

"When my mother meets me," he said, "I want to smell like a doctor."

CHAPTER 5

OUR LONG CLIMB to the summit—to become doctors and so protect man as long as possible from death—began by being admitted into a room filled with twenty cadavers.

As students, we expected it. To learn anatomy, it was necessary to take the body apart and physically note its separate nerves and muscles and organs. Yet the vision of twenty bodies, each on a marble-top table, was so overwhelming that I almost had to turn back into the corridor of the anatomy building.

There were so many of them evenly spaced in neat rows it seemed as though a graveyard had been laid bare, exposing its buried inhabitants once more to the world, stripped of coffin and clothes, so that we could merci-lessly witness their naked passage in the final rendering of self, to whatever awaited them.

It was this, the invasion of the privacy of death, that was so alarming—as well as the size of it. The presence of one or another corpse might be encompassed in a brief glance or the time it took to walk past it while holding your breath. This was something else. Here was a whole field of bodies that could never be overlooked or sidestepped. We had to go through them, breathing it all in—indeed, we had to encamp among them for weeks, months, a whole year of classes. How could we survive it?

And how—with horror, it came to me—how could *they* accept us? Surely, something more than death bound them together: mute rage and hate for those of us who had robbed them of the intimacy of their separate graves, laying them naked and defenseless on marble slabs to be stared at by students who would slowly pick them to pieces—not with the merciful speed of vultures but rather little by little in a slow tearing of tissue from tissue, nerve from nerve, until we eventually pulled up entire strips of muscle and whole organs.

I could not breathe, let alone look upon them. Closing my eyes, I had the sense of being closed within an Egyptian tomb, sealed off with its terrible secrets, its vials of poison, baskets of asps' tongues, teeth protruding through black skin and rotting linen—crumbling evidence that the mastering weight of time had reached down through tons of piled up stones and perfumed wrappings to chill and shatter everything, even we who were trapped within.

"God, this place stinks."

It was Harry Kahn next to me. I nodded mute agreement. The smell was so nauseating I felt I could not remain.

"It's the bloody formalin," he said.

"Oh."

"They've been pickled in it."

So it was that, I realized, and not the smell of death. It did not come with them from their graves, from the Other Side. It was a creation of man, HCHO, used to arrest death's continuing action—the spontaneous generation of living organisms from putrefying organic matter. It was something from Our Side, which we would have to live with. And if my classmates could take it, so could I.

"They do it in the cellar," said Harry.

"Yes, I know."

"Have you seen it? They pump out the blood and then blow them up with this stuff."

"Yes," I said.

I had not seen it. Yet I knew how it was done. Outside the building you could smell the odor of formalin being discharged by fans from the basement. We were in the anatomy and physiology building of the Medical School—the same complex of structures, huddled between the Groote Schuur Hospital and the graveyard, which Barney had pointed out the day he had picked me up at the station. For the next five years, I would study here, with eventual duties in the hospital. A few classes would be elsewhere —in the Peninsula Maternity Home, or the Valkenberg mental asylum— but the center of study, the inner ring of combat, was to be within these walls, beginning with anatomy and its counterpart, physiology. Where anatomy was the dissecting of plant or animal life to learn its structuring, physiology was the study of that same organism during life. This included a look at its chemical make-up (biochemistry), its tissues (histology), and how the parts worked (experimental physiology).

The attendant with an alphabetical list of our names began to assign us in groups of eight to a table. With the table, came the corpse. Harry and I were near the top of the list and would probably get the first table—but which one?

Frantically, as one condemned, I looked around me. Nearest to us was a white woman with only one breast, a scar in the shape of a cross indicating where the other one had nested its roving cancer cells.

Never, I thought, never could I go near that body.

Next to her lay a giant colored man, his blue-brown skin tight under the swelling of his big limbs and muscles, his mouth open as though seized while singing to the glory of God in my father's church. Nor could I cut him open, any more than I could stab one of the singing Morkels—never.

"Barnard, Christiaan, N. . . . B-a-r-n-a-r-d . . ."

"Chris . . . answer!"

"Yes . . . here."

"We got him," said Harry.

It was the first table to the left as you entered and "him" was a white man—thank God—with both his breasts and parts in full evidence. He was about forty and well-proportioned. His hair was dark brown, while under the arms and around the genitals it was lighter in hue—almost russet. His eyes had the brown and hazel of a wet willow limb—similar to those of my brother, Marius.

Could this ever happen to my brother or myself? What accident had ripped from such a man the harmony of pulsating life and then delivered him to us on this slab? Those arms once held a woman. Those loins had thrilled to the touch of another, the entire body had trembled in its coupling, all of it tensing into an arc of flight—then dropping sweetly, falling into soft oblivion. How many times had it happened to him?

In teams of two, we were assigned an arm or a leg. Harry and I drew the left arm. With scalpel and forceps, we were expected to begin the dissection, following instruction in our textbook—taking off first the skin, then exposing the muscles, arteries and nerves. Harry propped our book against the corpse, its blue cloth cover against white thigh. Together we read from D. J. Cunningham's *The Manual of Practical Anatomy*:

The Pectoral Region and Axilla—Dissection. Reflexion of Skin: Make skin incisions 1–4 shown in Figure 3. In making incision 2 avoid cutting into the superficial fascia and dividing the thin sheet of muscle, platysma, and the supra-clavicular nerves which lie deep to it (Fig. 4), both of which sweep down over the clavicle into the upper part of the chest wall.

Reflect the flaps of skin thus marked (A and B, Fig. 3), beginning in the median plane at one of the angles. Do not detach the flaps, but leave them hanging by their lateral ends, in order that they may be replaced when dissection for the day is finished. Leave the small patch around the nipple. . . .

"You want to start it off?"

"No, Harry, you begin it."

"You sure?"

"Yes, I'll pick up as we go along."

Harry made the first cut and, although I knew what had been done to the body, I was surprised to see no blood flow—only flesh the color of old fish gills.

"Here," said Harry, "hold the wrist a minute, Chris."

I put my hand on it—and instinctively pulled back from the cold, bloodless limb.

"Hold it yourself, Professor," I said.

I did not touch the body again that day, nor all that week. But gradually I began to do my share. Harry was very considerate and understanding. He also had a running sense of humor, which helped us all. One of the students working with us suggested our corpse should have a name and Harry supplied it immediately.

"Let's call him Chaim," he said, pronouncing it *Hy-am.*

"Why?"

"Short for I AM."

"I AM—what?"

"I AM THAT I AM," said Harry, with a wink for me.

Everyone laughed and agreed our cadaver should be known as Chaim or Hyam—short for "I am that I am." Quite obviously, none of them realized its origin. I was a bit shocked, knowing it from one of my father's recurring themes: Moses, asking God His name, received the answer: "I AM THAT I AM . . . Thus shalt thou say unto the children of Israel, I AM hath sent me unto you."

Harry, aware I would probably know this, had winked to suggest we keep it between ourselves. During the lunch break, I asked if he did not think he had been blasphemous.

"How do you dare suggest that the name of the God of the Jews belongs to an unidentified Afrikaner cadaver?"

"Why?" he asked, delighted at the challenge. He had a broad, intense face, with heavy eyebrows and eyes which blinked rapidly when listening.

"To begin with, maybe our corpse isn't a Jew . . ."

"Doesn't matter," Harry said quickly. "It means *being,* in the Judeo-Christian sense—or even *All Being.* Among the Gentiles, Thomas Aquinas defines *being*—that is, existing man—as including all perfections of being. So what better name?"

"You're saying there's a piece of God in every man?"

"No, I don't believe in God. I believe in man and life, and I believe that *being* is the highest and most comprehensive term we can use with any hope of reality."

After that day, Harry and I became friends. Often he would sit with me on the lawn, sharing a sandwich from my lunch tin, or treat me to a bite in the lunch hall. He loved classical music and sometimes invited me to the symphonies. He was also widely read, especially in the philosophies and social sciences, and we had long talks that inevitably went beyond medicine and music, to include politics and government, both in South Africa and in the world.

We agreed on most everything. The average man, especially the working man in South Africa, deserved a better deal. That included nonwhites. The treatment of nonwhite doctors, for example, was disgraceful. Matter of fact, the treatment of nonwhites in general had to be improved. The trouble lay in our economic system: The profit motive led to treating people as tools, rather than human beings. Wars were declared, making a handful of men rich while killing the youth of the nation. There was too much money in the hands of too few—idle money that should be used to improve living conditions of the poor. The middle class was especially guilty, for they had sold out to the rich.

I agreed to it all, especially the part about the betrayal of the middle class who in Beaufort West wanted to close down my father's church. This was enough for Harry.

"You agree with Karl Marx."

"I do?"

"On the evil concentration of wealth in the hands of a few, lack of political rights of the suppressed working class, war as a weapon of capitalism, the use of money to pervert the nature of labor, robbing man of his dignity and his identity with work, the exploitation of the underprivileged nonwhites, and the sellout of the middle class to the bosses of the industrial revolution."

"Did I say all that?"

"Well, didn't you?"

"Maybe—but in your words, or those of Karl Marx, it doesn't sound like me."

We were sitting on the steps of the walk across from the Anatomy Building. It was comfortable in the sunshine. Inside the anatomy laboratory, we had just begun to dissect Chaim's thoracic wall—a particularly tedious exploration of muscle, membrane, nerves, and arteries that would take two days.

"Are you a Communist, Harry?"

"Yes, Chris."

"You think I'm one, too? That is, potentially one?"

"Yes, I do."

"I don't know," I said. "I never read Karl Marx. I never knew a Communist in my whole life."

"Well, I'll introduce you to some," he said.

I met a few of his friends, but did not enjoy it very much. They spoke with shorthand references to works they had read, using phrases that were hard to follow. Also, I had a feeling they did not trust me—as well as some of their own companions. Despite this, I liked Harry and seriously considered joining the party. Dialectical materialism had an ethical substance; the manifesto of Marx tackled real problems, proposing real action and reform. All of this appealed to me, and I told Harry I thought I would join.

Before that could happen, however, two events occurred—one with Ninky and the other with Harry.

Even though we had not seen each other during the summer, I wrote to Ninky several times and upon our return to Cape Town we began meeting again on monthly movie dates. I was still crazy about her, though she seemed less interested in me—as though she liked me too much to refuse to see me, yet not enough to want to see me more often. Several times, in fact, I called at her home—only to discover from her parents that she was out with other boys. To learn this from them was a bad sign. If a girl is really crazy about a boy, she does not allow her parents to say the truth so bluntly.

Then I saw her one day while walking to school. By this time Joyce and Barney had moved into the home my father had helped them to acquire in Pinelands—four miles from Medical School. There was no direct bus or train service and, besides, I needed to save my allowance to take Ninky to the movie. So I often walked the eight miles, carrying my books and a sandwich tin. It was not too bad during good weather, especially in the early morning when I could review the day's studies. Coming back was more of a chore, because I was anxious to get into my books. Occasionally, I shortened the hour of return by running most of the way.

When it rained, however, I could neither draw profit nor save time in either direction. To avoid becoming drenched, I would run from one bus shelter to the other, or duck into any convenient entry. Despite this, I often reached school completely soaked, with no chance of changing into anything else. Both my wool jacket and pants began to shrink, yet somehow I never caught cold or suffered from it, other than the discomfort or the ordeal—and one painful encounter with Ninky.

It happened in the middle of a downpour, while trying to run across a street. A sports car approached, driven by a young man with a girl in the front seat. It was Ninky. She saw me suddenly and, as the car came alongside, our eyes met—unbelieving and fixed upon one another in the shock of the moment, her face against the car window, mine drenched in the rain. Quickly she turned back to the young man, as if to tell him to stop, but they drove on, and only then did I notice I had been splashed up to my fly.

I had decided to treat it as a joke, to tease her for not at least waving as she went by, but Ninky brought it up first, in a clumsy way, during our next movie date.

"You poor thing," she said, "what were you doing in that rainstorm?"

What sort of remark was that? I was not a poor thing. Also, she knew what I was doing there. She knew I had to walk to school and that I still had over a mile to go when they wet me.

"I asked Danny to stop, but he wouldn't do it," she said. "It was mean of him."

She gave me a nervous little smile and I recalled her startled face against the car window and suddenly felt sad for her. She claimed to live by instinct, but it was the instinct of others that controlled her. She could not say: "Stop the car, there's a friend of mine getting wet." She could not even roll down the window and holler. It was too sad and I decided to change the subject.

"What do you know about Karl Marx?" I asked.

"He's an old bugaboo and the father of Communism."

"But have you read anything he wrote?"

"*Das Kapital*," she said. "But I haven't really read it. Tell me about it, Chris."

So I told her, using more of Harry's phrases than I ever realized I knew. After a bit, I stopped because Ninky began to look at other tables in the Savoy Café.

"You're just angry," she said, "because you don't have a car like other students. So you want to take it away from them."

"Not at all," I said, "I think everybody should have cars. I don't want to take anything from anybody."

"But there aren't enough cars for everybody. So who gets them—the Communists or those who are the brightest and best ones?"

"Also the meanest?"

"That's not nice. He's not really mean."

"You said it, not me."

"But not like that."

She sucked for more soda through the straw, even though there was nothing but strawberry foam.

"I know there are not enough cars for everybody," I said, "but until there are, everyone should have an equal chance at what's on display."

"You don't sound like yourself."

"I'm being myself all right. I am that I am."

"Would you tell your father you are a Communist?"

"I'm not one—not yet, anyway."

"If you become one, would you tell him?"

It was a good question, but she destroyed its possibilities by once more looking at a nearby table. This changed the question into a declarative fact. There was, she felt, no use waiting for an answer. She assumed I would not be able to tell my father.

I wondered if it were true. He was, without doubt, one of the people I carried inside me, while she claimed to be free to move by instinct. And though it was the instinct of others, more than her own, she undoubtedly had an illusion of freedom as long as she could keep changing the basics— hemlines and hairdressers, toothpaste and news analyst, pop songs and movie stars, parties and men taking her there. Perhaps that was why she was so sad in the car. She realized she could not get out or ever be free of other people who gave her the sign of what was beautiful and bright and true.

"Why are you looking at me like that?"

"Nothing," I said, forcing a smile.

"When you smile, it melts me."

"Yes?"

"Yes," she said with a sigh.

After that, it was hard not to smile at her. I suspected she had maneuvered me, but I loved it anyway and it saved the evening for us—making our walk home and the protracted good night kiss just as sweet and intimate as always. Yet something was gone or going, and there was little we could do about it, other than continue our cycle until one day when one of us would say, "I'll be seeing you"—meaning at a distance where the whispered word would no longer be heard.

A few days later, Harry said Chaim should have his name changed to Chaim-Not. This broke up our table and practically everybody else in the hall, since it applied to every cadaver. The field of bodies had been decimated. Arms and legs had been incised, exposing the bones. Abdomens were opened, their contents removed. Kidneys and livers, severed from their connections, lay shriveled and lacerated atop backbones. Chests were exposed with the hearts cut away, leaving the great vessels dangling for want of a homing chamber.

We had all done part of the neck and now, from two sides, each team was attacking the face. At our table, the four students opposite us were dissecting for nerves and muscles, while we sought vessels and muscles.

To facilitate the work, we soaked cotton wadding in alcohol, then inserted it under the eyelids, cheeks and lips. The margin of the lips was sewn together with a fine needle and then we began. Since the scalp had already been lifted away, only one vertical cut was necessary, going upwards from in front of the ear until it met the earlier coronal incision of the scalp.

The skin was free then to be reflected forward as far as the middle line of the face and so removed entirely by both teams working on each side.

"Poor Chaim," said Harry, as he freed our half to reveal the first fibers of the platysma, going upwards to the fascia.

"He is no more. He's just Chaim-Not."

Amid the laughter, I felt a slight nausea and with it a little resentment at this ridiculing of a human being, this abrupt dismissal of the remaining evidence of his existence.

"You can't do that," I said. "You can't declare him nonexistent. He was, he is, he always will be."

"Where?" asked Harry. "In our notes, maybe—but when we lose them, it's Chaim-Not."

This created more laughter as Harry made a mess of our eyelid, tearing up some of the areolar tissue and subjacent muscular fiber.

"I don't think so," I replied, though unable to explain exactly what I felt.

"Why not?"

"It doesn't make sense, Harry. Nothing can come into being out of nonbeing—or pass out of being into nonbeing. Chaim might not be here, actually, but he is somewhere. I mean *potentially* he is."

"All right," said Harry. "When we finish with our dissection, what's left of his flesh and bones goes down into the cellar where they clean up the bones and put them into boxes for other schools. Suppose our femur stays here, another goes to Bloemfontein, the skull to Pretoria, and so on. Where the hell is Chaim at that point?"

This brought on more laughs—then a silence as they waited for my answer.

"At that point," I said, "he's not real—I mean an *actual* reality. But he is still an *ideal* reality at least."

"Where—how?" asked Harry. "In your head, in our notes—where?"

"Yes, there. And before God."

"So," said Harry, "all this time you've been thinking our Chaimie was a Christian?"

"The odds say yes."

"And on the day of the Resurrection, when his body is supposed to join his soul, who's going to run around and pick up all his scattered bones and ashes?"

I had never considered this before—the physical logistics of the Resurrection—and wondered what my father would say. I imagined he would say that only by realistically accepting death—total obliteration such as this postmortem crucifixion of Chaim—can we still hope for life with God. Jesus went into it with nothing more than a promise from God. He had no guarantee there was anything on the Other Side—nothing except God's promise that, as Creator, He would call the dead back to life. I did not know how or in what form everybody would show up in Heaven—or even if it would happen. But I did believe in God's will making itself manifest in some way and that every man carried within him an immortal seed which could never be taken from him, even by eight students picking him to pieces.

Our anatomy professor, Matthew Robertson Drennan, entered the hall and we stopped talking. Professor Drennan was my ideal—a man of grace and knowledge and physical courage. The corridor of the anatomy building was lined with heads of wild beasts he had shot at close range. He had a knowledge of anatomy that was astonishing. In classes, he would illustrate sections of the body by drawing the nerves, vessels, muscles, and bones on a blackboard using colored chalk and drawing with both hands at the same time. The finished work would resemble an etching from a textbook. Also, he had a Victorian elegance that we all admired. His assistant was called Archie and, needing some part of the body to illustrate a point, Professor Drennan would call out: "Archie, the bones, please!"

"That's the parotid gland," he said at our table, pointing with a pair of forceps to the exposed salivary gland between the lower jaw and the ear.

"And Stenson's duct," he said, tracing its course from the gland over the massetor muscle, finally going into the mouth through a small opening at the summit of a small papilla.

"Exquisitely designed, don't you think?"

"Yes," I said, along with the others, wondering how one could witness the infinite complexity and infinite beauty of the human body and not marvel at the power of the Creator—let alone doubt His existence.

Harry and I continued our talk during lunch.

"The difference between us," he said, "is that I'm more of a realist. For me, there is only one reality—what can be received by the senses. In the light of Descartes' *cogito*, the self is the only criterion of reality. I've never seen or touched God, so he doesn't exist."

I recalled sitting with my father on the hill above the dam and the train whistle with its invisible separation of sound and steam.

"Seeing is not everything," I said. "Your idea of reality is too restricted. We can conceive of possibilities not realized in this world. We can imagine things which do not exist in nature."

"Like what?"

"Like math equations, like Einstein's theory, like ideas in science and art."

"But they are eventually used by man—either proven or enjoyed—and so made real."

"Is that not true of God?"

"God for me is as dead as Chaim. He does not exist. Karl Marx was right. Religion is an opiate of the masses."

Marx meant religion was *used* as an opiate, but I did not know this at the time. I thought only of my father's love of God and how interlaced this was with his work for the colored people and suddenly it was clear that Harry and I could never agree on this subject.

"What you're saying is that my father was a drug peddler."

"I'm sorry, Chris, I didn't mean that."

"It's all right," I said.

Yet it was not all right. I continued to be friendly with Harry, but we never again discussed Karl Marx or my joining the Communist Party. Ninky had been right in her own way. My father's life could not have been in vain. He did not love a dead image. God was alive for him—and for me. And, I thought: for you, too, Chaim—wherever you are.

The drama and challenge of that second year at the university—the first real year in medicine—was not alone confined to anatomy, nor to Ninky, nor Harry-Chaim. Admittedly, they brought about a major shakedown. They drove me to look at myself, my interior self where Ninky claimed others also dwelled. And this gave me the strength to turn away from a girl I had loved and a young man I had admired.

There were also other theaters holding smaller dramas. These were of much greater potential, though I did not realize it at the time. In experimental physiology, for example, we pithed a frog. This is done by sticking a needle through the brain and down the spinal column, allowing the heart to beat and the nerves to react, while leaving the animal without a brain. The frog, in effect, becomes a heart-lung preparation—a situation later explored with other animals in studies for the heart transplant. Our experiments in class were outwardly simple—such as hooking a frog muscle up to a stylus and drum, then applying electric current to the nerve, causing the muscle to contract and so register on the drum—yet they gave us a working knowledge of how the muscles and nerves and organs functioned while in life. In a sense, it was Chaim before he became Chaim.

This encampment within living bodies, rather than the piecemeal seizing upon dead tissues of a corpse, also allowed us in histology to look through a microscope at normal tissues of a living being until we knew what to expect from normal skin or how to recognize a perfectly functioning mammary gland. Just as the roots of an oak are uncountable, so are the circuits of comprehension of the human body. Yet this gave us enough to be familiar with a functioning organism, to know what to expect from it and thus prepare ourselves to do what every doctor must eventually be prepared to do—leap from the known to the unknown.

It was part of the long and tedious climb to the summit. And as in any protracted and massive attack on an unscaled peak, there had to be moments of rest and laughter. We took them where we could find them, along the way.

When we came to study the human mammary gland, for example, Cunningham noted this of the female nipple: "A curious change of color occurs in this region during the second month of pregnancy. Of a delicate pink tint in the virgin, the nipple and areola become brown from the deposition of pigment at this time, and they never again resume their normal appearance."

"Now I know what I'm suffering from," said Harry. "The taut, upright roseate hue has been lacking from my life. I'm being suffocated by flappy old brown."

So ended the second year. I received a second-class pass in anatomy. Physiology was an eighteen-month course, ending in the middle of the third year. There were only three first passes in that and I was fortunate enough to get one of them. Life—its functioning and its fated cycle of existence— drew me on, filling my thoughts in class, my studies late at night, and even my occasional eight-mile walk to and from school.

We also began the study of bacteriology, which led us to recognize organisms causing diseases, as well as pharmacology with its drugs to combat these invasions of the body. This prepared us for the next eighteen-month expedition into the most bewildering and fascinating subject up to that moment: pathology, the study of how the body reacts to disease.

We were one-third through this when the third year ended—ending also our constant confinement to classrooms. Beginning with the fourth year, we were to split our studies between the college and the hospital where we would work with patients for the first time. Before that happened, however, something else occurred that led me to believe I could never become a surgeon.

CHAPTER 6

EVERY SUMMER I had returned to Beaufort West, to be with my parents and a new circle of friends. Among them was Dr. Jacobus van der Merwe—a very big and kind-hearted man with powerful shoulders and large hands, known to everyone as Great Koos. Like most small town general practitioners, he did a bit of everything, including minor surgery.

As a favor, Great Koos allowed me to go with him on his round of patients, both in the hospital and on trips to distant farms. It was valuable training, for I learned from him that acute attention to the smallest details, to the tiniest clues, can lead to success—and also that no doctor knows it all.

"Listen Chris, when you get to be a G.P. one day, remember you divide temperatures into two groups. First is the group that responds to aspirin and about that you don't have to worry. The second is the group that doesn't respond to aspirin. When that happens, you need a specialist!"

One day he asked if I would like to assist at an appendectomy and I accepted—excited at the chance to witness my first surgical operation. My sleep that night was broken by dreams of Great Koos in immense difficulty as he bent over the operating table in the glare of lights, calling for my help.

When finally I awoke, it was late and I had to hurry to the hospital hastening along the same streets I had run as a boy with hot soup for my father. A sister helped me dress in gown, cap, and mask, then showed me into the theater where the patient—a young girl—was being anesthetized by use of ether and the open-mask technique. Great Koos was already there and nodded at me—his eyes smiling over his white surgical mask. Another sister was bathing the abdomen with iodine and spirits.

The anesthetist with the mask lifted it away for a moment from the girl's face and I discovered that I knew her. She was the younger sister of Dawn, a girl I once dated. I had seen her last summer in town, but at first had not recognized her. She was walking with red shoes, her blonde hair bouncing, and as I began to pass her I wondered if the face would be as delicious as everything else in the rear. It was indeed—all bubbly with dimples and naughty gray eyes and a saucy little nose—a real sweetie.

Then, as I went by, she spoke to me.

"Hello, Chris!"

"Hello?"

"You don't remember, I'm Dawn's sister."

"Well, how are you?"

That was about all that happened and now you could see how she was, without the red shoes and with her bouncing blonde hair stuffed into a white cap, her lovely little abdomen being painted iodine brown and then Great Koos laying on the sterile white towels, covering it all up except a little patch of her tummy which would be the operating area.

As Koos prepared to make the first incision, I could visualize where he was going. In anatomy we had explored every part of the human body and I knew it was relatively easy to make an opening and reach the appendix. I stood opposite, on the patient's left side, eagerly watching each detail and secretly hoping my dream would come true—that he would need me to hold a retractor or assist him in an emergency.

Suddenly, there was one—but it was within me, not the patient. At the sight of blood pulsating from the open wound, I became nauseous. The odor of ether was overwhelming, my knees went weak, and bells began to ring in my ears. There was a chair in the corner, and I staggered to it just in time, sitting down with my head spinning, dimly aware that I was about to faint.

A scrub nurse helped me to leave and I went across the hall to the doctors' tearoom, where another sister offered me a cup of sweet tea. I accepted it weakly, feeling ashamed of myself and also quite worried. If I could not witness a simple appendectomy, if the sight of blood caused me to faint like a schoolgirl, I had no business planning to become a surgeon. I had been at it for three years, with three more to go. Yet if I was going to faint each time I saw blood in an operating room, what good was it?

I drank my tea and tried to figure it out. A roomful of cadavers had been almost impossible to take. Yet I had done it and gone on to dissect three bodies. I had also handled living tissues and organs from animals—all without trouble. So why this sudden inability to take the next step?

There was one major difference: This girl was alive. When cut, her blood came out, pumped by a beating heart. Yet it was not this, not the blood alone. Something else lay behind it.

"Feel better?" asked the sister.

"Yes, thank you."

I felt terrible but was not going to say so. I nodded toward her, and she nodded back. This left us grinning at each other like two mute fools, and I wished she would go away.

"Don't let it worry you," she said. "I've seen it happen to hundreds of students."

"Thanks."

"It's the ones with the most imagination who get hit the worst. And some of them make the best doctors."

"*Dankie*—thanks, sister."

I got up and went back into the theater—just in time to see Koos closing up the wound. He looked up to give me a friendly wink, then went on with his suturing. The sight of the open flesh, the towels red with blood, and the smell of the ether still hit me, but I kept it under control. Next time, I knew, it would be all right.

The sister had said it was too much imagination. Fine. But what had I imagined when I saw the blood pumping out? Was it death of the patient on the table? If so, perhaps my fright sprang from this fear of death. Maybe that was my biggest fear. Maybe I wanted to be a doctor for that reason alone—to make sure I knew how to dodge death's appointment, to know enough not to run off to Samara where he would be waiting for me in the marketplace. Thus I was not driven by a desire to help others, as I had always imagined, but rather by fear and an egotistical projection of my hidden self.

All of this made me feel quite depressed. Great Koos said nothing in the hospital, as though it had never happened. Finally, going home in the car, he spoke of it.

"The same thing happened to me the first time, Chris."

I nodded, hoping he would tell me more.

"After a couple of times, you don't notice it."

"Notice what?" I asked. "I'm trying to understand why I should react this way after having done anatomy and physiology."

"Those were dry runs. This is the real thing."

The real thing, of course, was life. We held it in our hands on the table—and this included me.

"Even if you were not actively operating, Chris, you were there. And with your knowledge of the body, it was the same for you emotionally as though you were actually doing the job."

Then he said: "You got buck fever, boy."

"I never heard of anybody fainting from buck fever."

"No, because the object on a hunt is to kill, and here it's to save a life. There's also this other difference. You don't identify with the animal. Otherwise, you couldn't kill it. But you can identify, especially in the beginning, with the patient. That's why doctors, surgeons mainly, let others do their close of kin."

So it happened to the best of them. The closer it came, the harder it was. Yet what caused this? Death could not leap up from the patient to grab the surgeon. It would simply lay there on the table, under his hands—mocking him, rupturing his sutures, ridiculing his skill, humbling his pride. So it was this—the professional disgrace, more than anything else.

That was how it had seemed at Beaufort West during the summer. Yet upon returning to school for the fourth year, the question came back again in a most awesome manner. And the answer was not good enough.

The pathology course now included the study of postmortems in the morgue of the Medical School. There were to be twenty of them, bodies ravaged by all variety of diseases. None of us looked forward to this and each one braced himself in his own fashion. I skipped breakfast, going with the other students into the postmortem theater where we took seats on a series of inclined benches to peer down at a body on a white enamel table.

Only when seated did I notice the sex. It was a young woman, a blonde with rather fair features. She might have been Dawn's kid sister, projected a few more years after surviving that first round with Great Koos, to find herself once more stripped of her clothes for us to witness her final and total dissection.

Unlike the cadavers we had handled in anatomy, she still possessed her life's blood, but I looked in vain for some color in her thighs, her flat belly, and her strangely shaped breasts. All of her had a strange yellow-white hue, as though she had been found drifting along an ocean floor. Beneath her, the bed of the dissecting table was slanted slightly and imbedded with grooves, as on a meat platter, converging in a drainage tube at the lower end. Her head was propped up on a wooden block and her hair hung down as though she had indeed been raised from a watery grave.

The pathologist stood on the other side of the body, waiting for us to quiet down. He was a big man, big as Great Koos, but without his smile—as though Koos had really lost that girl on the operating table. He was unshaven, and beneath the beard stubble his face appeared pale and yellow. Constant search through the entrails of the dead was investing him as well with their own special color. He wore a white theater gown and brown rubber gloves, and as he began to talk he touched the body before him as though it was a work of art that alone he had created and was now displaying for the first time.

"This young woman died, as we shall see, from cancer of the breast [points to one breast, then the other]. It proliferated through her body, affecting without doubt her liver [touches belly just below rib cage] spread through the endocrinal system [moves finger from mons veneris up to heart] and probably we will find traces of it in her brain."

This last bit was accompanied by him sliding around to the end of the table where he took the girl's head between his two hands, in the manner of an osteopath about to give it a good twist.

"The instruments, please," he said to an attendant, who handed him a scalpel and a hand saw.

"Regardless of what we suspect, we always begin with the head and removal of the brain," he said, incising the knife around the rear of the skull, drawing it from the top of one ear to the other.

Three or four rubber-brown fingers were then inserted underneath the top half of the scalp. This gave him something to hold and he pulled it, peeling it back on itself and over the brow. When it came up, he used a knife to separate the tissues from the skull, as you do in skinning antelope. In this fashion the scalp was pulled back over the forehead and down over the face, so that it lay there like a pale pink mask with no holes for the eyes. At first, it was not down far enough and the pathologist was forced to make a few more cuts around the ears which allowed him to yank it down over the nose as well.

The top half of the skull, white with no trace of blood, was now exposed. Similarly, the rear half of the skull was peeled back so the cranium was ready for opening.

"The saw, please," he said to the attendant who retrieved it from under the shoulder of the girl.

It was a hand saw like those butchers use when lopping off a leg of mutton, and he began to cut around in a line as though following the edge of a big skull cap—sawing first around the front, then turning the head to the side and finally cutting from below. This last action caused the body to rock so that both arms moved off the table to hang stiffly out at each side. The attendant put one back in place, then ran around the table and put the other one back.

Laying the saw aside, the pathologist began next with hammer and cleaver. The hammer striking the steel cleaver caused a high ringing sound. After encircling the skull, this began to change until the blows drew only hollow echoes, as when cracking the outer shell of a coconut. At that point the skull was severed.

To pry it loose, the instructor next used a steel wedge with handle, turning it inside the circular crack. This caused a sudden sound—woooosh! —similar to that of an arrow leaving a bow. It was followed by smaller sounds resembling the breaking of young tree limbs—tissues being pulled loose from their moorings. Finally, the skull came off onto the table like an empty gourd, leaving the brain exposed, its nodules and separate compartments streaked with purple veins and covered by a white mucous veil.

"And now for the removal," he said, inserting one hand in between the skull and brain, pulling it back and down until with another whoosh it, too, came loose—hanging for a moment by its attachment to the spinal column until that was cut, allowing the brain to fall into his brown hands.

"And there it is!" he exclaimed.

There was left only the empty skull, divided into two compartments by the membrane that once had separated the sections of a thinking human being—walls of a house with the roof blown off, empty of everything except tiny pools of red blood.

The next major action was to run a scalpel from the vagina, slitting up the belly to the throat—followed by a lifting out of the girl's viscera. With this, I hastily rose to leave.

"There goes Barnard," said someone.

"What's wrong Chris—anybody you know?"

I turned back once, to see him washing off the viscera with the hose as though watering a monstrous tropical flower. The pink eyeless mask still covered the girl's face, mercifully shielding her eyes from this last great indignity upon her body. Despite this, her mouth had come ajar, it alone appearing to register one final, silent cry of shame and rage.

I recount all these unpleasant details, recalled so vividly after many years, in order to convey the despair of mind and spirit that afflicted me after that experience. Making it worse, I had no one to talk to at that time—no one close enough to confide my deepest fears.

Why, I wondered, was I unable to witness this? The nurse at Beaufort West had said it was too much imagination. Yet imagination really had nothing to do with this. It was something else, and it was related to death. All along, I had been revolted by death, or possible death. It was not, as I had thought earlier, the fear of death in the family or of professional failure on the table. It was some aspect of death which disturbed me—but what and how?

I had to think it out and I tried it while walking along the beach at Sea Point, but it did not help. I strolled in the park by the school, watching the feeding grysbok, and that was not much better. Finally, I returned to the postmortem theater. It was empty and I sat once more on the bench, looking at the table where the girl had lain. But the smells depressed me and I left, walking up toward Groote Schuur. Behind the hospital, between the doctors' residence and that of the nurses, higher up on the hill, there is a little chapel.

It was open and empty, and I went in and sat down. There was nothing to look at, except the arched pine roof and one long colored glass window with Christur Redemptur at the top. I had a lot of questions to answer and did not expect Him to do it for me. I had to do it myself, and this was as good a place as any.

To begin with, one element united each of my traumatic experiences— the operation at Beaufort West, the postmortem, and, earlier, the anatomy class. They displayed the human experience in three stages: on the edge of death, just dead, and long dead. All dealt with the transition from life to death. To understand my anguish, I had to clarify what I thought about this—how I understood death. Instinctively, I looked up at Christur, then shut my eyes, telling myself to keep this in the realm of the known and provable.

All right, I thought, we start with basics. The entire physical world—all of it, with us in it—can be proven to be a world of energy. The atoms of all substances are in motion. That included man and everything else. In this, nothing could disappear or become lost. The law of the conservation of energy proved it: *All changes of matter are accompanied by transformations of energy, and energy, like matter, cannot be created or destroyed; however, energy can be changed from one form to another.*

So death was contained somewhere within that action. The energy in the human form left it going into another form. The form of the living body— determined by the arrangement of the matter—changed as matter changed. Matter was destined to do this. Matter was the mother of changing things. The receptacle in itself was the principle of generation or change. Thus the final change of matter, and subsequently of form, was to be accepted with death—the Prime Privation.

What was not acceptable was the untimely change of form by disease or error. A girl dying while her hair still bounced in golden waves, or death by cancer of the breast, or even the abrupt disembowelling of someone just dead was ugly and fearful for it forced the change of form before its proper time.

This applied to every man. It especially included me because it applied to every doctor, too, since each of us was potentially a physician of all men. Thus what was not acceptable for a single man, in his living or his dying, could not be acceptable to any doctor. My anguish and rage—and yes, my fright—stemmed from this premature privation of form, this loss of life before it had run its span. It was not an isolated fear of death. Death was to be feared and treated as an enemy, depending upon when it came. At the right hour, it was no longer to be held back—indeed, it was welcome. *Father, into your hands I commit my spirit.*

I looked up at the Christur and rose to leave the chapel—telling myself that I had arrived at my credo by the strength of my own reason. At the door, however, I turned around to look at Him once more.

"Thank you," I said.

Armed with this mechanical formula for change, conceived in an empty chapel and nourished by a belief in a continuing God, I went on to study nineteen postmortems of the most disfigured sort. Surgery also was no longer a problem, and I began to hang around the operating theater of the hospital for the chance to occasionally assist one or another surgeon. This meant holding a retractor and little else. It allowed me to witness operations at first hand, however, and slowly my confidence grew. Little things meant a great deal. Students, for example, wore used surgical gloves, while surgeons had new ones. When there were no used ones, we were given a new pair, and, drawing them on, we had the exciting sense of being closer to the chief surgeon.

Other fears also came tumbling down. At the hospital, we were given patients to diagnose under supervision. My first one was an old lady suffering from rheumatoid arthritis, a disease that was later to afflict my own body. I began to examine her—nervous and shy before a female patient. But she was very kind and helped me gain a confidence which carried me on to meetings with other patients.

The fifth year was one of those that come along every so often, momentarily exposing a lifetime by suddenly revealing what has gone, what remains to be held for a little while longer, and what to seize upon, among an assembly of new identities, with the hope that it might last forever— even though it never did.

We could trace the stars in flight, cross two mathematical unknowns for a known, and plot the heart and brain with electric impulses. But we were ill-equipped to follow the course of time in our own lives. We took occasional snapshots of things and places and people, doing this eagerly at the moment of recognition (stand there, don't move, hold it!), putting them on the wall of memory as though fixed and established for all time. After that, we never again looked close enough to see them curl and fade. So they remained, despite occasional warnings to take another look, that time was passing: a train station coming down, the death of a favorite movie star, a junked auto you once made love in, a stranger sitting on the *stoep* of a friend's home, tangled line on a forgotten fishing reel.

Finally the moment arrived, as it did now for me, when there was a wholesale changeover of images in the gallery of your life, a momentary updating of reality. You hung the new ones with excitement, and you pressed the old ones into books—though not without some tears.

One day early in the fifth school year, Michel Rossouw phoned to say he was in a nursing home at Rondebosch—ill with tuberculosis. Alarmed, I said I would come right over. It did not seem possible. Over the years we had drifted apart—he was just ahead of me in school and had graduated from Stellenbosch as a teacher—but the previous summer we had spent a wonderful week together, swimming and fishing at Strand, the resort near Cape Town. Shortly after that he married and took a teaching job. So it did not seem possible that he could now be ill.

But he was, with bilateral pulmonary tuberculosis, and it had ravaged his system with incredible speed. His eyes were sunken, his face pallid, his arms wasted and thin. When I arrived, they had just finished pumping air between his lungs and the chest wall and he could hardly whisper.

"Chris . . ."

"Yes, Michel?"

I bent over to hear better.

"They're trying . . . to turn me . . . into a balloon."

I laughed. It was either that or weep. So I laughed and tried to pretend it was nothing.

"They pump . . . and pump," he said. "But I never take off."

"It's the air in Cape Town," I said. "If you were in the Karoo, you'd be floating fine."

His eyes were so deep and so sad, you could drown in them.

"Chris, you remember the day we dumped Piet Theron into the river?"

"Ya, and how he came yelling up the bank after us."

"And how old Jaap used to buy back all the feed sacks?"

"Ya . . . you think he knew we stole them?"

"Sure, he knew . . ."

"Man, you sent them sailing over the fence like they were shot from a cannon. You were great at that, Michel."

He began to cough, pale thin hands holding a tissue against the mouth, the cheeks turning sudden red, then quickly slipping the tissue under the covers. He wanted a drink of water, and I helped him with it. After that, he smiled weakly and offered me some chocolates from a candy box—just as he had always shared his sweets with me.

"I've been wondering why we did some things," he said. "Like whistling for the wind."

I had forgotten that. We used to go to a place down near the river where we whistled to bring the wind, hoping this would cause a windmill to turn and so fill up a little dam nearby where we could go swimming.

"It never worked," said Michel. "But we did it anyway—why?"

"Sometimes it worked," I said, though I could never remember when.

"No . . . it never worked. But we did it anyway."

I had to leave for class and so I said good-bye, promising to come again soon. Then, going out the door, Michel whispered something.

"What?" I asked, coming back to his bedside.

"I'm whistling," he said.

"So am I, Michel," I said, hurrying out before he could see my eyes.

Michel had given me more than I could ever return. His whistle outside my window was a call to another world on a hilltop, a home where everyone laughed, and a friend who gave me half of everything he owned— including his heart. I could never repay him for this. The least I could do now was to visit him as often as possible.

Yet the doubling of classroom studies and duties at the hospital made it difficult. Apart from gynecology and obstetrics, we had many minor subjects including psychiatry, medical jurisprudence, public health, ophthalmology, and related diseases of ear-nose-throat. To save time covering the eight miles each day to Pinelands, I had moved into a private boarding house on Clee Road, just below the hospital. This gave me an extra hour and a quarter a day, but it still was not enough for our widely scattered studies. The course in psychiatry took us to the insane asylum at Valkenberg. Other classes were at the Peninsula Maternity Home where we assisted at childbirth. And this, in turn, led to the birth of another great friendship in my life: Professor Eric Crichton, who taught us gynecology and obstetrics—a man whom I respected and enjoyed and who often reminded me of my father projected onto another plane.

Despite the distances of these new frontiers in my life, I still managed to return from time to time to see Michel. When I could not see him, I would phone to leave a message, saying when I would come. One evening, however, there was a message from him. I had worked at the casualty department of the hospital all night and, returning home around three in the morning, learned one of the sisters at the Rondebosch Nursing Home had phoned. The message was very brief: "Michel wants to speak to you."

I called early the next morning and they said Michel had died that night. I did not believe it could be true, and I repeated his name several times. It was true.

"But why didn't you call me?"

"We did call you."

"But why didn't you say he was dying . . . why didn't you let me know?"

"We did."

"You said *'Michel wants to speak to you'* . . ."

"He did."

"Oh, Jesus," I said, and hung up.

He needed me, and I had not been there.

Michel wants to speak to you.

For years I had wanted to return a small part of what he had given me, a handful of love, an embrace, a kind word—and when he called for me I was not there. I was helping to administer plasma to drunks and bums, to fix in plaster and splint the human wreckage of the highways, to coddle and cure all the other broken pieces of humanity that pour into the casualty section of a hospital. When my friend was dying and needed my help, I was tending to others whom I had never seen before and would never see again—swimming through a broad stream of humanity while he was left alone to drown by himself.

Michel wants to speak to you . . .

What else was friendship but that? It was the right to call a friend at three in the morning and expect a reply—not at nine or eight or seven or six, but at three.

Hello, Michel, are you all right?

Hello, Chris, I just wanted . . .

What? What's that?

Just wanted to say good-bye, Chris.

No, Michel, don't say that. Please don't . . .

I loved you, Chris.

Michel . . . oh, Michel, I loved you, too.

I went to the funeral with Joyce. It was at Stellenbosch, and it was winter, and it rained all day. I was one of the coffin bearers, and we bore it through the rain up to the grave where the fresh earth was wet and muddy. There was water in the bottom of the grave pit, and we lowered it slowly— a light brown coffin with bright brass handles—until it reached the water. I hoped it would stop there, but it did not, and the water came up to the brass handles.

His mother was there, hysterically calling for Michel and begging every- one not to take her child away, sinking then to her knees in the mud to speak to the coffin half under water. The clods of dirt began to fall and I turned to leave—seeing then his young wife, also turned away from the grave, staring mutely into a mud puddle.

Ninky and I had long since ceased seeing each other and for almost two years I dated no girls at all, excepting when home on holidays. In the fifth year I began again, helped by a second-hand Austin I had bought from a friend at Beaufort West. It was dark blue, shaped like a box, and very light. On corrugated roads it would bounce along until we often ended up sideways. I loved it and took it everywhere—even up the steps and into the hospital one night. This sort of mobility, especially under that roof, inevitably led to my dating a few of the nurses.

One of them became ill and I went to see her. It was on C floor, where eventually I was to have my heart patients' ward, and in a large room that one day would also hold Louis Washkansky.

She was a cute blonde and a good dancer and liked to tease me.

"Any more husbands climbing in the window, Chris?"

"No, I've been a good boy, waiting for you."

At the rooming house, I had been caught kissing a young woman by her husband who jumped through the kitchen window with a pistol. He was prepared to shoot us until his wife told him this would inform the whole city that he was both a horse's ass and a cuckold. The poor man sank bewildered into a chair, dropping his gun on the kitchen table next to the teapot.

"My brother has a gun, too, Chris."

"I'll take my chances."

"All right," she said, "but he tends to shoot low."

She laughed and I laughed and the nurse in the bed next to her seemed to be laughing, too—at least her eyes seemed to be laughing. You could not see any more because the sheet was drawn up over everything else.

"Hello," I said.

They blinked back at me—big and brown and full of wonder.

"That's Louwtjie."

"Hello, Louwtjie."

The sheet slid down then, slowly revealing a cute little nose and then the mouth.

"Hello," it said.

She was not smiling, after all. Her eyes smiled at you, but the mouth did not.

"How are you?" I asked.

She nodded as though born in silence, a child of it, and was now waiting to speak and touch for the first time. A love, I thought, this is some love.

She withdrew her arm from under the cover to take something off the table, turning and revealing her breastline and hips. She had a lovely body.

"Would you . . . could you, mail this for me?"

It was a letter and I took it—one more of humanity's messages: *Michel wants to speak to you, Louwtjie wants to speak to you.* What did any letter or book or poem or work of art say other than: *I want, I need to speak to you, let's speak, hold me, say something to me, tell me, speak to me . . .*

"Louwtjie what?"

"Louw."

"All right, Louwtjie," I said, holding up her letter as though I was going to carry it myself to South West Africa. Then I gave my little blonde a kiss and left.

I returned several times after that, looking in on both of them, especially the strange dark Louwtjie. Finally, they were both discharged. I had promised a date with my blonde friend, but when I phoned, she said she still did not feel up to going out. Her friend did, however.

So Louwtjie and I had our first date. We saw Charles Laughton in "Henry VIII" at the Savoy, where Ninky and I had always gone. After the show we drove back to the hospital where she was due in by midnight. The front entry was locked and we had to use the back one, behind the hospital. I parked the car and walked her toward the tunnel leading to their quarters. On the way, next to the little chapel, I kissed her. I recall her face looking up at me.

"Are you gentle?" she asked.

"Yes," I said. "At least, I think so."

She kissed me then and I knew it was going to be something that would go on for a long time.

We saw each other often during the remainder of that year and regularly during the last year—a school year spent in intensive preparation for final exams. Louwtjie came to my graduation, and sat with my parents in Jameson Hall as I walked down the aisle, wearing black cap and gown— Bachelor in Medicine and Bachelor in Surgery—sitting next to my father as though she were already my wife.

As I walked by, her eyes were smiling for me and her mouth trembled a little. My mother appeared very proud and in control of herself and you knew she was going to tell God all about it that night. My father was overcome and his eyes seemed moist for he was blinking and biting his mustache. I remembered the day at the station when he had waved good-bye and how I had prayed I would not fail him. I had made it, but only to find myself facing something much larger. For that challenge had been confined to the grounds of a university. Now it was without limit. It was the world.

PART III
YOUNG DOCTOR

CHAPTER 7

AFTER THE CEREMONY, parents and relatives of the graduates surrounded and touched them as though each one, by some miracle, had won his race against all the others. They mingled together inside the auditorium and they walked out through the great doors of Jameson Hall, beneath the white pillars, onto the long flight of stone steps from where you could see the city far below.

I waited for my parents and Louwtjie on the steps, recalling how I had climbed them six years ago, wearing Michel Rossouw's jacket, my brother's pants and a tie of the wrong color. The bully on the stone wall beside the steps—a young man sat there now in a graduation gown, laughing with his girl—long since had gone into the limbo of dropouts. A thousand other things had fallen into that limbo, too, and twice as many had taken their place.

Six years. It had been a long time, longer than all the years before it—longer than all the races I had ever run, or all the days on the dry Karoo. It had been six years of eight miles with books and a sandwich tin, of sitting up through the night, of working alone in laboratories, in the viscera of the dead, in the eye of the living, in hospital wards, in empty corridors, in the chapel alone, always alone with a drive inside me to reach the top—the top of these steps looking down onto the city and, beyond that, the world.

Yet now that it had happened, we were really at the top of nothing at all. If anything, we were at the bottom of the medical fraternity. That's where we were, all of us, and there was a lot more climbing to be done as we went down the steps to the scattered towns and cities and hospitals of South Africa. It was to be an interior climb in three steps and it had to be accomplished before any of us could truthfully claim the title of doctor or mastery of our most difficult art.

We had already made the first step upon graduation, emerging with the ability of *conception*—that is, to apprehend the essence of the biological properties of life as well as their pathological forms in disease. The next step, which we were now about to take, was the use of this training to form *judgement*—the second act of the mind which unites or separates concepts by accepting or rejecting one or the other. Once this was done, the last step remained—*reason,* which was the passing from one judgement to the other.

That was why all of us now so urgently needed experience. It was impossible to exercise judgement, and so arrive at the play of reason, without first handling patients. The art of medicine required this—experience of the sort that makes multiple use of memory, leading up to the crossroad of judgement. This also led to self-confidence—as necessary for a doctor as for an artist or an athlete. Inevitably, it was lacking in the very young who questioned their own judgements—such as we did—and the very old who had gone too long without asking new questions.

To begin my experience, I had applied for a six months' assignment as houseman, or intern, at Groote Schuur with Professor Crichton in gynecology. This seemed a good approach to both medicine and surgery. Besides, I loved the professor and wanted to be with him in my first months. Fortunately, he also liked me and had honored me with accepting my request.

"Hello, Doctor."

It was Louwtjie, smiling and wrinkling her nose with happiness.

"My doctor," she said, cuddling up.

Even if I did not yet feel like one, it was nice to hear it.

"You know," she said, "until today, I never thought you were very handsome."

"What did you think?"

"I don't know. For one thing, I thought your ears were too big."

"And today they shrunk?"

"They're getting smaller," she said and bit me on one.

I tried to grab her but she ducked away, laughing. At that moment my parents found us, and I embraced my father first. As I held him, I saw my mother nodding at me and for the first time noticed she was getting old. She wore a dark skirt and jacket and a square gray hat, and she seemed smaller than I had ever remembered her. I did not want to look at my father and see the same thing, so I continued to hold him in my arms.

"I wish you could come to Beaufort West, even for a few days," he said in my ear, his voice high with excitement.

"No," said my mother.

"He needs a rest," said my father.

"No," she said. "He wants to get started right away."

She was getting old, but nothing was bending that spirit. Her boy did not need a rest. He had only started to conquer the world. There was no time to be lost sitting around doing nothing.

"Do you have to go right away?" asked Louwtjie.

"Tomorrow," I said. "But tonight we can have fun—all of us together."

Louwtjie squeezed my hand to say that half of the night was not going to be with everybody. Then she dug her nails into my palm and whispered it into my ear.

The next morning I boarded a train for Usakos in South West Africa. A month lay between graduation and the start of my internship with Professor Crichton. So I had decided to use it by relieving a doctor of his practice in a country town, believing this would provide both practical experience as well as extra money for dating Louwtjie.

Dusty and exhausted, I stepped off the train—three days and 1,300 miles from Cape Town—to find the doctor at the station, openly surprised at my youth. He could hardly believe I had just turned twenty-four—but was too impatient to begin his vacation to lose time worrying about it. His car was there, packed and ready to go, and quickly we went to see his home and office. He showed me the registry for the patients, the bed where I was to sleep, and gave me the keys to the house. That was it.

"Good luck, old chap," he said, leaving me in the middle of a remote town—and in the middle of a series of crises, beginning the moment he disappeared.

A woman arrived that afternoon, bringing a son with two badly infected molars. They obviously had to come out—under general anesthesia. I had never removed a tooth, but it did not matter. I got out his list of phone numbers, found ANESTHETIST, dialed it—and got a Roman Catholic nun.

She arrived, all starch and smiles, and using an open mask with dripping ether we put the boy to sleep. I began then to extract the first molar and almost immediately ran into trouble. By the time it was out, the boy was awake and screaming. That left the job only half finished, but it did not seem wise to put the boy under ether again. So I told the mother it was not necessary to remove the second tooth immediately. We could wait and see what happened.

She gave me a disgusted look.

"He's going to keep yelling until it comes out."

"Let's see."

"He's going to yell all night and tomorrow I'll have to come back."

"Let's see."

She was there next morning, with the boy still screaming. I summoned the nun who put him to sleep. This time the tooth came out easily and the mother left—only to be followed by another woman in advanced labor with evident stress of the fetus.

This meant a forceps delivery—something else I had never done. I called the nun again, grateful to have such an immaculate and efficient little savior. Once more she gave an anesthetic while I fearfully took forceps in hand, knowing that if I mangled this baby I might as well take the long ride back to Cape Town. Luckily, the boy child came out healthy and unhurt, though the mother was torn. I stitched her up—fortunately, it resulted in a perfect recovery—only to hurry off to treat a boy with snake bite.

So it went for three weeks, until the doctor returned, and I was free to return to Cape Town—more than ever aware of the need for additional training in the collective security of Groote Schuur, beginning under a man as wise as Professor Crichton.

I was wrong about the collective security. Life in the hospital was a collective experience. But this did not provide security against the single act of judgement, of deciding the right or wrong of an infinite number of details that in turn affected larger ones made by the professors. These never let up and they grew in size with time and experience. Often we moved as do those working their way through forests and inevitably our judgements were not always right. Sometimes they were grossly wrong—as occurred the night I decided to end a woman's life.

She was a colored woman, about thirty-five, suffering from severe abdominal pain. Her name was Maria and she had come into the Casualty Department as an emergency case and I had decided to admit her to our ward. That was one of the duties of the intern. Frequently it meant finding beds for patients in other wards when we had none left. And too often it meant turning them away for lack of space. This was hard to do because they were usually desperate, and in refusing them entry you just about said: "I'm sorry you must go home and die."

After bringing Maria to our ward, I took her case history—another routine task of the intern. It always amazed me that the formula for this has changed so little since laid down 2,360 years ago by Hippocrates, the Greek physician. The doctor, he said, had to make an inquiry into the background of the patient's life, his antecedents, his occupation, his temperament, "his habits, regimen, and pursuits; his conversation, manners, taciturnity, thoughts, sleep, or absence of sleep, and sometimes his dreams, what they are and when they occur; his picking and scratching; his tears . . . from all these symptoms we must form our judgement."

My judgement, noted at the bottom of the sheet, pending further examination by my superiors, was that Maria had something more than infection of the uterus—probably cancer. Sadly, it proved to be true. She was treated by radium and X ray, and each day I checked her progress. This meant keeping a chart of her temperature, pulse, respiration, bowel action, blood count, treatments, and medicine.

A lack of registrars, or resident doctors, gave the intern greater responsibility in those days than he is allowed today. For example, we handled patients bleeding from normal abortions, requiring a scraping of the womb. There were many such cases. The more complicated ones, calling for major surgery, were given to the chiefs. Yet we also assisted at these operations—another job normally handled today by the registrar.

For Maria, however, there was to be no operation. Her cancer, at the cervix of the uterus, had advanced too far. Not only were the nerves infiltrated, causing extreme pain, but it was also believed to have proliferated to the rest of her body. Her treatment was intense, yet with little hope of recovery.

They put her in a private room, in the A-9 Ward, and my nightmare began. Even though she was closed off, you could hear her sobbing and crying from pain in between sedations. It was especially bad at night when the hospital became silent, excepting for an occasional moan or mumbled word reaching the dimly lit corridor. In this silence—as on an ocean floor, broken only by the roll of breaking wave and striking rock—Maria was something else. She lay apart, alone in her private room, her cell of pain and sorrow, with its view of a green lawn and one white ionic column. In a way, it was our room, our cell, for I went there often, to hold her hand. I had never seen anyone suffer so much pain and found myself drawn with increasing frequency to her bedside, where I did whatever was possible to relieve the increasing agony of her inevitable crucifixion.

One night I found her in such distress that she could hardly speak. She wanted something to deaden the pain, but this had already been administered and she was not due anything else for several hours.

"Oh, doctor," she said.

I waited by her bedside, hoping the previous drug would give her some relief. She had rather nice features and once, I knew, she must have been quite beautiful. Her skin was light and her eyes were hazel, the color of mine, with dark, sweeping lashes.

"I can't continue," she said. "There's no more in me."

"You must, Maria."

Another flash of pain seized her and she grabbed my arm.

"No-no, no-no!"

"Maria, be quiet, you'll wake up the other patients."

"NO-NO!"

She shuddered and held on even more fiercely.

"Please God, please God, oh-oh JEEEEEESUS!"

"Maria, be quiet!"

I put my hand on her mouth and she bit it. I pulled it away and she bit her own lip until blood came. After that she spoke more easily as though the spasms had lifted.

"Did you know?" she asked.

I nodded, thinking she referred to her illness.

"You did know? I just found out."

Obviously, we were talking about two different things. She knew she had cancer. So this was something else.

"I didn't know it was going to happen to me, but now I know it."

She thought she was going to die.

"You know, I'm not afraid. I knew it had to come, I was always wondering and, you know, Lord, I was scared . . ."

The pain was returning.

"I'm not scared any more, no-no, no-NO!"

She began to scream until the pain reached the point where it broke even her cries and she went under it making incoherent sobs, mumbles, and little yelps—a puppy being drowned in a toilet.

"Please do something," she said. "Please, please, oh please."

"Yes."

"Did you speak?"

"Yes, I spoke."

I left the room to get some morphine. Before going to the drug cabinet, however, I began to walk back and forth along the gray linoleum of the corridor, asking myself what was the best way to help this woman. Here was a human being in extreme agony, caused by an incurable disease that would eventually kill her. She would wither and shrink and her soft face would wither, too, into an ugly grimace—a mask over a skull.

That was her destiny: a tunnel of horror and pain. Yet why did she have to go through it? Pain was nature's cry of alarm. It told you something was wrong. It was a summary call of the psychic complex against the onslaught of a stranger. Yet here the stranger had already won. He had entered the gate and, sadly, the battle was over. The alarm was obsolete. Despite this, the pain had continued to mount until it had gone beyond the level of a scream, reaching a high decibel of suffering that—like sound beyond the threshold of human hearing—was also beyond the registry of human feeling. So it had become something else: an ally in the camp of the enemy, a part of the disease itself.

There had to be a humane end to it. Otherwise, she was going to continue toward still more senseless suffering and eventual disfigurement. To turn away from this was to stand without mercy before her readiness to die. She wanted it now—not later. She wanted it as a recognized, final step in the natural process of death. She asked only to be helped along, to be hastened through the corridor of horror to her final destination.

Mercy death: What was it if not a recognition of the inevitable, conjoined with a Christian hand helping the sufferer along his way? She asked for this help, pleaded for it, prayed for it. Could those who held her in charge turn away from her words, her prayers formed by lips wet with real evidence of an interior hell? Duty called for a cure by using all means.

If no cure was possible, the doctor was required to alleviate as much pain and suffering as possible. And for the supreme relief of the supreme sufferer, there was only one lasting answer.

From the drug cabinet I took down a bottle marked MORPHIA GR. ¼ and shook out twelve tablets. Three grains would normally be enough. From my palm, I slid them into a spoon with distilled water and held it over a flame until it had dissolved. Then I drew it up into a syringe and walked back down the corridor to Maria's room.

The Hippocratic Oath forbad this. I had sworn to it, the code of the medical profession, upon becoming a doctor: "To none will I give a deadly drug, even solicited, nor offer council to such an end." Yet it also said: "Likewise, to no woman will I give a destructive suppository"—and what drug store did not carry them? No—one was the beginning, the other the end. Neither prevailed against the overwhelming problem of our time.

She was asleep, under the double effect of the earlier drug and her own exhaustion. Her mouth was open, its lips swollen. She was perspiring and some of her dark hair had become matted along her cheek. I lifted it away and then took her arm, pulling up the nightshirt. It was a delicate arm and her hands were shaped in a gentle mold—light brown against the white sheet. In the Hippocratic Oath we had also sworn to Apollo and the Greek gods and goddesses, but ours was another Judge of Mercy.

Judge me, O Lord, for these my acts.

I took the arm and pinched it up to plunge in the needle—looking once more at her face, the mouth open, eyes closed. And then I saw her not in life, but in death—dead at my own hands.

It was a flash and it was over at the same instant. I let go of the arm and lowered the needle. This was a grotesque disfigurement of myself. I was violating not only the laws of social man, but also my own most personal ethic, born of despair and hope in a chapel under Christur Redemptur: evil was the forced change of form and matter before its natural hour. Evil was to turn away from nature's hidden face. Death was the common enemy until its just hour. Yet who could pick the hour and who was the Judge? Nobody had helped Christur. He called out in doubt, but little was done to help. He went his way slowly, in pain, wondering if He had been forsaken while the others sat around rolling dice, weeping, beating their breasts. But they had waited.

I squirted the morphine into the sink and started to leave—just as Maria awakened.

"Thank you," she said.

"For what?"

"For helping me. I feel much better."

The next day she seemed to be better and six weeks later she left the hospital—free of pain with her disease arrested for a few more years. I watched her go, wondering how I had come so close to committing a tragedy. When I told Professor Crichton about it, he smiled as though he already knew of the episode.

"It happens to all of us," he said. "You are driven toward it by the same impulse for human relief that makes you a doctor. Some don't go as far as you did. Others go all the way before realizing they've crossed the line and made the Great Transgression."

"Between life and death?"

"Yes."

"But the doctor is still responsible for the alleviation of pain, even as the patient is crossing over. So how near does he come to the line—that is, how much do you alleviate, how much should you help him in the crossing?"

"You are responsible for saving a life, if possible. But you are not responsible for your patient having life nor for the pain that comes with it. That's his own inheritance. You did not give it to him, you cannot take it away."

"Are you saying we should not shield him from pain, especially useless pain?"

"No, I'm saying you are not responsible for what he has, no matter how ugly or violent it might be. I suspect this is a lesson you will never completely learn, Chris."

"Why?"

"Because you identify with your patients. I've noticed that. You transfer not only your skill, but also some of yourself to each of them."

This hurt me, for it implied that I had learned little since fainting before an appendectomy at Beaufort West and being unable to witness a post-mortem. I resented it but said nothing. We were having tea in a room next to the operating theater, and a couple of doctors came in to join us. After they left, I waited for Professor Crichton to continue but he said nothing more. He had soft blue eyes and white hair and the gentle manner of my father.

"So you think I'll never learn my lesson?"

"What lesson?"

"About not transferring."

"Who says that? How can we not transfer? It's like asking a woman not to touch a child—at least for those who are born healers of men and you are one of them, Chris. It's not done, can never be done all the way without leaving a little of yourself behind in each one."

"Until there's nothing left?"

"No, I think an exchange takes place. You give a bit of yourself and you take a little of each one of them so you gain strength and enlarge your feeling as you go along."

He was right, and he understood because he suffered from it as I did—as we all do. It was impossible not to feel a shared responsibility for other lives, even though we had no part in their creation or in their damnation up to the moment of finding them before us in the Casualty Department, in the ward room, or on the operating table.

One night a young woman came in with her boy friend. She was a pretty little creature, about eighteen, and he was thin and dark with the crew cut of a swimmer. You knew right away they were in love from the way they took hold of one another, almost by turns. You could also see they were not married and were in trouble. Finally, the girl explained it. She had become pregnant by the boy and then, to get rid of the fetus, had put an instrument into her uterus. This had perforated the womb, and now she was bleeding internally.

We had to go in and do something about it, and Professor Crichton's son Dirk did it, opening the abdomen. She had so mangled the uterus—God only knows with what sort of stick or spoon and in what frame of mind— that we had to remove it. Then something went wrong. She turned blue and died on the table. After that, we could only close her up and go out to the boy.

He was sitting on a bench, as though waiting to be called for an eight-hundred-yard freestyle relay, and when he saw us there was a little smile —the sort that asks for a return smile. When none came, he stood up, alarmed. Dirk had the responsibility to tell him.

"My boy, I have very bad news for you."

He looked at me, hoping I would say it was not true.

"She is gone, we could do nothing."

"What gone . . . where?"

"I'm sorry, very sorry."

The boy stared at us—first at Dirk, then at me, trying not to accept it.

"She's not dead, she can't be."

"I'm afraid she is."

"But she was here, standing here only a minute ago . . . standing on her feet, right here . . ."

He began to cry then. He was ashamed of it and turned away to the wall.

"It's my fault. I did it. Dear God, I did it."

Dirk put his arm around the boy, but he continued to talk to the wall.

"She wanted to have it but I said no because it would shame her mother and father—what would they think of me? But she wanted it anyway, she said she didn't care what people said, she wanted it. She said, 'It's ours, Billy, it's our own, the first thing we ever made together.' And I wanted it, too, but I was afraid. So I said no, and she said 'What can I do?' and I said, 'I don't know, there are many ways, you have to do something.' That's why she did it, because I made her do it. Oh God, I did it . . . I killed her!"

"No, you didn't do it, Billy."

"No? Who did it then?"

He began to tremble and we tried to get him to sit down on the bench. But he would not do it, and then he left us—going out the door and down the corridor, returning alone to the city and to the old streets where a few hours earlier he had walked, holding a pretty girl by the hand, telling her everything would be all right.

Dirk and I went back to the tea room.

"Our society is guilty, not the boy," I said. "They loved each other and had sexual intercourse. At their age it was a natural act. Nature demands it of them. But we deny it, we find it shameful. So we drove them to do it, we aborted that girl, we killed her—not the boy."

Dirk shook his head. "Between social order and life, which do you choose?"

"Life," I replied.

"Then the girl must be guilty because she took one life and her own with it."

"But society, that is, her parents and the world she lived in, would not approve of a child."

"Yes, but they would approve even less of her aborting herself. No, she was guilty because she and the boy did not have the courage to live with the result of their love—even though it would be hard. They committed the same Great Transgression my father discussed last week. They crossed the line and played God. You simply cannot do that. You cannot find any justification for taking life—unless it will take yours."

In the days that followed, I kept thinking of that boy and his feeling for the girl—his love, yet his inability to do anything about it. Professor Crichton had been right about transference. A part of that boy, and his guilt, stayed with me and I felt a part of myself had gone to him and his girl.

I told Louwtjie about it and she immediately took the part of the girl.

"You're too soft on that boy. He's as guilty as I'm sitting here."

We were sitting in the Doll's House, next to the Mouille Point Lighthouse, having a coffee.

"Imagine what he must have said or done to drive that girl to that point. Do you think a woman sticks a knife or fork into her uterus because she is afraid of what her mother will say?"

I thought about my mother. I had always been frightened of her, afraid of making a mistake. But I would never have destroyed myself to avoid her anger. On the other hand, the girl probably thought it was a simple thing to do.

"The boy told her to do it," she said. "He's guilty and it's typical of you men to say the girl is guilty—and even guilty of double murder, as though one wasn't enough."

"I said society was responsible."

"It's the same thing. You mean the boy is blameless."

"I felt so sorry for him."

"Why? What did he ever do for you?"

"Come on, Louwtjie, that's no way to talk."

"That young woman was a mother, Chris. Think of it that way—a mother. Don't you men ever feel any responsibility for the women you pretend to love?"

I said nothing. Then she said she wanted to go home.

"Why?"

"You know why. I'd like to go home."

We got into the car and I drove down near the lighthouse, stopping at our usual place.

"No, Chris, I want to go home."

"Just a few minutes."

"I'm tired. Either take me home or I'll go myself."

"Why are you so upset?"

"Why shouldn't I be? How long do you think we can keep doing this?" Obviously, I should never have told her about the boy and girl.

"Do what?" I asked, trying to be nice.

"Don't touch me," she said. "I'm not that girl and I'm not going to get caught the way she did with somebody who will say it's all society's fault, or my fault."

"I'd never say that."

"What would you say? Maybe I'd better hear it now."

"I don't know," I said, starting the car.

What, I wondered would I say? We had been going together for about two years and our lives had begun to follow a pattern of love—or rather, a reverse pattern determined by the masterprint of our working hours and fixed by flipping towels at each other. I lived in the doctors' bungalow and she lived in the nurses' quarters up on the hill, the second window along the top balcony. We signaled to each other by waving towels because the phone was always busy. Up and down meant yes and the number of snaps set the hour. Back and forth indicated no—meaning one of us had to sleep or go into an emergency.

We had spent some wonderful times together. Louwtjie had come to Beaufort West to see my family, and I had met her parents who owned some cattle farms in South West Africa as well as a little house at The

Strand. We were alike in many ways and where we were different, it seemed to be designed that way, so that we could help one another. She was very sharp on people and always right in warning me about one or another person in my work. She did not like to dance, which was too bad because I loved it. She was also very jealous at times and had a terrible temper. But she was a love anyway, just as I had imagined she would be when I first saw her eyes looking over the top of a bedsheet.

All the nursing staff, including the sisters, who were a rank above the nurses, had to be home at certain hours—either ten o'clock or midnight, depending on the evening. The checkpoint for this was an entrance to a long tunnel that went sloping upward into the mountain at the rear of the hospital. At the end of the tunnel, an elevator took the girls up to their quarters. A tiger of a matron ran the checkpoint at the tunnel entrance, controlling every arrival. She generally had no idea who was out, but she knew when anybody came in because there was no other entrance at night.

Very often, as could be expected, we never got to the tunnel in time. Nor did other housemen with their dates. When this happened, we all stayed in the doctors' bungalow until 5 A.M. when they unlocked the tunnel door. At that moment, with the tiger-lady gone, we set in motion Operation Home Flight.

One houseman would go up the long tunnel to its end and hold open the elevator. Another would be stationed at the entrance, and another at a point where we could see him from the bungalow. A three-way signal would then be flashed to us, releasing a covey of girls who would race out of the bungalow, turn into the tunnel and scamper like bunnies up its long incline to the houseman holding open the elevator. A few minutes later, they would all descend again, dressed in white like little angels, ready for work.

One morning, as Louwtjie started to make the homeward flight with some friends, I held her back.

"Let me go, you idiot!"

"Wait a minute, I want to ask you something."

"I can't wait!"

She broke away from me and began to run for the elevator. I ran alongside, trying to get her to stop.

"Please, Louwtjie, it's very important."

"What is it?"

"Will you marry me?"

She stopped and looked at me, blinking her eyes like a little girl.

"You fool!"

"What do you mean?"

"I never thought of anything else!"

We kissed then, even though it was daylight and everyone could see us, and we were going to miss the elevator. When we looked up, there was the little chapel and we smiled at each other and kissed again as though it was, indeed, the real moment of our marriage.

That was how it had been and how we had left it a few months ago. And now, in the car, Louwtjie wanted to know what was going to happen next.

"The trouble," I said, "is money. We have no money for it."

"Money isn't the question."

"Yes, it is."

"Do you want to get married or not?"

"Yes, I do. You know I do . . . eventually."

"Then money doesn't matter. We can get engaged and marry when you go into practice."

"All right," I said. "If that's what you want."

"Well, don't you?"

"Yes, yes . . . of course, just as much as you do."

Three days later I sold my little blue Austin to buy an engagement ring. Louwtjie had seen one she liked and we went to look at it in the window of a jewelry shop. There were several of them, and at first I could not determine the one she wanted.

"That one," she said. "The one in the middle that looks like it's smiling at us."

"Smiling?"

"Don't you see? Now it's laughing."

"I'm glad somebody's laughing."

She took her arm out of mine.

"Aren't you happy?"

"Yes, delirious."

"You don't sound like it."

"Sweetie, how in the hell can I identify a ring when you say it's laughing at me?"

"Not at you," she said. "It's just happy with us."

We stood there a while longer, staring at the ring. Finally she spoke.

"Well, shall we go in?"

"I feel embarrassed."

"About what?"

"That man in there. He'll know we're going to get married."

"What's wrong with that? Aren't we?"

"Yes, but it's sort of strange. You know what I mean?"

"No," she said, saying it in a way that was flat and final—like a box being snapped shut.

We went inside and bought the ring. That night we had an engagement party in the billiard room of the doctors' bungalow. We put towels over the billiard table and served beer. There was a piano and a friend of mine,

"C.G." De Villiers, played oldtime Dixieland jazz. It was a great party, and Louwtjie was very happy and openly proud of her ring.

"It's a great beauty, all right," said C.G.

"I've always dreamed of one," said Louwtjie.

"Instead of waving towels at Chris, you can now flash that rock at him."

Everyone laughed, except Louwtjie. C.G. plunged onward.

"Hell, man, if you caught the sun right with that rock, you could train it right through Chris's window like a lighthouse."

Louwtjie hesitated a moment, then joined the general laughter—but only out of politeness. C.G. had wrapped the truth with a joke. The ring was just that—a constant alert and searchlight into my bachelor's quarters. But it was also something else: a bright pool of memory where the two of us ran alongside one another to stop before a chapel and kiss and whisper words of love. And this also stayed with us, wherever we went.

CHAPTER 8

AFTER SIX MONTHS in gynecology, I was offered a similar training period in general surgery. This was quite an honor, extended to only a select few of the graduate doctors. I accepted and joined the surgery department, headed by Professor Cole Rous. Below him was a senior surgeon. Below that came three junior surgeons. At the bottom of this heap were three interns—myself, Jacques Roux, and Pikkie Joubert.

As can be imagined, competition was most fierce at the bottom. Since we were in surgery, there was every incentive to carve our way to the top—that is, by doing more operations than any of the others. We were allowed only minor undertakings, such as removal of an appendix or reparation of a hernia—and even these were assigned to us only after we had proved ourselves capable.

So we fought for every chance, seizing each one with the speed of eagles. Competition was keenest between Jacques Roux and myself. Many an evening he left me saying, "By God, you've pinched them all for yourself again today"—only to grab them all for himself the next day.

This came to a dramatic climax one morning after I had prepared a patient for removal of a gall bladder. The intern's job was to bring the patient into the theater, see that he was properly anesthetized on the table, and then open up the abdomen—waiting then for the surgeon to take over.

When I reached this point, the surgeon had not yet arrived. So I continued to the next step, which is dissecting down to expose a small artery to the gall bladder, as well as a cystic duct through which the bladder sends its bile into the pancreatic duct and so into the small bowel. Once these two major links were defined for dissection, the bladder could be removed.

After I had done this, Dr. Jannie Louw, one of the junior surgeons, came into the theater. He wore his white shirt and trousers, with gum boots, mask, and cap—but he still had not put on his surgical gown and gloves. So he merely peeped at the table from over the top of the anesthetist's curtain.

"What have you done?" he asked.

"I've exposed the bladder, the artery, and the cystic duct."

"Well," he said, "since you've nearly finished the operation, why don't you go ahead and do it?"

He remained there, looking over the curtain, while I clamped the artery and the cystic duct. Then I lifted up the bladder and dissected it off its bed in the liver. This practically concluded the operation and I glanced up to see Dr. Louw smiling over the top of the curtain.

"Well, close the abdomen," he said, and walked away.

I put in a drain and closed it. Then I sat up all night looking at the patient in the event anything went wrong. I was terribly excited. No intern in the hospital had ever done an operation of that importance—not even to this day. Jacques Roux took it well, congratulating me with the grace of a gentleman. We have remained lifelong friends.

The operating theater was not, however, always an arena of personal triumph. Shortly afterward, I had to do an appendectomy. Louwtjie, then in theater training, was to assist as instrument sister—the nurse responsible for passing instruments to the surgeon.

I have always been nervous and keyed up at the onset of any operation. With Louwtjie next to me, I became even more tense. There was a sense of intimacy between us that did not belong in the theater. It was something electrical, a sort of involuntary interlocking of our projected selves that she could not help any more than I could. Inevitably, this was a disturbance at the operating table where the ritual of command and the interlacing of hands and instruments demands a totally different relationship. Men and women at a surgical intervention are instruments or extensions of instruments—including the surgeon who is an instrument of nature's law. Anything that slows down or deflects this is a blunting of the total team action.

It began almost immediately. Our hands, which the night before had been pressed upon one another in love, now met and touched in sterile gloves.

Thin rubber was never intended to insulate such sensations. There was also the ring, cuddled atop her left breast. Rings could not be worn under sterile conditions and Louwtjie, following common procedure, had pinned it beneath her sterile theater gown—a little bulge that had been a blue Austin, a kiss in the sunlight, and a pledge that could only be redeemed by making more money than I was now earning as an intern in a hospital clinic.

Then it happened—an artery forceps slipped off, allowing blood to pump out into the operating area. Quickly I put it back and turned on Louwtjie.

"That was clumsy of you."

"What?"

"Good God, girl, didn't you even see it?"

I had never spoken to her like that—but she was not Louwtjie. She was a clumsy nurse, a break in the chain, a crumbling block in the total pyramid. She had to see this, to know that she was two people, I was two people, and we were now on two sides of a knife.

Brown eyes flashed hate over the white mask, telling me everything. I had violated something as sacred as the life under my hands. I had cut her adrift. The lady of the castle had been treated like a servant. She was wrong, of course, because this was not our castle. It belonged to the man on the operating table. We were his servants. There was no room here for any of us, except as servants. There was no room for the touch that remembered last night or a ring which promised tomorrow.

She handed me a needle holder, moving precisely and mechanically from years of discipline, but within there was the cold rage of a Boer opening the front door of her manor house to the occupying troops of Sir Bindon Blood.

"Your incident occurred while my back was turned, getting you this—Doctor."

You could feel the choked laughter all around the theater, followed by a silence that penetrated and isolated us from each other. It remained even after the operation, lasting several days. I sent her a bunch of roses and that evening began to once more wave a towel toward her little window high on the hill. After a few minutes, another towel was waving back at me in the valley.

There is an element of violence in surgery that began to bother me. We had three wards—B-1, B-4, F-4—three tragic fields where, amid the slow harvest, some plants were forever subject to sudden withering and death. We worked there and in the theater until we were ready to collapse. The calls never ceased, and when one of us was absent the load become still heavier. Besides this, we also checked admissions from Casualty, and assisted senior surgeons in the Out-Patients' Department.

In all of this, there was a constant crisis that was resolved most often by radical surgery. One day I had to tell a little boy it was necessary to take away his leg—a hindquarter amputation that would leave nothing, not even a full hip. That is a massive destruction of the human body and for a little boy it was like telling him he was going to die. He cried in a very sad way, all choked up, trying to be brave at first, then dissolving into tears, saying over and over: "If I can't run with my friends, who will be there to play with me?"

During the operation, as the surgeon slowly dismembered the young body, I realized that the boy was asking us much more. His question was something else: "Doctor, please tell me now, when you are finished with this, who I can walk with, live with . . . love with. . . . Please tell me so I can know what to do!"

Afterward, talking with Pikkie Joubert in the tearoom, I said I felt guilty.

"Of what? That boy would have died of cancer."

"We have dismembered a young life."

"You didn't do it. He came to you that way."

It was Professor Crichton's argument. *They* came that way. *We* could do no more.

"But we should have some answer, other than cutting it off."

"Like what?"

"Like putting on another leg—something constructive."

"Yes," he said. "In the year 2000."

"Sooner," I said. "Sooner than that. At any rate I don't like the destructive aspect of surgery."

"You have to look at it from the positive side," he said. "At what is left."

"That's just what disturbs me—what is left, what we haven't done."

Pikkie had a flat face, the flat gray-brown eyes of a fighter, and a very tough intelligence. One day he had a toothache and no time to go to a dentist. So he pulled his own molar. Then his father was admitted to my F-4 ward for removal of the stomach. It was not a common operation in those days and he developed both pneumonia and an infection from a leak in the small bowel anastomosis. We did everything possible, even locating some streptomycin, which was rare at that time. But eventually he died.

Pikkie insisted that a postmortem be performed on his father, saying he wanted to see what had really happened. I went to the mortuary to witness the examination and was surprised at his cold, clinical manner. How could he allow strangers to witness a piecemeal dismembering of his own father— limbs which had cradled him, loin that had delivered the seed of his life, brain that held all the hopes and dreams for his son? There was something almost inhuman in the whole spectacle. When I discussed the findings with Pikkie, I watched his face and tried to understand what he was really looking for—beyond the broken hinge of his father's life. Was it perhaps to find within the torn flesh, the running blood, the uplifted intestines, a glimpse into his own interior? I did not know and afterward could not bring myself to speak to him about it.

At the end of my six months' training in general surgery, I was offered a doctor's residency at the Peninsula Maternity Home and accepted it with great relief. It meant the end of what I felt was too often destructive surgery, the lack of any answer other than the cutting away of the human body. It meant a return to birth, to the beginning of life before it was violated by man, destroyed by machines or diseased by age. It meant the use of whatever skill I possessed to help deliver onto this planet whole human beings with a promise of a better life, rather than those broken by life and bankrupt of promise. Finally, it meant a return to a hospital where I had lived and worked briefly as a student, placing me once more in a working relationship with Professor Crichton.

This fountain of life, however, was located in one of the most violent sections of the city—District Six. If Cape Town is a tavern of the seas, this is its bar, bedroom, and basement with no walls in between. It is packed with Malays, Indians, coloreds, and many whites who love the colorful district as a vanishing piece of history. All of them are tumbled, one atop the other, into a boiling cauldron of races, languages, dialects, religious beliefs, and superstitions. It is a show that never ends. For since there is hardly enough room to sleep, most of the living is done in the streets. It is the sort of living that has more crime, vice, laughter, love, compassion, and prayer than anywhere else in the city.

A world by itself, the District seems to have been flung together with bits and pieces of other cities of the world. The architecture has the tumbledown grace, like old ball gowns, of the Vieux Carré in New Orleans. The streets slope up and down, giving you intimate views into back yards and bedrooms, as in Montmartre or San Francisco. The market has the spicy aroma of Tangiers, and the wind blows in from the sea as it does in Bombay. The mosques have drifted in from scattered Islam, the synagogues from Sephardic shores, the chapels from northern Europe and Calvin's guilt dreams. The street violence is from everywhere and native to the heart of all desperate men, but in its intensity it has few counterparts—except in New York City.

Shortly after arriving, I looked out of a second-story window onto Primrose Street and saw two youths arguing with a young girl. They spoke in a low, urgent way, but the girl only shook her head. She wore a bright turquoise blouse and when the knife appeared it was like silver on turquoise—just a flash of it as it plunged three times into the girl, all of it happening without sound, the girl backing off across the sidewalk each time the blade went into her breast, until her handbag fell first, making most of the racket. After that she sank to her knees and for a moment sat upright. Then without a murmur, she lay down as though going to sleep on the sidewalk. It happened so quickly, I had no time to do other than watch. Then the two *skollies* began to walk away slowly, as though nothing had happened. I started to yell at them, but a nurse pulled me away from the window.

"Don't shout!"

It was Sister Naude.

"Excuse me, Doctor, but if you yell at them, they'll think you are on the side of the police."

"Well aren't we?" I asked, running for the street with the nurse following me.

The young woman was still on her back, blood already matting on the bright turquoise blouse, running around the collar and dripping into the gutter. She had died when she went down onto the sidewalk.

We returned to the office and phoned the police. After that, Sister Naude explained whose side we were on.

"We're on the side of the police," she said. "Of course we are. But we're also on the side of their babies, maybe even a little bit more on the side of the babies, so we don't yell at them from windows. That would upset the arrangement."

The arrangement held up in a most amazing manner. To assist women giving birth at home, we went into the worst areas at all hours without ever being molested. If we needed help to find our way, boys and women would appear to lead us onward—a sister and myself carrying a case with our instruments, including a little rubber bag for the placenta.

Always it was a crowded room. We would find a woman giving birth in one corner, while the remainder of the chamber was filled with sleeping bodies—only a few of them bothering to sit up, dazed and mute, to stare at the spectacle before them. On the walls and floors and in the beds were cockroaches, lice, fleas, and rats. When there was no electricity, we delivered by candlelight. Sometimes the membrane broke as we began to examine the patient, dousing the candle and plunging us into the darkness amid shrieks and cries to Allah or Elohim or Jesus—drawing in return a mixed chorus of guttural curses from the sleepers.

Yet even as they cried out, the women were generally splendid creatures —accepting pain with a deep knowledge of its link to pleasure, as though these were not simply sensations, such as color or sound, but something deeper, linked to a separate set of nerve ends buried in the vital chambers of life. They bore the breech of the world and the link of all mankind was in them.

The men were less interesting—mute and powerless before the miracle of birth and often amazingly primitive. One woman tore while giving birth, a peroneal tear, which we closed with dermalon stitches, to be removed after one week. Two days later, we returned to do a dressing—only to find the stitches had been removed.

"What's happened here?" I asked.

She was a handsome Malay woman, about thirty-five, and for a moment she looked at me in silence.

"*Niks daar nie,*" she said finally, in dialect, meaning "Nothing there."

"I know there's nothing there. Where did it all go?"

"*Kan nie kla nie,*" she said, meaning "I can't complain."

"Very well," I said. "But I'm complaining. Where are all the stitches?"

She told us then. Her husband had pulled them out, saying they tickled him.

There were equally primitive remedies for most every illness. For a headache you put vinegar-soaked rags or sliced potatoes against the temple. Children with tummy aches had raw eggs smeared over their bellies. Open sores were treated with carrot and cabbage leaves.

The superstitions were assembled from all over the world. A cat washing its face meant someone was coming for a visit. If a knife or fork fell down or if a lid was left off a pot on the stove, it also meant visitors were coming. It was unlucky to have in the house horns of animals or artificial flowers. Pictures should never hang over doorways, nor should children crawl under tables or put shoes on them. You never sewed on a button while a garment was being worn, unless the wearer chewed thread during the sewing. Nor should anyone use hammer or nails on Good Friday. If cobwebs were brushed off walls while someone was ill, death would follow. A candle dripping down one side also foretold death, as did cupboard drawers left open like coffins.

If you were in trouble, a *doekum,* or Malay witch doctor, could fix you up by the shuffling of mystical objects, charms, and burning papers with secret symbols over dark graves. Behind these conjurers rode a whole legion of folk tales, featuring cat-women, wolf-men, and the *Kwaaiwind*—a vicious wind which sears the face and neck and causes paralysis. Filth, disease, and lack of proper food did nothing, of course. It was the *Kwaaiwind* or maybe the cat-woman.

The more serious maternity cases were handled in the hospital, which once had been a private home, known as Buckingham Lodge. There was about it still the feeling of a once elegant manor home, now overrun by a lusty battalion of poor relatives who had gradually driven away all the servants, broken the china, stolen the silver, ruined the rugs, and now were slowly turning the living room, library, study, and even the hallways into bedrooms for the endless multiplication of their kind.

I lived in a small, pea-green room, which looked onto a garden through double bars against night prowlers. Dr. Tos Roux, the only other resident doctor, had a room next to mine. The nurses' quarters were across the garden on the other side of a magnificent loquat tree. Wrought-iron grill ran like lace between slender columns with baroque capitals, giving our little living area an old-world atmosphere.

The work was enjoyable, though it took us out at all hours. It brought a clean and wonderful feeling, walking back at dawn through the narrow, empty streets, knowing that you had left behind another human being—born well and healthy and perhaps even bearing your name, assumed in a bright moment of triumph and happiness.

And then, without warning, a call came one evening from Pikkie Joubert. He was in Ceres, where he had gone to take over the general practice of a doctor who was away on a year's leave.

"Chris," he said, "there's more work here than I can handle. Why don't you come over and join me?"

I laughed at the idea.

"No, Pikkie, I'm signed up for six months here, and I'm thinking of specializing in obstetrics and gynecology."

"We got that too. Babies coming in all the time. On top of that, there's a little hospital and surgery. It's a nice town, Chris. Nice people. We can share the practice—what do you say?"

"I don't think so. I hadn't planned to be a general practitioner."

"Think about it, Chris. We know each other. I'd prefer someone I know."

When I told Louwtjie about it, she thought it would be a good idea. It would allow me to make more money—at least more than I was getting at the maternity home. And with that, we could get married. That was what she wanted, but I was not too sure about it.

"Why not?" she asked.

"I don't know. I have a feeling it isn't right."

"How can it go wrong? There's nothing you can't handle now. You've done pediatrics, medicine, and surgery. You even pulled some teeth at Usakos. . . ."

"It isn't that."

"What is it then?"

"I don't know. Maybe, I'm looking for something else."

"Maybe you're not looking for anything. Maybe you've settled into a rut—have you thought of that?"

"How can you say that?" I asked.

"What else is there to say?"

A few days later, Louwtjie was waiting for me to take her to a movie. There was trouble in one of the wards, and since we were short of nurses, she cheerfully pitched in to help out. At one point, she was holding a little baby boy in her arms when I turned to take the child. For a moment, she held onto him, the tiny head nestled against her breast. We said nothing. We did not have to speak. We knew what we wanted—but when?

Within a week I called Pikkie Joubert to say I was ready to join him in general practice at Ceres.

"Great," he said, "It's the best thing you've ever done, Chris."

"I hope so," I said.

"What are you worried about?"

"Nothing."

"Are you sure?"

"Yes, Pikkie, I'm sure."

"All right then, come right away."

I was not sure, however. There was something wrong about this move, but I did not know what it was . . . not at the beginning, anyway.

CHAPTER 9

THE DRIVE TO CERES took only two hours but it was like going to a land cut off from the world. You felt it happening as you came down from Mitchell's Pass toward the little town that sits in a crater cupped by blue mountains—a valley quilted with fruit orchards and laced with fast-running trout streams. There was also game in those days and every so often a leopard streaked down through the foothills to plunder a flock of fat Merino sheep.

Other than this predatory fury, no violence reached Ceres to break the soft cycle of its seasons. Fierce storms lashed the Cape barely 100 miles away, only to exhaust their violence against encircling mountains. In the winter it rained, but between you and the sky there were tall, interlacing oaks and there were pines, too, marking the speed of the wind. Beyond this, higher up on the mountains, there was snow that never reached the valley to fall upon brown leaves clinging to winter limbs.

In the summer the sky was a deep blue and the valley was ripe with fruit—apples so fat that juice squirted out at the biting, peaches as golden and heavy as honeycombs, and pears with a delicate flavor that could only come from the blossom of the fruit being buried within them. It was a valley named after a Greek goddess, a valley of wonder—especially for a young man from the Karoo who once had whistled for the rain wind.

Yet more than all this, something else happened that converted the cupped valley of Ceres into a boundless new world. For here my relationship with patients underwent a radical change. In a general hospital, such as Groote Schuur, a doctor receives patients he has never seen before, with never enough time to know them well. They pour in, an endless stream, afflicted with all variety of ailments, which are met under full attack—much as one encounters an enemy on the battlefield.

This has an inevitable result. Lacking an intimate link with a doctor, the patient is driven to place his trust elsewhere, generally in the hospital itself—the aggregate of buildings, doctors, nurses, equipment, and even such peripheral elements as the neatness of the corridors, the color of the room, or the starched linen of the nurses (starch = cleanliness = efficiency = protection against germs). These symbols of security are anxiously seized by the patient to meet his unsleeping fears, his unending hope to have not only the best possible treatment, but also to see that the dice are loaded at least a little bit in his favor. Such a display of security symbols is most important in private hospitals where patients pay larger sums of money and expect a larger return.

In a small town this matters less because the patient goes directly to the doctor. There is an immediate you-me relationship, even among welfare cases, that does not exist in large cities—except among the rich who can afford the running intimacy of a doctor on call. The rich can also afford to pay for a physician of such high calibre and training that he is by virtue of his intelligence and social standing a family confidant, a friend at the dinner table, a member of the wedding. This type of relationship is impossible among urban workers and the middle class. It exists, however, between a general practitioner and his patients in a small town.

Ceres was exciting because of this. Previously my patients had been found in wards or private rooms, cut off from the world which had produced and delivered them with their afflictions into my hands. In Ceres I became part of the total experience of human beings I would treat—part of the web, the corner, the roof of their existence.

It was no longer necessary to take a patient's personal history in order to learn "his dreams . . . his picking, his scratching . . . his tears." You saw it as he walked down Acorn Street or sat in Main Church. You observed it across his dinner table or while playing rugby together. Perhaps you had brought him into the world and knew secrets of his mother and father, which they, in turn, never told one another.

This immersion into the life of the community was so overwhelming that I quickly forgot my premonition that it would end badly. In a way, it was comparable to a young minister receiving his first parish, his first experience with human beings on a pastoral level. Similarly, I had my first parish of human life.

It would be misleading, however, to say I saw all this as I began work in Ceres, or even that I realized what was happening to me. At first I saw little, other than each experience as it came along—beginning on the day I arrived.

I had made the drive from Cape Town in the first major investment of my new life: a dark blue Chevrolet sedan. A country doctor needs a car and this one, bought on a bank loan from C. P. Nel's in Beaufort West, looked as though it belonged to a man who had a good hold on life and was making a success of it. A 1948 model, barely one year old, it was the first man-sized car I ever owned, and the day before my trip I had proudly washed and polished it myself.

Loaded with bags and books, plus a box holding a few instruments and my framed diploma, I pulled up in front of the residence of Dr. Tim O'Maloney shortly before noon. This was both the home and office of the doctor whom Pikkie Joubert and I were to relieve for one year—or until he returned to claim his practice.

It was a pleasant, double-gabled house with bay windows and a porch with red steps and four white columns—a hybrid Victorian which transplanted easily to this valley. To the right of the house stood a giant oak and next to it were rose trees. On the opposite side were hydrangea shrubs with immense white flowers as though their roots had found some secret level of loam and water untouched by any other plant. Before all this lay an immense lawn encircled by a hedge. The front gate was made of birch limbs and next to it was a stone block with O'Maloney's name in bronze letters. Beneath it, Pikkie had put his: Dr. Joubert. Dr. Barnard was going to be at the bottom of the list.

The drive was around at the side and as I pulled into it, a colored house boy emerged to say Dr. Joubert had gone out on an emergency but would be back soon. His name was John, and together we unloaded the car.

Inside, the house was large and comfortable with plenty of room— except it had only one bedroom with a double bed. Next to the bed was the phone, which started to ring as I stood looking at it.

I picked it up and heard a woman's voice.

"Dr. O'Maloney?"

"No, this is Dr. Barnard."

"Where is O'Maloney?"

"He's gone away for a year."

"A year? I can't wait that long," she said, and hung up.

Quite obviously, we were not going to be the automatic inheritors of all O'Maloney's patients. The phone rang again and it was another woman.

"Hello, Dr. Joubert?"

"No, this is Dr. Barnard. What is it?"

"Oh, Dr. Barnard. We've been expecting you. Welcome to Ceres."

"Thank you."

We were, I decided, making progress. At least this one was not hanging up and she even knew my name.

"I'm Sister van der Merwe at the Nursing Home. Would you tell Dr.

Joubert that the lady from Prince Alfred Hamlet is going into labor now?"

"Yes."

That sounded more like it. I began to unpack, but before I could finish the phone rang two more times. One was a woman who thought her little girl had the measles. I took her name and address and said I would soon be there—my first patient. The second call was from a man at a distant farm, to say they were bringing to the hospital a woman who had been clawed by a leopard.

"A leopard—is the woman alive?"

"*Ya,* but she's scratched up bad."

"When will she get here?"

"In about forty minutes, maybe less. Her husband, van Rensburg, just left here with the truck. He said to phone Dr. O'Maloney and say he was on his way. He didn't have time himself after he found them."

"Them? How many more are there?"

"Just the wife. *Ya,* he found them both in the kitchen. With the leopard dead next to her."

I hung up, wondering what would happen next. Maybe an elephant herd would stampede down Munich Street. Or a battalion of baboons would take over the City Hall. Some little town, I thought. No wonder Pikkie had called me.

He came in shortly after that and I gave him all the messages.

"I'll deliver the baby," he said. "You patch up the leopard lady."

I nodded.

"I figure we go fifty-fifty on everything," he said. "Share the work, share the profits—right down the line."

I nodded again.

"As for the house, the first one who marries can have it."

I told him he was going to lose on that. Louwtjie and I had decided to marry in November if all went well at Ceres.

"That's only six months away," I said.

"*Ya*—and I don't even have anything in sight."

He sighed.

"There's hardly any time to hunt pheasants, let alone find a wife. As you said, this is some little town. It's loaded like a double barrel."

The two barrels, he said, were the two classes of patients in town. There was, first of all, a big backlog to be treated under the government medical program—poorer cases, mostly coloreds.

"There are hundreds of chronic hernias, appendices, tonsils—you can name it," he said. "For years nobody has touched them. Doctors here have been interested mainly in private cases. So I'm telling you, man, this is virgin territory for surgery. We can do two or three a day until O'Maloney comes back and still not clear them all up. It's not much—five pounds for abdominals plus two guineas for the anesthetic. But if we get it rolling fast enough, we can clean up."

This was immediately intriguing. It meant we could do some good work, bringing our skill—all that we had learned at the Groote Schuur—to help a group of people who belonged to the extended chambers of my father's church. That gave it substance. It meant also that we would not have to take money from these people, or even demand it when they did not have it, since the government would pay. Finally, it meant I could get a vast amount of experience, working through a hundred, maybe a thousand, abdomens and chests and throats, confirming what I knew and going beyond that to what I thought could be changed or improved.

"There's also the private practice," said Pikkie. "But it needs to be built up."

"Do they hang up the phone on you, too?"

He nodded.

"It'll take time to build that up—confidence in a new doctor, especially a young one. The people here all know each other and it takes time. But until then, we have this government backlog. And once they see what we can do, they'll know we've got what it takes—right, Chris!"

"Right Pikkie . . . where's the hospital?"

If I was going to treat a lady clawed up by a leopard, I wanted to be there when she arrived.

"Come on," he said. "I'll show you."

On the way out the rear of the house, Pikkie pointed to a separate bungalow in the back.

"That's where O'Maloney has his office and also receives private patients. There's room for both of us and even a little emergency room for small interventions."

In the car, he explained the hospital was quite small—six rooms and an operating theater, plus offices for the staff, which included three sisters with one of them doubling as secretary. It had been set up as a private hospital by a doctor with a sure formula for making money. He specialized in tonsillectomies, requiring his patients stay at least three days in the hospital. His bill included food, but since the patients were forbidden to eat the day before their operation and their throats were too sore afterward, he made more money on food than anything else. After removing every available tonsil, he moved on to fresher territory—and the little unit was converted into a provincial hospital.

It was a low, rectangular building of yellow stone with a corrugated metal roof bright as silver. Roses grew outside against the yellow wall, and overhead giant oaks extended their limbs across the street—Acorn Street.

Pikkie introduced me to the nurse on duty and hurried off to the nearby nursing home. Shortly after that, a truck arrived with Marie van Rensburg.

She lay on a mattress in the bed of the truck with a blanket over her, and next to her sat a young man who was her son. She had regained consciousness but was in shock from blood loss. Her dark blue flower-print dress was ripped down the front and matted with blood.

We carried her into the emergency room, removed her clothes, cleaned the wounds, and prepared for treatment. She was about sixty yet had the rugged, muscular build of a farm woman who had chopped wood and carried immense burdens. Her body was cut and clawed in a way which could only have been caused by a beast, such as a leopard. There were some serious lacerations on the abdomen—fortunately none through the stomach wall. There were others on the chest, shoulders and even the neck. By some miracle, her face had not been torn. But most everywhere else there was an opening.

To alleviate her shock, we gave plasma and injections. Then I began to slowly sterilize and suture fifty-seven wounds. As I worked, I tried to figure out what had happened. No man could singlehandedly fight and kill a leopard—not even this tough old lady. Besides, no one in his right mind would pick a fight with a beast many hunters feared more than the lion. Finally, after I had closed all the wounds and put the woman in a private room, the husband and son told me the story.

Their dogs had tracked the leopard to a cave and the son had gone there with a gun. From the barks and excitement of the dogs, he knew what was inside—the same leopard that had been killing their sheep. So he smoked it out, his father helping, until the leopard suddenly burst forth in leaps so high and long it never seemed to touch the ground. Both men shot, hitting the animal in the neck and shoulder, but not enough to bring it down. So with the dogs behind, the wounded beast raced onward, looking for some refuge—down the canyon and toward the farm about a mile away.

Marie van Rensburg had spent the morning first in Bible reading with her husband and son, then making butter and kneading dough. After putting some loaves into the oven, she heard the dogs coming toward the farm and barking wildly. She went to the kitchen door just as the leopard bounded into the farmyard. Weak from his wounds and lack of blood, the animal headed for the only possible refuge in sight—the kitchen.

Marie barely had time to recognize it was a leopard before it leaped. She met it there in the doorway—the beast which had killed her husband's sheep and now wanted to enter the kitchen where she was baking bread.

As the leopard landed on her, Marie fell backward with it on top, her powerful hands finding its throat while her legs hooked around the animal's lower half. In such a murderous embrace, the two rolled about on the kitchen floor, Marie driving her thumbs into the windpipe while the dogs snapped wildly at the leopard's tail and ears—until the animal went limp and expired just as Marie herself lost consciousness.

Mr. van Rensburg and his son came running up, to be met first by the barking dogs racing out to them from the kitchen. Upon entering, they found Marie on the kitchen floor, unconscious yet still embracing the dead leopard.

After making sure the patient was resting well, I began to leave for the lady whose daughter supposedly had measles. Mr. van Rensburg was waiting at the door to pay me. I told him there would be an eventual hospital fee for her bed and board—but none for the doctor. South Africa had been settled and built by people like the van Rensburgs. I could no more accept money from them than I could charge my father or grandfather for services.

In such a spirit, I knocked on the door of the home with the sick child. A woman holding an apron in her hand opened the door.

"Mrs. Swarts?"

"Yes."

"You called for the doctor?"

"Yes," she said, "where is he?"

This was such a surprise I hardly knew what to say. Understandably, she had called for old Dr. O'Maloney and drawn a young man, medical kit in hand, who could have been her son.

"I'm Dr. Barnard."

"Oh," she said, looking me over, then reluctantly letting me in.

The little girl did have measles and I prescribed the treatment. Mrs. Swarts accepted it, but not with any show of confidence. Quite clearly, it was going to take some time to obtain the support of the people in this town. Where a farmer would accept me, a middle-class town family would not. I recalled the middle class of Beaufort West who wanted to close down my father's church—how suspicious they were of anything new, how quick to discredit anything that touched the edge of their lives or their prejudices.

It was very discouraging and my spirits, which had been so high, now plunged to an all-time low as I drove back to the hospital to check on Mrs. van Rensburg—and from there to the home that Pikkie and I were to share.

At dinner I realized I had not eaten all day, and after a glass of beer began to feel better. Pikkie was openly delighted I had come, and he did not share my fears that we were going to find it difficult to build up a private practice.

"First of all, consider how that woman felt. She opens the door and finds you there—a young man in place of an old one she has known for years. The point is, she let you in. Now her child will get well and she'll tell everyone you did it. That will bring more of them. Besides that, we can also get patients another way."

"How's that, Pikkie?"

"Charge less than anyone else—say seven and six a visit. People will do practically anything to save money, including trust a young man who looks like their son."

He was right. Pamela Swarts recovered from her measles, but not without two of her friends also getting it. I received one of these as a patient. In this way, the private patients began to arrive in the reception room of the little bungalow behind the O'Maloney home—at seven and six a call.

Fanie Bekker, who had become an insurance salesman, brought Louwtjie over for a weekend and we all had a good time together. She liked Pikkie and the little town, and she seemed to believe it would be ideal for us. That meant we could go ahead with the marriage plans.

"Shall I tell my parents?" she asked.

"I wish I were sure about this."

"What do you mean?"

"That it will work out. O'Maloney is liable to come back and kick us both out."

"Not for a year at least. By that time, you will have your own practice. Once these people realize what kind of doctor you are, they'll all ask for you."

"Are you sure of that?"

"Yes, Chris."

"All right," I replied—two little words which said nothing in particular, yet everything.

They meant I was ready to trust this town with my future, that I felt confident enough to succeed, and that I was ready to marry Louwtjie in November. Life's major decisions were often made that way—two mumbled words as though you were saying: "All right, two lumps of sugar."

"My father and mother will be so happy," Louwtjie said. "Maybe I'll take a leave and go home for a visit."

That meant she would be in South West Africa, some 1,300 miles away.

"No," I said. "You'll be too far away."

"Too far for what?" she said, with a mischievous smile. We were alone together, in the car parked at the top of the pass, looking down into the valley.

"Umm," she said after a bit. "Maybe you're right. I don't think it's safe to leave you alone. Not until after November 6, and even then I'll worry."

"About what?"

"About all the young girls, the nurses, and Fanie Bekker. He always has an extra girl."

"That's his problem, not mine."

"So leave it like that. Don't help him with his problems."

"Never," I said.

"The way you two laugh when you're together makes me nervous."

"Nervous about what?"

"I don't know. Like I was being left out."

"Out of what?"

"Left out of you. Like there was a part of you I could not touch."

"Is there some place we haven't touched?"

"I mean inside you."

There it was again, just as Ninky had seen it—a part of me that was not touchable. Yet there had been a part of her, too, which was beyond my grasp. And there was in Louwtjie something else—a running, uncontrollable tide of emotions, pulled by forces forever beyond my reckoning. It was a part of her that I could not touch. A human being was a house of many chambers and some of them were never opened, even by the owner. Fools and lovers had this in common—they wanted the keys to all the rooms and the right to lock them off or to enter them whenever they felt like it.

"I know Fanie is your boyhood friend. But you're no longer a boy, Chris. You're a man, my man."

"Like you're my woman, Mrs. Barnard."

"Oh, that sounds nice," she said, cuddling up. "Say it again."

Louwtjie and Pikkie appeared to be right. As the town got to know us, the practice grew. The phone rang day and night, often calling me out to distant farms. There were so many of these farm visits that soon they began to blend, one into the other. Two of them remain distinct in memory, however, probably because most of the others tended to fuse into them.

One occurred shortly after I began to work in Ceres. It was an urgent call to attend a woman having a difficult birth at a farm forty miles away. I left immediately and by the time I arrived it was early evening and the young husband was waiting for me, surrounded by barking dogs, on the steps of his home.

His wife—dark, young, still not heavy from the weight of farm work—had been in labor eight hours. Examination showed, however, that both she and the unborn baby were in good condition.

"There's nothing to worry about," I said to the husband.

He grinned with relief. He was a good-looking boy and had studied agronomy at college—one of the younger generation who would probably build his farm into a showplace.

"It's just one of those long ones," I said. "You'd better get some sleep."

"Will you call me?"

"Yes, I'll call you."

The labor pains were weak and infrequent and to prevent further exhaustion of the young woman, I sedated her. Then I took a magazine and sank into a sofa to begin the long wait—every so often listening to the heart of the unborn child to determine the onset of fetal distress. Shortly before dawn, I began to detect trouble—a gradual increase in the heart rate. This continued to mount until I knew we were going into an emergency. In order to save the child's life, it would have to be extracted with forceps. And this could be done only under general anesthesia.

I went into the living room where the husband lay asleep on the couch—waking him up.

"What is it?" he asked.

"I need your help."

"Ya, is it a boy or a girl?"

"It's nothing yet. Get yourself awake. You have to help with the delivery."

He jumped up, threw some cold water on his face, and was ready. I explained there was no cause for alarm, but it would have to be a forceps delivery—and he had to help anesthetize his wife.

He had pale blue eyes, and they looked at me with total trust. Thank God, I thought, for my training at the Peninsula Maternity Home.

I put the mother to sleep by placing a mask over mouth and nose, then dripping ether from a bottle onto the mask. After this, I showed the husband how to continue with the slow drip and prepared for the forceps delivery.

It was very quiet. The hush of the world before dawn lay over us and we worked in silence, the husband holding the drip while I carefully applied the blades of the instrument to the head of the child. Slowly, with intermittent traction, a little girl emerged, weighing about six pounds. Her sudden infant cry broke the dawn's silence, then settled into little gulping sobs as she began her life. Outside a cock crowed, then a hog began to grunt. The world was waking up. I looked at the husband whose blue eyes were wet with tears, and it was hard to hold back my own.

We had made it, I thought, and began to help the mother—only to discover she was still in labor.

"How do you like little girls?" I asked the husband who was peering at his first-born wrapped in a blanket like a papoose.

"Oh fine," he said, smiling. "Just fine."

"That's good, because it looks like you're going to have two of them—at least, a twin is on its way."

Half an hour later, the little sister arrived on her own—as though determined to catch up with her twin who had preceded her into the world by waking up roosters, pigs, and the rest of the barnyard.

After a cup of coffee, I began the forty-mile drive back through the dawn, feeling that all my seven and a half years of study and training had been worth that one moment when the little girl woke up a rooster.

A couple of months later, I was called to another farm about thirty miles away. Once again, I arrived toward evening, and there was the comfortable sensation of farm life preparing itself for the night as the sun went down. The cows were being herded back from the fields, the chickens had gone to roost, and even a goat, tied to a pole on the front lawn, looked at me with sleepy, yellow eyes.

Inside, I found a farmer with double pneumonia. He had it in an advanced stage and was quite toxic, with a temperature of 105 degrees. I began treatment and did all I could. He was an elderly man and he reminded me of Professor Crichton whom I still saw from time to time when he came to Ceres to join me on a pheasant hunt.

The wife was a gentle-mannered woman with gray hair—very quick to help with what was needed and outwardly in control of her emotions. But you could tell from her eyes that she had been weeping in private. The death of a husband or wife, who have had the great fortune of an enduring love, is more than the loss of one human being. It is the end of life between two people, a life created over many golden years, and in a way it is a double death. For one partner lingers on, alone in the old house, amid the belongings of the other one who has gone on ahead, occasionally looking at a photo, a walking stick, maybe an old cup and saucer, asking a question never asked when they both were alive: "When?"

Such a double tragedy would begin tonight with the death of this man—unless he could possibly survive. Either way, it would occur during the night. There was nothing else to do but wait and continue with whatever help was possible. We kept at it, checking him regularly, though there was no sign of improvement or that the medicine was taking effect. Finally the wife made a suggestion.

"Tell me, doctor," she said, "have you tried everything you know to save my husband's life?"

"Yes, of course—why?"

We were sitting in the kitchen before two cups of coffee which neither of us had touched.

"I mean you've tried all you know as a medical doctor?"

"Yes."

"If you have, then why don't we try a farm remedy for inflammation of the lung?"

"What is it?"

"We believe heat is very helpful. We kill a goat and skin it and quickly wrap the skin around the chest and this draws out the inflammation."

"So that's why you have a goat in the front yard?"

She nodded.

"Strange thing, it was born on my husband's birthday—three years ago."

I shuddered. It was like the sacrifice of a son to propitiate a God—Abraham and Isaac. There was a faith for you, a faith built on rock: a father lifting his sword to kill his own son.

"Let's hold on to our faith a bit longer," I said.

The wife nodded, but her eyes implored me to accept this, to try the remedy—otherwise, she would be left with the feeling that we had not done everything to save her husband.

"All right," I said. "It's three o'clock. If your husband is not better by four, we'll do it."

She agreed and at four we took his temperature. It had fallen to ninety-nine degrees and he was slowly showing signs of passing the crisis. An hour later, he was sufficiently free of danger for me to leave.

On the way out, I passed the yellow-eyed goat on the lawn.

"Goat," I said, "I saved your life—and God saved two others."

In town, the practice also enlarged. We did private work and surgery in the morning, and in the afternoon gave consultation on provincial welfare cases. Pikkie would operate while I administered the anesthetic, then we would change over. As a team, we became exceptionally adept and fast. Appendices took anywhere from seven to ten minutes, hernias twenty, with tonsils averaging five to ten minutes—provided, of course, there were no complications. We had our share of these, too, including one serious one.

One evening, examining a man with a pain in the lower right half of the abdomen, I accepted his case history which described him as suffering from inflammation of the appendix. All the symptoms concurred and I decided, much too quickly, to remove it immediately. Within an hour, we had him on the table, anesthetized by Dr. Joubert. Assisted by a nurse, I proceeded to expose the appendix.

It was normal. There was evidence, however, of some inflammation inside the abdominal cavity. So I enlarged the incision to discover an acutely inflamed gall bladder. Since the trouble was there, I prepared to remove it—starting with exposure of the artery to the bladder. Almost immediately I ran into trouble. The artery began to bleed profusely. I sought to control the flow, but it continued with no sign of letting up.

At this rate, the man would die. Experience consists in the multiple laying in of memory and in the few seconds of the crisis I raced back through everything I had learned—recalling an incident at Groote Schuur when Dr. Van Zyl had opened an infected stab wound in the neck of a man, causing a drum-tight abscess of blood to burst forth like a geyser, splattering everyone, including the operating lamp from where it dripped down on all of us. Dr. Van Zyl had calmly padded the area with swabs, pressing down to stop the hemorrhage. I did that now and the rate of flow diminished. I put some more on, again with pressure, and slowly the bleeding ceased.

Pikkie broke the silence.

"We're in trouble, Chris, I told you . . ."

"Never mind what you told me. Just keep this as stationary as you can for a minute. I'll be right back."

I ran to the phone and put in an urgent call to Dr. Jannie Louw. It came through quickly and his voice was like talking to God. Quickly, I described my situation, only to hear a chuckle on the other end of the line.

"Chris, you've done just right up to this point. Now leave the swab there for another half an hour. That should insure it. Then close him up and bring him in here in a week and we can do it together."

"Thanks, Dr. Louw," I said, and hurried back into the theater—to do as he directed.

Ten days later I took the patient into the same theater in Groote Schuur where I had removed my first gall bladder while Dr. Jannie Louw observed a confident young intern. This time I watched him do it. The inflammation had subsided and the operation was relatively simple.

In the tearoom afterward, I again thanked him.

"But tell me, why did you laugh when I called you?"

"Did I? Maybe because I expected it."

"You expected me to get into trouble?"

"Not at all. But I knew that if you did get into a fix, you would call me, or someone else—without taking a chance. You could have lost that man if you'd gone ahead. Instead, you stopped just as I had expected you would. Chris, you never take a chance—the patient takes it."

These kind words and the security of being again in the big hospital left me with a sudden feeling that I was going in the wrong direction. Perhaps I really belonged here, building up my surgical skill and knowledge of medicine. Perhaps I had gone too quickly into the world and was spreading myself too broadly in general practice.

"What's the matter, Chris? Did I say something wrong?"

"No, Dr. Louw, I was only wondering if I'm going the right way."

"I don't know either, Chris, but I think you should know if you're going the wrong way."

If it was wrong, then everything else with it was stacked up the wrong way—including Louwtjie, the marriage, the whole investment. It was hard to know if this feeling stemmed from some special insight at this moment or if it was only another surfacing of my oldest enemy—doubt, doubt of the unknown, of what was coming next.

I said good-bye to Dr. Louw with a sense that he was a real friend, secure enough in himself and his profession to give others a chance. I returned to

Ceres, telling myself that this was an experience which had to be seen through to the end, whatever it was. After all, there had been many profoundly rewarding moments, as well as some delightful ones that lightened our heaviest hours with laughter.

The spacing of our work meant we seldom got to bed until quite late. And even then, the phone usually rang. It was on my side, and often I was tempted to pass the tough cases or distant calls to Pikkie. Some were distinctly for him, some for me—but when they were unspecified, we took turns. Pikkie suspected, however, that I was jumbling it up so that all the difficult ones came out on his side. This was not true—except once when I could not resist it.

A frequent visitor to Ceres was a farmer named Reggy Bacon. He had a wooden leg and he was a heavy drinker—generally getting drunk in Ceres before starting to drive back to his farm forty miles away. Reggy came to town one day during a rainstorm. It rained all day, and all day Reggy poured down the drinks. Toward nightfall he staggered to his car and started home.

At one point, twenty miles out, a stream ran alongside the road and then crossed it. In making the fording, Reggy confused road and stream, driving down the stream bed until he sank into a hole. The storm had raised the water level so that it flooded the engine and even came up to the floorboard inside the car. To prevent his wooden leg from getting waterlogged, and thus difficult to operate, Reggy unscrewed it and threw it over his shoulder. This effort, together with all the other excitement of the day, so tired him that he fell asleep.

The first we heard about any of this was a phone call after midnight which I sleepily answered. On the other end was a man's voice, speaking in a most excited manner.

"Doctor," he said. "You have to come quickly—there's been one helluva wreck. This chap's stone dead in his car with a leg torn off and hanging over his shoulder!"

I sat up in bed while Pikkie stirred uneasily.

"Tell me more, where is the accident?"

He told me, and I figured it must be Reggy drunk again.

"Jesus, how awful," I said into the phone.

Pikkie rolled over and I repeated it.

"How terrible, something incredible."

"What is it?" asked Pikkie, now fully awake.

"It's for you, man," I said. "It's your turn—a terrible accident."

Pikkie took it and from the way his face began to wrinkle and crease, you knew he had not thought of old Reggy.

"Be right there," he said.

"Don't hang up," I said quickly.

"What is it?"

"Ask him if he's got a bottle of whisky."

"Are you mad?"

"More than anything else, I think Reggy will need a drink."

We checked and it was Reggy—alive and indeed in grave need of a drink.

Very often, especially among the colored community, the men complained that they were getting weak. This meant they could make love only once or twice a night, instead of five or six times. Among them was a man named Josephus who became a chronic pest—arriving with a provincial certificate for treatment every Saturday at the peak hour.

I had tried everything without effect and finally decided to use a bit of psychology. With Josephus sitting before me, I took some dark iron tonic solution and put it into a bottle.

"This is an iron tonic to make it strong," I said.

He nodded.

Next, I took some yellow vitamin compound and poured it on top of the iron tonic.

"That's to make it stay strong," I said.

Finally, I poured in some red liver extract.

"That gives you some extra supply."

Josephus nodded again, smiling with wonder at the marvels of medicine. I slammed a cork into the bottle, shook it up until it was bright with foam, and handed it to him. He then said his wife had a complaint. So we received her while he waited in the reception room. I remember seeing him sit down and carefully put the bottle on the window ledge. It looked like dark red wine in the sunlight.

I had hardly finished examining his wife, when we heard an explosion and I leaped to the door. The reception room was empty. All the patients were outside, wiping the medicine off their clothes. It had even splattered over the walls.

Then I saw Josephus, alone in the corner, holding the broken neck of the bottle.

"Doctor," he said, "you made that medicine real fine—but it was just too powerful for the bottle."

There is a residual element of psychology in every diagnosis, if only in the doctor convincing the patient that he understands the ailment and is in full control. This relationship, once established, helps relax the patient and puts him in closer harmony with himself in the battle to correct a pathological imbalance of nature's forces. Sometimes I was successful, sometimes not.

There was another chronic nuisance named Sam. He walked with his head canted to the right, his eyes rolling, shuffling into the outpatient clinic with a magistrate's slip entitling him to free treatment.

We tried everything. He complained of stomach pains and did have a bad appendix. So we took it out. Two weeks later he was back again, with a chest pain. We fluoroscoped his lungs and found no trouble but gave him multiple vitamin shots. Finally, he returned to report that he was surrounded at night by goblins and ghosts. Obviously, something had to be done to give him peace of mind.

"The trouble is your eyes," I said. "Most people can see through ghosts, but you can't."

"That's bad, isn't it?"

"Very bad for you when there are ghosts. What you need is a pair of glasses so you can see through them."

"What will that do?"

"Helps you realize that ghosts are harmless. If you can see through them, they are too weak to do anything. You've seen many ghosts. But has one ever personally put a hand on you?"

"No, *baas.*"

"You see!" I said, with an air of triumph that amazed me, since I have always believed in ghosts.

I gave him an eye examination and wrote a prescription for a pair of glasses. He left quite happy. But when I saw him in town a few weeks later, he was shuffling along in his usual way—without the glasses. That meant he would be back again next week. So I stopped him on the sidewalk.

"Sam, we go to all the trouble to locate the cause of your disturbance. Finally, we prescribe a pair of glasses and everything seems fine. Then what happens? You go around without them—why?"

"Oh, Doctor," he said, "I'm keeping them safe at home, 'cause if I wear them they might break, then I'd be in trouble again."

The day of our wedding gradually came upon us until it was there, sudden and big and white like an immense close-up photo of the face of the moon. And as when one sees the craters and meaningless shapes on the moon's surface, so were the faces of everyone looking at us in church, causing an immense and unfathomable space between myself and those around me. Only Louwtjie was there, ready to be touched and held in a space of our own, looking tiny and precious yet warm and very familiar as she came down the aisle in white on the arm of her father, the organ suddenly blasting out with the *Lohengrin* wedding march. Each time it hit a deep chord, I could see the little marker on the string plunging downward in our Kerk at Beaufort West. For a moment, I felt sorry for any little boy who would have to pump so hard for us, then realized it was all electric here in Cape Town's famous Groote Kerk where they prized their organ as the most spectacular in all Africa. Then she was beside me, her eyes smiling as they had on the first day we met, as though by some miracle of faith and love's chemistry we were now beginning all over again.

"Hello," I said.

She said nothing, turning to face the minister above us in the pulpit.

"Hello, Mrs. Barnard."

Still nothing.

"If you don't say hello, I'm going to say no when he asks me to say yes."

"Ssshhh!"

"Well?"

"Hello," she said.

Then she said hello again with her lips as though saying it to herself on the inside. I squeezed her hand and she squeezed back. That was it for me. Marriage was a mutual contract between two people, a private contract, and we had made it at that moment. The rest was now going to be for the benefit of all the other craters and bumps on the face of the moon.

The minister stood high up in a pulpit supported by two huge lions carved from red Indian teak. The lions had their mouths open, as though roaring dutifully to wake every sleeping sinner in the city. Each beast held up a chaplet of leaves with one front claw, while the other rested on a parchment scroll. What was in that scroll? Something we should not read? Or was it to be read only by a pride of lions? Why couldn't one ever say a pride of husbands? The answer had to be somewhere. Maybe it was with that red teak anchor, hanging above the lions—reminder that the virtuous husband and true member of the Dutch Reformed Church never strayed anywhere. Virtue consisted in staying put.

"Do you, Aletta Gertruida Louw, take this man as your lawfully wedded husband, to have and to hold forever?"

How could you measure forever? With what instrument could we calculate the open and loving heart—or the growth of doubt in the closing one? Forever was from now on out, until the end—but the end of what? Was it the end of the world or the end of us or maybe only our ability to love? Somewhere they had to feed into their calculations a law strong enough to harness the outline and shape of forever. A basic element was *now*—a sense of immediacy. It had to be there since the concept of *forever* could exist only as long as there was this sense of *now* buried within the moment of touch, in the tremulous extension of hands shaping the moment and so creating their own private space. Somewhere in that space lay Forever.

"Yes. . . ."

She had said it very softly. I thought she was going to say it louder. Again, it was as though she had spoken to herself alone.

"Do you, Christiaan Neethling Barnard . . ."

"Yes."

"Then I do pronounce you man and wife."

The organ began to play again and there were people shaking my hand, patting me on the back—Professor Crichton, Dr. Jannie Louw, my parents, my brother Marius, colleagues from Groote Schuur, and many patients from Ceres.

The reception was next door at the Koffiehuis. Everyone toasted us, and I made the worst speech of my life. Then Louwtjie left with her father, as is our custom, to get ready for the honeymoon. Eventually, I left to pick her up—jumping into the car, waving good-bye to everyone, and starting off.

Fanie Bekker was among those at the curb, and as I drove away I saw him laughing in a familiar way that could mean only one thing: he was playing some trick on me. I heard no rattling tin cans in tow and could not imagine what he had done—until I had gone two blocks and had a flat tire. So that was it. With Louwtjie waiting for me at the hotel, I had to get out on Adderley Street, in the middle of Cape Town, and change a tire while wearing striped pants and tails. I was furious, of course, but as I went to work, a little crowd gathered. With a few laughs, some men began to help me—married men who could not resist advising me that my bride would never understand and so be angry with me.

They were right. Louwtjie was waiting, ready to go and not at all happy. I did not tell her it was Fanie Bekker who had played the prank, but she knew it by instinct.

"That's typical of him," she said.

"It could have been anybody."

"Nobody in my family and none of my friends," she said.

"Maybe it was nobody at all—just a stray nail."

"Named Bekker. Fa-nie Bek-ker."

I decided to drop it. We stopped in Elgin, at a delightful little hotel. That same night, Johnny Ralph, South Africa's heavyweight champion, was to fight Bruce Woodcock, the British title holder. I wanted to hear it very much, and while Louwtjie was asleep I went down into the lobby to take in the match. Woodcock knocked out Johnny Ralph and I went back to my room feeling very depressed about it. When I got there, Louwtjie was awake and sitting up in bed.

"Hello, sweetie."

She did not speak.

"Johnny Ralph was knocked out."

"A prize fight," she said, angrily.

"It was only a few minutes, sweetie, while you snoozed."

I got back into bed.

"It was a knockout, all right," she said, rolling away from me. "A knockout for everybody."

I tried to hold her, but she would not let me.

"Come on, Louwtjie."

"No," she said. "No, Chris, stop it."

I did not stop anything, but I knew she was right in her way.

"I'm sorry, Louwtjie. As a husband, I was wrong. But as a man you must understand me."

"I married a husband."

"You married a man who has to learn to be a husband. Do you think it happens immediately?"

"Well, please start learning."

"All right, now come on."

"Will you promise?"

"I will. I'll do my best, but you have to help with some understanding."

We spent the honeymoon at The Wilderness. We took boat trips up the lagoon and baked in the sun and got sunburned. The days and nights folded into one another until it came time to return to Ceres. We drove it in one day, crossing the Karoo. Then, as we came over the pass into Ceres, Louwtjie began to weep.

"I'm frightened," she said.

"Frightened of what?"

"I don't know anybody here."

"You know me."

"I feel alone and afraid," she said.

"You shouldn't. We have many friends here."

"I've never been a wife before."

"You'll be the best one that ever was."

"Will I?"

"Yes."

"You have to help me, Chris."

"I will, I'll help you."

CHAPTER 10

MARRIAGE CHANGED MY LIFE in Ceres, bringing me more friends, mainly married ones. It also widened my practice to include older patients who seemed to feel that a married doctor was a wiser one. Louwtjie was a great help, both at home and socially. The attorney Evelyn Krige and his wife became part of our lives, as did their daughter, Ann, and her husband, Bill Theron. We saw a lot of the Joubert Botmas, too, and the Dutch Reformed Missioner, Reverend Ernst Holtzapfel, who was a constant source of strength and counsel.

We lived in Dr. O'Maloney's home, with Pikkie staying on as boarder. Louwtjie transformed the house from an encampment of men into a home. At Christmas gifts poured in from everywhere, especially from patients in the country who sent twenty-three chickens, five turkeys, one suckling pig, and five sheep. Such a providential harvest had to be shared, and we took most of it to the hospital for a Christmas dinner with patients and staff.

Eventually, Dr. Tim O'Maloney returned from his overseas tour, ready to reclaim his practice. We had hoped he would ask us to stay on with him—and he did. The practice had trebled in his absence and could well occupy three doctors working full time, in partnership. Dr. O'Maloney agreed.

"There's enough here for all of us," he said.

"And the town is growing," said Pikkie.

"If you left me alone, I'd never get any sleep and would soon be calling you back," said Dr. O'Maloney, with the nearest expression he could get to a smile—a sort of freezing of all features, including the eyelids.

We were in the kitchen of his home, drinking beer. He was a middle-aged country doctor and looked like one—graying hair, sober face, neat dark suit, and a precise manner. You could tell from the way he put his glass down, in the same place each time, that he was a man of fixed habits within a fixed world. He also walked with a limp.

"Obviously the house is not large enough to ask you to stay on," he said, carefully.

"We're fine," said Pikkie.

We had moved across the street into a boarding house called Holiday Inn. It was all right for Pikkie, who was not married, but I was going to need a home and had already found one on sale a couple of blocks down the street.

Leaving Dr. O'Maloney and Pikkie, I walked down Munich Street to look at it once more. It seemed to be made from bits and pieces of my past. Perhaps this was why I had first stopped to stare at it and then discover it was for sale.

It was encircled by a hedge, as had been my home at Beaufort West. Outside, along each side of the street, there were irrigation streams similar to those I had played in as a boy. There was also a rivulet of red steps up to the porch which had four white columns, as did *Petra*—the home of Michel Rossouw. And in the garden there were rose bushes like those my father tended in our front garden in the evening until his hands were bleeding from the thorns. Finally, on the inside there was an arrangement of rooms reminiscent of Michel's home, large enough for a family with children, whenever we could afford to have them.

Above it all, giant oaks rose on each side. These, too, were part of my past for in the Karoo I had dreamed of such trees and now they were there, making a blue-white lacework of the sky. One of the oaks, a giant one, stood at the corner, next to the gate. It was immense, yet soft to the touch. Its bark, grey and brown and flecked with black, came up if you pulled it. Underneath, however, it was hard and durable as the bones of an elephant, the ribs of a mountain. Down below, at its base, the roots had swollen until they had broken the sidewalk, tilting it up and down like a crazy rooftop, even breaking through and constricting the flow in the cement casing of the irrigation stream between the sidewalk and the street. I walked over the uplifted cement, above the swollen power of the white fiber sinews of root—and decided to buy the house.

Back at Holiday Inn, Louwtjie was not in the room. I called Mr. Krige and asked if he thought I could make the purchase with a mortgage. He felt it could be done, and we made a date to discuss the terms. After that, I went into the garden to find Louwtjie.

She was in the back, looking at some African parrots in a large cage. They had red beaks with green and blue and yellow feathers.

"They're like rainbows," she said. "Little rainbows caught in a net."

Then she looked at me and knew what had happened.

"O'Maloney agreed," she said.

I nodded.

"So I phoned Mr. Krige about the house. He thinks we can swing it."

She was quiet a moment.

"Are you sure?"

"Sure about what?"

"About O'Maloney."

"Yes—why not?"

"Do you like him?"

"How do I know?"

"It's important."

"He's no Crichton or Jannie Louw. He's a plain country doctor. He walks with a limp."

Louwtjie spoke as one of the parrots began to screech and I heard nothing. We walked away from it.

"I said can you work with him?"

"Yes," I said.

"Look, Louwtjie, why aren't you happy about this?"

"I am—very."

"You don't show it."

"Chris, I want you to be sure of yourself—only that."

"I'm sure. I went to look at the house, and I liked it very much."

"The house," she said, "the house is not as important as Dr. O'Maloney. Did you like him?"

"I told you—yes. At least, I think so."

"All right," she said.

Later that night she again asked me if I was going to be happy with O'Maloney and buying a new home.

"Yes, why not?"

"How much, how big?"

"What do you mean, Louwtjie?"

"How big is what I mean. How many people?"

"You and I," I said.

"And why not someone else?"

I could hear her breathing and in that space of time I suddenly realized this was the inevitable development of the promise of Dr. O'Maloney, of the giant oak, of the house, and of our own love—our first child.

In the months that followed, we settled into our new home and began to prepare for the new arrival. Baby clothes came to us from many friends, and the Joubert Botmas sent over a lovely cradle covered with white tulle, like a little ship forever sailing through mist. Louwtjie was radiant and our home under the giant oak seemed to be putting down its proper roots.

The practice continued to expand, and we shared it all together, regardless of the work load on one or the other of us. Pikkie and I had many patients. Many were new ones, but, unfortunately, some were Dr. O'Maloney's former patients who began to ask for us.

Occasionally this was a bit embarrassing. One day I entered the office to find him talking with Mrs. Swarts and her daughter Pamela whom I had treated for measles on my first day in Ceres. I said good morning, and we chatted a bit. As I prepared to leave, Dr. O'Maloney stopped me.

"Mrs. Swarts wants to see you."

"All right," I said and smiled at her and the little girl. After her measles, Pamela had experienced influenza, a bad tonsillitis, and a flare-up of the appendix which probably would have to come out. We were going into the consultation room when O'Maloney spoke.

"They didn't think I could handle them anymore."

I turned to look at the old doctor, shocked by his words, only to find he was shocked by them as well.

"I'm sorry," he said and left.

Mrs. Swarts was understandably upset.

"He told us it was all the same, that it didn't matter which doctor we went to."

"He's right. It doesn't matter."

"But it does—at least for him. He seemed hurt."

I did not know what to say. I smiled at Pamela, and she smiled back.

"Pam said she wanted Dr. Barnard—so here we are."

"I'm happy Pam feels that way."

I was not happy, however, about the rebuff of Dr. O'Maloney. Afterward, I looked for him but he was gone and I did not see him until later that day at the hospital. I wanted to say I was sorry about the incident, but he spoke first.

"Why did you order a salt-free diet on that woman with liver trouble?"

"Because I suspect she's suffering from coronary disease."

"She has recurrent infection of the bile tract. I've treated her for years and know the symptoms very well."

"Have you examined her heart?"

"Yes, I did, but it doesn't prove you're right."

"Don't you think we should at least X-ray her chest?"

"No, I don't, Doctor Barnard."

He had always called me Chris. Now there was a wall between us and I felt very sad.

"I'm sorry," I said. "I had no right to examine your patient. I only wanted to help."

We said no more and a few days later the patient was gone. I inquired and learned she had been sent to Groote Schuur for cardiac treatment.

About that time I helped deliver a child—not my own, but one that was almost as close. It was the first child of Lex Rankin, a young woman who had worked for Pikkie and me, doubling as nurse and secretary and even doing some housekeeping. We had followed the gestation of her child with anxiety and had considered the possibility of having her cared for during pregnancy and childbirth by a specialist in Cape Town—as I planned to do with Louwtjie. Her family, however, wanted me to deliver the baby in Sister van der Merwe's nursing home. Lex was delighted.

"They don't trust anyone except you," she said.

"You know better than that."

"No, Chris, I don't. I'm completely happy in your care."

"All right, but you have to promise me. No twins or triplets."

"Yes," she said, laughing. "I promise."

The baby, a seven-pound boy, arrived on Saturday afternoon. I showed it to Lex who smiled happily—one of those incredible smiles that come from women whose features only a few moments earlier were contorted in pain. The husband and the relatives all had a glimpse of their first grandson and then he was taken by Sister van der Merwe into the baby ward.

With this done, I went off to a Western movie with Louwtjie. We had just settled down to the first volley of gunfire, when I was called to the phone.

It was Sister van der Merwe.

"Lex's baby is not doing well."

"What is it?"

"You'd better come quickly. He's gasping for breath."

The nursing home was only five blocks away, but when I got there it was almost too late. The child was gray-blue, breathing with difficulty, and the little pulse was hardly perceptible—all signs that the heart was failing.

Sister van der Merwe stood beside me.

"Start mouth-to-mouth breathing," I said and prepared to inject a stimulant into the infant heart. This caused a brief improvement in circulation. Then the pulse became fainter and fainter—until it stopped. The little life that meant so much to the young mother, to her family and relatives, had ceased to exist.

Sister van der Merwe looked at me, at the lifeless body—then turned away. Next to the ward, in a private room, Lex lay waiting to hear me tell her that the sister had been overly alarmed, that her baby was well. I walked to the door of her room and stopped, unable to go in. Outside, on the street, a car raced by at top speed. Then a dog began to bark. Slowly, I opened the door. Lex's eyes met mine and she saw it.

"My baby is dead."

"Lex . . ."

I was unable to say more. I wanted to tell her of my sorrow and sadness in being unable to save her son. But I had no words for this and left the room.

I drove out of town, going up the mountain road toward the pass, and parked near the top where I could look down at the lights in the valley. I sat there for some time, thinking that down there among those lights, a little child lay dead—a boy who might have been saved and grown into a man, if I had been a better doctor. I was not responsible for his birth with a defective heart. He had entered the world that way—unable to live for more than an hour. Yet that was sufficient time for me to be responsible for him. He came to me—defective, but alive. He came, asking for a new heart. I could not give it to him. Modern medicine had no means for this. But it did not absolve me—all of us—from our charge. He had asked for life from those of us who should have been able to give it to him. We had not. We were guilty—not only for this little boy, but all the millions before him who had died in a similar way, including my little brother, Abraham.

My home down in that valley, my real home, was not under an oak tree where my wife was waiting her turn in birth. It was inside the heart of that dead child, somewhere within its chambers where the great vessels were transposed, where a valve was malformed. Wherever that heart failed, there was the seat of my existence, the center of my life. For as I stood outside that boy's death chamber, so I stood outside myself.

I drove slowly down the mountain and back into the valley, realizing I did not belong there. My future was somewhere else, and I still had to find it. Somehow, I would have to explain this to my wife—after the birth of our child.

Louwtjie moved into Cape Town a fortnight before the baby was due, to be close to the Booth Maternity Home where she was under the care of Professor James Louw who had replaced Professor Crichton at the university. I remained in Ceres, taking care of patients, until Professor Louw called me late one afternoon to say that Louwtjie was about to begin her labor. I turned everything over to Pikkie who wished me Godspeed to a happy bedside—and then leaped into the car, only to run out of gas as I was going by a gas station. That seemed to be a lucky sign, and I drove happily on through patchwork fields of the valley, toward purple-blue mountains.

At the nursing home, Louwtjie was not yet in advanced labor. There were dark circles under her eyes and she was pale and strained—but without panic.

"I'm so glad you're here," she said, taking my hand.

"Everyone says you're a brave girl."

"I'm not. I'm scared."

I squeezed her hand.

"I'm a scared girl," she said.

"That's normal," I said.

"I want it to happen soon. I want to see what our baby looks like."

"You will, you will."

But it was not soon, and toward midnight Professor Louw suggested I get some rest. He would phone me when the moment came. I went to Dr. Jannie Louw's, grateful to have such a friend. More than sleep, I needed to talk to him about many things, especially my belief that I had to leave Ceres in order to come closer to my profession and to myself.

He was waiting up for me with a drink and seemed to know beforehand what I was going to say.

"I expected this," he said.

"Do you think I could get a post at the hospital?"

"We can try."

We drank a bit in silence. Then Dr. Louw nodded as if this was the thing to do.

"So you make a decision to leave. It's a moral one and important since they are the only real decisions of our life. Everything else is an arbitration of convenience."

"Dr. Louw, I'd like to return to surgery."

"Surgery, eh? That won't be too easy."

"Can it be done?"

"Anything can be done, man, if you do it yourself. Nobody will tell you to do it or give you a hand. You have to cut your own path."

I had always cut my own path. This was going to be no different—except now I had a family and needed a base to pay for the essentials.

"We'll go to work on this, Chris. There's no urgency, I suppose—other than your desire to move into another field?"

I nodded.

"I mean there's nothing that compels you to move immediately?"

"No."

The phone rang. It was Professor Louw.

"Congratulations, Chris, it's a girl."

"How does she look?"

"In full possession of her faculties, which is strange—considering the father."

I laughed, relieved.

"Are you coming?"

"Yes—right away."

I expected Louwtjie to be excited but she had her usual calm manner and when I came into the room she gave me a patient smile as though I was late for dinner.

"How is she?" I asked.

"Fine."

"What else . . . what does she look like?"

"Oh, Chris, like I've always hoped she would."

That meant she resembled Vivien Leigh as Scarlett O'Hara. Louwtjie had seen the film four times. Finally, a nurse brought a small bundle into the room, and we pulled back the cover to look at Scarlett O'Hara, age forty-three minutes. I found a little face looking at me as though it knew all about Scarlett, and a lot more. The features showed no sign of labor trauma, the skin was white and smooth. There were long, sweeping eyelashes that would have startled all Dixie, and slowly they unveiled two of the most wondrous brown eyes I had ever seen.

I was amazed.

"It is Scarlett!"

"Umm," said Louwtjie. "Let me hold her again."

"I must have delivered a thousand babies, but I've never seen one like this before."

"You fool, you've never been a father before," she said, finally smiling as though enjoying it.

She was right, of course. I wanted to hold the child, even though I knew it was better not to do it. Then I realized I had been seized by a new emotion—the love of a parent for his child. I had never felt anything like it before and was surprised at the suddenness of its arrival. This was a love different from any I had known.

The nurse returned for the baby and we were alone again. For a moment we sat in silence, each with his thoughts of the child. Then Louwtjie got down to business.

"So, what shall we name our little beauty?"

"Something pretty. Beautiful little girls should have names to match."

"Chris, this is the first female grandchild in my family."

I nodded and she continued.

"Is there anybody in your family whom we should especially consider?"

"We don't feel strongly about names," I said.

"We do," she said.

"What do you have in mind?"

"My mother."

After a pause, Louwtjie said: "Dedrika Johanna."

I looked down at the floor. It did not sound right.

"It's sort of heavy," I said.

"It's my mother's name," she said, a little hurt.

"I know, but isn't it rather heavy for such a delicate child?"

Louwtjie laughed.

"Do you think she's going to be tiny all her life?"

"No, but she just doesn't look like that kind of name."

"All right, what does she look like?"

"I don't know, something lighter."

After a moment, Louwtjie said, "We could do it the French way—Deirdre Jeanne."

We began to say the names out loud, doing it fast and slow, then whispering it as though we were putting the child to sleep, finally shouting it as though she was already being naughty. Every way it sounded perfect. I said I liked it and Louwtjie smiled happily. Then I kissed her good-bye, to return to my patients in Ceres.

"Hurry home. The place is empty without you."

"You haven't said that in a long time. It must be Deirdre."

She said it as though the name had always existed between us, even before Deirdre was born. I was glad we chose it and kissed her again.

"Chris, you seem preoccupied. Is something wrong?"

"No, Louwtjie. Everything's perfect."

So I left without telling Louwtjie of my decision to eventually leave Ceres when a post became open at Groote Schuur. Nor did I talk about it immediately upon her return. I wanted to be sure I had something first. Before this happened, however, Louwtjie became pregnant again and I decided to wait until we had our second child before making the move. Then one morning Dr. O'Maloney asked me into his office.

"It's now clear," he said, "that this practice requires only two doctors—not three."

"What does that mean?" I asked.

"It means you've always wanted to specialize and now's your chance."

"Are you asking me to leave?"

"Well, let's put it this way. Dr. Joubert and myself have decided we can handle the work without a third person."

"Why isn't Pikkie here to say as much?"

"He's busy at the hospital."

"Then why didn't you wait until he was here to discuss it among the three of us?"

Dr. O'Maloney sat behind his desk, opening and closing a ballpoint pen. It went click-click as he talked. When he stopped talking, it went on click-clicking.

"There's nothing further to discuss, Dr. Barnard. We've decided we can do it this way. You were the last to arrive, so it must be you who goes. I'm sorry, but that's it."

Click-click, click-click went the ballpoint.

"Well, it's not it. I'm not going at your bidding and you can't force me to do it."

"What will you do?"

"I'll stay and practice here as long as I like."

"Not legally," he said. "Legally, you can't touch one patient of my practice. They don't belong to you. You can't even practice in this area for five years."

"I signed no contract with you. I'm free to do as I wish."

"I'm sorry you're taking it this way. You'll regret it if you try."

Click-click, click-click, click-click.

I got up and left. Pikkie was at the hospital, operating. I had taken Louwtjie on a vacation to Mossel Bay. It was her first vacation after the birth of Deirdre and it had rained all the time. I had hardly seen Pikkie since my return, and now, as he came out of the operating theater, I could tell from his eyes above the white mask that he knew Dr. O'Maloney had told me to leave.

"Why didn't you let me know about this?"

"You saw O'Maloney?"

"Yes, why didn't you tell me?"

"I didn't have a chance. You were away."

"You could have written or phoned or left a note."

In the dressing room, Pikkie looked at his shoes, his tie, the mirror—everything except look me in the eyes.

"Dr. O'Maloney says you agree I should go. He says it was a decision between the two of you."

"That's not it, Chris, and you know it."

"What is it then?"

"Dammit, man, haven't you seen it coming? You've humiliated O'Maloney ever since he returned. You go all out for a patient and it doesn't matter whose toes you step on, you do what you want. The old man can't take it. He said: 'Chris has to go, I can't take it any longer!' "

"And then?"

"He asked me to stay on with him and I said I would."

"I see."

"Chris, don't be hurt, please. I like this work. I belong here. You don't really. You've always said you wanted to further your studies."

It was true—but not this way, not by being kicked out of town.

"That's Dr. O'Maloney's line. Don't try and get off the hook with that, Pikkie."

"I'm not really, but what else can I do?"

"What else?" I felt my voice rising and tried to control it. "You could have said no to him. You could have stuck with me."

"And do what?"

"We could continue together with a practice of our own. Practically all the patients are ours, anyway."

Pikkie finally looked me in the eyes.

"I couldn't do that to O'Maloney. He asked me to come here to help him, not ruin him. I couldn't do that and live here."

"But you asked me to come here. How about that?"

"I know and I'm sorry about it. But maybe it's better this way. Maybe it's better for you to go than stay."

It was better, and I knew it. But not this way. Never.

"Listen, Pikkie, I'm not going just because one day you two decide to tell me to get out of town. No, sir—I'll stay as long as I like."

"Of course, Chris, take all the time you need."

"You're damn right, man, and it might just be that I'll be here a lot longer than either of you."

"Chris, don't feel like that, please don't."

I left him there in the dressing room with his tie half done. At home, I put in a call to Dr. Jannie Louw. He was in the operating theater. Louwtjie was out, probably shopping. So was Lizzie, the maid, with Deirdre. I walked around the house for a while, then I went outside into the garden, under the big oak. After a while, the phone rang. It was Dr. Louw calling me back—but he had no news.

"Nothing in sight yet, Chris . . . but we are working on it."

"How long do you think?"

"Who knows?"

He told me of two doctors who were waiting for appointments to other hospitals before leaving Groote Schuur. There were also a couple of others waiting for research grants.

"So you see, it can happen any time. We just have to wait. Okay?"

"Okay."

"I'll call you soon as there's the slightest sign."

"All right."

"Anything wrong?"

"No . . . I just want to get ready."

"Right then, I'll let you know."

"Thanks Dr. Louw."

I wanted to tell him what had happened but could not bring myself to do it. Besides, it would weaken my chances at the hospital. Also, I could not leave now—not while they were trying to drive me away. I could never leave under such a humiliation. The only answer was to stay for a while longer, treating those patients I had treated, those many families who had become friends of ours. Dr. O'Maloney and Dr. Joubert would quickly learn the meaning of loyalty and dedication. I had given everything to these people. They all knew it. They would not let me down.

I called the Swarts first. Mrs. Swarts was very friendly. She said her husband was on his way home and suggested I come immediately and stay for lunch. When I arrived, they were both waiting with drinks. I explained the situation, and Mr. Swarts began to look like a man who has just been informed that he has a leak in his roof.

"So you intend to set up a separate practice against O'Maloney?"

"Not against, just separate."

"And what do you want us to do?"

"I'd like to count on your support."

Mr. Swarts turned to his wife, who nervously patted at a lace runner on the armchair, smoothing it with her hand.

"Pamela is very fond of Chris," she said.

"I'm fond of Chris," said Mr. Swarts. "We're all fond of Chris and Louwtjie. But dammit, that's not the question. O'Maloney's been our family doctor since we came here."

"Maybe we can go a little to one and a little to the other," said Mrs. Swarts.

"We can't go to two doctors," said Mr. Swarts. "Let's be realistic. Dammit, Chris, isn't there some way you can strike a deal with O'Maloney?"

"I'm afraid not."

"And Joubert is staying with him?"

"Yes."

"Did they say why they want you out?"

"It's a personality question."

"I saw it," said Mrs. Swarts. "I saw it with Pam that day, plain as the nose on your face."

Mr. Swarts heaved a big sigh and shook his head. This was not as plain as the nose on anybody's face.

"Chris, have you seen your other patients?"

"No, you're the first."

"Well, after you see them, let me know what they say. I want to think about it a bit."

"All right," I said, and left.

They did not ask me to stay to lunch, and I did not want to stay—not if they were not going to support me. When other friends came to my support, so would they. There were many who would—men and women whose lives I had saved, whose children I had brought into the world. They would rally behind me.

Yet no one did. I went from house to house, suffering one humiliation after another, unable to stop under the shock and incredulity of what was happening. No one would take the initiative to stand up for me. Some agreed at first, then withdrew after making a few phone calls.

There were a handful of exceptions, such as the Kriges, the Therons, and the Botmas—but not enough to ask those few to expose themselves against the growing unity of the community. Eventually, news of what was happening went ahead of me—so that when I phoned, my patients knew what I wanted and began to say they were on their way out, or otherwise avoided meeting me. Finally, I called the Swarts again, to suggest they summon a meeting of everyone where I could present my case. Little Pam answered the phone and, after a pause, said her parents were not at home. This was more than anyone could take.

I went home, to find Louwtjie in tears. She was now in her fourth month, and this strain was hard on her.

"This would never happen in South West Africa."

She repeated it again and I said nothing. There was nothing more to say. We sat alone in the living room.

"People I know don't behave like this," she said.

"It is strange," I said.

"Our friends, people you've treated. People we trust. It's like we were criminals."

She began to cry again. In the basket next to her chair was a half-finished needlepoint she had been working on for the church bazaar.

"I knew it," she said, "when we came here after our honeymoon, I knew something was going to happen."

I had felt it long before that, but there was no use talking about it. Now something had to be done, some solution had to be found. Finally, one appeared a few days later. Another doctor in Ceres offered to sell me his practice. I considered it for a while, then went to see Dr. O'Maloney and Pikkie in our old office. We sat on the same chairs, among the same furnishings where we had worked as friends and colleagues. Yet now faced with the prospect of my direct opposition, they no longer behaved as friends and began to attack me openly as an enemy.

It was a particularly sad scene. I did not mind the hate of Dr. O'Maloney, but could not bear Pikkie Joubert also turning against me. Unable to face them any longer, I left the office for the last time and went to see Reverend Holtzapfel who had always been close to me—one more in an endless chain of substitutes for the living reality of my father. He was loyal as ever.

"Chris, if you stay on, I will remain your patient. So will my family. We will go to you and to no one else because what they have done to you is wrong."

"Thank you, I . . ."

He interrupted me.

"But I don't advise you to start a battle because the bitterness of it will spoil everything else."

"I can't accept defeat this way."

"You can, and you have to learn to do it."

"No, it's impossible."

We were sitting in the living room of the parish house, next to the old gothic church. The bell rang for evening service, but he did not move. He smiled as if to say the entire congregation could wait until we had decided on what I should do.

This gesture and his offer of solidarity brought me to sudden tears. I had not broken down at any point but now I no longer had any defense left.

"What have I done? What have I done to deserve it?"

"You don't deserve it, Chris."

"These people, I held them in my hands. I sat up nights with them. Do you know what I mean? I neglected my life, my home, everything for them. And now when I ask them to help me, they turn their backs. How can they turn away from me?"

I could not go on. Reverend Holtzapfel waited in silence for me to finish but it was not possible.

"They don't want to do it, Chris. They don't want to humiliate you."

"But they are, and they know it."

"They're afraid to do anything. So they do nothing."

"But they prefer me as a doctor. They've always asked for me."

"Yes, when you were working with O'Maloney. But now you want them to go against him, and they can't do that."

"Why?"

"Because he has become a symbol of the community. So you're asking the community to go against itself."

"I'm asking only that they accept me."

"But a community never accepts anyone—not really. What happens is that the individual accepts the community."

"I don't understand."

"When a stranger is assimilated, the group does not adopt him. He adopts the group."

What else had we done, if not that? I belonged to the clubs and played rugby with the first team of Ceres, even in the big game against Worcester. I served the Old Crocks at cricket and played tennis for the town. And Louwtjie had done her share, too, until her needlepoint had fallen into the basket.

"But we did adopt Ceres. We belonged to everything."

"It's not a question of belonging, Chris. An individual is known by the social bonds that hold him. I ask you to consider this: What are yours?"

It was true. No one in Ceres held my bonds. They were elsewhere. They were in the blocked heart of Lex's dead baby. They were in any hand moving across a medical frontier, seeking new ways of preserving human life. That was what held me, not the men and women of Ceres, whatever their collective fears or unspoken loves.

"Chris, there is in all people a hidden code of behavior. It appears under pressure and often it surprises them as much as you. Many of your patients have come here, deeply hurt and disturbed by this. Some have even wept in this room. But there is no way out for them, other than an action they cannot take. Society is founded on an unspoken, mutual trust. And this issue about you has reached a point, beyond you and beyond them, where what you ask is a breach of trust."

"How?" I asked.

The bells started again and the minister paused, but he did not get up.

"How did it happen?" I asked. "A child needs a doctor. I'm the best one here—not because I say so, but because they've said it. Now, if my child needed a doctor, I'd go to the best one . . ."

Reverend Holtzapfel interrupted me.

"If your child was in real trouble, you'd take him to a specialist. Let's face it, Chris, a general practitioner is like a minister. They are both an expression of the community life, of the common trust—and always replaceable. If I was unjustly accused and replaced by another minister, do you think these people would get together and block it?"

"Perhaps," I said. "But certainly you wouldn't accept such failure without fighting back."

"What failure? My mission is to bring men nearer to God—not break them into fighting groups. If I could leave this town, saying I have saved a few souls, I would go with peace of mind . . . and under any condition. Your mission is human life and you have saved many lives here. So you can go with your dignity and honor intact."

The bell rang again with insistent urgency. Reverend Holtzapfel looked at his watch and rose to go.

"Remember, anyone who is not against us is for us," he said.

I shook my head.

"All you've told me is right," I said, "but don't ask me to accept so much. As you say, I have only one duty and one love—human life. You can't have it without also hating sickness, disease, and people who, by their living, by doing nothing, hurt others."

"I am with you," he said.

We stood there, unable to say good-bye. Then we embraced and I left. As I went around the side of the church, they were singing my father's favorite, "Rock of Ages." Bitterly, I wished it had been any other song but that one.

PART IV
THE SEARCHING YEARS

CHAPTER 11

DRIVEN FROM CERES, we had one place to go—one refuge where we could live while beginning a new life and also preparing for our second child. This was the little home of Louwtjie's parents at The Strand, a resort town thirty miles from Cape Town. Fortunately, it was empty at this time, and we quickly prepared for the move—packing our belongings to be moved by truck, while we went by car.

It rained the day we left, a heavy rain falling in such torrents that it was hard to see the road. Louwtjie sat in the front seat holding Deirdre, and neither of us said anything as we drove through the gray downpour and out of the town where we had lived for two years—leaving first our empty home under the old oak, then Dr. O'Maloney's house where my name had been stripped from the pillar, and finally, the hospital which would seek me no more, not even should some patient call my name. The gothic church where our first child had been baptized was closed, and so were the homes of people we had known, homes where once the porch light had burned in the night. No one waved good-bye. No one was in the rain to wave to us, or not to wave.

The rain cloaked it all—good rain, sweet rain, covering our departure, our expulsion. So we rode, a man, a woman, and a child, leaving a garden valley where we had made our first home. How had Adam and Eve left their garden, if not in silence—silence filled with shame?

Reverend Holtzapfel had said I should go with dignity, proud of what I had done for the men and women and children of this town. Yet it was precisely this, my pride in what I had done, that also produced in me a sense of guilt, of failure. I did not want gratitude or thanks. But I did expect to have some human touch, some hold of a hand to ask me to linger—some recognition that I had been wanted.

Before leaving, we had been entertained by a few friends—but only a handful. The majority of my patients, the bulk of my parish, had looked the other way. On the street they had smiled and nodded but passed on by, as though we had already said good-bye and any further delay was mutually embarrassing. And now, in the gray rain under the gray sky, there was no one in sight, and we were packed into a steamy little car. The big Chevrolet had been exchanged for a smaller, cheaper Prefect, and we were leaving in it—a huddled family going with a sense of bewilderment and bitterness in our hearts.

"Did you turn off the water main?"

"Yes."

"And the electricity?"

"Yes."

"And you left the keys with the Kriges?"

"Yes."

They would sell the house for us—maybe to another doctor. Reverend Holtzapfel had said we were all interchangeable. One minister or general practitioner, one lawyer or dentist was as good as the other, accepted or rejected by the common trust of the community. If one did not work, you threw him out like a cracked billiard ball, a broken washing machine, a sucked orange—it did not matter.

A truck passing in the opposite direction threw a sheet of muddy water against our windshield, and Louwtjie uttered a little cry, drawing Deirdre close to her.

"When we came here that evening, you remember?" she asked.

"Yes."

"The sun was shining, and I was crying."

"Yes."

"Well, now it's raining, and I'm not crying anymore . . ."

She was not crying, perhaps, but still it was not easy to talk.

"I just hope it keeps raining until it floods the whole town and washes them all into the Indian Ocean."

I laughed—then stopped, recalling my terror upon seeing a flood at Beaufort West. The rain had come down without end, more and more of it, until suddenly the Gamka River climbed its banks to pour down New Street and then into Donkin. Fanie Bekker and I scrambled to a rooftop to watch it—coiling and twisting like a monstrous snake made from the rock and iron and red clay of the Karoo, one of the desert's prehistoric beasts awakened after a sleep of centuries, glistening red under the suddenly clearing sky, taking away with it bits and pieces of our town. Gas tins came drifting out of the Karabas Garage, one after the other as though moving in obedience to some primordial call, followed by a mattress that appeared at first to be a fat woman with no clothes over her swollen belly. Then we saw a rubber boot, a chair, a yellow hat, and finally a cat in a wash bucket, meowing wildly with fear as it drifted toward the raging river—until the bucket passed near enough to a house to be stopped by a woman with a broomstick. Further down the street, Steven Theron, who paid us for our dead mice, stood on top of his little baby Ford. Someone had thrown out a green garden hose to pull him to safety but old Steve kept shaking his head, saying he was afraid to get off his car because it might drift away. Suddenly they pulled him and he fell into the water, holding onto the hose, struggling and yelling in the red current like a giant fish with a man's head.

Afterward, my father talked about it in church. He explained that some people had thought it was the end of the world—and, indeed, one of the Pienaars did drown, and a number of homes were washed away. But we must remember, he said, that God had promised Noah there would never be another deluge. The windows of the sky and the fountains of the deep would never again open and return the earth to chaos. God had made his covenant, his promise. Noah had been forced to leave his brothers and his relatives and his friends behind to be drowned. That was very sad. But never again would a man be asked to do this. Instead, everyone would help the other, as they had done at Beaufort West during its flood—each man helping his brother.

And they helped the cats, too, I thought, as I listened from the rear of the church, unaware that my father was saying something else which everyone else had quickly understood—that each man had helped his brother, regardless of the color of his skin.

Recalling this in the car as we left Ceres, I felt a sudden sadness. Once, I had belonged to a town, to a community where the families were linked as in one family. Among them I had walked with my father, and none of my friends had ever closed their door on me.

"One flood," she said again, "to wipe them all away."

"God promised Noah it would not happen again."

"A little flood," she said. "He didn't say anything about little floods. Anyway, they'll live to regret this. By God, they'll regret it. When you come back with your London degree, they'll realize whom they sent away."

I had decided to become a Fellow of the Royal College of Surgeons, a degree that would be a great help to me at Groote Schuur, or wherever I worked.

"Don't you think you should get a job at the same time you're studying for the degree?"

"No. We'll make it all right."

"How, Chris?"

"We'll manage. I'll get a loan if necessary and when we sell the house we'll have something. We'll make it."

To obtain the F.R.C.S. I had to write two examinations. The first was in anatomy, physiology, bacteriology, and some pharmacology. Normally, it

would take six months or more to do both. I figured I could do it in four
with one-half of it spent in Cape Town preparing to take the first exam as
soon as I reached London. We had to do it this way. If I tried to do it while
doing other work, it would take a year or more.

"I'll study fast," I said.

"Maybe I should try and do something, at least part-time nursing."

"No."

"For a month or two."

"No, Louwtjie."

She was almost five months pregnant. It had not been easy the first time,
and there was no reason to assume this one was going to be any different.

"If I worked, we wouldn't have to worry so much."

"If you worked, I'd worry more."

Deirdre awakened and wanted to be fed. The rhythm of her little life,
regulated by its own internal awakenings, was impervious to flood, betrayal, and bankruptcy. A little pink mouth opened for its mother's milk,
and then the eyes began to blink slowly as though each gulp required a
separate, interior dialogue, incapable of being understood by the world.

So the new life began with a return to studies. Once again, I went from
laboratory to textbook, from microscope to formula, from the witnessing of
biological phenomena to learning the laws that governed them—shuttling
back and forth with the same restless searching that had carried me through
medical school. And once again, there was a great gap between home and
school—thirty miles, which I did by train, reading my books as I rode back
and forth.

It was during university holidays and I was alone, but I knew what I had
to learn and so I charted my own courses. A few cadavers had been left in
the anatomy hall, for others like myself doing special studies, and I worked
on them—reviewing all I had learned and then going into a more detailed
exploration of anatomy. Often I withdrew to the anatomy museum on the
second floor. No one came there and I could work undisturbed at a table
next to a case filled with jars holding human hearts which had suffered
from valve defects and various diseases. I never forgot that assembly of
hearts and recalled it vividly years later when critics attacked the rectitude
of putting a heart in another human being yet did not question the arbitrary
placement of one in formaldehyde on a museum shelf.

Each evening I returned to our little home at the Strand, arriving in time
to play horsey-horsey with Deirdre, then have dinner and study in the
living room while Louwtjie and Deirdre slept.

After two months, I was almost ready to go to London for the first
examination, which would be followed by my staying there for another two

:ar, however, that this was going
uld manage it. Louwtjie was only
cond child. Each day seemed to
Also, Deirdre had included me in
 a part of mine. I would begin to
n, kicking open the wooden gate
oom where she would be waiting
 and walk around with her while
e raced faster and faster, always

m alone at this time. Besides this,
we were running short of money.
 out a loan, which only added to
o a showdown one morning as I
wn. Louwtjie needed some money
enough cash to leave with her.
er bills this month and next?" she

ake a loan."

here we're going. You keep saying

was in her negligee, sitting on the
edge of the bed. I was dressed and ready to go. If I did not leave immediately, I would miss the train.

"I have to go, Louwtjie. We can talk it over tonight."

"Why doesn't Dr. Louw get you a place on the hospital staff like he
promised?"

"He's tried, but there's no opening yet."

"Did you tell him we were desperate?"

"Not exactly."

"What did you tell him?"

I had seen Dr. Louw several times, and he knew I wanted a post as soon
as possible. But I was careful not to appear desperate. He thought I had
left Ceres on my own volition. I saw no reason to change this since it could
be easily misunderstood and used against me by others who also wanted a
post at the hospital.

"What did you tell him, Chris?"

"I said I was ready to come as soon as possible."

"Tell him again. Tell him we need the opening now."

"That won't create one and it could do us harm. Try and not worry about it, sweetie. You're tiring yourself for no reason."

"I'm tired all right—tired of being married to an unemployed doctor."

"Louwtjie, I'm doing this as fast as I can. I can't do it any faster."

"And I can't stand any more of this!"

She began to cry, and I knew I had lost the train. I sat down on the bed, and after a bit she stopped crying.

"I'm sorry," she said. "I'm sorry I'm not stronger."

"You're all right, Louwtjie. You're splendid, really."

"No, I'm not. I'm weak and afraid and ashamed of myself because you're trying so hard."

She dried her eyes and tried to smile. It was a little smile, waiting to be caught by someone. I did nothing, and it sank into a pool of loneliness and was gone. After that she seemed to be asking me only to touch her, to take one of her hands that lay open and empty in her lap under the bulging weight of our unborn child. For a moment I hesitated before this, too, feeling helpless and lost and unable to make the slightest gesture—a lifetime of them would never fill that pool of loneliness, that ocean of doubt and fear. And then, guilty and sad, I took her into my arms. For a moment we clung to each other without words. None were needed. Finally she spoke as to a fellow passenger.

"You'd better hurry. You'll miss your train."

I hurried, perhaps more in an effort to catch myself than any train. I was totally confused, and when I found it was too late, I stood alone on the platform, feeling that I had lost much more than a train.

I was losing control of my life, of my sense of direction and purpose. My failure at Ceres had led me to seek a degree that would prove my worth. Yet I was about to fail at this, too. For I could not leave Louwtjie in her present condition—certainly not until she had given birth. And this delay, coupled with our continual failure to sell the house at Ceres, meant I was going to have to find a job somewhere. Inevitably, this would delay the London degree, perhaps forever. It was sad. Yet even worse was the prospect of looking for a job somewhere, a job with no goal or purpose behind it other than making money for my family.

For the first time in my life, I felt lost. Something had entered my existence for which I was not prepared and only now was beginning to understand. From childhood, I had been conditioned to the hostility of the material world around me. As a boy, there had been a lack of real things— money, food, clothes, even rainwater. In school the struggle was just as real and visible, played on a field of recorded knowledge with fixed rules for gain and loss. Depending on how much ground was covered, you either failed or graduated. And work in the hospital as an intern was essentially a projection of this.

Trouble began when I entered the world at Ceres. At that moment, the hostility of a material environment was replaced by something else—people. Other people became my problem—not the world. The people of Ceres had failed to join me, or I had failed to join them. Regardless, they were detrimental in causing my departure and with this I seemed to have lost my road. Now I needed the time and freedom to find it again. The only way to do this, it seemed, was to get a job, some medical post which would lift off the pressure at home and so allow me to see my way clearly once more.

Another train pulled in and on the way into Cape Town I found a notice in the Medical Journal stating a post was open at the City Hospital for Infectious Diseases. I phoned them that same morning and a few days later was ushered before an examining board of five doctors at the City Hospital. They included the hospital superintendent, Dr. Frikkie Wicht, the health officer of the city, Dr. Olaf Fredrick Fehrson, and his assistant, Dr. Edmund Cooper. Dr. Fehrson had a red nose and smiled in a friendly way.

"I'm Dr. Fehrson from Beaufort West. You probably don't remember me."

"How could I forget? You delivered me."

"Bravo!"

We laughed, and I decided he was ready to deliver me once more—from the street into a hospital job. That was 20 per cent of the vote in my favor before they even asked to see my credentials. I smiled at him again. He had left Beaufort West, and I hardly knew him, except by name. Yet here he was, sunk in the hierarchy of hospital and city, examining a boy he had delivered thirty years ago. And thirty years from now, would a child I had delivered at Ceres or on a remote farm find me also with a red nose and a baggy tweed suit, sitting in a bare office of a city hospital for infectious diseases?

I shuddered and turned to look at the rest of the examining board. They were pleasant enough and, after half an hour of questions, asked me to step outside while they interviewed other applicants.

I began to wait in the matron's office, but there were others there, also wanting the same job. Their silent stares made me so uncomfortable that I went outside, going down some wooden steps into the central courtyard of the hospital. It was large as a rugby field and quite pleasant, lined with azaleas and tall palm trees. Around the sides were half a dozen large barrack-type buildings, undoubtedly separated for the different diseases treated here—tuberculosis, diphtheria, measles, scarlet fever, meningitis.

I wandered into one of the first barracks on the left and found no one in the corridor. From the far end came the sound of children crying—strange, muffled cries as though they had been doing it so long that they were at the point of exhaustion. I continued until I opened the door, to find a large, high-ceilinged ward, filled with what at first appeared to be iron baby cribs. Then I saw they were actually little beds with bar sidings of black iron.

Behind the bars of each bed was a colored baby or child in some stage of deformity. Many of them had little bodies with heads as big as basketballs. They could not easily carry such a load and lay on their backs, eyes blinking from massed flesh—vacant stares as if they had seen an abyss of such frightening horror that it had left them mute with awe and fear. A few kicked stiff little legs into the air, their sobs and cries seemingly directed at the legs, telling them to run faster. Others lay with backs arched upward, heads jerked back, so that they remained fixed like pulled bows emitting tiny cries asking for release. Still others had legs and arms stretched out stiffly in spastic extension, their faces also paralyzed with only the eyelids moving—opening and closing at regular intervals in the only free expression left to their rigid bodies and frozen minds. Still other children sat upright, or clung to the edge of the iron cribs, heads not yet wholly deformed, jumping up and down in dumb rhythm as though the brain felt the first touches of its eventual, monstrous deformation and so was telling the child to escape if it could from the hell that was soon to claim it: tuberculous meningitis.

Never in my life had I seen such a field of human suffering. That these were little children did not diminish the massive weight of their total pain, but rather more seemed to magnify it. There lay upon it a ruin, a wastage of the promise of life that would not have been there if these were older people who had already lived. Here was the beginning of life, the seeds of a society twisted and bent and turned into a hideous perversion of life. Over it all rode their plaintive cries and sobs, none much louder than the other, as though pain and disfigurement had reduced them all to the same level, fusing it all into one long, unending wail. The corridors of hell must echo with such sounds.

At the rear of the ward were two women in white—one of them obviously a sister. They had lowered both sides of one crib bed and, as I approached, the sister picked up a little girl in a pink nightie. Kneeling on the bed with both legs, she positioned the child in her lap so that its back was exposed in a curve. The other woman prepared to do a lumbar puncture, but stopped upon seeing me.

"Hello?"

"Hello, I'm Dr. Barnard."

"Dr. Barnard? Oh yes, Dr. Wicht said you might be the new resident—are you?"

"I don't know. They're talking it over now."

"Oh," she said. Then she smiled as though she knew they would choose me. "I'm Dr. Rabkin, and this is Sister Gillespie."

Sister Gillespie, kneeling on the cot with the child over her thighs, said hello in an open and easy manner, as if we were meeting at a football game. She was blonde and rather tall, but well-shaped and good-looking. Dr. Rabkin was smaller, dark and more intense and terribly alone amid all those beds. Together, they were like day and night.

Dr. Rabkin continued with her lumbar puncture at the fifth vertebra, drawing off five cubic centimeters of fluid.

"Good," she said. "We've been getting some blood from Lilly, but now it's clear.

Lilly had pigtails, and they hung down, limp as her little arms, while she sobbed one name over and over.

"Weeny, weeny, weeny, weeny . . ."

"As you can see," said Dr. Rabkin, "there's nothing but tuberculous meningitis here, and even upstairs. If you join us, you'll probably be given this ward."

She looked at me closely to catch my reaction. I had been right. She was one of the dedicated ones.

"What are you preparing to inject?" I asked.

"Streptomycin."

Slowly with a syringe she put five cubic centimeters of drug solution where she had withdrawn the spinal fluid. Then Sister Gillespie sat Lilly on her knee, pulled down the pink nightie, gave her a big kiss—and put her into the cot. After that, both women pulled up the iron grill on each side. From behind her bars, little Lilly looked at us with wet eyes and slowly shook her head as though we did not know what we were doing. Gillespie laughed and picked up a toy elephant and gave it to the child. Lilly seemed to be about four. There was already some swelling at the back of her head. She was about to enter the house of horror.

"What are her chances?" I asked.

Dr. Rabkin shook her head.

"They either die or become vegetables. If we get them early enough, there's a chance. But we rarely get them early enough."

In a bed nearby, a girl larger than Lilly began to jump up and down, singing "Yankee Doodle." She wore a blue nightie with a design of daisies, and as she bounced, her eyes looked like daisies, too.

"That's Flavia," said Gillespie. "She's the gayest of the lot."

In another bed next to the wall a boy began to take his feces into his own hands and stuff it into his ears and nose.

"No, no," said Gillespie, quickly taking the child into her arms and heading for the washroom while Flavia sang away: "Yankee Doodle came to town, riding on his pony . . ."

Dr. Rabkin shook her head sadly.

"They do that, some of them," she said. "It's a sign they are going into the 'S' stage."

"You have no cure for this?"

"We also give intramuscular streptomycin and PAS—paraminosalysylic acid. But the brain is generally always damaged. Do you think you'll come here?"

"I don't know. I hope so," I replied, suddenly aware that the board might now be waiting to see me.

We walked together toward the door of the ward. Dr. Rabkin stopped there.

"I hope you do come," she said.

I thanked her and we said good-bye. Then she turned back to the children in beds like prisons, and their unceasing wails covered her as would the immovable fathoms of the sea.

The meeting was still in session, with the matron looking for me. The board had sent out word that I could leave and would know their decision within a few days. This seemed to be a polite way of not saying no immediately, and I went home believing I had failed to obtain the job. Louwtjie, however, was certain I would get it.

"That hospital is run by the city. Did you ever hear of a city doing anything in one day?"

"I keep thinking about those babies with tuberculous meningitis," I said. "There's no effective cure for them, and there are so many in their iron prisons."

"And I keep thinking of you spending all day with those infectious children, then coming home at night to play with Deirdre."

"Don't be foolish, Louwtjie. You can't take home most of those diseases, and with the others we are always careful."

"It couldn't have been a normal hospital, or a maternity home," she said. "No—it had to be one with infectious diseases, which have no cure. That's us, all right."

The next day, Dr. Wicht called to say I had the job. Further, he would be grateful if I could come to work immediately. I did, packing a bag and taking the Prefect. There were living quarters in the residence building and Dr. Wicht promised to see about arranging a small apartment for my family—probably after the birth of our child. Until then, I could spend weekends at The Strand with Louwtjie and Deirdre.

I was given the tuberculous meningitis ward and almost immediately began to seek some answer, some exit from the nightmare of their suffering. I had four other wards—typhoid, diphtheria, measles, and pulmonary tuberculosis—and occasionally these also provided challenges. In the pulmonary cases, for example, we occasionally removed a lung. This was my first exposure to surgery inside the chest, and I learned much from it. Yet my real interest was elsewhere, and as soon as I cleared my other wards, I hurried over to Ward 15, overflowing with its tiny victims.

I began my attack by studying the origin of the disease—a germ inhaled by the child, generally from a parent or relative with pulmonary tuberculosis. The germ then settles in the lung, causing a primary focus. At this point it is not yet serious. Practically every child in South Africa gets a primary focus that remains localized and eventually heals, leaving a certain amount of immunity against further infection. This natural cycle is broken with undernourished children who lack the strength to fight off the germ. So it is spread by the blood to the body and finally infects the meninges or the three membranes surrounding the brain, causing a meningitis.

Once this occurs, the child is set for its terrible destiny. Inflammation creates an exudate or deposit of protein material at the base of the brain. This blocks a free flow of the cerebral spinal fluid—a fluid secreted in the ventricles of the brain whose flow is used to cushion both brain and spinal cord. The brain then begins to suffer, for it continues to secrete fluid that no longer has an exit. As a result, pressure mounts, compressing the brain and expanding the skull like a balloon—hydrocephalus. It is this which turns the children into such grotesque monsters suffering from neurological lesions, hemiplegia, and decerebrate rigidity. Also it is this that causes such pathetic acts as stuffing personal feces into the nose and ears, as though the brutal blockage of one orifice to the brain drove them to complete the deathly process by using their own self-product to dam up whatever openings remained.

Some way had to be found to halt the inflammation before it created the exudate that sealed off the brain. The accepted method of treatment was intrathecal injections of streptomycin by lumbar puncture, as well as intramuscular injections of this same drug. Yet this seldom, if ever, removed the deadly block. As a result, there was a tremendous death rate and those who survived were left with a destroyed brain, resulting in stiff limbs, big heads. Quite often, they were little more than human vegetables.

It was not easy to see this happen. One after another of our little patients slipped away from us as we continued to make the rounds. One morning we found Lilly having convulsions. I had been particularly interested in this little girl ever since seeing Dr. Rabkin treat her the first day. Yet despite everything we tried, her condition had deteriorated to where her limbs were stiff, without any movement except at the wrists and ankles. And now her little body was wracked with a fit. We gave her a mild sedation and, after noting an improvement, proceeded to treat another patient—Flavia, the girl who sang "Yankee Doodle."

Sister Gene Gillespie got onto the bed and expertly bent the child's back, preparatory to my drawing out the spinal fluid for eventual analysis of protein, chlorides, sugar, and cell count. It was vital to hold the child correctly. Otherwise, you got blood instead of fluid and the whole test would be spoiled for days because the blood remained in the spinal fluid. Gene did it beautifully, holding Flavia against her magnificent thighs as I drew out the fluid. I next prepared to put in the streptomycin and glanced over toward Lilly. She was motionless—with no sign of breathing.

"My God!"

Gene saw it, too.

"Oh," she said. "Little Lilly."

During the rest of that day, I thought of how Lilly used to shake her head at us as though we did not know the answer and that night I went to see a friend of mine—Dr. Mark Horwitz.

"Chris," he said. "Maybe your answer is cortisone. It dampens down inflammation and probably could diminish protein exudate which is your big problem."

Mark was then working in internal medicine at Groote Schuur. We had met during student days, on a train to Beaufort West. He was two years ahead of me, and so we had not seen each other often. Yet I had always admired his abilities. And when I discovered he had a bachelor flat at Mouille Point, near City Hospital, we began to visit one another.

"Cortisone is a steroid, as you know, and has a strong action," said Mark. "I use it often on arthritis, with dramatic results."

"But as a steroid, it'll stop the body's localizing defenses and allow the tuberculosis to spread."

"Yes . . ."

"We can prevent this by giving streptomycin and PAS at the same time to kill the germ."

"Looking at your mortality rate," said Mark, "I'd say it's worth the try."

We were in his apartment—a place I would visit often in the coming months as Mark's friendship and counsel became increasingly important to me. I was ready to try cortisone but uncertain whether I could get it through my own hospital.

"I'll see what I can get, but if I have any difficulty can you help me?"

"Yes, Chris."

I could hardly wait to begin the treatment and walked home in a state of excitement. By this time, Louwtjie had given birth to our second child, André Hendrik Barnard, or "Boetie," and we were all living in a small but comfortable apartment in the residence building of the hospital. Dr. Ray Rabkin had a smaller apartment next to us, and we often dined together with Ray's boy friend, Victor Holloway, a sports writer.

I wanted to talk about the new treatment, but everyone was asleep. So I woke up Louwtjie and told her about it.

"A degree," she said, sleepily.

"What?"

"You remember what Robbie Slome told you? Use this time to do a thesis."

"Yes."

"You can do one on your search for a cure of these children."

She was right. Dr. Slome, who had preceded me, had done a thesis on tetanus. I could also do one as part of the requirement for the M.D. degree—Doctor of Medicine.

So we began with a selected group, using cortisone with streptomycin and PAS. Flavia was among those selected and first results seemed to help her and the others. Temperatures dropped, and there was a settling of proteins and cells in the spinal fluid that also became less viscous. Despite this, each patient slowly followed the usual pattern. As they died, I did the postmortems, making multiple coronal sections through the brain. At the base of each one, there was a dense exudate. Flavia, after thirty-three days of cortisone with antibiotics, still had exudate on the pons and midbrain.

Gene Gillespie had worked with me on all of these and when I had Flavia opened on the table, I telephoned her to come down and look at it.

"Chris, it's after midnight."

"It doesn't matter. You've got to see this so you know what's going on inside the brains of these children . . . you've got to see this to understand why we're treating them."

"Chris, it might surprise you, but most human beings need some sleep."

"So you won't come?"

"Yes, I'll come."

"Hurry."

We did postmortems in a little building, small as a chapel or tool shed, at the far end of the garden. The nurses slept nearby and Gene was there in a few minutes—without make-up and her blonde hair touching her shoulders.

"Look," I said. "Look at the exudate. Nothing has happened. The cortisone did not work."

She looked at the cross-section of Flavia's brain.

"But it wasn't supposed to remove it—only stop it from happening."

"That's right. Perhaps we began the cortisone after the exudate had started. But the point is that we did not remove it, and this girl got progressively worse until she reached this point."

We both looked at the final point of Flavia's arrival—her brain on the table, while nearby lay the little girl with her cranium now void of its sensorial seat of life.

"We need something that will dissolve this away," I said. "Something to remove this block."

"And I need a coffee—or something," said Gene.

She smiled, but it was a forced smile, and I could see she did not want to stay any longer. So I put the brain sections in a jar to preserve them for photographing later at the Medical School, and we left for the Doll's House at Mouille Point. In the car, I noticed tears in Gene's eyes.

"I'm sorry," she said.

"What is it, Gene?"

"You remember how Flavia used to sing "Yankee Doodle"?

"Yes."

"I know it's not professional of me, but I just can't separate the human being from the experiment."

She was right and I felt a sudden sense of identity with her—close and intimate. At the same time, I felt threatened, as though she was about to clobber me with a cricket bat because she did not know the rules of the game. This was something I had suffered through for years. She could never know how much I had suffered over it. Then I wondered: Was it possible I had gone too far toward the other side and become insensitive to the separate weight and value of single lives? I was handling so many children—we now did forty lumbar punctures a day—and so many were dying that perhaps I was losing my sense of respect for the single life. Before I could decide, she started again.

"The jar where you left the brain. It didn't say Flavia—only *Case 53*."

"What do you expect me to put there? Each case has to be numbered. You can't make a graph with names. It won't work."

"But the human being gets lost as a number on a jar."

"Gene, we're doing this to save human beings, not lose them. Don't you see that?"

"Yes, I see it," she said.

Yet it was not that simple, and she was right in a way. We had to be careful to remember that these were human beings whose single lives were no less precious than all the lives put together. They were part of a mass human experiment, but this could never diminish their separate identity and single worth. There was no question about the experiment itself. Our regard for life required we do all possible to save it. This meant making experiments. Nor was there any ethical problem involved in this—as long as our work involved no danger to the patient. It could only arise when our experiment might possibly endanger the patient's life—something I never expected to happen.

Yet it did happen as soon as I found a medical product capable of dissolving the exudate blocking the brains of the children. It was a purified crystalline trypsin derived from animal pancreas, called Tryptar. Unlike other enzymes that attack proteins, this only acted on dead matter, without injuring normal cells and tissues. It had been used medically to clear blood clots, fibrous strands, and purulent lesions. But it had never before been injected into the spinal space thus reaching the brain. Inevitably, this contained unknown dangers since we did not know what it might do to the nervous system. In some of the cases, for example, there was vascular brain damage. Would Tryptar further harm such brains? We did not know, and I discussed it beforehand with Mark.

"Do you intend to try it out?" he asked.

"Yes—in limited amounts and only on moribund patients."

"You'll get parental permission?"

"Of course."

"Then I don't see any reason not to go ahead. You're going to lose the patient anyway. This way, you might have a chance to save him."

The situation was similar to one that applies to all patients suffering from incurable diseases. Were we justified in undertaking an experiment with a view to saving his life—or at least prolonging it? I believed we had this right, as long as we also had the permission of the patient, or his relatives if he was physically incapable of giving it. This concept was eventually adopted as an ethical guideline by the World Medical Association at Helsinki in 1964.

Yet it did not lessen the drama of our first use of Tryptar. We chose a two-year-old boy in an advanced stage of the disease, with enlarged head and spastic limbs. Gene Gillespie helped, as usual, and we gave him one twentieth of the intrapleural dosage. Within four minutes the boy began to vomit and twitch. This settled down within an hour, but that night the child went into convulsions with a 105-degree temperature.

Desperately sad, I thought he would die. Throughout the night, I returned to his bedside, looking for some sign of improvement. Slowly the temperature settled, and the following morning the boy seemed better. After another treatment, with less reaction, we tried it on another child with the same result. I continued treating both cases and they lived longer than other patients at the same stage of the disease. They died, however, but their postmortems were startling—the grain exudate had been cleaned away. Death came as a result of damage before its removal. Obviously, treatment had to be started earlier.

It seemed safe to proceed with cases in the initial stages of the disease and I began treatment upon a select group of twenty-five. Most of these were less than three years old, but four were over twelve. This included Richard, a handsome youth of seventeen, who came to us with rigid limbs and deafness—yet without any visible deformation of brain or skull.

Richard soon became a favorite of Gene's. Every day she put him into a warm bath to loosen his muscles, working his light brown limbs as though she knew he would get well. There was much pain for him in this, but Gene kept after him, speaking to him as if he were not deaf and could understand every word.

At first we injected Richard and the others using the spinal route. Then I decided there was no reason why we should not go to the brain more directly. Instead of the drug coming up through the spine, it could be administered through the skull. Babies have a natural opening at the top of their heads, called the fontanel, which generally closes at eight months. It remains open, however in many cases of tuberculous meningitis. With these, it was a simple matter to insert a needle through the brain. But this was not possible with others where growing bone had closed the opening. To achieve this in a select few, I called Professor H. L. de Villiers Hammann and asked him to open two plugs in the skulls of some older children, including Richard.

"Why?" he asked.

"I need it to inject medicine into the brain ventricles."

"Are you mad?"

"Let me explain it. Come to lunch and also see them."

He came, he saw the children—and he made the plug openings which we left covered with skin. Richard was among these, and three weeks later Gene came running out to meet me.

"Richard can hear!"

"If you shout like that, anybody can hear—even the deaf."

"Oh, Chris, it's so beautiful!"

She hugged me with joy, and we went in to find Richard with an alarm clock on the pillow next to his ear.

"I think I also hear the ticking," he said.

"Now watch this," said Gene.

The boy could bend his arms now, yet only with difficulty. So Gene did it for him, setting off the alarm and replacing it on the pillow next to his ear. Richard then smiled happily, as though hearing beautiful music. We stood there, watching his smile fade as the alarm gradually ran down. Gene had open tears of joy, and I had to struggle to hold back my own. Suddenly, all the days and nights of labor, all the sacrifices of self and family, were shown to be worth it. It was there before us, visible in the face of a boy with an alarm clock at his ear.

Richard was one of the lucky ones. His hearing returned, and, with physiotherapy and warm baths, his arms and legs regained movement. The combination of Tryptar, cortisone, and streptomycin brought him slowly back to normal. These drugs and similar bath treatment also worked on a few others. Yet tragically these were only a few exceptions. Tryptar cleared the brain of blockage, either totally or in part. It also extended the life of all those who received it. But it did not change the final result sufficiently to establish a clear breakthrough. This was a disease that had to be prevented before it presented itself for a cure.

I did not give up, however, and continued to test other adjuvants, such as tuberculin and isoniazide, until I had a clinical study of 259 cases over a period of two years, March 1951 to March 1953—the largest inquiry ever made in this disease. I was helped by Professor Jan François Erasmus, neurosurgeon and chief of surgery at Groote Schuur, who arranged for photographing the graphs and postmortem findings. With all this material, I prepared to write my thesis. At the same time, my work had created enough interest at Groote Schuur for them to finally act upon my application and I was asked to accept a post as resident doctor in medicine.

I took it with joy, for this would allow me to complete my studies in internal medicine. City Hospital had been a bottomless cradle of suffering and sorrow, a frightful realm ruled by an unconquered disease—and a laboratory of human life where I had tried to meet that disease. I had fought with weapons new to me—research and scientific inquiry.

Now I wanted to continue with them at Groote Schuur, broadening their use. After I had finished my thesis and obtained the M.D., I would prepare for still another—the M.Med., or Master of Medicine, required for specialization in internal medicine. With these, I would have covered medicine sufficiently to proceed toward surgery and its use in the laboratory to increase our ability to save patients beyond the reach of medicine. My life, which had seemed without destiny after Ceres, once again had goal and purpose.

CHAPTER 12

I RETURNED TO GROOTE SCHUUR like someone coming home from a long trip. I knew its corridors better than those of my own home which was constantly changing. Its doctors and nurses and patients were a part of my larger family—and far more demanding than my own. Even the vision of the hospital on its hill stirred me in a more profound way than had any front gate under a giant oak.

Groote Schuur in Afrikaans means "Big Barn." Actually it resembled more an immense health resort hotel, with double wings of evenly spaced windows while high atop the central building a statue of Hygeia, Goddess of Health, stands against the sky. Seen from the highway, it sets deep into the slopes of its pointed mountain, Devil's Peak—blue-green forests cupping the white structure as though it not only belonged there but had taken root and become a part of the mountain itself.

From the highway, ambulances race day and night up to two portico entrances, one for Europeans (white) and another for non-Europeans (nonwhite). If you stand at either entrance, you can see Cape Town below and, beyond that, Cape Flats with the blue sea to the left and far in the distance the purple of other mountains blocking the view to the tip of the African continent.

So the hospital sat above the city, linked to it by screaming ambulances, each one bearing its pitiful load, its latest, most urgent cargo of violated life, lifting it by bits and pieces from beds, wheelchairs, car wrecks, factories, sports fields, bar rooms, love pads—an inexhaustible warehouse of spent and broken human life. In this way they poured into the hospital, and once again, in the middle of such a flood, I realized I had been right before returning.

There were just too many patients beyond the reach of medicine. They were sent to us because they were beyond repair by the general practitioner. Yet too often there was little we could do, other than cure infections with antibiotics. There were no lasting remedies for most of the serious body disorders—other than cutting them away or blocking them provisionally with medicines.

Diabetics were given insulin to control the sugar level in the blood—but it never cured the diabetes. Cancer was burnt or cut away, if we got it in time—without knowing where it came from or when it would return. Failing organs, such as heart or kidney or liver, were treated—generally without knowing the initiating cause of the illness. Or if we knew it, there was little we could do about it. Patients with congestive cardiac failure were treated and then sent home—only to return two weeks later with further failure. After more treatment, we sent them out again, knowing there were lasting defects we could never repair. While this was happening, the patient tended to convince himself that he was improving or at least holding his own. Yet we saw it another way—a floundering between life and death in an area beyond our reach. As such, it sometimes took years to run its course. And sometimes it required only a few minutes.

One morning they brought in a man with a heart block. His pulse was low—thirty-five to forty beats a minute—and Professor Frank Forman requested he receive special care. As I began the examination, he suddenly went into a fit and had a Stokes-Adams attack—something I had never seen. In this, the heart stops beating and the patient becomes unconscious until the heart starts again, usually within a minute or so.

Unaware of this, I was shocked to see the patient shaken by a coughing seizure, then suddenly roll up his eyes as though he was dead. At that same moment, he ceased breathing. I felt his pulse—no pulse. I listened to the heart—no heart beat.

"This man's dead," I said, and hurried to phone Professor Forman that we had lost his special patient. Yet as I waited for the call to go through, the nurse came running up.

"Doctor, the patient is alive again."

When I reached the room, he was sitting up and asking for an aspirin to relieve his headache.

What, I wondered, were we doing with such people? Of all the barriers before us in the search to make medicine a better servant of man, perhaps the most challenging lay here—in the area of the heart. How could we enter its chambers and repair its valves without killing the patient? The main difficulty was not in touching the heart, but rather in depriving the brain of its need for a continuous supply of blood. More than any other part of the body, the brain needed sugar and oxygen carried to it by the blood. The heart muscle could survive without it for an hour or more. But brain tissue could not go beyond three to four minutes without death of the higher centers, while a longer period of twelve to fifteen minutes brought total brain death.

Open-heart surgery, with a cessation of blood flow through the heart, was thus limited to three or four minutes—too brief an interval for any extensive work inside the heart. There were, however, two conceivable methods of obtaining more time. One was to use a substitute pump for the heart while it was being opened and repaired. The other was to arrest or slow down body functions sufficiently to allow a safe interruption of blood flow for longer than three to four minutes.

Eventually, the heart-lung machine was to become the universal answer. An American pioneer in applied physiology, Dr. John H. Gibbon, of Philadelphia, had been trying to build one since 1935 and, beginning in the spring of 1953, he had used it on several human beings. But they had all died, except for one fifteen-year-old girl, and by the end of the year many felt the heart-lung machine was still too dangerous to use in the operating theater. So for us at that time, the second method seemed safer and nearer at hand. Medical journals reported doctors in Canada and Holland had discovered that a lowering of body temperature allowed the blood flow to be cut off and the heart opened for twice the usual period—and perhaps longer—without serious damage. At a subnormal temperature, the brain needed only one-half to one-fifth its usual quantity of oxygen and so could endure at least twice as long without a blood supply.

This set off a frantic search in the medical world for the best way to achieve hypothermia—popularly called "frozen sleep" or "artificial hibernation." One method was to put the anesthetized patient into a tub of cold water or cracked ice. Another was to wrap him in a blanket containing built-in, water-cooled coils. Both systems seemed clumsy and difficult to use under totally sterile conditions. Looking for another method, I decided the same result could be obtained by inserting a rubber balloon for cold water circulation into the stomach. Since the stomach wall has a rich blood supply, its contact with cold water would quickly lower the body temperature. It seemed safe and efficient, and I was anxious to try it with open-heart surgery on animals.

But before moving over to surgery, it was necessary to finish my studies for those degrees required of a specialist in internal medicine. I had finally written the thesis on tuberculous meningitis and been awarded an M.D. Besides this academic degree, a clinical one was needed—the M.Med. —and I prepared for it while working at the hospital.

Because of this and my anxiety to begin with surgical research, I often studied through the night in the doctors' bungalow without returning to Louwtjie in our new home in Pinelands. This anxiety continued into the day of the M.Med. practical examination before a group of doctors. After grilling me for several hours, they appeared to be going around in circles. Their questions seemed senseless—an insensitive delay of my return to surgery. Unable to stand it any longer, I rose up, saying, "Gentleman, you know enough about me by this time to either plug me or pass me. I leave it to you."

They awarded the degree, qualifying me for the specialist registry in internal medicine. After that, I applied to become resident in surgery and this was also granted—the job I had so desperately wanted three years previous, upon being banished from Ceres. In a way, it now meant stepping down. From high on the ladder of internal medicine, I went to near the bottom in surgery. Yet I took with me a deeper knowledge of medicine than most of my associates, and it was immediately helpful. It was also a pleasure to be again with Professor Jannie Louw. He had become an associate professor and senior surgeon, under Professor Erasmus. So once again, after six years, I assisted him in the operating theater—as a registrar.

My real life, however, began in the evening when I could withdraw to the animal house to begin my experiments. How can I begin to describe the excitement with which I first entered the little animal building, stuck in between the medical school and the graveyard? It smelled of guinea pigs, rabbits, and hundreds of mice. Yet it was like heaven, and even today those odors excite me with memories of our first days, so filled with hope and dreams—and bitter anguish.

There was little to work with—no surgical laboratory, no equipment, not even a formal nod from the hospital that this could exist. We were given two bare rooms on the second floor by Professor Arthur Kipps, head of the bacteriology department, who agreed to look the other way at night. The mice and rabbits and guinea pigs, as well as the building itself, were used by his unit for routine laboratory tests. There was no provision for surgical experiments on animals—yet we could do it in his animal house, provided we did it quietly at night.

Besides Professor Kipps, others believed in the work and soon came to labor through the night in a bare room, where the smell of mice and guinea pigs intermingled with the ether of an operating theater. They came, as I did, with the belief that we were going to find a medical truth. Being young, we did not question the origin of our belief. We had it, we felt it, and it was this which drove us on through that year to its dramatic end.

The first project was to be heart surgery on dogs whose body temperature had been lowered by means of stomach balloons filled with cold water. Since the animal house had no dogs, I bought them from the city pound—

taking only stray mongrels that were unclaimed and about to be destroyed by gas. If they had to die, this was at least in the service of science and mankind. If they lived afterward, we would find homes for them. With this in mind, I loaded four dogs into my little Prefect and drove them all to the animal house.

Before attempting surgery, we had to determine if the gastric cooling system would work. From the hospital pharmacy, I drew a supply of condoms after determining they could be expanded sufficiently to fill a canine stomach while also being thin enough to transfer contrasting temperatures to the stomach wall. To help me at this stage, I had two colored attendants from the animal house, Boots and Appel, who quickly became expert and invaluable aides.

After a few attempts, it became clear that the system needed to be controlled by a refrigeration unit, with automatic temperature controls and a cut-off. So I built one, with the help of the university engineering department, using a cooler donated by the Fuchs Refrigeration Ware—another example of how people were ready to help. The finished unit was relatively simple. It circulated ice water through a balloon inside the dog's stomach. Overextension was prevented by a level-sensing device in the tank. This continued until we had lowered the body temperature to the desired level recorded by a thermometer in the dog's rectum. The dogs were full of fleas and, when the temperature dropped, the fleas would begin a mass exodus—hopping onto the operating table and onto us, so that we inevitably went home covered with them.

Once we could cool the dogs and control the process, we were ready to begin the first surgical experiment. Eventually we were to get our own equipment and linens, but in the beginning we had nothing—so we just took it. Two nurses volunteered to help, packing sterilized instruments from the operating theater into a sealed drum and bringing it after dark to the animal house along with sterile linens, swabs and some intravenous fluids. They were Marlene Voges and her sister, Nel Voges, and they came with a sense of excitement, tinged with conspiracy. Before dawn, we would have to clean everything up and get back to the hospital.

With quiet efficiency, the girls quickly transformed the bare room into a surgical theater. Saline drips went up. Sterile linens on the wooden table converted it into an operating base. A ceiling lamp that could be raised and lowered on a pulley was our source of light. Dr. Sarel Knipe arrived to give the anesthetic. And Dr. Robert Casserley, a thoracic surgeon, was there to open the dog's heart and sew it up again—within the eight-minute limit allowed by our cooling process. At that time I was not sufficiently skilled to do such an operation.

We chose a light brown, short-haired mongrel and, after it was shaved and anesthetized, we inserted the balloon with its double lumen tube into the stomach. Flushing began and when the temperature reached eighty-two degrees Fahrenheit, Dr. Casserley began the operation, cutting through the skin, fat, and muscle to enter the rib cage. I helped with the retractors, clamping the bleeding points, and swabbing. Pulling away the lung, the pericardium covering the heart came into view. This was opened and the heart was exposed, turning on itself with each pump.

We were ready and, after checking the temperature and noting the time, we clamped off the major veins to the heart. Dr. Casserley then began to open the heart—cutting into the right auricle, exposing the tricuspid valve for an assumed stenosis, then sewing it up again. Within eight minutes, the auricle was sufficiently closed to release the clamps and allow a free return of circulation. We began then to run warm water into the gastric balloon, bringing the temperature up to normal. The dog seemed to have taken it well enough and we returned him to his cage. The girls and I then spent another hour cleaning dog hairs out of the linen and about 4 A.M. we all went home.

Despite the late hour, I could not sleep. I wanted to talk to someone and tried to awaken Louwtjie, but she only rolled away. So I lay awake for some time, thinking about what had happened.

It was the first time in my life that I had gone into a live heart and left it still beating and able to sustain life. It was fascinating. The heart was like a remote, unclaimed country. Yet you could be very definite in your diagnosis of it—unlike other organs. In diabetes, for example, it was assumed that the pancreas was not secreting insulin. Or if producing insulin, something else prevented it from being effective, such as a disturbance in the metabolism of the liver, or altered activity of other glands, or other causes behind causes—often without end.

On the other hand, there was some order about the medicine of heart disease. The heart was a mechanical pump and it worked like one. When there was a blockage, certain things happened. When there was a leakage, other things happened. The heart existed unto itself, within a special area. It could be heard by the ear, calculated by mathematics, tracked by electric impulses, measured in all its chambers by catheter, and witnessed by the eye. Finally, we were coming into an era when it could be touched, opened, and repaired. It was exciting to think about this, and I did not fall asleep until dawn came upon me—suddenly, like a forgotten guest.

The next morning, en route to surgery, I stopped by to see how the dog was doing. Appel met me on the stairs.

"*Nee,* doctor, the dog is dead."

I could not believe it and ran up the stairs to see that it was quite true. Heavy with exhaustion, I felt the weight of failure even more. Where had we gone wrong?

"Shall I burn it?" asked Appel.

Dead animals were placed in the incinerator.

"No," I said. "I want to open it up tonight and see if we can find the mistake. Maybe the sutures were not close enough."

Yet they were close enough. There had been no internal bleeding. So I did not know what had caused it, unless the hypothermic technique was wrong. Nor did I learn much more on the next two dogs, for they both died. Miserable but determined, I proceeded to the fourth—altering the technique slightly. In the last two cases, the heart had gone into brief fibrillation. Believing we might have been too severe in the cooling, I kept the temperature at 86 degrees Fahrenheit, or about 12 degrees below normal. The machine worked perfectly and the animal seemed to accept it well. Dr. Casserley and I both did the intervention, opening the pulmonary artery to expose the pulmonary valve. After closing the wound, all seemed well. It was a big black dog, and we put him in the cage with a feeling that we had finally succeeded.

Yet the next morning, when I stopped by, Appel again was sitting on the steps, shaking his head.

"Nee, doctor, the dog is dead."

"No—really?"

"Ya, Dr. Casserley was by before. He said put it in the bag."

We placed the dogs in a bag before putting them into the incinerator.

"All right," I said, sadly. "That's that, Appel."

I hurried on to the hospital where I was due in A Theater to assist Professor Jannie Louw. We had to do two gastrectomies—removal of the stomach. I was tired from working all night on the dog, depressed by its failure, and hardly ready to submit to one of Professor Louw's bad-tempered days.

He was already there and very quickly we entered the theater. I helped with the retractor, holding back the liver, and it seemed to be going quite well. But Professor Louw did not like it and began to complain.

"Pull it away from me, man."

I did as directed and he growled at me.

"Not that way, the other."

I pulled the other way.

"You still haven't got it—pull this way!"

He shoved my hand. I obliged but did no more—holding the retractor in place and waiting for him to tell me what to do next. Since everything I did was wrong, this seemed to be the safest course. Instead, it caused him to explode.

"What's wrong with you? If you don't feel like helping me, then you can get out of the operating room."

He accompanied this by shoving my hand again. If he had not done that, I might have stayed. But the final shove, as though he really wanted me to go, was more than I could bear. I turned and took off my gloves and

walked out of the theater—the same one where one day I would transplant
a human heart. As I left, there was total silence, broken only by the
patient's breathing and Professor Louw finally calling to the instrument
sister.

"A Pott's clamp, please."

I got into my car and drove up the slope of Devil's Peak to Rhodes
Memorial. There I parked, looking down at Cape Flats and the mountains
in the distance. I thought that my career was finished—at least at Groote
Schuur. I had walked out on a surgeon who was cutting away two-thirds of
an ulcerous stomach, leaving him without an assistant at a critical part of
the operation. It was unethical and unforgivable—even though he could get
another surgeon immediately. Yet he had no right to treat me as he did
when I was trying to do my best.

Eventually, I returned to the hospital and as I entered the ward, Professor Louw was just emerging from the operating room. He was with Dr. Jim
Pittuch, who had taken my place.

"You should apologize to me," he said, curtly.

I looked at him but said nothing, and he went into his office. Dr. Pittuch
tried to calm me down.

"I know how you feel," he said, "but perhaps you should tell him you're
sorry."

"It wasn't my fault. I tried to do my best, but he kept at me and then
invited me to leave."

"Yes," said Jim. "He was wrong. But you were wrong to leave him and
you know it."

I knew it, but could not bring myself to apologize to Professor Louw. At
that moment, a nurse called me to the phone.

It was Appel and he was excited.

"Doctor," he said, "the dog's alive."

"Alive? You said it was dead."

"*Ya,* Doctor, but he's alive now."

"Didn't you burn him up?"

"*Nee,* Doctor, the incinerator would not start. So I left him there in the
bag until it got hot. Then when I came back I saw the bag walking around
and I did it."

"You did what?"

"I opened it up and there was that black dog trying to get out."

"Jesus."

"Now he's back in the cage and looks hungry. Can I give him anything?"

"Appel," I said, "go across the street and buy him the best ground filet
you can get."

Jim saw me coming back.

"Good news?"

"Yes," I said. "Where's Professor Louw? I think you're right, I should apologize."

Going toward his office, I thought how easy it was to be graceful—if you were a winner. He was looking at an X ray.

"I'm sorry, Professor Louw. I had no business walking out on you—no matter what."

He stood up and smiled with a slight nod. Then we shook hands.

"Chris, I was . . . I admit I was obnoxious today."

I hoped that would end it, but he went on.

"It's just that I expect more of you."

Now what did that mean? Was he going to start it all over again?

"I have such a high regard for you, I sometimes forget you don't have all the experience."

He sighed and glanced at the X ray.

"Also, I'm depressed today. We lost that little boy with intestinal atresia."

"That's too bad."

"Now I have to face the parents. That was on my mind, too."

"What happened?"

"How the hell do I know? We lose nine out of ten—you tell me why."

I knew only that intestinal atresia was a congenital disease. Babies were born with a gap in the bowel. It either ended in a dead end and then began again with no link, or also there was a slender strand of fibrous tissue like an earthworm between the two gaps. Either way, the child had a blocked bowel and unless it could be relieved, it would quickly die.

"You must have some idea why it isn't working," I said. "At least from autopsies."

"We open them up and there's the bowel we have joined—free of mechanical obstruction, yet obviously with no power of propulsion. That's what kills them. Why can't we anastomose a bowel in a baby when we can do it in an adult? I don't know. Chris, I just don't know."

"Do you have any theories?"

"Maybe it's due to a vascular interference. Children might be born that way because the blood supply to that segment of the bowel has been cut off. So a segment of bowel disappears. That's what I think, but I can't prove it."

"It shouldn't be too hard to prove," I said.

"No?"

"No, I can do it with dogs."

Professor Louw squinted his eyes as though trying to see a puppy with intestinal atresia.

"I don't see how," he said.

"If this comes from a blocked blood supply before birth, we can produce it artificially in an unborn fetus."

His eyes widened as though seeing a ward full of dogs with the disease.

"Hell, that's a bloody good idea, Chris."

Excited, he rose up on his toes.

"If you can prove this, it'll be a major event in pediatric medicine. It will give us a basis to finally get hold of it."

"All right," I said. "I'll do it."

Going back to the animal house, I began to think I was losing my mind. After fighting with Professor Louw and walking out on an operation, I had gone on to promise a medical discovery of world importance—using dogs. Yet I had lost most of my dogs and this was going to be far more difficult than anything I had ever attempted.

I had to open up a pregnant dog and expose its uterus. After that, the uterus had to be opened and the puppy removed. Then the puppy had to be opened up in order to tie off a portion of blood supply to the bowel—and so create an infarct which would disappear and create a gap, proving that intestinal atresia came from this defect. Then the whole process had to be done in reverse—the fetus closed and replaced in the uterus, then the uterus closed and replaced in the dog and, finally, the dog itself closed up. All of it had to be done in a way that would not kill or abort the fetus, allowing for its natural growth in the womb until the day of birth—hopefully with a bowel defect.

Obviously, this was going to require much patience, skill and time—months, maybe years. Suddenly it seemed too complicated to ever be possible. Why had I ever promised to undertake such an experiment—especially before Professor Louw? It was a mad gesture, born of my sense of guilt for having walked out on him.

Burdened with such doubts, I slowly climbed the steps to the animal house. On the second floor, I found the black dog that had survived both the heart operation and the threat of an incinerator. He lay on his side and looked at me and banged his tail on the floor of the cage.

"Hello," I said, and he banged his tail even harder, finally standing up. I opened the cage and he came out, a bit unsteady, and sat down before me.

"Take it easy, old boy. You have to get well."

I got a stethoscope and listened to the heart. It was normal and the reflexes seemed all right, too. Appel came in, and the dog stood up on all fours.

"I gave him some steak," said Appel.

"Good," I said. "Now we must find a home for him. He's done his share."

At least, I thought, we had achieved this. The stomach balloon, as a technique of hypothermia, had worked and doubled the operating time on the heart. It could also be used on brain operations—and, indeed, it eventually was at Groote Schuur, while also being modified later in the United States for treatment of gastric ulcers.

Looking at the black dog, I suddenly realized we could use this same technique in the search for the origin of intestinal atresia. By cooling down the pregnant dog, I would also reduce the demand for blood to the fetus—and so have a greater margin of safety. Maybe it would work. Maybe we could prove it.

"Appel," I said, "find a home for this dog right away. We've got to make room for some others—pregnant ones."

So we began, hoping that hypothermia would help. It became quickly evident, however, that there were more pitfalls than I had ever imagined—too many and too involved to be helped by body cooling. With the first half dozen dogs, I was not even able to finish the operation. Upon opening the uterus, the fluid escaped, the uterus contracted, and I could not return the puppy because there was no longer room for it. Also, two puppies, fifteen days from birth, began premature respiration, making it impossible to return them to a fetal state inside a uterus. Obviously, a puppy could not be removed from its womb. We had to find a way to do it without removal and without cooling, since it was possible that this also affected the unborn fetus.

At the next experiment, I made an incision from the tip of the twelfth rib to a midpoint between umbilicus and pubis, split the abdominal muscle parallel to the fiber, and opened the peritoneum. The uterus was then gently brought out of its cavity to allow easier handling. In a dog, it is shaped like a horseshoe and I felt for a fetus in the middle of the right horn. My plan was to rotate it in such a way that I could position the dog with its belly away from the placenta and next to a portion of the uterine wall. In this way, I could cut through to the fetus without damaging the placenta.

The fetus was thirteen days from its term and sufficiently formed to determine head, limbs, thoracic cage and tail. When we had it rotated, my assistant held it in position while I made a three-quarter-inch incision through the uterine wall and membranes. This immediately exposed what appeared to be a patch of fetal belly, and I seized its loose skin with a pair of forceps, drawing it into the opening in the uterus. In this way, the fetus served as a stopper, blocking the escape of its own precious amniotic fluid. Looking closely at the patch of fetal skin, I saw palpitations of its little heart and knew we were at the correct costal margin.

Using a pair of iridectomy scissors, a half-inch opening was made through its abdominal wall. It was a bit too high and I found myself immediately hampered by the large fetal liver which had to be retracted. After that, it was easy to obtain a loop of small intestine and I picked it up with trembling forceps. Victory seemed to be so near. All that remained was to obstruct the blood flow to that section of the bowel. This was done by tying off a pair of mesenteric vessels. Immediately, a part of the bowel turned blue, indicating that the blood supply had indeed been cut off.

Nothing else was needed. Gently the bowel was replaced in the puppy, the peritoneum and muscle layers were closed with catgut sutures. The skin was joined with black silk which would not be absorbed and so help us find the puppy after birth. Then the uterus was sutured, replaced, the abdominal wound closed—and we were finished.

For three days we gave penicillin injections, and all seemed well as we waited anxiously for birth. It occurred ten days later, but before we could get to the puppy the mother had eaten it up. I could hardly believe it was true and, after hearing the news, ran over to the animal house. Appel and Boots were looking at a litter of six puppies climbing over each other as they blindly sought their mother's nipples. I carefully examined each one. None had silk stitches on the belly.

"She just ate the other one up," said Boots.

"Impossible," I said. "Dogs aren't cannibals."

"Yes, Doctor, they cannibals all right. If they think anybody's messed around with their own, they'll just eat them up like cannibals."

I looked at the mother bitch with my puppy inside her and felt like weeping. There were not enough troubles in this. We had to be opposed by the mother, too. I could see her doing it: the tongue licking its offspring one by one until it felt one with the black silk stitches. Sensing something was wrong, the mother had eaten it up—rather than allow it to take milk into a blocked intestine and eventually die. There were so many forces in nature, and we knew so little. Instinctively, the mother was right. Yet we had to stop her.

"Appel, I'm going to make you and Boots dog nurses. Next time you sit up with the patient to make sure this does not happen again."

"Yes, Doctor."

The next one was born macerated—indicating what had happened to the other. The mother had eaten an offspring that showed no signs of life. This was unpleasant to contemplate, but it was a relief to know that the first one had not been eaten alive. Yet it did not solve our problems. We still had to obtain a living puppy.

We tried it again and once more it arrived macerated. The next dog aborted the entire litter the day after the operation. We continued, doing eleven others yet obtaining nothing more than abortion, death, or no puppy at all—probably eaten by its mother.

That totaled twenty attempts—each one ending in failure. Desperate, I began to read all the literature I could find on intestinal atresia, beginning with Meckel who also sought to explain the origin of the disease in 1812. Since then, hundreds of doctors and scientists had advanced conflicting theories—none of them proven. Two years previous, Professor Jannie Louw had published a paper reviewing seventy-nine cases and suggesting the disease might be caused by interference with the blood supply. This was not new. Denney and Sloan in 1932 suggested much the same. And Laufman in 1949 thought that strangulated bowel loops resulted in fibrous bands or simply disappeared, leaving a gap in the bowel.

Despite these many theories and the failure of so many before me, I became more than ever convinced we were on the right track. Atresia was initiated by interruption of the blood supply to a portion of the fetal bowel. This could be caused by stoppage in the mesenteric blood vessels to the bowel. It could also be caused by a volvulus or twisting of the intestine during its formative period.

This last theory led me to begin tying the intestine into loops, as well as blocking the mesenteric vessels. Yet I could not get one puppy to live after I touched it. We gave the dogs special foods and vitamin injections to make them stronger. We cut the operating time by one-third and we intensified the postoperative care. Yet nothing broke the terrible chain of abortion and death. It went that way through the winter and into the first spring days of September as our failures grew in number from twenty to thirty—and then forty.

Desperate, I went over every step in the operation—to see where we went wrong. One possibility remained: by moving the uterus, however gently it was done, we were interfering with the blood flow through its main vessels—and thus affecting the entire litter. I therefore tried it without allowing any portion of the uterus out of the peritoneal cavity. I did it this way on the forty-first dog and it died. The forty-second aborted. I intensified care and feeding, doublechecked on sterility, and went into the forty-third attempt. It was a black and white spotted mongrel due in fifteen days, and all seemed to go well as we returned her to the cage.

A few days later, a colleague told me he had won a Nuffield Scholarship in London. We had both applied for it. I felt I was more qualified, but it had been given to him.

"After I finish," he said, "I'll be professor of gynecology and obstetrics at another hospital."

"I hope you make it."

"It's in the bag, man. It's been confirmed."

"How can you say that before you're qualified?"

"I'm qualified already. I speak Afrikaans and my children go to an Afrikaans school."

"What does that mean?"

"It means a lot, Chris."

"I don't understand. What does language have to do with your getting a professorship?"

My mother tongue was Afrikaans. At the university, we had studied in both languages. Yet to write my thesis on tuberculous meningitis, I needed my intern, Dr. Eugene Dowdle, to help me put it in proper English.

"Also it's important to belong to the Dutch Reformed Church," he said.

This was even worse—a misuse of faith and church. I derived strength from prayer, and I could never sustain my life, nor nourish the memory of my father, if I did not believe in God. Yet to use this as a qualification for a professorship was beyond my ability—perhaps because it was never intended to be used in this way.

I had wanted that scholarship very much as the next step in my career. Louwtjie had helped me fill out the application and write the letter. She felt I would win since I had more experimental experience. I had a doctorate and a master's in internal medicine, as well as experience in surgery and pediatrics. I had also done research, including my current project to discover the cause of intestinal atresia. Perhaps I would be the first in the history of medicine to breach that tragic gap. Yet with all this I had lost the scholarship, and no one had asked me to be a professor of anything. I was professor of over a hundred dead puppies and their mother dogs.

"It shouldn't be hard for you either," he said. "Your father was a minister. You speak Afrikaans. And your children go to an Afrikaans school—no?"

"No, English. So they can speak to somebody else."

"Oh," he said, and stopped talking—perhaps because he saw my anger, even rage, at the misuse of a national tongue and a love for one's country. I felt then—and later, after having traveled, I became confirmed in this thought—that we were too provincial in South Africa, too out of touch with the world. It was like the springbok we found in the Karoo after fences had been erected. Unable to run free, the animals inbred and became progressively smaller. We had a similar problem—too enclosed in ourselves. Our fences had to come down.

"No," I said. "There's no future in that sort of thing."

"You don't feel Afrikaans?"

"Very much, but not that way. Not by putting up fences. That can only lead to little people."

"You mean the government policy?" he asked, referring to the separate development program of the government for colored and white people—apartheid.

"No, I'm talking about a mentality that finds its identity and security in a single language, a single church—anything single. That's a weakness . . . and you know it."

"I don't understand you," he said.

After he left, I felt more than ever alone, yet somehow stronger. On the way out, I went by the cage of the spotted dog.

"Do it," I said. "Do it in Afrikaans or in English or in any language, but do it, dog—for God's sake, do it."

It occurred when I was in J Theater, removing a kidney stone. Boots called me urgently.

"Doctor, the puppy's come. We have the puppy."

"Our puppy with stitches in it?"

"Yes, Doctor. Appel is standing by to make sure the mother doesn't eat it up."

"Don't do that. Go tell him to take it away. Tell him to put it in a separate cage. You hear me?"

"Yes, Doctor."

I began to shake with excitement and fear. Why, after all these months, would they still allow a puppy to remain in the same cage with its mother?

"She might gobble it up before we can stop her. You understand?"

"Yes, I hear you."

"I'm coming right down," I said, hanging up.

Professor Jannie Louw met me as I rushed from the dressing room. Since we were both due in theater in half an hour to remove an acute appendix, I was obviously going in the wrong direction.

"Where are you going, Chris?"

"Be right back . . . I think we made it!"

"My God, really?"

Running down the hill toward the animal house, I realized Professor Louw had known what I meant without my saying it. In a way, he was running with me and I laughed and ran faster. At the house, I climbed the stairs two at a time and found the boys sitting in front of the cage. Inside was a little black and white spotted puppy, lying on a yellow shirt. Then I saw Appel wore a work jacket over an undershirt. The yellow shirt was his own. How, I wondered, could they talk about putting up fences when these were ready to take off their shirts?

I opened the cage and took out the puppy. Along its belly were three interrupted 4-0 silk stitches—stitches I had put in fifteen days ago. The little dog curled about in my hand and for a moment I held it against my chest. Dear Lord, I thought, thank you for this little one. Then I put it back and closed the cage door as gently as would a night nurse in a ward.

"*Nee,* Doctor?"

"*Ya,* it's the puppy. I'll come back as soon as I can get away from the hospital. Don't leave the dog for one moment."

"*Nee,* Doctor, we're not going to move, and we're waiting for the celebration."

When I returned four hours later, they were still sitting there. Inside the cage, the spotted puppy lay asleep on Appel's yellow shirt. And next to the cage door something else had arrived—a little saucer of milk with an eye dropper.

I looked at the boys and said nothing. No words were needed. Between birth and death, there was to be no hunger. The illusion of life had to be kept, even though it came from an eye dropper and ended in a blocked bowel. It was the common covenant of the living: Life was more precious than death because it was there, before you. It lay curled up on a yellow shirt. You had spent a year trying to create it and now it was there and could not go hungry. Eventually the doctor was going to kill it and look at its intestines. But this would happen later, when the doctor came. Meanwhile, the little dog would live forever—even if forever was only going to be four hours.

"So we're ready?"

"Yes, Doctor."

"All right, bring it to the table."

We put it to sleep and opened it up—and there it was.

"My God, look at it."

I began to tremble. We had made it. It lay in a little spotted puppy on a wooden kitchen table—the end of a bitter parade of the death of dogs and dreams. It was the promise of life for thousands of babies. It was a devascularized puppy bowel with proximal and distal blind ends—classic intestinal atresia.

"Appel, Boots, *ons het dit gemaak* . . . we did it!"

They grinned happily.

"Dankie," I said.

"Dankie," they said.

"Can we do it again, Doctor?" asked Appel.

"Yes, I think we can do it now whenever we want."

It was almost true. After that, we succeeded eight out of ten times—doing it at various stages before birth to determine the full course of the disease, and proving what we had believed: (1) strangulated bowel resulted in a diaphragm that blocked the bowel, (2) a relatively small shutoff of blood supply resulted in interruption of bowel with a wormlike strand in between, and (3) larger closure caused complete severance of the bowel.

In surgical terms, this meant that Professor Jannie Louw and his colleagues around the world had lost eight of ten babies with this disease because they had sought to join pieces of bowel which had insufficient blood supply. This was because the extended ends of the blood vessels ran to the bowel like the delta of a river, spreading out far beyond the immediate area of the bowel gap. To successfully join such a segmented bowel, it would be necessary to cut back and discard at least fifteen to twenty centimeters of intestine, perhaps more. The new juncture, having a blood supply, would live, as would the child. So it seemed, and so it proved to be true. Professor Louw lost no more children. From his hand alone, thirty-five human beings are alive today who otherwise would probably not bear witness to the wonder and mystery of our world.

A few weeks later, I happened to meet Professor John Brock after lunch on the lawn before the medical school.

"I've been looking for you," he said. "How'd you like to go to Minneapolis?"

"Where?"

"The University of Minnesota at Minneapolis, to work with Professor Wangensteen."

I had no idea where Minneapolis was in America. It sounded like the place where they had the auto races. I had heard of Wangensteen, however, because we had a suction apparatus by that name.

"I just left there," said Professor Brock. Professor Wangensteen is very high on Alan Thal. He said if there are any more South Africans like Dr. Thal, to send them over."

He paused, squinting in the sunlight.

"You're the only one I know, Chris."

He waited for an answer. In the sunlight, on the lawn before the medical school where I had first learned the rudiments of medicine, where I had eaten my student sandwiches and talked of Karl Marx with Harry Kahn, now another door had been opened—America. How could I not accept it? But where the hell was Minneapolis?

"What do you say, Chris?"

"Yes."

"Are you sure?"

"Do you recommend it?"

I watched his lips shape the words. They came, as from an oracle pronouncing my fate.

"Oh yes. They are doing fantastic work in heart surgery, and they have built their own heart-lung machine. You will see medical history being made every day."

"Then I'm doubly sure."

Louwtjie agreed I should go. She said it on the phone, and we talked about it when I went home that evening. She was in the kitchen getting dinner.

"How long will you stay there?"

"I don't know. Alan Thal is still there and he left about two years ago."

"Will you be that long?"

"They're doing pioneer work in heart surgery."

"So what does that mean?"

"I'll stay as long as I need to learn all that's possible."

"All right," she said. "I'll keep my job here and you can apply for an Adams Scholarship. When we get that, I'll come over with the children."

Later, at dinner, she was very quiet. I tried to cheer her up, but nothing helped. Maybe, I thought, it would help to talk about it.

"It's strange," I said, "how I was ready to go. As soon as he asked me, I was ready to go."

Louwtjie said nothing.

"If we had not found the answer to atresia, I would never have felt free to go. But now I do—you know what I mean?"

Freedom went two ways. It went into something and away from it. It went into the search for the origin of atresia and there was no going away from that. Yet when the answer was found, there was freedom to go elsewhere, to choose another enclosing area of engagement. Freedom was the elective ability to choose your own cell, and an illusion that you could choose your own dreams.

"So I did not hesitate," I said. "And now we're going to America. Aren't you excited?"

She still said nothing.

"What's wrong, Louwtjie?"

"I know you have to go."

"And you, too, as soon as possible."

She bit her lip and avoided my eyes.

"It's just that I have to get used to being alone now and it's . . . it's hard to think that way."

In America, we were to have some difficult times. Yet none of it could ever diminish the splendid way Louwtjie accepted my sudden departure and the courage with which she set about to hold our family together.

PART V
AMERICA

CHAPTER 13

THE FLIGHT TO the new world of America was cradled in old and familiar emotions. Once more, there was the wonder of the boy leaving the garden of childhood, of the youth leaping across river rocks onto a new path toward high school, of the young man waving good-bye to his father as a train took him across the Karoo at night to the university at Cape Town.

It was again the leaving of all that was known and loved for the unknown—facing a challenge that was always greater than the one before it. It went that way and it kept happening, no matter what you did about it. At Beaufort West I had waved good-bye to my father and wondered why pigeons were trained to fly home while I had been taught to fly away from it. Then I had created my own home and filled it with a wife and children —only to have to wave good-bye to them, too.

Besides this, I had also said good-bye to Groote Schuur—the Big Barn. The hospital had been variously my classroom, training ground, battlefield —and home. Indeed, the Big Barn had been the Big Home. It had sheltered and fed me. It had shaped and inspired my dreams. Most of all, its charge of patients and doctors had given me the stimulus, perhaps even the strength, to keep going ahead. Yet I was leaving this as well, to begin again in another hospital where I would have to prove myself before some of the world's most skilled surgeons.

There was always somebody on the track ahead of you—another Daantjie Rabie. No matter how hard you ran it, he was up there in front. And when you closed in on him, he assumed different forms—a dogfish in the laboratory, a corpse in the morgue, a closed door at Ceres, an exudate in a child's brain, a puppy in a dog's uterus—and now a place alongside surgical pioneers in a foreign land.

On the plane, I tried to sleep but it was impossible. Besides the future challenge, there was a sense of being a prisoner of the plane and unable to turn back. It had been the same on the train to Cape Town, except that from its window you could see passing landmarks, and these helped prepare for the arrival. In the air, however, there was nothing but trackless clouds or empty blue space or total blackout—a mixup of day and night as if we were being shot through a tunnel, racing ahead of even the sun itself, only to land floundering at each airport along the way.

At New York a porter put my bag and overcoat on a trolley and together we worked our way through hundreds of people toward a money-change counter. I had never seen American currency and in the confusion tipped the porter ten dollars. He slipped it quickly into his pocket, put down my bag, and left. Then I realized my error and also that he had forgotten to leave my overcoat.

I ran after him and when I caught him, he turned about slowly to stare at me. He was a big Negro and he waited for me to speak first.

"Look, I've made a terrible mistake. I think I gave you ten dollars and I can't afford it. I want to give you one dollar."

For a moment, he said nothing. He was much darker than our Cape coloreds, and his eyes were the color of ebony in white pools streaked with yellow.

"Yes, you gave me ten," he said, and returned it to accept one dollar.

He had not said *"Baas"* or "Sir." It was simply "you"—as though we were equals, and perhaps it bore a suggestion that he was the superior one. Most certainly, these were not like the Cape coloreds. They were more Bantu, or one of the dark-skinned African tribes—tough, proud, and filled with an untouchable substance of self. It was going to be interesting to see how these white Americans lived with their Negroes.

The plane for Minneapolis touched down at Detroit and Milwaukee and by the time we arrived it was dark. It seemed as though we had landed in a white tunnel and when the door was opened, I saw that it was snow banked in high drifts along the runway. Never in my life had I seen so much snow—or felt so cold.

In the airport building it was warm and noisy, and I looked for someone waiting for me. There were people playing pinball machines, reading papers, sleeping in chairs, punching tickets behind counters—but no one for me. I got my bag and asked the airline clerk if there was a message.

"Your name again?"

"Dr. Barnard."

"No," he said and went on working without asking if he could help. This, quite obviously, was a very busy country. People did not have time to help each other. Professor Brock had given me a number to call at the university and I did it—learning what a nickel and dime were by how they went into the phone slot. I got through and eventually was met by Alan Thal, the other South African doctor. I did not know him well, but in Minneapolis it was like meeting a brother and we spoke Afrikaans.

"You must be cold," he said.

"Frozen . . . how can you stand it?"

"It's hard at first. Like some tea?"

I nodded and we drove toward his apartment, the streets a gray slush, the snow still white on the sidewalks and piled up into strange shapes on the trees. There was a frozen stillness and then, going over a bridge, we were hit by a wind that cut through car, overcoat, and underwear—colder than any wind to ever touch the Cape. They would never need my gastric balloon here. For hypothermia, all you had to do was open the window.

Over tea, Alan explained the arrangements.

"Until you find a room somewhere, you can stay in the doctor's bungalow where the interns live."

I nodded.

"And the Chief wants to see you tomorrow."

"The Chief?"

"Wangensteen."

It was a city where people were too busy to talk to you. But when it was necessary, they wasted no time.

"Have you met him?" asked Alan.

"No."

"He's incredible. Gets a new idea every minute."

"We have his decompression apparatus at Groote Schuur."

"There's that," said Alan, nodding, "and his peptic ulcer surgery and now the second-look business with internal cancer. He opens up old patients to see how they're doing, rather than take chances. A lot of boys say its unwarranted, but he doesn't give a damn. And actually he's saved a lot of lives doing it."

Thal was tall and blonde and at first had seemed rather shy and reserved. But he had no trouble talking about Wangensteen whom he had worked under before being transferred to another department.

"He refuses to accept anything as final and this can drive you mad. But it has made him the greatest teacher of experimental surgery today. Under him, Walt Lillehei and Dick De Wall built a bubble oxygenator that's done close to forty open-heart operations. There's something new here all the time."

"Sounds like what I want."

"Then you're lucky. How'd you manage it?"

I told him and only then did I realize that if I had won the Nuffield Scholarship, I would be in England now and not on this American frontier of surgery. Life was strange that way. It dealt you cards you could not read until after you had played them—or after they had been played for you.

Professor Wangensteen was much smaller than I expected and in a startling manner resembled my father. There were the same delicate features and white hair. The eyes were like my father's, too, and as he rose from behind his desk he looked at me as though we had met somewhere before.

"I've heard of you," he said.

I did not know what to say. The resemblance was unnerving.

Fortunately, the phone began to ring, mixed with brief appearances of his secretary. He waved me into a chair and took one call from Washington, asking someone for $5,000 to do research on a membrane oxygenator. In another call from Memorial Hospital in New York, he discussed a cancer patient. Next, there was someone I could not identify who caused him to laugh and to become angry within one minute. His voice, I decided, was sharper than my father's and more caustic. Also unlike my father, his mind raced ahead of subjects, like a scouting bird dog, rather than linger over them. Thal had been right: This man was a hunter.

Finally he faced me with a sigh and a smile.

"I gather you've been doing research on dogs."

"Yes, for intestinal atresia . . . establishing that it comes from vascular deficiency."

"Really?" he asked, immediately interested.

I described my experiments to him and he nodded with obvious pleasure. He interrupted at a few points, to understand better the technique I used, and from the way he asked the questions I could tell that my first impression was right. He looked like my father, but inside he was a hard taskmaster—like my mother. After a bit, he nodded as though he knew enough and had made up his mind.

"Good," he said. "I'd like you to continue these sorts of experiments. We need a new method for joining the esophagus and I have a project that needs to be explored . . ."

We were interrupted again by his secretary, and in the brief interlude I decided that I had made a mistake to talk about my work with dogs. He had the impression this was what I wanted to do and was therefore giving me more of the same. But the gullet of a dog did not sound the least bit interesting. Before I could find a way to tell him this, however, he began to enthusiastically explore the problem of replacing a section of the esophagus below the trachea.

"All right?"

"What?"

"Can you handle it?"

"Yes . . . of course."

There seemed little else to do other than agree to it and see what would eventually happen.

"Fine, you'll work in the surgical laboratory. My secretary, Mrs. Hans, will make all the arrangements. Check with her, and if you need anything else, come and see me."

He said no more, and I rose to leave.

"Happy New Year," he said.

"Yes, Happy New Year also to you, sir."

It was a day before the end of the year, yet he was already racing ahead of that, too.

After a brief fill-in from Mrs. Leontyne Hans, I left the building feeling somewhat lost and depressed. He had not asked how I wanted to extend my earlier work or studies. Instead, he had given me a problem in gastro-intestinal surgery that held no special interest or meaning for me.

I walked for a while along icy streets until I came to a block overlooking the Mississippi River. Dark and immense under the grey sky, it moved through a frozen world of snow, beyond the reach of seasons or the touch of time.

I felt very alone, and this feeling did not leave me. The next evening I went with some doctors to a New Year's Eve party. At midnight, everyone fell into each other's arms while I could only remember how Deirdre had cried when I left Cape Town. She had cried to see me go. Louwtjie had not cried because she was like my mother that way. But Deirdre was like my father, and she had cried for me.

The Minneapolis laboratory of surgical research was better equipped than anything we ever dreamed of having at Groote Schuur. Yet I felt lost in it. There were others working there—a Texan, a Philippine, a Burmese —yet each had his own project and I was alone, more alone than I had ever been before. In Cape Town I had two boys to help me and occasion-ally there were volunteer nurses and doctors. Here there was no one. Not only did I have to collect my own dogs, but also had to sterilize the instruments, put on the gown, and finally go into the operation without assistance.

I did the operation on the dog's gullet as requested—and the dog died. I prepared for another one, but with little feeling that this was going any-where. I did not like it, yet at the same time did not know what to do about it.

In the late afternoon, after everyone left, I stayed on, working up the experiment or simply sitting there doing nothing. When the cleaners came in the evening, I watched them sweep out the debris, and then they would go away. Around one o'clock, I would leave, walking awkwardly in over-shoes through icy streets to a little room I had found on East River Road. It was two miles away, but I went on foot to save bus fare as I had done years before at the university.

The room was a lonely place, and I wrote many letters home. When some came for me, I would read them over dozens of times—especially those from my father with news of old friends at Beaufort West. Louwtjie wrote of her work as a social welfare nurse, the children, some friends— and debts. We had never learned to write love letters to each other.

I became friendly with an intern, Jim Storey, who was from Dallas and fond of Dixieland music. We listened to records in his room and occasionally went in his old car to the River Road Inn where they had a jukebox, and we bopped about. My favorite was Dean Martin's "Memories Are Made of This," which seemed to wrap up everything for me. It was like living in a world seen through a wide-angled lens that was somewhat blurred. Finally, one day it was suddenly narrowed down into sharp focus on an event that dragged me back into reality, showed me what I wanted, and sent me once more into Professor Wangensteen's office to ask for it.

Another laboratory next to ours was used by Dr. C. Walton Lillehei and Dr. Vincent Gott, a young resident surgeon in charge of Dr. Lillehei's heart- lung machine. Vince Gott at that time was developing a method of retro- grade coronary perfusion—pumping blood backward through veins of the heart to facilitate operations on the aortic valve. This interested me and since he also had no assistant, I occasionally gave him a hand. After a bit, he asked me if I would like to watch him run the heart-lung machine in the operating theater. Having never seen this, I quickly accepted.

Perhaps I should have been prepared for what followed. After so many years and so much searching along the blunt anticline of life and death, it should not have made such an impact. Yet it did, and even now I can recall the details of that morning, the first time I witnessed the life of a human being held in a coil of plastic tubes and a whirling pump.

It occurred about two hours after the patient had been brought into the theater. He was a dark, hollow-eyed youth with a graceful body, and they quickly put him to sleep. After that, he was scrubbed from neck to thigh by a nurse, painted with an orange antiseptic, hooked up to electrode leads for heart and brain readings, entered with tubes into the bladder, a needle in the forearm, an electric thermometer in the rectum, covered with green towel- ing except at the chest—and then cut open in an oxbow incision from armpit to armpit across the fourth pair of ribs.

All of it was normal ritual in preparing the patient for chest surgery so that he would suffer as little damage as possible from all the ills that accompany knife wounds—even sterile ones. There were, however, a few features in this Minneapolis theater—Operating Room J—which we did not have at Cape Town. One was a glass dome in the ceiling that allowed students and surgeons to look directly down into the operating area.

To obtain this luxury, however, the surgeons had to pay a price. The dome, with its direct downward view, made it impossible to use the tradi- tional overhead lamp. Around the dome were a ring of bright lamps, but they were too far away and too diffused to wipe out shadows in deep heart surgery. To overcome this, Dr. Lillehei wore a headlamp with which he peered into the deeper recesses of the youth's chest as he and Dr. Richard Varco cut toward the heart.

It was a curious arrangement, for Lillehei moved the lamp with his head while the head itself had been deprived of the usual array of supporting tendon and tissue in the left neck—cut away with his lymph glands six years previous to remove a malignant tumor. Without this usual support, resulting in a declivity in his neck, one expected at first that his head would topple over to the side. It did not, of course, being sustained by auxiliary muscles and, even more, by an interior strength of mind and spirit that only later I would come to know and respect. At this moment, however, I was fascinated by the top-heavy assembly of lamp on a head that seemed to be perpetually lopsided, yet moved continually from one side to the other like some strange bird sensing a danger it could not see.

I could not look into the cavity of the young man. An observer in the glass dome with a pair of opera glasses could see more than either Vince Gott or myself sitting behind the waiting heart-lung machine—halfway between the operating table and the gray tile wall where there were light boxes holding X rays of the young man's heart which had an interatrial defect—a leak in the wall between its two upper chambers. An X-ray tab carried his hospital number and name. It was Greek, with so many consonants jumbled together that I could not even pronounce it. The first name was indicated by the initial "A." Did this stand for Achilles—bravest, handsomest and swiftest of the army of Agamemnon? And did they perhaps dip this youth by his heart rather than by heel into the same waters of the Styx, making his entire body invulnerable, Achilles tendon included—excepting for the heart whose unbathed upper atrium lay open as the one door of death?

So I wondered as we looked across the machine primed with four five-hundred-cubic-centimeter bottles of blood. And though unable to see directly into the operating area, I have since observed so many hundreds of hearts that it now seems I saw this, too, on that first day—the opening of the thin pericardial sac with the heart suddenly in view, twisting with each beat in its private world, its universe created twenty-three years ago in some womb's dark chambers where it began with a first beat that was to take it out of its cavernous cradle and into the world, beating at its own rhythm in perpetual midnight until this moment when Dr. Lillehei exposed it to the glaring blaze of his electric headlamp where it lay, autonomous and unheeding of this intrusion, as though all the poets and philosophers of the world had been right to consider it with wonder and awe. Here, indeed, was the seat of life, the base of all existence, the beginning and the end, the giver and the receiver, the springboard of life and death, the living animal inside the animal, the prime pump. . . .

"Pump on!"

It was Dr. Lillehei, looking at us now to see that the command would be obeyed, his head cocked at an angle with the lamp incredibly still in line, its beam falling now on the floor somewhere between our machine and the surgeons around the table.

Dr. Gott threw the switch, and the motor began, the oxygenator whirring into action, steel fingers of the pumps milking blood through the plastic tubes, which suddenly jumped as though they had actually become the great cardiac vessels of the human being on the table.

"What's the blood pressure?" asked Lillehei—and then, getting it, nodded his lamp.

"How much flow?" he asked Dr. Gott.

"Two thousand cubic centimeters."

The lamp nodded again, and then was beamed into the cavity as Lillehei began the final shutdown of the heart, tightening tapes around the caval veins, which sealed off any further flow of blood to the heart chambers.

We had it then. The machine took over for both heart and lungs. A motor in the center drove two pumps. One picked up the used venous blood, before it reached the heart, and brought it by tube to us to do the work of the lungs, while another pump sent the oxygenated blood back into the body through a tube attached to the left subclavian artery and so into the blood system. That was the heart. The lung was in the middle of this cycle: a column tube into which oxygen was bubbled—some of it going into the blood, some forming leftover bubbles. Since bubbles in the blood are lethal, it then passed into a debubbler coated with a chemical agent to break them up—going finally into a spiral tube or helix that removed any leftover air while also serving as a reservoir for oxygenated blood.

So the dark red liquid went through yellow plastic tubes, rolled onward by steel fingers, from machine to patient and back again—blood that would soon fill the empty heart, stir the wakened brain, pump through running legs, race with the touch of love, and swell in the tumescence of passion. The immensity of the spectacle was staggering, and the longer it ran, the more exciting it became.

This was more than a machine. It was the gateway to surgery beyond anything yet known. While it stood in for heart and lungs, vast repairs could be made inside the body. New valves could be put into the heart, maybe even a whole heart itself. We had already begun to transplant kidneys—why not a heart? Or even both heart and lungs? With improvement, this apparatus could also be used to save people from acute heart attacks. It could even hold in life those who had suffered heart death, keeping them alive long enough to make a testament, say good-by to their loved ones, a family, or even a nation. There was no visible end to where it would take us.

It could also be a gateway for my return to South Africa with training in open-heart surgery. Quite clearly, that was what I should be doing, rather than sewing up dog gullets. I had to learn how to operate this machine and then how to use it at the operating table, like Dr. Lillehei.

A new figure had come onto the track—latest successor to Daantjie Rabie. He wore a headlamp and he was out there ahead of all of us. But the race was only beginning and to prepare for what lay ahead, I needed to talk to Professor Wangensteen.

He received me the next day. It was not his usual visiting day, Thursday, but I was new and he was ready to be as helpful as possible. He wore a bright blue bow tie, like a spring bird, and on the desk before him lay a model pump for draining stomachs.

"How's the work on the dogs?"

"We've lost two, but maybe it'll be better with the next one."

"Good. We meet here every two weeks to report on our progress. You can fill us in then."

I nodded and knew the moment had come to tell him what I wanted, including dropping his experiments on dog gullets.

"Professor, I'd like to begin work on my Ph.D. in surgery, so that I can register at home and become a specialist surgeon."

"Very good. You know what is required?"

"Yes."

"It takes six years, but maybe you can do it in five."

"I don't have so much time, Professor. I have a family and children and very little money. I have to do it in two years."

"Impossible," he said, and began to toy with the stomach pump.

"I think I can do it."

"How can you?" he asked. "You have to spend a year in either physiology or pathology to get your minor. Then there's two years clinical service for your major. And then there's two years in a laboratory for your thesis —plus mastering two foreign languages. After that, you write the exams. It's five or six years, any way you look at it."

"No, not necessarily."

He squinted at me, and I realized I should have been less abrupt. This required careful handling. Yet, there was only one way to say it.

"You see, Professor, I've done most of it. I've done a hundred postmortems for tuberculous meningitis, so pathology can be my minor. I've done over two years in a laboratory and am ready to do a thesis on intestinal atresia with some important findings never published before. I've spent over two years in ward service and also done surgery. So that is done. As for the languages, Dutch is like Afrikaans and I'll learn German. So I can study pathology and languages for a year, prepare the thesis in the next one and be ready for exams within two years."

"No, we can't accept your two years spent in another clinical service or postmortems done elsewhere. You have to work at least two years in our hospital."

"All right, I'll do that and at the same time do everything else."

"You want to work all day in the hospital, and at the same time study pathology, do postmortems, prepare a thesis on atresia, learn two languages and be ready for exams in two years?"

"Yes sir."

"When will you sleep?"

"I don't need much."

He smiled and for a moment said nothing. Then he nodded.

"All right," he said. "Let's see what happens. For a start, you can switch over to my service."

I smiled, and he stood up, giving me his hand. As I took it, I knew from the way he looked at me that he expected me to succeed, and I could not fail him. It was a relief to feel this and to know that it was there.

"Stick to it, and you'll make it."

They were almost the words my father always said to us before a big exam—*sterkte, hoor!* I did not know how to reply and, in a confusion of emotions, could hardly mumble my thanks before leaving.

Once outside, I felt like flying and shouting to the world. Everything was in its place—even winter. The sun was shining and the icicles were as bright as Kimberley diamonds. Two quarreling birds fell from a tree into the snow, then flew up again in a shower of powdered crystals. On a hill, some children playing with sleighs shouted happily as they zoomed down its slope. And then one of them spilled, rolling over into the snow. I ran up to look at her and she lay there laughing—just as Deirdre used to do when we played horsey.

Walking on toward the river, I thought that winter could be swept away with a pair of wings or a laugh—but not a memory. Memories were made of toughter stuff. And this one would never die. I had everything but it. I knew where I was going at last. My goal lay ahead—two winters away. But until Louwtjie came with Deirdre and Boetie, there was going to be a little bit of winter everywhere.

CHAPTER 14

A NEW LIFE BEGAN after Professor Wangensteen transferred me to his service. He handled all the major cancer operations—most of them desperate cases—and many patients died. This depressed me greatly. Also, the method of working was different than ours in South Africa. We took notes differently, used different terms, and even ordered drugs in another way. On top of this, I was given menial tasks and allowed only to assist at operations—hold retractors, put up intravenous drips, and do dressings as though I had just graduated from medical school. It was particularly painful to be subjected to this when Professor Wangensteen was in theater. He must have known I was more than an intern. Yet unlike Professor Jannie Louw, he never helped me go beyond my role in the ritual of his service. Quite obviously, I was going to have to seize whatever I wanted.

In the evenings, after a day with patients, I was free to begin experiments on intestinal atresia, reproducing all the conditions I had achieved at Groote Schuur. This time they were to be photographed and recorded for my Ph.D. thesis. Also, here I knew what I was doing and, despite the difficulties of always having to work alone, began to enjoy the laboratory—regaining at night a sense of personal worth that I lost by day.

Yet the nights were always lonely, especially when I was not busy with an atresia experiment, and occasionally I went out with Dr. John Perry, my chief in Professor Wangensteen's service. He had a girl friend, Jenny, who shared an apartment with some other girls, and sometimes she asked me over with John for a dinner of Indian curry with beer. It was a pleasant relief, but the walk home to the empty room on East River Road was always melancholy and filled with apprehension that Louwtjie would never arrive in America.

And then one evening I found a letter waiting for me on my bed. It was written by Louwtjie and I knew this was it, even before reading the first lines:

Everything is happening here. All of a sudden they told me you have the Adams scholarship. Some of your so-called friends didn't want you to have it, but you got it anyway, which shows you that God is on our side . . .

This sounded too much like my mother claiming God played only on her team. I raced on through the rest of the letter to find out what else had happened—with or without God's help.

. . . They tell me the cheapest way is this little cargo ship. It's called *African Star,* and leaves here June 6th. That seems okay, since its after the children finish mid-term. I've never been on such a boat, but . . . it arrives in the U.S.A., Boston U.S.A., at the end of the month.

I don't know how to begin to get ready. There's all that snow you talk about and the children have no clothes for it . . .

This allowed less than three months to prepare for them and very quickly, it became evident that I was going to need all of it. Furnished apartments were too expensive. The only solution was to take an empty flat and fill it with second-hand furniture—or whatever I could find. After two weeks, I discovered a vacant half of a duplex on the outskirts of town, near the airport. Airplanes came in for a landing over the rooftop, but we would have to get used to it—it was all we could afford.

I began then to haunt the second-hand shops for old furniture—especially the Salvation Army. To get the money needed, I shoveled snow off walks in the neighborhood of my rooming house. This shook my landlady: "You're a doctor with lots of degrees and here you are, shoveling snow like someone on welfare."

I laughed and kept shoveling. When the snow melted and the lawn needed cutting, I did that, too. I also washed cars and did other odd jobs. Still, this was not enough, and at the hospital I began to work as a night nurse. Wealthier patients wanted extra attention and were ready to pay five dollars a night. So instead of studying in the laboratory, I brought my books into the rooms of cancer patients and carried on, between the duties of a male nurse.

Some of the resident doctors thought this strange and implied it was beneath the dignity of a doctor. My dignity, my pride was not measured there. It lay in being able to have a home for my family when they arrived. Others understood this more easily. My landlady gave me some chairs, a few shelves, and a box that she said was perfect for special papers. The woman in the house next door lent me some sheets. And even the manager of the University Bank broke protocol—lending me all the money needed for a 1956 blue Chevrolet.

In this way, with the help of others and by a great deal of scrambling, our new house was assembled. To make it easier for Louwtjie landing in a strange country, I arranged for the American Express to meet her when the boat arrived and help her onto a direct flight to Minneapolis. Since the arrival of her cargo ship was not certain, I expected a phone call from the travel agency, with details of her flight.

I was in the cancer ward with a dying patient when a call came from Boston. It was Louwtjie and she was very upset.

"Hello, Chris."

"Hello, sweetie, how are you?"

"I'm miserable. I don't know what to do."

"What's wrong?"

"They're calling me," she said.

"Who's calling you?" I asked.

"En daar roep hulle my," she said, thinking I could understand it better in Afrikaans.

With that she hung up, leaving me in a state of frenzy that lasted about six hours until another call came through—this time from New York.

"I have to catch a plane," she said.

"What are you doing in New York? You're supposed to be on your way to Minneapolis."

"I'm miserable," she said again.

"Louwtjie, what are you doing in New York?"

"There's no plane to Boston—I mean from Boston to Minneapolis. They put me on this one."

"Who did?"

"A Negro porter. Now they say I must go to Chicago. I told them I don't want to go to Chicago. That's where all the gangsters are. But they say I have to go because it's closer to Minneapolis than New York. I don't know what to do. I don't know what I'm doing here. I'm miserable."

"For God's sake, Louwtjie, calm down. Let me talk to the airline people there. Where are the children?"

"Here," she said, and a man came on the line, giving me details of her connection.

The flight was to arrive at three o'clock, and that night I polished the floors of the flat while looking at a boxing match on the television set I had gotten as a surprise for Louwtjie. Then I turned down all the beds and laid out the surprises for the children—a train and cowboy suit for Boetie, a doll's house for Deirdre.

I drove to the airport ahead of time because every time a plane zoomed over the house, I thought it might be them. I did not want to be late—not for this experience that had become so precious to me.

I saw them enter the terminal before they saw me. Louwtjie looked tiny, and her face was hard without a smile. Deirdre was dragging a little doll, and Boetie looked at every man he saw as though it might be his father.

"Hello, hello!" I said, running up to them.

Louwtjie saw me and walked the last two yards with her eyes closed, shaking her head. It was not going to be good. Once in my arms, she let it out.

"I hate this country. When can I go home?"

She was tired, I knew, and she did not know what she was saying.

"Hello, my *skattebolle,"* I said to the children, grabbing them as though they were indeed little treasure bundles.

There was a wild fright in their eyes—harvest of their mother's panic. I kissed them again, but it did not help. They did not even seem to recognize me.

"I hate this place," said Louwtjie. "I want to go home."

"I have a lovely home for you," I said. "I have furniture. I have a TV, I have a little train for Boetie . . ."

"I don't want to know about trains," said Louwtjie. "I just want to sleep for at least twenty hours."

I had not mentioned the car. Walking toward it, I thought this surprise would certainly delight them all. With this car, we could drive out of the city and see the lake country. We could even go to Duluth, or almost anywhere.

"There's our car," I said.

Boetie was in my arms, and I held Deirdre by the hand. Both of them blinked at the car and then at me.

"Where are the bags?" asked Louwtjie.

"Here they are," said the porter.

"It's our own car, Louwtjie," I said.

"I feel sick," said Boetie.

"Me, too," said Louwtjie.

I looked at Deirdre and she looked back at me while hugging her doll. She was six now.

"You like it, Deirdre?"

She nodded and smiled, and I bent down to kiss her, but the porter broke that up, too.

"Where you want these bags, mister?"

Once in the car, I thought Louwtjie would be able to relax—but no.

"This is insane," she said. "Everybody drives on the wrong side of the road. Do you know how to stay on the wrong side of the road?"

"Yes. I'm doing it."

South Africa, like most everywhere else in the world that had been stamped with a commercial imprint of the British Empire, went on the left.

"It's been that and everything else," she said, "from the time I entered this country. In Boston there was not a solitary soul. American Express weren't there. There were only two people, and they were speaking Afrikaans—two missionaries. Afterwards this American Express chap came along and said, 'I'm terribly sorry, Mrs. Barnard, this boat is late—you have missed your flight to Minneapolis.' He left me and I got into a taxi which went on the wrong side of the road, like now, with the two children—it's on the wrong side of the road as far as I'm concerned, and I thought, 'Ooh, where am I going?' I went to the airport, the first person that I saw was a Negro, and I thought I'm going to ask him, that reminds me of home. So I went up to this bloke, and I said, 'Look, I don't know how to use the phone here, I wonder if you could put a phone call through to my husband in Minneapolis. So he first said to me, 'There's no plane to Minneapolis now, the best thing for you is go to New York.' I said, 'New York? But that's further away.' He said, 'Yes, go to New York, catch a plane from there and try to get to Minneapolis.' Then he said, 'But there's nothing at the moment, so you just sit and wait.' So I sat there, and this Negro was very kind. He said, 'All right, Ma'am, I'll put this call through.' So I got through to the hospital, you see, and the woman said, 'Sure I'll call your husband, he's waiting to hear from you.' Then I said, 'Hello, Chris,' and you know what happened then. They said, 'Mrs. Barnard, if you don't board flight so-and-so you'll miss this plane to New York.' So I got onto this plane with the two kids dragging along, and we got to New York. They said to me, 'Now you have to go to the Idlewild Airport.' I said to them, 'But my luggage, what's happened to my luggage?' It comes down the chute and goes round and you've got to grab, but I don't know these things. In the end I realized, well, this thing is going round and round, I better grab while I can, so I got hold of my luggage and got hold of a Negro again, and he called a taxi for me. I said I had to go to Idlewild Airport if I can get a plane from there. By then it was dark, and the children were miserable. I got into that taxi and I thought, 'God, where am I going? This country, I don't know it, I don't know the people, I know nothing.' "

Once in the house, I thought, she would relax. When she saw our home, the fear would fall away and she would feel secure. She would have a sense of being in the center of our lives and lose her panic.

Unfortunately, when we arrived there seemed to be an unusual number of planes coming in for a landing—red and green lights, black shapes against the sky, descending with a roar that seemed interminable.

"My God," said Louwtjie, "do we live on a landing field?"

"The airport is not far away," I said, unable to think of anything else.

"Sounds like it's in the back yard," she said.

"Mommy, mommy," cried Boetie.

"I know how you feel," said Louwtjie.

"Wait till you see inside," I said. "You don't hear so much in there, and it's very comfy."

Inside, I took Louwtjie from one room to the next: two bedrooms, a lounge, a kitchen, and a pantry.

"There's a basement, too," I said.

"Basement?"

"Cellar. Everyone has a cellar here."

"Why?"

I didn't know why except you could put bags there. I began to feel very sad. Even this brought no smile, no word of happiness, only suspicious questions indicating it was not perfect or not wanted. It was like my mother going over the linoleum floor after I had polished it, finding a little speck of dust: "Look at this, you missed it and here and here"—tumbling down one castle after another and not even knowing it. Perhaps that was the most painful part—they were unaware of what they did because your feelings did not count.

Without bothering to unpack her bags, Louwtjie got into bed and continued her story as though she had seen no car, no house, and no furniture that had been obtained by moving a ton of snow, serving a landlady, mowing lawns, washing cars and emptying bed pans before the smirks of other doctors.

"Then I got to Idlewild Airport, and I asked the taxi driver, 'How much?' He said 'One dollar fifty.' Look at me, I was on that boat for three weeks and should have learned all about the money—but not me—I had a jolly good old time and I never worried about the Yankee money. Well, I don't really know what a dollar fifty is, so I give him a five dollar bill. He said, 'Thanks for the tip,' and then I realized, 'Look, woman, now you've got to keep your wits together because they might think you are a wealthy woman traveling around here and everybody is going to take money from you.' "

In bed, I chuckled.

"What's so funny?"

"I did the same thing and had to run after the man to get it back."

"Well, I walked into this Idlewild Airport, and it was the maddest and most terrible experience I have ever had. Millions and millions of people milling around, and in one corner there were people gambling, you know, they were playing dice and things. That looked bloody silly in an airport, you know, and the kids said they were hungry, and I thought, 'Oh, my dear, I must go and get some food.' So I went up to one desk, and they said, 'No, you've got the wrong desk.' In the end I got to the right desk with all my luggage. And they said to me, 'Look, there's a plane at ten or eleven o'clock tonight as far as Chicago.' I said, 'Chicago! I don't want to go to Chicago. All I know about Chicago is the underworld gangsters . . .' "

I do not know where she ended. I fell asleep more or less at that point. I know all of it because she recounted it again the next day. And whenever anyone would listen for months afterwards, she went through it again.

The trip had been a traumatic experience, and I expected it to wear off. But events and people seemed to combine against it. Four days later, an airplane failed to make a proper landing and crashed three blocks away from us. I heard about it by phone when I was again in the cancer ward.

"Chris, when are you coming home?"

"Why?"

"A plane just crashed next door and killed three families."

"What?"

"Three families, except one little boy who went fishing. Just killed them all. What do you think about that?"

"Think of it?"

"Yes, think of it. After all, it's your family that's out here on this landing field. Only here, that's what I say."

"Only here . . . what?"

"Only in America could this happen. I was looking at the TV when it happened. The whole house shook. The iron nearly fell off the board. It's awful."

It was awful, all right. When I got there, there was a crowd around the ruined houses, people waiting to see a corpse brought out of the rubble.

"It's terrible the way people look at things like that," said Louwtjie.

"Then why are you looking?"

"Because it's next door, that's why. You know what that means? It could happen to your wife and children."

I said nothing, and she went on.

"How can people live like this? It's like going to sleep inside a motor. That's America for you . . . airplanes crash on houses."

"Maybe," I said, "and maybe there's something in it that's of value. A desire to go on and on, looking for something new, rather than hold on and wait for it to happen to you."

"Well, this little American family didn't go anywhere. It happened to them sitting at home and it came right through the roof."

For her, the dangers assumed varying shapes. A hand without an engagement ring, a town of strangers in a valley, an unpaid bill in the mailbox, a contagious disease hospital, and now an airplane through the roof.

Nor did this strange land have a particular understanding of Louwtjie's world. One morning she came to see me at the hospital. The children were with her, and a doctor heard her talking to them in Afrikaans.

"You're Dr. Barnard's wife?"

"Yes."

"Is that Zulu?"

"Zulu?"

"You're speaking to your children in Zulu?"

"Yes, Zulu," said Louwtjie, flaming with anger. "We always use it before stripping off our clothes for a raiding party."

She was still fuming like a Zulu when I arrived with John Perry.

"These people think we're all barbarians. That neighbor of ours, Mrs. Skinner, came by this morning with some cookies for the children and a newspaper showing Table Mountain. 'Here,' she said, 'is that lovely Table Mountain you always talk about.' I thanked her for it, then I saw there was another photo, a policeman arresting some coloreds. It said, "South Africa —the Beautiful and the Sad," and I told her this paper didn't know what it was talking about. You know, she said that everybody knew we arrested all our blacks at night and locked them up, otherwise they wouldn't come to work. I thought of our little Lizzie, and how I loved her, and here was this awful woman. I almost threw her cookies in her face."

"Did you?"

"When she left, the doorbell rang and there was a young Negro selling magazines to go through college. I was still furious with the Skinner woman, and I thought, 'Hell, here's a Negro, and let's see what he says.' So I asked him in and I told him it was the first time I could talk to a colored person. 'Naturally,' he said. 'You live in a restricted area.' And then he told me no Negroes were allowed in our neighborhood. They could come to the door and sell magazines but they couldn't buy a house because if they bought it, the value of all the other houses would go down. Can you imagine it? We have airplanes crashing on our heads, but they worry more about keeping away Negroes than airplanes!!"

John Perry sighed. "It's sad and true," he said. "We still have a long way to go."

"You see, Chris? They have apartheid—only it's hidden. Ours is out in the open. We have five nonwhites to one white so we're afraid they'll take over. They have ten whites to one Negro and are frightened of the same thing but won't admit it. I prefer our honesty. We haven't solved the problem, and we admit it. They haven't either, but won't admit it."

Louwtjie's belief that America was a dangerous place to live was further confirmed on the first day of school. She dressed Deirdre and Boetie in the school uniforms they had worn in South Africa and sent them off. They came back that night, bruised and beaten by other schoolchildren.

"They were beaten up because they looked different," she said.

Deirdre had a black eye, and Boetie limped.

"This is a violent country and a violent people. You have to be the same as everyone else or they beat you up. That's how it is, and they say we're cruel to the blacks!"

Despite this, the children loved it and, unlike their mother, quickly adapted. When winter returned, I took them ice skating, and almost immediately they began to skim over the ice. I had a hard time. My feet hurt terribly, and I clung to the rail hoping the pain would leave. A little girl skated by and said, "Why don't you let go and skate—are you chicken?"

I tried to do it, but the pain was too much. I had borrowed my skates from John Perry and told myself it was that. The pain continued afterward, however, and one toe became swollen. I thought I might have fractured a small bone, but did nothing about it.

There was no time for it. What with family, work, and studies, there was little left for myself and often too little for the family. With Professor Wangensteen's help, I had been transferred to surgical pathology. It was required for the degree and a full-time job. In the laboratory, we examined surgical specimens taken from patients with diseases—cutting them up, making sections, and slides for projection. Eventually, there were over a thousand of these, and we had to know them all.

Meanwhile, I had to also continue my atresia experiments with dogs as well as study German. To do this, Dr. Lober, the head of the pathology department, allowed me to spend a couple of hours in the animal laboratory, and also attend an occasional German class on the university campus. Nights were spent on research for the thesis or once again in the animal laboratory.

Early in the morning I studied pathology slides with another doctor, Gil Campbell, who was preparing for his board exams in surgery. We used to meet in a diner at 6 A.M.—for a stack of pancakes with maple syrup and hot coffee. Someone would put a nickel in the jukebox, and the place would rock with jazz. At that hour, there was usually some chap half asleep drinking a cup of coffee, another eating bacon and eggs without enthusiasm, and someone else figuring out the day's races. The jazz used to wake me up and gave me energy, and I liked it. There was something distinctly American about this scene—lonely men, ham and eggs, and the music blasting away, "Annie doesn't live here any more . . ."

After breakfast, we would go to the pathology department and study our slides for an hour and a half. The remainder of the day was divided into lab work in pathology, experiments on dogs, and classes in German. Besides these labors, there was something else—constant, relentless, and almost monstrous in its finality. These were postmortems, which also formed part of pathology. We had to do them at all hours and many at night. In Cape Town a patient dying after dark is placed in a refrigerator until the next day. But Americans want it done immediately. So the phone often rang at night, waking up both Louwtjie and myself, forcing me to get dressed and drive to the hospital or some remote funeral parlor.

During this period, the pain in my foot spread to the joint, then to the other foot. I decided it was a touch of rheumatism and did nothing about it. Then my hands also began to swell and developed pain. Finally a specialist at the medical center gave me an examination and the terrible verdict: rheumatoid arthritis—a crippling disease with no known cure.

It was the same affliction that had deformed the first patient I had treated as a student: an old lady whose terminal state necessitated her being bathed and fed by others. This was what lay ahead; and before it occurred, there would be the slow crippling of my hands.

I tried not to think about it, but it was there all the time, reminding me of its continuing progress by flashes of pain. What was the use of continuing, if my hands would soon fumble in the tying of a simple overhand knot, or even tremble with a scalpel? At night the pain seemed worse. You could feel it going through the muscles and swelling the joints. Often I turned on the light, while Louwtjie lay asleep, to try and measure the extent of its hold upon me—telling myself it was nothing. Yet in the morning, my feet would be so enlarged I could hardly get into my shoes. Eventually, it spread to my shoulders and Louwtjie began to help me put on my shirt and coat. Every step, every act was made with pain.

We tried various medicines, even guava leaves and brake fluid, which Louwtjie claimed had miraculous powers. Yet nothing helped, and I dragged myself through each day, convinced that there was nothing else to do other than go on to the bitter end.

After a few weeks, however, the disease appeared to level off. My hands remained swollen, but they did not get worse. I returned to the specialist.

"You seem to have a high resistance to the disease," he said. "Perhaps it will stabilize at this point. Perhaps it will not cripple you. We can only watch it—and stay active. The more you move, the better it is."

So there was a chance of not becoming a cripple. The pain would be there, deep as old roots. But if the disease went no further, some years remained.

I walked out of the doctor's office feeling greatly relieved, almost elated. Before it happened, before I had to accept people looking upon me as a pathetic bundle, some time remained. Years later, looking at terminal heart patients who believed that a valve might save them from total disaster, I could understand how important was this promise of a little bit of time—a month, a year could seem like a lifetime.

If it was helpful to keep moving, there was every reason for improvement. For there was no chance of rest, especially with constant calls to handle postmortems in various parts of the city. One of these came on New Year's morning when we had planned to drive out to the country. I tried to get out of it, but it was impossible. Many Americans had killed themselves celebrating the New Year, and their bodies were scattered about in morgues and funeral parlors all over Minneapolis. I had to go.

It was on the outskirts of the city, and there were many delays before I could begin. There were other delays as I did the autopsy—an old lady with disseminated cancer of the breast—and it was dark when I returned home. Louwtjie was very angry.

"The dead come before the living in this house," she said.

"Listen, sweetie, that's not true, and you know it."

"The only way I can be sure you'll keep a date with me is to drop dead."

Earlier, someone had sent flowers to the house, but Louwtjie had sent them away.

"Did you send me flowers?"

"No."

"That's what I told the man. My husband wouldn't send me flowers. But he insisted and showed me my name."

"Are you sure they weren't from someone else?"

"Who would send me flowers? I don't know anyone in this country. I'm in Siberia, that's where I am—living in an igloo."

"Maybe someone did send them to you. Did you open up the card?"

"No," she said.

She learned it the next day.

"They were from South Africa," she said. "From my office, from every-one in the office. I asked them to send me the flowers again, but it was too late. They had sent the money back, saying Mrs. Barnard didn't exist."

She began to cry, and I knew it was going badly in a way I had never expected.

"I think I should go home, Chris."

"No, Louwtjie."

"Yes. You are never here. I'm tired of living on a breadline. We have no money. My parents might die, and I'll never see them again. The children have awful American accents, and I'm miserable."

"No, Louwtjie, no."

I convinced her to stay, but it did not last long. A month later, I came home to find her furious with Mrs. Hans, Professor Wangensteen's secretary.

"She heard that I want to go home and came to tell me this would be a terrible mistake. 'Your husband,' she said, 'has a great future in America. You shouldn't take him back to a backward little country like South Africa.' Backward! Oh God! I told her off. In South Africa, airplanes don't crash on our heads. Our children aren't beaten up at school. We don't cheat on apartheid. And we are not a rude people."

She had booked passage home. It was done, and there was nothing I could do to make her stay.

"You finish your studies and I'll be waiting for you there," she said.

In order to be with them a little longer and also spare Louwtjie the nightmare of a return flight, I obtained leave from the hospital, and we drove East. The children wanted to see Washington and we stopped there first. Of all the monuments, the Lincoln Memorial was most impressive—especially for Deirdre. She had learned about Abraham Lincoln and the American Civil War in her school at Minneapolis, and now, suddenly, he was before us in Georgian-white marble, sitting in a great chair, immense as a god—yet with a very human face.

"He looks so sad, Daddy."

"He was sad much of the time."

We were alone. Louwtjie had taken Boetie to try and get some cherry blossoms for her scrapbook.

"Why was he so sad?" she asked.

"Well, there was the Civil War that you know about."

"To free the slaves and . . ."

Her voice trailed off. On the stone wall opposite, was carved a tablet.

"Come," I said, "let's read it together."

We read it slowly, word for word. She read the parts that were easy, and I read the others:

Fourscore and seven years ago, our fathers brought forth on this continent a new nation . . . conceived in liberty, and dedicated to the proposition . . . that all men are created equal . . .

I paused, and Deirdre stopped, too, while we both looked up at the massive figure with the sad eyes.

He must have known that all men are not created equal. They had different colors, unequal abilities, and varying chances of survival. Actually, all men were created unequal but with the common goal of a free life. In that struggle, they should have equal rights. This was what Lincoln meant: All men were created to have equal rights. It included the freedom to mix—but also the freedom to *not* mix.

How could you hold onto both freedoms in the American South—or South Africa? Should it be given to those who might abuse it? It was easy to write editorials or to tell high school students that law and order could protect the minority and insure the rights of all men. It was also easy to ask where on earth had this been tried and long endured. It was more difficult, however, to do something about it—to continue a search for the solution. Everything was there, in the search, and it had to go on. Apartheid, as a holding action—as a no-search—was wrong. As a system of continuing separate development toward equal rights for all, it was something else. Perhaps it was not the best answer, but for the moment it was the only one we could handle.

Deirdre began to read again, and some of the words were strange to her. So I read them slowly.

. . . that we here highly resolve that these dead shall not have died in vain . . .

"The Negroes?" she asked.

"Yes, and the white men who died for them. But it means more than that, Deirdre. It means everybody who fought for freedom. That includes your Boer ancestors who crossed into the Transvaal in covered wagons like these Americans. They fought, too, at the Battle of Blood River, and they had their Alamos. And as you know, daughter, we are also highly resolved that they shall not have died in vain."

Deirdre nodded and began to read on by herself.

. . . that this nation, under God, shall have a new birth of freedom—and that government of the people, by the people, for the people shall not perish from the earth.

The boat was to sail from New York, so we had a few days there, too. It was Boetie's birthday, and we got him some toys. Louwtjie wanted to take home a pair of shoes bought on Fifth Avenue, and we spent one day looking for these, as well. I had car trouble and ran out of money with nowhere to cash a check. Several banks refused me, until I became desperate and insisted that one of them phone the University Bank in Minneapolis to clear a fifty-dollar check—which they did with little grace. New York is no place to be without friends or money.

Eventually I put my family on the boat—it was now the *African Planet* —and said good-bye, leaving quickly; I could not bear to see Deirdre cry again. Nor did I want her to witness the tears of her father.

It was about a thousand miles to Minneapolis. I drove all night, and the next morning slept for an hour in the car next to a highway diner. Then I went on through that day and again into the night when I ran into a violent snowstorm.

It was nearly midnight when I got home—or what had been my home and was now empty. I walked from one room to another, knowing that every sound I made was all there could ever be. Never again would there be the murmur of their voices, a sudden laugh, a little cry. On the floor in the children's room was a toy Indian, its head knocked off. In the kitchen where we stacked dishes, lay Deirdre's red hairband. Louwtjie's closet had a pair of worn sandals I had given her last summer, and on the dresser was an empty jar of face cream.

As I got into bed, a plane roared overhead, and I remembered how it was—almost a year ago—when every plane carried a band of angels while I polished the floors, laid out the toy train and cowboy suit, and then raced to the airport. What had happened? How had I failed them? I did not know, but in the dark I knew I could not live in this house any more. I had to find another home, another place to live and finish my studies.

CHAPTER 15

A WEEK LATER I relinquished the house, sold the television set with some furniture, and gave the rest of it away—moving into the home of Mrs. Shear, an elderly lady who no longer had husband or children, and in exchange for company gave me a comfortable room and use of the garage. She was both gentle and kind, and I stayed in her home for the remainder of my time in Minneapolis.

It was also the time for other changes. Finally, I could go into heart surgery and learn how to use the heart-lung machine. Professor Wangensteen agreed, and in preparation for this I was placed in the service of Dr. Richard Varco as a senior resident. This was an advancement over my earlier work with Professor Wangensteen, where I was only a junior. Now I could assist directly with the operations and it was immediately rewarding.

Dr. Varco was the first major surgeon to take an interest in my surgical technique. Above all else he taught a respect for the human body and its tissues. His major lesson has remained with me.

"Nothing must be crushed or tied or burned unless there is a reason for it. Eventually, the body must repair every trauma you create. If it has to use energy to recover the damage you have done, it cannot use it to fight the essential disease we want to cure."

He was a short, stocky man with short, fat fingers, and you would never guess that those fingers could be so beautiful and delicate inside a wound. I spent a pleasant three months working with him. But he did less heart surgery than Dr. Lillehei, and when offered the chance to go on the Lillehei service as a senior resident, I quickly accepted.

So began eleven crucial months of training under Dr. Lillehei. In the first phase, I learned to operate the heart-lung machine. It was the role Dr. Vince Gott had when I first saw the machine in operation. Floyd Hamrick was still the pump technician, and together we assembled the pump every morning before an operation. A favorite of his was *"Mélodie d'Amour,"* and we used to sing it while hooking up the pump apparatus before the arrival of the other doctors and nurses.

After a few weeks I could hook up the machine blindfolded, as well as anticipate every demand to be made by the operating surgeon. At that point Dr. Lillehei moved me over to his side at the table, and into the ward as his chief resident. This put me finally in the thick of it.

In the morning I would come in and make the rounds of Dr. Lillehei's ward, then prepare the patient for surgery—weigh him in, see him positioned onto the operating table, and open his chest in preparation for coupling to the heart-lung machine. After that Dr. Lillehei would scrub, connect the patient to the pump, do the operation, close up the chest, and then leave. We would then take the patient to the recovery room—staying there for a few hours until his condition stabilized. By this time it was evening, and Dr. Lillehei would return to check the patient, and together we would do a round of his ward—ending at 9 P.M. a day that had begun at six, generally by shoveling snow off the drive to get out to the street.

Dr. Lillehei was a great teacher, an inspiration—and, above all else, a sensitive human being. He had the grace of Daantjie Rabie, who took me onto the track, the patience of Professor Crichton, who guided my hand, and the confidence of Professor Jannie Louw, who trusted me to do it alone.

All of this was revealed one terrible day when I made an error in preparing a seven-year-old boy who had come to us for the repair of an imperfectly developed ventricular septum—or hole between the two lower chambers of the heart. He was a slender, dark-haired boy from South America, and after we had him in position on the table I learned that his father was among those looking down at us from the glass dome above.

My job was to make a transverse thoracotomy—or oxbow incision from left to right armpit—opening the chest and exposing the heart, then inserting tapes around two big veins bringing used venous blood to the heart. Once looped, the two veins—inferior vena cava, and superior vena cava—would be ready to hook onto the heart-lung machine when Dr. Lillehei arrived. Until he came, I was in charge, assisted by another doctor, Dr. Derward Lepley.

There was no trouble at the beginning. We opened the chest, exposed the heart and prepared to loop the two veins. The superior vena cava came into position easily. But in putting an instrument around the inferior vena cava I found a bit of tissue in front of it. Turning to Dr. Lepley, I gave the fatal command.

"Cut that, will you?"

He gave a cut with the scissors but it was not quite enough. He cut again and that did it. Blood spurted out as though driven by a pump—and indeed, it was a pump. We had cut into the heart.

"Give me an artery forceps—quick!"

I got it and tried to clamp the hole but only tore it further. The blood poured out now in a flood, filling the cardiac cavity. The heart continued to beat at its own irreversible pace, pumping its precious liquid, not into its own chambers but rather outside the heart itself. So it went, like an animal drowning for want of help, until it was almost submerged and I could not see what I was doing. The pool had to be drained, and I began to do it with a sucker.

"Call Dr. Lillehei . . . now!"

As we sucked away the blood, the heart continued to pour out more of its own life until the pressure started to fall. At this point, the anesthetist began to call out the awful figures.

"It's below eighty . . . seventy, now it's sixty-five . . ."

That was approaching the alarm point of sixty and frantically I reached my hand into the cavity, filled with blood, trying to find the hole in the heart.

"We're still going down . . . it's below sixty now, fifty-eight, fifty-three, forty-nine . . ." I could feel the heartbeat getting fainter.

"For God's sake, get Dr. Lillehei!"

"Forty-two and still descending," said the anesthetist. Then he said, "I've got no reading. Pressure below thirty-five."

The heart had stopped. Blindly I reached in and began to massage it, hoping to start it again. But it did not respond, and each successive squeeze of my hand only drew out more blood into its dark lake of death. I could not help but look up once, seeing the faces of those in the dome looking down at me, including that of the father, his eyes wild with fear. Seeing me, he shook his head as though to say: "Please say it is not true . . . say it is not my little boy, say it is not his heart that you have in your hand . . ."

Lillehei came, and we connected the patient on the heart-lung machine. The cavity was drained, and I saw where we had cut a hole into the left atrium. With the heart still not beating, but the boy held in life by the machine, Dr. Lillehei began the operation—opening the heart and repairing the leak in the wall between the ventricles. After this, he closed the hole we had cut into the upper chamber. Through it all, I prayed that the child would be all right—that when we ceased supporting him with the pump, the heart would again take over and sustain his life.

"All right," said Dr. Lillehei finally. "Loosen it, let's see what we've got."

The heart did not start, and they began the pump again with some massage and direct stimulants to the muscle. Still it did not take over. More stimulants were tried, but nothing would help. The boy was dead.

"Close the chest," said Dr. Lillehei, leaving the theater and leaving me with Dr. Lepley to stitch up the chest of a boy who only a few hours earlier had been alive and laughing and confident that he would soon be able to run and play with other boys. Now he lay, limp and dead, beneath my hands.

"I'm going," said Lepley, leaving me to finish the job, beneath the petrified gaze of the father in the dome above. I did not look at him. If I had, I would not have been able to continue.

When it was over, I left the theater—but not the hospital. Lepley had gone home, but I could not do that. I had to stay and face whatever was left. So I wandered through the corridors of the hospital, without speaking to anyone and no one spoke to me. You could tell from the way they looked at me, however, that everybody knew what had happened. Finally I phoned Dr. Lillehei. He was in his office and said I could come over.

I must have looked very upset when I entered, because he quickly asked me to sit down. I shook my head and remained standing. I had no right to sit anywhere.

"Listen," I said, "it's no use my saying I'm sorry, because it won't bring back that child's life. The child is dead, and I don't know what I can say or what I can do. It's not your fault, but it's your patient. It's my fault. I am the cause of that boy's death."

"Chris, will you sit down, for Christ's sake?"

I sat down.

"Look, Chris, we've all made these mistakes that cost the lives of patients. You've made the mistake this time. The only thing you can do is to learn by your mistake. The next time you have bleeding, remember you can stop it by putting your finger in the hole. That gives you time to prepare and consolidate yourself, to get calm, and think of what you have to do."

I nodded. He was right. I had known this once before—why had I forgotten it? Perhaps it was because this was the first time that it happened to me with a human heart.

"All you had to do was put your finger in that hole. Now it's a lesson that you have learned, and I still have confidence in you, because I've made the same mistake in my life—you hear me?"

I nodded again.

"I have full confidence in you. So tomorrow go ahead and open the next patient's chest. We'll do the same thing. You go in and loop the venae cavae and I'll wait for you."

The next day I did just that and Dr. Lillehei stayed away until the last moment. Then he came in with his cocked head lamp and peered into the chest.

"Good job," he said.

"Thank you," I said, and thought: "Thank you for giving me the chance to recover. Thank you for understanding how it is to lose, and how important it is to have the illusion that you can win."

The death of the boy was tragic because it was needless—a visible mistake. Yet there were many other deaths caused by mistakes we could not see or by an incapacity to correct a known deficiency. This occurred most often in our attempts to repair damaged heart valves.

My brother Marius phoned one day from Rhodesia, where he had gone into practice with another doctor. He described one of his patients, a young woman with an aortic stenosis. Could we do something about that? I said we could and to send her over.

She came with her mother, and she was a wonderful-looking creature—a brunette with dark brown eyes, lovely figure, and all of it full of life and laughter. She had suffered from heart trouble on and off since having had rheumatic fever as a child, but it had not prevented her from leading a fairly normal life. It became a problem, however, when she wanted to become an air hostess for Central African Airways. They examined her and detected the trouble. Further tests revealed she had an aortic deficiency.

"Marius said you would fix me up like new," she said. We had met in the reception room of the medical center and now were in the cafeteria having a cup of coffee.

"You don't look like you need any fixing up," I said, and she burst out laughing.

Her mother smiled, too. She was an older edition of the daughter—same height, same dark eyes but without the laughter. Also, her voice was lower in tone.

"Marius told us about you working with Dr. Lillehei. He said there was only one place in the world he would recommend for Yonsie."

I looked at Yonsie.

"Yes," she said, "that's my name—Yonsie."

I smiled again and she thought I was looking at her earrings.

"You like them? They were for my twenty-first birthday, and Marius pierced my ears. That was his present to me."

Everybody was ready to give her presents. The Rhodesian State Lottery even helped pay her fare over. And now we were going to give her a new heart. It went like that when you were young and you had the looks of this girl.

In those years, the patients were not scheduled for operations. They lay around in wards waiting for their turn. Sometimes they waited two or three weeks. We expected it would be at least that long before Yonsie could be moved into the theater. Meanwhile, we put her in a ward for observation.

The next day Professor Wangensteen called me to his office.

"Chris, I've just come from Houston where I saw De Bakey and Cooley. Boy, you've never seen such vascular surgery in your life. They're magicians, especially that Cooley. You've got to see it."

I thanked him for the suggestion. He encouraged us to do this whenever possible. On Saturdays we often drove to the Mayo Clinic—Sam Hunter, Derward Lepley, Juan Gonzalez, and myself—to watch John Kirklin. We considered him exceptionally brilliant, and from these Saturday morning trips we learned many shortcuts and safeguards. There was a rivalry between Minnesota and Mayo, and we joked about it. But Kirklin never held anything back. Thanks to his knowledge, we changed catheters, suction systems, and he taught me how to close a ventricular septal defect without causing heart block.

We had learned all this from Dr. Kirklin, and now I hoped to learn even more from Dr. Cooley and Dr. De Bakey—if it were ever possible to get to see them.

"Tell you what," said Professor Wangensteen. "It's so important you see them that the department will foot the bill for you to go there for a week."

This was typical of Professor Wangensteen. He would criticize and scold and drive you until you were ready to break. Then he would do something like this—a gesture so overwhelming that there were no words to thank him for it.

I said good-bye to Yonsie and promised to be back for her operation.

"Send me a postcard from the Alamo," she said.

"All right," I said, and kissed her on both cheeks.

In Houston, I found that Professor Wangensteen was right about Dr. Cooley. It was the most beautiful surgery I had ever seen in my life. Every movement had a purpose and achieved its aim. Where most surgeons would take three hours, he could do the same operation in one hour. It went forward like a broad river—never fast, never in obvious haste, yet never going back. Some surgeons drove themselves, their hands groping for a solution to the imbalance before them. Dr. Cooley's hands moved effortlessly, as though he was simply putting everything back in place. This allowed him to make direct and often dramatic entries that would seem daring if done by anyone else. In dissecting the femoral artery, for example, one normally would make a small cut, then another and another, until it was exposed. Dr. Cooley simply made one slit, and the femoral artery lay open. No one in the world, I knew, could equal it.

Dr. Cooley's skill was matched by his grace and kindness toward me. He invited me into the theater, showed me everything, and politely answered all questions. Dr. De Bakey was more difficult to approach. When I finally obtained permission to watch him at work, he treated it as an intrusion and even shouted at me for being too close to the table. I thus learned little from him.

After three days, I returned to the hotel one evening to find that Minneapolis had called several times. One message said Yonsie was going to have her operation ahead of schedule. Another, marked urgent, said please call immediately. I did and learned it had not gone well. Yonsie had been on the table for six hours and was now in a serious condition. When I phoned an hour later she was dead.

I took the next plane out and in Minneapolis went immediately to her mother. She was sitting in her room in the hotel, staring at a newspaper clipping with a photo of Yonsie. It said: "Salisbury Girl to U.S.A. for Heart Repair."

"This is all I have," said Mrs. Herbst. "I don't have a real photo of her with me."

It was getting dark outside, but she had not bothered to turn on the lights, and in the room she remained seated in the chair looking at the newspaper photo of her daughter.

"I don't want to ever forget what she looked like. I'm afraid I might forget."

"You won't forget," I said.

"They asked me what to do, if I wanted to take her back as she is or did I want to cremate."

I waited for her to continue.

"I said to cremate."

She began to weep then, silently.

"Did I do right? Was it right to say that?"

"Yes," I said, "you were right."

The image of a final obliteration by diesel flame of this girl who had been so lovely was almost too much to bear. It was even worse at the airport when the mother walked to the plane carrying a little brown wooden box. A week earlier, she had walked across this same stretch of tarmac, arm in arm with her daughter, both of them secure of what Marius had told them: *Chris will have you fixed up like new.* She had been fixed up, all right. She was in a little box, under the arm of her mother who was now returning to the house where her clothes were still hanging in the closet and her shoes were there, too, in neat little rows. So the mother walked to the plane, a single woman with a brown box. She did not weep and was very strong—stronger than I was.

Before this occurred, it was clear to all of us that some way had to be found to repair faulty heart valves—or else replace them with artificial ones. At Professor Wangensteen's suggestion, I had already begun to work on this. And after the death of Yonsie, it became a personal, almost sacred mission—inevitably linked to my feeling of responsibility in her death.

Of the four valves of the heart, the one that caused us most trouble at that time was the one that claimed Yonsie, the aortic. Through it, the heart pumps fresh blood to the body. If it is stenotic—that is, narrowed—not enough blood will be allowed out, and the heart must therefore pump harder than normal. This places a strain on that chamber which does the pumping—the left ventricle—leading to eventual heart failure.

There had been numerous attempts to repair damaged valves by grafting on human tissue, only to fail through shrinkage or fragmentation. Because of this, I decided to use plastic materials in repairing the damaged valve and, if possible, to create a whole new valve.

It seemed simple enough. What we needed to replace was very small in size and one of the simplest creations of nature. Three leaflets, or cusps, shaped like half-moons, folded down on each other when the valve was closed and opened up when the heart pumped fresh blood to the body. The blood came upward from the left ventricle, driven by the contraction of the heart muscle, causing the three leaflets to open up like a flower and so allow the blood to enter the great aortic vessel, which then directed it to the rest of the body. After that, the pumping ventricle relaxed in order to receive more blood for its next cycle. When that happened, the little leaflets slammed shut—causing the *dubb* in the heart's *lubb-dubb* sounds—thereby preventing a return of the blood back into the ventricle.

Nothing could be simpler. Man had created far more complex instruments. He could fly blind through the night. He could project his image across space. He had harnessed the atom, split the heavens, and with DNA was touching the origin of life. Surely he could create something to replace three little leaflets that simply opened and closed in passive response to the pressure of flowing blood.

So it seemed and so it was, except for one essential. This artificial creation had to coexist within a living body. It had to serve the human system, and, in doing this, it should not damage it.

The demands were suddenly enormous. First of all, the valve had to be small enough to fit in below the coronary ostia, in the root of the aorta. Next, it had to be sufficiently flexible to respond to the flow of blood that would open and close it. It had to do this gently, without damaging the components of the blood. And it had to be so designed that no blood remained in its area to stagnate and cause clotting, embolism, and eventually death. Finally, this sensitive, flexible, fluid-smooth instrument had to be stronger than rock. The pounding it would take was staggering. The little leaflets had to open and close seventy times a minute, 100,800 times a day or over a million closings every ten days. And all of this had to endure for many years.

In order to study the functioning of valves, I built a machine to watch them in action—a mechanical pulse duplicator. It was quite simple: two plexiglass boxes, one atop the other, with a disc in between that could hold the valve. Water from a faucet was pulsated into the lower chamber by a system of solenoid valves simulating the rhythmic flow from the heart. In this way, the seated valve could be seen opening and closing as if it was inside the human body.

This allowed us to make film documentaries of normal and diseased valves taken from cadavers, as well as test artificial ones for durability. When a valve performed adequately within the machine, it was then tried on dogs—the only method possible to determine whether it would be tolerated in the circulation without promoting clotting or damaging blood elements.

I worked at night and whenever free during the day. Once again, I found myself trying to duplicate a simple equation of nature. And once again, it required infinite care and precision. First it was necessary to find a plastic material both flexible and strong enough to take the abuse of millions of diastolic poundings. For this, I went to Professor Fulton Holtbey in the university's department of engineering. He suggested Mylar, and together we built a mold in his basement workshop. After that, we went to the Minnesota Mining & Manufacturing Company, where one of their engineers, Richard Larson, cast a three-cusp valve in Mylar.

It seemed to have all the qualities we needed, and excitedly I began to test it on my machine, working through one entire weekend. Professor Wangensteen, who had been greatly impressed by the work, heard about this and exploded. In an emotional scene, he forbad me to enter the laboratory on Sundays. It was, he said, playing hell with the cleaning service. Mankind was desperately in need of an artificial aortic valve but, by God, it had to be created on a day other than Sunday. Like a pope or a king, Professor Wangensteen was a prisoner of palace ritual.

Despite its promise, however, the first Mylar valve did not stand up under pressure and also caused clotting. None of the dogs survived longer than a few days. A similar valve, made from Sylastic with the help of Dow-Corning, did not tear as easily, but under tests it proved unable to endure the pounding that could be expected from the human animal and his anxious soul. Also, it contained stagnant pockets that caused clotting. Dogs with this valve inserted in their descending aorta died within ten to fourteen days. A two-cusp butterfly-type valve was little better.

Despite this setback, I continued—helped greatly by a grant from the National Institutes of Health. Working with Oliver Moe of Remington Rand and Orville Ross of Honeywell Regulator Company, we built a Sylastic flap-type valve, which was to help the functioning of a diseased valve rather than replace it. This worked, but it was a compromise. I had wanted to build an entirely new valve—not an adjunct to a sick one. Eventually, I was to do it—but this was as far as I got in my research at the University of Minnesota.

Using this material, I wrote a thesis on the problems of making and testing an artificial aortic valve, and was given a Master of Science degree from the university. Previous to this, I had submitted my thesis on the etiology of congenital intestinal atresia, as well as undergoing exams in pathology, and the German and Dutch languages. These were all accepted and in February 1958, I was awarded my Ph.D.—Doctorate of Philosophy in Surgery.

Professor Wangensteen was openly delighted and asked me into his office.

"By God, Chris, you made it."

"Thanks to your help, Professor."

"Nobody could have done it for you. One thing still puzzles me—when did you sleep?"

"On Sundays, after you kicked me out of the animal laboratory."

We laughed. In the last months we had become close friends.

"As a favor for me, would you cancel your return to South Africa and stay with us?"

We had been through this several times. He felt I had a great career before me in Minneapolis—and, in a way, I did not want to leave. In two and a half years, it had become my world, a place I knew with a sense of belonging. It was a world filled with friends—the Jorgensens, Perrys, Hanses, Roods and many others. South Africa seemed remote, distant—another world. Even Louwtjie had begun to write less and less. Yet my roots were somehow still there. At least, it seemed that way. So I could not stay without first returning to my country.

"Are you sure, Chris?"

"Yes," I said, though I was not all that sure.

"How are you going to do advanced heart surgery there without a heart-lung machine?"

"I don't know yet."

"You're going to need one," he said. "Why don't you go and see what it'll cost to ship one across the ocean?"

I could not believe it.

"To South Africa?"

"Does anybody else in Africa except you know how to use one?"

It seemed incredible. Yet he had said it, and now he was laughing at me.

"Go on, Chris, stop staring at me like a fool. The stores might close."

Floyd Hamrick helped me select the essential elements: pumps, canisters, tubing, and other accessories. Each time I touched one of them, I felt a thrill. The next time I saw them would be when they were unpacked in Cape Town. That was going to be some homecoming—Ph.D., M.S., and H-L all at once.

I returned to Professor Wangensteen the next day.

"With $1,000 we can get the equipment."

"One always underestimates these things," he said. "You'll probably need double that, plus help in the first years of your research . . . Mrs. Hans! Please get me Washington."

He had Washington and the National Institutes of Health within two minutes.

"Hello, Bill? I've got a young South African who's worked with us. He's done some wonderful work. That's right . . . he's the one you gave a grant for valve work. I think we ought to help him get started back home. We'll need $2,000 for a bypass machine and $2,000 a year for three years."

A minute later he hung up.

"You've got it," he said, with a smile.

Years later, many people around the world, including President Lyndon Johnson, would ask me how it happened that the first human heart transplant occurred in a nation as small as South Africa. It was made possible in that two-minute phone call, by the generosity of the United States government, and by one man's faith in me. The pioneer is always a lonely man, but he is never completely alone. He carries others within his heart. And in mine there is written, along with a few others, this name: *Owen Harding Wangensteen—father, teacher, friend.*

It was a bright April morning when I drove out of Minneapolis, heading for New York. It seemed a century had passed since I had first arrived, being driven through the streets of snow—a time longer than all the years before it. And now, it was spring. The trees would soon break into green forests, the birds would be back, and once again the squirrels would scamper across the campus lawn.

Why was I leaving? Louwtjie had been right. I transplanted easily, and now this seemed to be my home. I had come as one pulled along in a flood, unable to do other than be washed up onto these shores of the Mississippi. And now I was going back the same way, once more swept away from what had become a new home. I did not know the answer and I drove slowly through the streets as though perhaps I would find it there—yet there was none.

In New York, I put the car on a boat and caught a plane for South Africa. At Cape Town, a northwest wind was blowing, and we came in over the sea with the waves close below.

Louwtjie was there with the children. I had written little in the last two months, yet I was unprepared for her greeting.

"Why did you come back? Why didn't you stay in America and never come home again?"

There was no longer any smile in her eyes, and her lips seemed to wait for nothing.

Oh God, I thought, I've made the most terrible mistake of my life.

PART VI
THE RETURN

CHAPTER 16

THE SEARCH FOR an aortic valve had delayed my return by about four months. Essentially, it was nothing. If we ever built such a valve, its value to medicine and mankind would be beyond measurement—perhaps beyond the lifetime of any single man. Most certainly, it was beyond four months of my existence. Louwtjie, however, claimed it could be measured.

"Don't look so surprised," she said. "We gave you up. We decided you were never coming back."

"It was only a little delay . . . I wrote you about it."

"You wrote once a month to say you weren't coming home. That's what you wrote."

"We were building valves—aortic valves."

"You were also building a family," she said. "I mean, once upon a time you were building one, until you dumped it into my lap."

We were in the car, on the way to a flat she had found in Pinelands. For a moment we said nothing and I thought of Minneapolis—of those whom I loved there and how I had turned away from them to come home—only to be told I did not mean it. It made no sense. Louwtjie had acted this way in Minneapolis because she felt insecure in America. Yet now we were in South Africa, and she was behaving the same way.

"Why are you so upset?" I asked.

"Because we have ceased to exist for you."

"That's not true."

"All right—what did you bring the children?"

This was more difficult. Now she was hitting out at me—but why? Why did she have to be that way? She did not know of my loneliness and struggle in Minneapolis. She was striking at a void.

"Didn't you bring Deirdre and Boetie anything?"

"No—I didn't have the chance."

"In a year and a half you had no chance."

I had intended to get them something special in New York, but there had been last-minute delays in shipping the big surprise for the whole family—our new Chevrolet station wagon. After that, I had planned to find gifts for them in Cape Town—better ones, perhaps, since I would know what they wanted. I tried to explain it.

"Tomorrow we can get something they really want—and you, too."

"Never mind," she said. "I bought them bicycles and said they were from you. I did that so they would think that their father remembered them."

"Do you really think I forgot them?"

"I know only what you tell me."

That was it—but what could I tell her that would not be questioned until it, too, became as meaningless as a repeated I-love-you on a stuck record? I wanted to say that I came home because I loved my children and believed I loved her. I did it because I felt it. And going with it, I knew we would find the substance of our love. Yet we could not question it—not now. If we did that, we might lose it altogether.

It began to rain. The city was gray under a gray sky. It was winter in Cape Town, and in Minneapolis, the spring was already there. Along the Mississippi, the trees were a splashy bright green—brighter than anything we knew in South Africa. In the fields there were wild flowers and once again the pheasants were running across the roads. How was it possible to lose a whole springtime? It had to show up again somewhere else. So did love.

At the hospital the next morning, Professor Jannie Louw was anxiously waiting for me. He had never doubted my return and for weeks had told everyone what was going to happen: Chris Barnard was returning with a heart-lung machine that would allow the Groote Schuur to be the first hospital in all Africa to perform open-heart surgery with cardiac bypass. A new era was to begin. Barnard would start it with all the techniques he had learned from the American pioneers in Minneapolis.

"Where is it?" he asked, meaning the pump.

"Coming by boat—in about two weeks."

"Good. How long will it take to get it working?"

"We have to train a team to run it," I said. "Then we have to test it on some animals until we're sure of it. After that, we should be ready."

"How long?"

"If we get the help we need, maybe two months."

He nodded and leaned forward, obviously disturbed.

"Chris, we have to make sure it works. I'll tell you why."

It was not a pleasant story. Nine months before my return, another surgeon had bought a Cooley-type pump in the United States, tried it out with water to see if it worked mechanically, and then—with no previous training—hooked it on to a patient. The blood ran out onto the floor and the patient died.

"After that," said Professor Louw, "I told them to do no more open hearts until Chris comes back."

I looked at him sitting behind a desk with photos of his family facing him. Next to these were letters bearing his name, linked to ponderable degrees of learning, each one buttressing his current position of power: Chief of Department of Surgery. Here was a man at the top, secure in his world. Yet within it, he was not so safe—not now.

The disastrous experience before my arrival, and Professor Louw's canceling any further open-heart surgery, had focused the hospital upon me and my ability to run the machine. It would have been safer for Professor Louw to say: "Let's wait until a better machine comes along." Instead, he had said: "Let's wait until Chris comes back."

Eleven years ago, looking over the top of an anesthetist's curtain at an exposed gall bladder, he had said: "Well, why don't you finish it?" Now he had looked across an ocean and decided. His arc of faith was getting longer—and more exposed. He could quickly repair a faulty gall bladder job. But if anything went wrong with the pump, he could only sit and witness one more death in the operating theater—structured this time by himself.

The heart-lung machine, when I finally moved it into the theater, would carry within its coils not only the life of the patient but also something integral to the lives of two men who had brought it there—my reputation and his faith in me.

"We'll do it, Professor Louw. Don't worry, we'll do it."

"I know you will."

We discussed then how to form a team to operate the pump. It would be based within the surgical research laboratory, which currently was without a chief surgeon.

"So you take over that unit," he said. "It includes a young technician, Carl Goosen, who is very bright. Will you need someone else?"

"Yes, Professor."

While Goosen ran the machine, I had to have a surgical assistant.

"There's another one, doing general surgery under me—Malcolm McKenzie. Go and talk to him. If he wants to join you, I'll arrange it."

Two weeks later, when the boxes arrived with the De Wall-Lillehei bubble oxygenator, the team had already been formed—Carl Goosen, Malcolm McKenzie, and a colored assistant named Victor Pick. Together we began to open the boxes in the surgical research laboratory—two rooms in the pathology museum building and across the street from the animal house—laying it all out onto the floor: tubes, connectors, bolts, plates, antifoam. I knew every piece of equipment. I had held each one in my hands in Minneapolis, and now, spreading it out onto the floor, I knew how it would all appear when assembled—a creation of a dozen different sciences, harnessed into one unit to replace the heart and lungs of a human being. I could see this, all of it functioning perfectly—red blood pulsating through the yellow mayon tubes, little bubbles of oxygen rising up through a mixing chamber, flowing then across antifoam paste, steel fingers rolling it onward to the patient on the table, a red stream going from femoral artery through the body and returning back to us along the two venae cavae, while inside it all the motor kept humming on and on—the heart's indestructible stand-in.

So it would be, when it worked well. When it did not, it was an instrument of death. Each one of the pieces on the floor had its own threat, its own specific danger. Bubbles in the helix, a leak in the line, overheating in the warming bath, a slipped catheter, antifoam XC-2-033 in the blood and into the brain—how many hundreds of other leaks, drips, breaks and pressures lurked there, among the separate parts, ready to reduce a human being to a vegetable—or cause his death on the table? Dear God, one thing had to be clear. Before this machine was hooked onto a living person, we had to bolt every member of the team to the machine itself—most importantly, to its capacity to go wrong.

"Shall we start with the motor and build out from there?"

It was Carl Goosen with the pump diagram in hand, anxious to begin the assembly. After being trained, he would be the technician in charge, much as Floyd Hamrick had handled Dr. Lillehei's machine. He was a ruddy youth—meticulous with a high sense of responsibility, and I trusted him from the beginning. Malcolm McKenzie more closely resembled myself— perhaps as I had been four years ago when first entering the animal house. And like myself, he seemed filled with just as many questions.

"Before we start," he said, "tell me one thing. The pump sends the blood into the femoral artery. But how does it come back? How do we get the venous blood back into the machine?"

Good, I thought, he is already running ahead of the diagram. Even before the pump is up, he is looking for errors in its system.

"It returns by gravity," I said. "We set up at different levels with the operating table higher than the well holding the venous blood—twenty-five centimeters is enough."

"Do we start with the motor?" asked Carl Goosen again.

The moment had arrived to warn them of the dangers before us.

"Yes, but remember this about every one of these pieces. They all have a function to keep the patient alive. But they all have a capacity to kill him, too. Our job is to make sure that they don't do that."

Victor—Big Victor, as we came to know him—had said nothing. He had helped to open the boxes, doing it carefully without breaking any of them. He had listened to us, and I knew from his manner that he was going to be invaluable. Finally, after we had assembled the machine, he asked one question.

"Doctor," he said, "the boxes are so beautiful. May I have them?"

"Yes, Victor—why?"

"I can use them to make some furniture for my home."

It was a good beginning. The pump's casing would cradle life within a home. And the pump would do it on an operating table—beginning with dogs in the laboratory.

We lost the first dog through incorrect calibration of blood flow. The second one died from a connection allowing air into the line. After that, we lost no more and successfully did twenty-four operations, each one increasing in complexity and duration as machine and team became more coordinated. At first we ran it for thirty minutes, opening and closing the right atrium. This was extended to an hour as we went into the right ventricle. Finally, we ran it for an hour and a half, simulating operations of the most difficult sort, such as tetralogy of Fallot or a leaking heart valve.

Dr. Walter Phillips, head of the cardiothoracic unit, would occasionally look in to see how we were doing. He never stayed long, however, other than to say he was waiting for us to get ready.

I said little and continued to work—making sure the team and the machine were perfectly integrated. Finally, after a successful run-through with the twenty-fifth dog, I was ready to move into the theater and accept the risk of a human being. Yet before this could happen, I had an appointment with one of life's cruelest events—the death of a father.

CHAPTER 17

EARLY ONE MORNING at the hospital, I received a phone call from Knysna, the seacoast resort near Wilderness where I had spent my boyhood summers. My father and mother had gone to live there—staying in the home of his niece, Sarah. The call was from her husband Piet Kap.

"If you want to see your father alive," he said, "you must come immediately."

Oh, Lord not now, not so quickly . . .

"Chris, are you there?"

Please, give me some time, a little more time . . .

"Chris—do you hear me?"

"Yes, I hear."

"Are you coming?"

"Yes . . ."

"Hurry, because there's not much time."

"Tell him I'm coming. Tell him to wait for me. Tell him to hold on a little bit more."

"Yes, Chris, I'll do that."

Please tell him . . .

I was at the hospital, and after I had found someone to replace me in the operating theater, I called Louwtjie to say I was leaving. She did not reply, and I knew she was crying.

"What can I do?" she asked.

"Get Joyce and Barney and come up with them in their car. Telephone Marius in Salisbury and tell him, too."

"You don't want me now?"

"Not now—just come."

"All right," she said.

"Good-bye," I said.

She would not hang up.

"You'll be alone . . . all alone."

"Just come, Louwtjie, just do that for me."

"All right, I'm coming."

So I left—driving it alone, because there was no other way. Only the father knew his son—and the son his father. No one could stand in for them. No one could die for them. And before this happened, no hands, no eyes, no lips could replace their own.

Dear God, let me be in time. Let me see him once more. Don't take him away yet . . .

I raced the car over Sir Lowry's Pass heading for the coast road. It would take about seven hours—a long time, perhaps too long. I should have started long before this, for there had been ample warning. I had known it was going to happen after I returned from America.

There were messages waiting for me then. My father was not well and wanted to see me. I knew it was not going to be good, even before I finally went to see him—about ten days after my return. Yet I was not prepared for what I found in the little home of his niece overlooking the lagoon at Knysna.

When I entered, he walked out of the bedroom to meet me and it was visible in his face even before I touched him. He was thin and pale and his eyes looked into mine asking why I had waited so long.

"Hello, Chris—how are you?"

"Fine, Daddy—and you?"

"My stomach," he said. "It is not nice."

You could see it immediately—so swollen that he could not close his pants—as though all the life in his face and arms and legs had withdrawn to settle there, within the stomach, creating a separate existence of its own. I knew it then, even before I took him into the bedroom and had him lie down, only to feel it through the stomach wall—knobs of cancer massed around the liver.

I went cold with fear but tried to hide it. He saw it, anyway, in my eyes and knew it was not good.

"It's all right," he said.

"Yes," I said, trying to play it lightly.

"Don't worry, Chris. Don't worry about it."

I looked away from him, trying to calm myself. On the walls of the little bedroom were pictures of all of us. There was Dodsley and Barney together in the garden, the garden of my childhood. There was another one of Barney with our first car, the Willys Overland, and then one of me with a tennis racket and a trophy cup. Nearby there was one of Marius and me planting a tree at Wilderness. There was also the old photo of Abraham sitting on a cushion in the little chair, then the one of my mother by his graveside, and next to it the little angel waving good-bye as he went to heaven. On the dresser were others, mostly wedding pictures, including one of Louwtjie and myself taken at Michaelis Gallery, before we went to the reception. She was smiling—how long had it been since she had smiled like that? And how long since we had put our hands together with the palms touching?

"Don't worry, Chris," said my father again.

"Well," I said, "I think we should take you back to Cape Town to let Professor Louw look at you. I'm sure there's something he can do to help."

"All right," he said. "If you would like me to do that, I'll go back with you."

I had come in Louwtjie's little Austin, and with my mother we all returned to Cape Town. My father was cramped in the back seat but he never complained. At the hospital he joked with the nurses, telling them they were so beautiful he had decided to stay there forever. Then Professor Louw examined him, and my worst fears were confirmed. He was beyond any intervention. We tried to hide it from him, saying it was better not to operate for the time being—but he knew better. He knew the truth. He could see it in my eyes.

"I think it's better I go back to Knysna, don't you?" he said.

"Yes, I think so."

The new station wagon had arrived from America, and I put a mattress in the back so he would be more comfortable. My mother sat in front, and we went first to Ceres to spend a night with my old friend, Joubert Botma. The next day, as we left, my father lifted himself up from the mattress to wave good-bye to our friends who had come to see him. I remember him that way, raised up on his elbow and waving good-bye—like a figure on a Greek vase—while all the other scenes of that trip are similarly locked in memory, as though forming a procession to a final sacrifice. We drove through the night, stopping frequently because he had to pass water and also he felt nauseated. We stopped for tea at Swellendam, but he was too weak to get out of the car. Finally at Knysna, I helped him into the house. He slept until noon and then got up, saying he felt better.

"Good," I said, "don't stay in bed. Please move around because it's better for you."

He nodded.

"If you stay in bed you'll get terribly weak."

"Did you hear that, Daddy?" asked my mother.

"I didn't hear a word," he said, with a wink at me.

I left then, to return to the hospital. After that, I phoned several times, and my mother said he was not too bad. "Every day I make him get up and move around," she said, speaking with the same flat finality she had used on us as children. "He seems to be all right," she said.

All of this had happened before the heart-lung machine arrived. We began to test it then on dogs, in preparation for its first use on a human being. At the same time, I was doing general surgery at the hospital—and trying to bring some harmony and understanding into my life with Louwtjie.

So it had gone until the phone call came from Mr. Kap, saying there was little time left. Indeed, there was too little time. I drove all morning and got there in the early afternoon. But it was not soon enough. When I reached the house, Mr. Kap came to the door, shaking his head.

"The old father is dead," he said.

He held the door open for me to come in, but I did not move.

"I came as fast as I could," I said.

"He was going when I called you."

"If only you had called me sooner."

"We didn't know."

I said nothing. There was nothing to say.

"Come in. I'll show you where he is."

"No."

"He's in the living room. Your mother and Sarah have dressed him."

"No. I don't want to see him dead."

"Come this way, then."

He took me into the kitchen, and then my mother came in with Sarah. They had been with my father, and both looked exhausted. You could see that Sarah had been crying, while my mother had not.

"He doesn't want to see him," said Mr. Kap.

"I understand," said Sarah, choking up.

I embraced my mother, then she looked at me and shook her head.

"Sit down. I'll fix you some coffee."

She began to tell me what had happened. My father had awakened early, saying he did not feel well.

"Do you think Chris will be angry with me if I stay in bed today?" he asked.

"No, I'm sure he wouldn't mind," said my mother.

He lay back then and closed his eyes. Shortly after that, my mother found him sitting up in bed, waving good-bye to the photos on the wall.

"He said 'Ta-ta' to each one of you," said my mother. "And he called each of you by your names. He even said good-bye to Abraham. And then he said good-bye to you. You were the last one he spoke to, Chris . . ."

Of course, that was it. I was the last one because he was waiting for me. Until the final moment, he expected me to be with him. But no, I had done it again. Michel had called for me, and I had failed to arrive in time. My father had called, and I had not reached him, either. So he had waved good-bye to my picture because there was nothing else. He had wanted more—to hold me one last time, to hear my voice and to hear himself say good-bye and so be secure of what he was doing. Yet it was not possible. When he needed me most, I was not there.

Unable to endure any more, I took the car and drove out to the Heads. Knysna sits on a lagoon, formed by two arms reaching out into the sea— both arms ending in steep sandstone cliffs known as the Heads. They are close to each other, linked by shoals which allow the sea to enter but have wrecked a thousand ships. I went to Coney Glen, on the eastern side where I had gone many times as a boy.

From there I could look back upon land where my father had spent many years of his life. Below me and to the right was Ouplaas, the little village where he was born and had lived as a child. Beyond it was the Tsitsikama forest, where his father had dragged the giant stinkwood logs by ox team and where Adam, the frail son, had also worked before hearing the call of God. Still further away, on the far side of the lagoon and up on the hill, was the little house of his niece where he now lay dead in an open coffin in the sitting room.

Linking these landmarks of his life were two bodies of water—the restless sea crashing against rocks and the calm lagoon sleeping in its basin. In between this, purple shadows streaked down the face of a brown cliff to plunge into the white foam of black waves. So the two waters met under an early evening sky: one pounding urgently, insistently, upon rocks—the other a dark blue lake of unmarked time.

It came back to me then—the evening we had sat here on the cliff, when my father had explained these waters to me. He had pointed first to the treacherous shoals where at low tide you could see the wreckage of earlier ships—immovable as the rocks that had dragged them down to quieter fathoms. Then he had told me about his uncle, Great Koos Barnard, who would go to sea across the shoals while the men of Knysna shook their heads, saying that the bones of Great Koos would soon be drifting among the wreckage of a century of ships piloted by fools like himself. At this, my father laughed.

"Yet, he always came back," he said. "When there was a great storm, I would come here to wait for his return, and it was frightening to see it. The ship was so little that the waves tossed it like foam blown by the wind. Sometimes it would disappear completely, and we would hold our breaths until it appeared once more. Then somehow he did it, somehow he knew the exact moment, the freak moment of time when wind and wave and the little oars of his boat would all heave together and so cast him suddenly below us, in the middle of the shoals where he continued to row his way in between the rocks with mouths of monsters—arriving at last in the lagoon. We would cheer from the cliffs and wave to him. . . . He could not hear us, but he could see us and he always waved back, shouting the same words: 'Praise the Lord!' He was home, Chris . . . he was a man who had come home."

After he told me this, I had looked at the lagoon and at the sea and realized my father saw these as the two natures of man, the two sides of life—and that he felt it was better to be in the lagoon. But I did not feel that way. I belonged in the sea because inside of me were emotions like pounding waves. I did not belong in flat waters. Nor did I understand anyone wanting to be there.

Yet now it was different. Now I understood the meaning of the lagoon. For the face of my father lay there, on those waters. And so rested his soul.

I was on the other side—crashing with the sea upon rocks, floundering with wounds and pain because I had failed my father in many ways. Long before he died, I had practically disappeared from his life. Wherever I went, I carried his image within me and his words were forever mingled with mine. I had all this from him, guiding me through life. Yet I had given him little in return—too little.

All he asked was a little time, a few words. Yet even this I had not given—nor had our children. He only wanted to enjoy us, to have a little pleasure—and to give whatever he could. Louwtjie was fond of figs, and when he knew she was coming for a visit, he would pick tender little ones and put them in the refrigerator. When we arrived, there was excitement in his eyes and he would happily show Louwtjie the figs he had gathered— sweet juice oozing from green skins and red button bottoms. Finally, when we left he would watch us go and I could not bear to see the sadness in his eyes—even as he wished us Godspeed.

Why had I not given him more time? Why had I failed him as I had Michel—and maybe as I was now failing Louwtjie and the children?

We gave you up, Chris.

I wrote two theses and got two degrees in two years. I wrote you as often as I could.

You never wrote, except to say you were not coming home.

I was building a valve for humanity.

What did you bring for your children . . . or are they outside of humanity?

These others are sick, they need immediate help, they are in pain.

We're in pain, too, Chris. You give everything to the others, and leave us nothing.

I give you all I can, everything I have left.

That's right. You give leftovers: leftover love, leftover days and leftover nights. You're a leftover man and a leftover husband.

Don't say that, please don't. I give everything to my patients. To those who need most, I give everything.

Do you really? Your father wanted to say good-bye to you, and what did you give him except a picture on the wall?

I had no answer for any of it and, overcome with sadness and despair, I left the cliff to drive back to the house. There I found Louwtjie had arrived with Barney and Joyce. I met her as she came out of the room where they had lain my father. She said nothing. There were only her tears and her eyes looking into mine for some answer.

I could stand no more and went into the bedroom alone. They wanted to come in and comfort me, but I did not want them. I was beyond help. I wept for my father, and I wept for myself and how I had failed all those who wanted more from me than I could ever give them. There was no answer, none that I knew, and I wept alone. After a while, I felt a hand on my shoulder and turned to see who it was. There was nobody—yet somehow this was enough to calm me, and I fell into a deep sleep.

The next morning we carried my father's coffin out of the house and down the steps to the black hearse. I followed in the car, with my mother and Louwtjie and Barney. The church was simple and white and small, and when we put the coffin down in front of the pulpit, I turned around to see the balcony was filled with colored people from Beaufort West. I saw the Morkels, the Pienaars, and the Malcolms.

They stared at me without smiling. A few of the older men nodded and some of the women had handkerchiefs in their hands. The preacher would soon talk about my father but nothing he could say would ever equal this—the mute presence of these colored people who had come two hundred miles to see the burial of a white minister who had loved them as he had loved his own family.

"Chris, sit down."

Was there some answer for me in this? What could those eyes, those hands with handkerchiefs, tell me besides testifying to a love for my father —a love I also shared?

"Chris!"

It was my mother tugging at me to sit down. The minister had come into the pulpit, Reverend Burger, who was an old friend of my father. He looked at us in the front row, he looked at the colored people in the rear, he looked at my father's coffin—and then, after a long silence, he began to relate how many years he had known Adam Hendrik Barnard. He described some of his habits, including observance of the Biblical tithe for the poor.

"He continued it up to the day he died," said the minister. "He took one-tenth of his money each month—he only got eleven pounds [thirty dollars] —and gave it away. He did it in his own way, bringing groceries and medicine for those who needed them most. I don't have to ask you why he did this. You know why. That's why you came to say good-bye to him. So I wonder how we can best do this. Maybe we can do it by listening to the last words he wrote to me in this letter I have before me. It's in reply to our little note that we were praying for him to get well. He wrote back, thanking us for our thoughts and our prayers. And then he said:

Perhaps I am near the end. Sometimes I feel as ancient as Abraham, an old man full of years, and the words of the Lord are near upon me: "My little children, I shall not be with you much longer . . ."

Soon I will say good-bye to those whom I have loved and lived for—to say hello to Him I have loved and lived for. I pray that He will understand how I have tried to do my best for all who needed my help. I have failed many times, but I have tried and I keep on trying.

Of some things I am proud, especially my sons. Christiaan has just won new degrees of honor in America and will soon be coming back to see us. This will be a source of joy, and I confess that I can hardly wait for the day of his return . . .

It was more than I could bear, and Louwtjie took my hand to give me courage.

. . . Christiaan has honored me. He labors in God's name against pain and sorrow. He told me that in Ceres he had found a parish of human life . . .

Had I also failed there because I came too late? Too late for what?

There was no answer in the letter—other than my father's love, broad and wide, and in it was his special love for me. After the minister finished, we joined in a common prayer which ended with the little church suddenly filling with one word like a long, plunging wave:

"AHHH-MMENNN!"

We rose and again I thought they were looking at me as I helped carry out the coffin. Then I realized it was not directed at me, but rather at the brown wooden box with the brass handles.

We drove slowly to the graveyard, and many walked. When we reached the gate, the colored people came forward as though acting on common command—moving in between us and the coffin, and then taking it onto their shoulders. There were many of them and suddenly the coffin seemed to be floating above all of us.

We stood back and watched it go through the gate. The people for whom he had lived were those who now bore my father to his grave. They said nothing. Their faces were heavy with sorrow, but there was no sound. They bore him onward, as though he was a part of them. In the wooden box was a shrunken old man with white hair. They had dressed him in clothes I had not seen, but I knew it was the old dark suit with the little *strikkie* tie he always wore when walking through town on Sunday to bring God's patient word to prisoners in the city jail, later standing in the pulpit of our church like an old eagle peering down into a distant valley.

There were so many shoulders and so many hands you could not count them. Yet each one carried the weight as though it was a great burden, as though lifting up something more than a little old man. They were carrying a part of themselves to the grave—and with it went all their terrible sorrow. With it also went their unasked question and my question, too, which now found their answer.

The minister gave it at the graveside from the Gospel of John, after they had lowered the coffin and had begun to throw in the flowers.

> As the Father has loved me,
> so I have loved you.
> Remain in my love.
> If you keep my commandments
> you will remain in my love,
> just as I have kept my Father's commandments
> and remain in his love.
> I have told you this
> so that my own joy may be in you
> and your joy be complete.
> This is my commandment:
> love one another,
> as I have loved you
> A man can have no greater love
> than to lay down his life for his friends . . .

When I turned away, there was the thud of soil on wood. Off to the left was Ouplaas where he was born. And then closer at hand, were the Heads, where he had crossed over the shoals into the lagoon.

Thud. Thud. Thud.

"Are you going, Chris?"

"Yes, Louwtjie, we're going."

We said good-bye to my father's parishioners and then to our friends and so began the trip back to Cape Town. Louwtjie sat close to me, and for a while we said nothing. Then a truck bore down on us and I was almost forced off the road.

"Are you all right, darling?" she asked.

"Yes."

It had been years since she had called me darling.

"I loved your father," she said.

"Yes."

"He was like my father—more than my father."

Then she said: "Is it all right if I sit close while you're driving?"

"Come closer."

She lay her hand on me and we joined hands with palms touching.

So it happened that my father in his dying left me two gifts. He returned to me a sense of dignity, and through the people who bore him to his grave he answered the questions I had asked on the cliff. You found your life by giving it to others. You are most honorably borne in life and in death by the most distant members of the human family. Their pressing hands were your highest tribute.

With this, there was the second gift of understanding through love. Within it, he had returned Louwtjie to my side.

CHAPTER 18

THE MOMENT HAD COME to pick our first patient for the heart-lung machine. To make sure we would not fail, I chose a relatively easy case—a fifteen-year-old girl named Joan Pick who suffered from pulmonary valve stenosis. Little would be required other than put her on the machine, open the pulmonary artery, make three little cuts in the valve, close the artery, and turn off the machine. It would require a bypass of only a few minutes. Many surgeons were doing the same operation with hypothermia alone, and some even did it so quickly they needed neither hypothermia nor heart pump.

This seemed ideal for our first attempt. If we ran into trouble, if the pump failed, we had a good chance of pulling through anyway. It differed from the first tragic open-heart attempt, made before my return, when they had selected a tetralogy of Fallot—one of the most difficult cases possible.

We began the night before to prepare the machine. Its mayon tubing had to be sterilized in a dry, exhaust-type autoclave—otherwise it would cloud up and lose its transparency. There was none large enough for it at Groote Schuur. So we did it in the mattress autoclave at the Red Cross Children's Hospital, wrapping it in sterile towels and bringing it back across town.

The next morning at six o'clock, Carl Goosen and I began to set up the machine in the theater. After that, they brought in the patient and the anesthetist, Dr. Joseph Ozinsky, put her to sleep. Dr. Phillips also arrived to do the operation. Professor Louw watched from the crowded amphitheater.

After having calibrated the machine, I scrubbed and changed gloves to help at the table—working opposite Dr. Phillips. The patient was a colored girl, and we made an oxbow incision from the right to left chest, below the breasts, then cut the sternum and so pulled it apart to reveal the pericardium and finally her heart. I made two small holes into its right atrium, running two catheters into it and so into the superior and inferior venae cavae for drainage of used venous blood. Before this, we had made an opening into the femoral artery in the right groin to allow entry of fresh blood from the machine.

We were ready, and I ran over to start the pump. After making sure it was working well, with pressure and flow under control, I ran out to scrub up again and put on more sterile gloves to help with the remaining surgery. It began to take longer than expected, and as Dr. Phillips was seeking to close the pulmonary artery, Carl Goosen said we were in trouble.

"The blood supply is dropping."

"How much?" I asked, trying to help close the artery.

"Low," said Goosen, "very low."

"How much, man? How much time?"

"At this rate only another minute."

If we failed to make it, air would come into the line and either kill the patient or turn her into a vegetable. Quickly I helped Dr. Phillips put the last stitch into the artery and called out to Goosen:

"Cut pump!"

We had made it—with hardly any blood to spare. I checked the line and then discovered where it had gone wrong. A clamp had slipped off the lower end of the femoral artery incision, allowing the blood to run out onto the floor. Incredibly, no one had noticed it—and ever since that day I have always put two clamps on the distal end of the femoral artery.

Had this damaged the patient? Worse, had any of the dangerous antifoam slipped into the line and then into her brain?

Dr. Ozinsky, who was to become a major figure in all future heart operations, removed the drapes from the girl's face. He had kept her in the first and lightest plane of anesthesia, enough only to put her to sleep and so render her insensible to pain. In this way, when we were finished, she was already surfacing—indeed, she opened her eyes to look at him. This was exactly what we wanted.

"Close your eyes," he said.

She did it, and we knew her brain was undamaged. After that, I took her back to the ward to supervise the postoperative care. We had come this far, and I was not going to lose her by any more accidents. By this time, however, I was also ill. I had eaten nothing the night before, nor that morning. My blood sugar must have been zero for I had a splitting headache and extreme nausea. I knew I needed rest yet refused it for another four hours—checking pulse, blood loss, urine, drips, temperature, and all other indicators of postoperative recovery.

Finally arriving home, I barely made it to bed before collapsing. Louwtjie brought me tea and then something to eat. After that, I got up and went back to the hospital to be with the patient. The next morning, July 29, 1958, the newspapers bannered it in headlines, and Joan Pick was sufficiently recovered to hold my hand.

"I can't thank you enough," she said.

"You have," I said. "Your hand is enough."

Inevitably, we could not succeed every time. After the first victory, we did a few more relatively easy ones, such as holes between the upper chambers of the heart. This gave us the security to go on to the more complex cases, and we also handled these without loss, until we came to the twelfth patient—a little girl who was the sister of a staff nurse.

She had three heart defects—narrowing of both pulmonary and aortic valves plus a leak through the atrial septum, or wall separating the upper chambers of the heart. It was going to be a difficult operation, and I went to see the child the day before. It was Sunday afternoon and I found her out on the balcony, looking down over the Cape Flats—a blonde girl of twelve.

"Isn't it funny," she said, "that tomorrow this time I will not be here."

She said it calmly, without looking at me, her hands on the ledge of the balcony, her eyes fixed on the city below as though she wanted to see as much as possible in the little time she had left.

"Don't be a silly little girl," I said.

"Why?" she asked, finally turning.

Blue eyes looked briefly at me, then back again at the city. I held no answer for her.

"No," she said. "Tomorrow I will not be here."

She died on the table.

After that the strain under which I worked during that period became almost unbearable. For the first time in major surgery, I was alone—terribly alone. I had no one to guide me. No one around me knew bypass technique better than I did, nor what was needed in order to insure ourselves as much as possible against error and death.

Above all else, we had to create a team of people who could handle all the techniques needed in open-heart surgery. That meant, first of all, a team of nurses specialized in handling such patients. It meant more surgeons to help with the operations—especially after Dr. Phillips left and I took over the cardiothoracic department. It meant technicians who could run the heart-lung machine perfectly. Finally, it meant tying in with the ancillary services such as blood transfusion, biochemistry, bacteriology, and cardiology.

We already had an excellent cardiac unit, built through the labor and genius of Professor Velva "Val" Schrire, which was to be of invaluable help. The blood supply was provided by the Western Province Blood Transfusion Service, blood compatibility by Dr. Marthinus "M.C." Botha, the ward nursing by Sister Geyer, and the surgical staff was slowly increased. Dr. Malcolm McKenzie was followed by Raoul de Villiers, and then John Terblanche. The goal was to create a team of such strength, discipline, and technique that it could do open-heart surgery as well as or better than any other team in the world. In all conscience, we could not seek less.

A team of this sort required a heart-lung machine of equal quality, and we sought that, too—seeking to diminish as much as possible its capacity to kill our patients. It had this capacity from the nature of its operation as a bubble oxygenator. Tiny jets of oxygen were shot through the blood, perfusing its red blood cells with the quotient of oxygen needed by the body. In this way, the used blood was made whole again. At the same time, the process created bubbles that had to be removed before reentering the bloodstream—otherwise they could cause lethal embolisms. To prevent this, a greasy antifoam solution was smeared inside a tube through which the blood flowed—chemically altering the surface tension and so breaking up the bubbles. Occasionally, however, the grease itself entered the patient and either killed or paralyzed him.

It was a terrible threat, but eventually we found a solution. Dr. Richard De Wall, who first created the bubble oxygenator with Dr. Lillehei, described a method of dipping steel sponges into a solution of antifoam diluted with ether. The ether then evaporated leaving a fine coating of antifoam on the sponges. Blood flowing through these, inside a tube or canister, no longer collected any dangerous matter.

We made this modification, only to face other problems. One was how to get rid of bubbles when first priming the machine. We discovered this could be done by priming with very hot dextrose and water. As the solution cooled, we knocked it with a patella hammer. This caused the bubbles to vanish, since gas is more soluble in cold than in warm water. After this, we went on to another problem.

Many of our seriously ill patients developed arrhythmia—an irregular heartbeat that often led to death. It occurred mainly with patients who had been under treatment for a long time before coming to the operating table. What had been done to make them so vulnerable to the heart-lung machine? We suspected it came from a depletion in the body's store of potassium as a result of prolonged diuretics. In the operating theater there was a further loss especially when the heart-lung machine was primed using blood mixed with dextrose and water—a dilution of pure blood that helped prevent kidney complications. The low level of potassium in the blood after surgery made the heart muscle more irritable, especially in patients treated with digitalis.

This hypothesis was investigated in the laboratory by my brother Marius and proved correct. It became clear that the blood potassium level had to be monitored and additional potassium given when needed. This immediately reduced arrhythmias and deaths from such a complication.

We continued investigating other techniques—such as the introduction of moderate hypothermia with high flow perfusion, profound hypothermia with low flow perfusion, and even no perfusion at intervals. This last method, shutting off the blood flow, was especially helpful in dealing with large aneurysms, or extended swellings, of the aorta.

Each time a technique was perfected in the laboratory, it was applied in the operating room. These were small discoveries, yet they had real value. They gave us a greater freedom in the mechanics of open-heart surgery and allowed us to move into the most advanced and difficult operations.

There remained, however, many heart diseases for which there was no known remedy. Once again, the nature of our mission dictated that some answer also be found for these. It had to be done. Incurable diseases of the heart claimed increasing numbers of patients—and the rate was increasing.

The most common cardiac killer of infants was Transposition of the Great Vessels. The child is born with the aortic and pulmonary arteries transposed, creating two separate circulatory systems. In one, used venous blood enters the right side of the heart and then exits without being cleansed by the lungs. In the other, fresh blood from the lungs goes around in a closed cycle through the left side of the heart.

If there is a rupture in the septum, or heart wall, allowing some blood to be shunted from one side to the other, the child can live for a few years. My little brother Abraham probably had this, and it eventually killed him. If there is no opening in the heart wall, the two blood systems never meet and the infant is aborted or born dead. It was this defect that claimed the life of the baby boy of Lex Rankin, the nurse at Ceres.

The problem was how to alter this so that used blood went to the lungs and fresh blood came to the body. Surgeons had sought to simply cut both arteries and so transpose them to their correct channels but because of the position of the coronary arteries, this had universally failed. It had to be done within the heart—but how? A Swedish surgeon, Ake Senning, achieved it through a restructuring of the atrial septum. But this was not too successful, and when I tried it, the patient died.

One Sunday morning, while sitting in Cape Town's Groote Kerk, I was so bored by the sermon that I began to think about how to handle this operation. I had a child suffering from the disease at the hospital, and, unless something was done about it, he would soon die.

There seemed to be only one way to approach it. Since the two ventricles had the wrong arterial attachment, and since the arteries could not be switched, we had to accept the ventricles as they were and switch the kind of blood they received. Normally, the right atrium gives venous blood to the right ventricle, while the left atrium gives fresh blood from the lungs to the left ventricle. This had to be reversed so that the right upper chamber fed the left lower one and blood from the upper left went to the lower right.

Very well, I thought, we can use tubes and crisscross the blood supply through the two atrial chambers. In fact, we could cut away the wall between the two atria while laying in the two tubes. That would create one big upper chamber where there had been two. Yet it would also render the chamber useless, for it would continue to pump, with no blood. Supposing, however, we used only one tube—going left to right or right to left—while the enlarged atrium would continue to pump through the one remaining opening?

Excited, I could hardly wait for the sermon to reach its dreary end. That child's life was worth more than a million pious words—and now time was suddenly important. Something could be done.

A few days later, I inserted a tube from the pulmonary return into the right ventricle of the child's heart. At the same time, I removed the atrial wall, creating a single chamber where there had been two. Its contractions forced blood into the only remaining opening—sending it into the left ventricle, and from there into the lungs.

The child survived and left the hospital to begin a new life. I wrote a paper on it, and two years later, the Canadian surgeon, William Mustard, did a similar operation, running the tube the other way—from right venous entry to left ventricle. Today it is known as Mustard's operation.

Another cardiac killer is Ebstein's anomaly—a congenital misplacement of the tricuspid valve. Instead of being at its proper seat, between right atrium and right ventricle, the valve is attached partially inside the ventricle itself. As a result, the ventricular chamber is too small to do its job of pumping blood into the lungs. This puts the atrium above it in the same condition as a waiting room filled with too many people. In the heart, something has to give way. Pressure builds up until its walls extend and become paper-thin. Eventually, it leads to death.

Attempts had been made to cure this by plicating or diminishing the extended atrium—but this gave poor results and seemed to really solve nothing, since it did not correct the main problem: The ventricle, as a result of the misplaced valve, was too small to be effective. The only solution was to remove the diseased valve and insert a prosthesis, or artificial one, where the valve should really be.

I tried it on a boy of five—putting in a whole new valve. The result was beautiful. The little boy, who had been quite blue, was sent home without further trouble. He has since grown up and leads a normal life. Eventually, this became standard treatment for the disease most everywhere.

By this time—it was 1962—we had begun to develop our own valves. Here also we were forced into finding a new technique, because the treatment of acquired valve disease demanded that something be done. We had methods of repairing diseased valves, such as building up the posterior shelf. But the results were always uncertain, and there seemed to be only one valid answer: build a plastic, ready-made valve that would allow us to cut out the diseased one and insert a new unit.

The Starr valve had emerged that year—a ball in a cage, extending downward into the ventricle. We ran experiments and decided to eliminate the cage since it could irritate the ventricular wall and result in fatal arrhythmias. With no cage, we suspended the ball into the ventricle from a T-piece that shuttled up and down through a ring at the end of a suspension arm. The arm extended up into the atrium and was anchored to a larger steel ring that formed the valve seat between atrium and ventricle. We covered this seat ring with Ivalon and later with Teflon cloth which gave us a material to stitch through when anchoring the valve into place within the heart.

This worked well, but then we realized that only one side of the ball had any function—the side that closed against the seat ring under pressure from the blood. So we cut it down to a lens-like shape, leaving less bulk in the ventricle.

There were variations on this, depending upon whether it was to replace aortic, pulmonary, mitral, or tricuspid valve—but the basic mechanics remained the same. We called it the UCT or University of Cape Town Prosthesis, and it has served us well until this day.

Amid all these advances, one area remained beyond our reach—coronary heart disease. None of our valves or plastic tubes could repair it. Nothing prevented it from being the most deadly and treacherous of all heart ailments.

It killed in a direct and simple way. The heart, being a highly active muscle, needs a large supply of blood to continue its incessant beating. It receives this through two main coronary vessels—the right coronary and the left coronary, which branches off into two other arteries. If anything narrows these vessels, such as arteriosclerosis, the blood supply is diminished. As a result, there is not enough available blood for the heart when under stress. The muscle, needing extra blood yet not receiving it, suffers painfully.

This is angina, and the patient feels it in the center of his chest—a warning to slow down. If there is too great a stress, or a total occlusion of the blood supply, an ischemia results which, in effect, electrocutes the heart. There is ventricular fibrillation and the patient drops dead. If it is only partial or temporary, a portion of the heart will die, leaving the remainder of the muscle to carry an even greater load. The patient then begins to have quite serious trouble. So does his doctor, for there is little that can be done about it. A part of the heart is gone forever. The margin of life has been irreversibly reduced.

Various attempts had been devised to relieve this. One of these, the Beck operation, is accomplished by scratching both the heart and the pericardial sac around it with the hope of causing both to grow together—thus allowing some of the sac's blood supply to also flow into the heart. This is comparable to watering a plant by putting wet paper around its base.

Another approach, devised by Vineberg, consists in mobilizing a portion of an artery from the breastbone—the internal mammary artery—and implanting it directly in the muscle, allowing it to bleed freely into the sponge-like myocardium of the heart. Eventually it sprouts and reconnects with other blood vessels. This is comparable to burying a hose on one side of a flowerbed to water a plant on the other.

We did both operations but never with good results. The reason was simple: Once there was death of the heart muscle, nothing could bring it back. We could replace valves and even parts of blood vessels, but never the heart's precious substance—its muscle. Clearly, there was only one total solution: Cut out the heart and replace it with either a mechanical pump, or transplant the normal heart of a human being who had died from some other disease or accident.

I decided to discuss this in a talk to the students at the University of Pretoria on the past, present, and future of heart surgery. Before doing it, however, I went into the laboratory and told Victor to get two dogs ready for a heart transplant.

"I've got them ready and waiting."

"Aren't you surprised?"

"No, doctor," he said. "After you did that two-headed dog, nothing surprises me any more."

We had grafted a second head onto a dog and made a film of it before going to a conference in Moscow—an experiment that had also been done in the Soviet Union. Professor Louw had heard about it and rushed down to the laboratory to find the dog lapping up milk with both heads.

"What sort of monster will you create next?" he had asked.

"We'll let you know when we do it," I had promised.

Victor, recalling this now, asked: "Shall we tell Professor Louw?"

"Let's see if we can do it first."

It was easier than I expected. As soon as I released the aortic clamp, the transplanted heart began to beat.

"Victor," I said, "we can not only tell Professor Louw about this, we can also tell them in Pretoria."

I began to write my speech that night: "The future treatment of heart disease will include the transplantation of the human heart and most likely both heart and lungs. There is today no major problem in the actual transplantation. The difficulty is in how to maintain the existence of a foreign organ in a body without it being rejected. Yet even this will be overcome eventually . . ."

It was March 1963—nearly five years before we were to do the first human heart transplant. It took us that long to develop the technique to do the operation and create facilities to care for the patient after the operation.

During those years, I had wonderful times with my family. After the death of my father, Louwtjie and I had learned to preserve each other's personality. The children were delightful. Deirdre managed to capture not only my heart, but also many hours that would otherwise have gone into surgery or the laboratory.

CHAPTER 19

IT BEGAN IN A deceptively simple way—without anyone suspecting what would happen eventually to all of us. During a Christmas vacation at Knysna, Deirdre and Boetie started to water ski. Boetie was very adept, but Deirdre had a grace and ease that surprised everyone. Hentie van Rooyen, who owns a hotel at Knysna with docking facilities, said he had never seen anything like it.

"Look at her go," he said. "She's got the makings of a champion."

I looked. Deirdre was then ten, a little *pik* of a thing—a river reed with blonde tassel on top, flying over the water. It was 1960—two years after my father's death.

I thought Deirdre looked great, and said so. Then I went fishing and forgot all about it. The next year when we returned, Hentie started it again.

"You haven't done anything about that girl," he said. "Look at her now."

I looked again. She was on one ski this time.

"I gave her a monoski and she came right up on it. Look at that cross-wake cut!"

It did seem beautiful. A curious sort of wild freedom was obtained, within a very tight frame. Bounded by the laws of nature and the power of a machine, it existed on top of water, at the end of a tow line, and as far as you could go on either side.

"If you don't train that girl, it'll be a real loss. She could become a junior champion within two years, maybe one."

"You really believe that?"

"I know it."

I liked the idea of my daughter being a champion—even a junior champion.

"What do we need to start?"

"You need a boat, three pairs of skis, lots of patience—and a helluva lot of discipline."

I thought I had the patience and the discipline.

"I'll build you a boat at cost," he said. Hentie and his wife, Rita, had become close friends of Louwtjie. I liked them, too, and agreed.

So it began—at first, a pastime sport. Hentie built the first boat. It had a forty-five-horsepower Gale outboard and, being either naïve or a fool, I imagined it was all we would ever need. I christened·it *Louwtjie,* brought it to Cape Town, and began to train Deirdre. It was March 1961. She was eleven, and, remembering what Hentie had said, I figured we would soon be scoring in competitions.

I knew nothing about water skiing, so we began to learn together. The sport is performed in three events: tricks, slalom, and the jump. Before we got very far into any of this, however, Deirdre fell doing tricks and cut her knee on the patella. I took her to the hospital, and she was very brave. She looked at me with tears in her eyes, but she never cried.

"Go ahead, Daddy," she said. "Do what's necessary so we can begin it again."

That was my girl, and I sewed her up—my hands shaking like an intern's. Because of this, she missed most of the competitions. When we returned to Knysna, at the end of 1961, I bought better skis, and we began in earnest. Deirdre was fearless, but she was also a skinny little thing, and I worried she would hurt herself again, especially at the jump where the skier ascends a wooden platform, coming in on a curve at high speed. As protection, I encased her in a life jacket with pants and a jersey and a crash helmet. Besides all this extra weight, she rode on a pair of men's jumping skis, weighing twenty pounds. Finally, to insure her against further danger, I approached the ramp at fifteen miles per hour. Since it is impossible to effectively make a jump at less than twenty-four miles per hour, she barely made it up the ramp, then plopped into the water on the other side.

I raced up in the boat, to find her smiling at me from the water—blonde hair stringing down from a lopsided helmet.

"Don't worry, Daddy—we'll go a lot further than this."

"I know we will. With you, Deirdre, I know we will."

She had, I felt, the making of a champion. At that point, I was hooked on her career. I did not know how far I would eventually go in heart surgery. We were constantly at work, experimenting with valves and new techniques, but so were many other teams in hospitals around the world. Maybe we would make it, maybe not. There was no doubt, however, about this little girl. She was something incredible. Feeling this way, I bought her a skin-tight white suit, and on the water she looked like a nymph moved by invisible winds.

Harry Singer, commodore of the Cape Peninsula Aquatic Club, began to talk like Hentie.

"She's a natural, Chris—perfect balance, beautiful form, and she looks so damn nice. Enter her in the club championships, as a junior."

After that, I spent every minute away from the hospital either on the road heading for the water with Deirdre by my side and the boat on the trailer, or actually out there doing tricks-slalom-ramp, tricks-slalom-ramp. Sometimes the waves were so high we could hardly get the boat into the water. Sometimes my arthritis pained so much I could barely lift the sandbags needed to set the boat deeper and so create a larger wake for tricks. Deirdre was always willing, always laughing—and always a delight. By this time, I was wholly waterborne. When she flew across the water, I was with her.

She swept through the club competitions, easily winning all three events. I entered her into the Western Province Championships and again she won everything. Nobody could believe it. She was only twelve.

I then took her to the Transvaal for the South African Championships. She had been competing as a junior for only a few months, but everyone had heard of Deirdre Barnard. The contest was at Vereeniging, where they signed the Boer War peace treaty. It rained all the time and we stayed in our trailer and the Transvaal officials came through the rain to see us.

"You will enter Deirdre as a junior?" they said, hopefully.

"We'll see," I said.

The Boer War was over, but obviously another one was underway between Transvaal and Western Province. Our people wanted Deirdre to conquer as much as possible by going in as a senior. So I agreed—entering her at the last moment.

Her main rival was a girl called Elise Knox, and the first event was tricks. Deirdre came out, sun-brown in her white suit and my heart flew with her. I prayed she would not fall all through the first run. On the second, she fell only at the ninth trick and won the event by a couple of hundred points. On the slalom, Deirdre went first and started at twenty-six miles per hour—then twenty-eight—then thirty. At thirty-two, she missed the last buoy. It was four points on thirty-two and Elise Knox made the same score.

Elise began the run-off, starting at thirty-two miles per hour and managed only three buoys. This was a great piece of luck and I ran excitedly to Deirdre.

"Only four buoys! That's all you need—just four! Can you do it?"

"Yes, Daddy, I can do it."

She did that and won the jump, too, taking all three events and the South African senior girls' title—at the age of twelve. That night she was given national springbok colors—youngest girl to ever be so honored. She was also picked to represent South Africa at the Junior European Championships in Spain.

They made me team manager, and I pushed aside our work on mitral valves to take the squad to Bañolas, Spain. It was Deirdre's first foreign competition. She tried hard, and her second jump was tremendous—but she fell. Walking into the dressing room, she burst into tears.

"I don't believe in God any more," she said. "I asked Him really hard to help me, and He didn't. I fell, and I'm never going to pray again."

This upset me, and I tried to think of what my father would say.

"You know, you can't always understand why these things happen. Perhaps it's right this way. Perhaps you shouldn't become a champion so quickly."

It was not exactly as my father would have said it. He would have accepted the fall as God's will—but without the implication that it was only a small delay in God's over-all plan for Deirdre to become world champion.

She placed second in Spain and was sent to France for the world championships at Vichy. Here, for the first time, we encountered big-time competition, and Deirdre was outclassed: tenth in tricks, seventh in slalom, seventh in ramp. But at thirteen she was obviously a coming champion. So we returned to Cape Town, proud of her ability to stand up under world competition.

It now seemed to be only a matter of time before Deirdre made it. I told myself that we are all born with a certain amount of ability, and a champion not only had an extra amount but also stopped at nothing in the drive to become first. If Deirdre lacked anything, I was prepared to give it to her. I had enough, I thought, for both of us—with some to spare.

Every day I would leave the hospital to pick her up at school. It was Rustenburg Girls' High at Rondebosch and I waited at the corner in the car with the boat on its trailer. She would come out, wearing her school uniform—black skirt two inches below the knee, black stockings and lace-up shoes, dark blue shirt with blue blazer, and a derby hat. Her blonde hair was carefully pinned up to not touch the collar. If it did, you were fined two pennies.

Half an hour later, the same little girl was in a next-to-nothing swim suit, her hair tumbling down onto her shoulders, racing across the water at thirty miles per hour, and laughing as she always did when we played together—at least in this first period.

That year, 1964, she again won all the South African titles and went to Castel Gandolfo, outside Rome, for the European championships—placing third in tricks, second in slalom, and fifth in ramp. She saw the Pope, got a medal, and when she came home people began to speak of me as Deirdre Barnard's father. Somebody in the family, at least, was going to make it. I decided we needed a better boat to speed up the training, and we bought a sixty-five-horsepower Mercury engine.

In the autumn, after finishing a major operation at the hospital, I flew up to the Transvaal to see her in the South African Championships. Rob Steyger, commodore of the Cape Peninsula Aquatic Club, met me.

"Chris—Deirdre's had an accident."

It was her first serious injury. She had caught the skeg of her ski on the corner of the ramp and the foot was cut badly under the instep. They had pulled her out and put in thirty stitches. I found her in the girl skiers' dormitory. There were no chairs, so I sat on the floor next to her bed.

"Please don't be upset," she said.

"I'm not," I said, trying not to show it.

"It'll be all right. I'll be up soon."

"I know," I said. "We still have time."

We both knew what time meant—time to become a champion.

The foot healed, but she had lost some confidence, and I worked to give it back to her—driving the car to the water every day and coming back after dark. Finally, Louwtjie decided we had reached the limit.

"You'll have a breakdown if you continue this way," she said. "You get up at six to go to the hospital, and you come here at night, wet and cold. You'll both die."

"Nonsense," I said.

"If you really want to train Deirdre, let's get a house on the lake at Zeekoevlei so you don't spend so much time running around, dragging that boat behind your car."

I agreed, and that same day Dr. Ozinsky showed me an ad in the paper for the sale of a house at Zeekoevlei. We bought it, and now nothing was in our way. The boat and the lake were at our back door. The training became more intense.

Deirdre was chosen next to represent her country in the 1965 Australian trials. That meant an even bigger boat, and we got a 100-horsepower Mercury engine. This also moved me into even higher gear. I stopped playing golf, stopped fishing, and refused all social engagements. Every minute was spent with Deirdre, and at home we talked of nothing else. When she did well on the water, it was wonderful. When she did not, we began to fight and she cried and we would not speak for days—even while training.

As the time approached for her to leave for Australia, I began to worry about another leg accident that would again delay her moving to the top. Nothing happened to her leg, but she began to complain of ringing noises in her ears. I took her to a specialist and discovered she had a middle-ear infection. He would have to open up both ear drums and, as a result, she would be unable to go to Australia.

"Hell, man, she's going anyway," I said.

"I advise against it . . . not with both ears open."

"We're opening nothing," I said, and took her away.

Louwtjie's mother made a home remedy from South West Africa—boiling up the feet and leg joints of sheep. From this brew, she drew off an oil and poured it into the infected ears, and they both healed.

Deirdre went to Australia and did quite well—second in slalom, second in jump, fifth in tricks. This gave her a world rating. It was followed by a competition at Cypress Gardens in Florida, and then in March 1966 she returned to Australia to win the Victorian State Championships and the Moomba International. In the Moomba she jumped 115 feet—thirteen feet beyond the world record though it was not recognized because she was not in a world competition.

Deirdre's picture was in all the papers. I was wreathed in her glory—and my son, Boetie, began to suffer from a sense of exclusion. I felt it and tried to compensate. He was growing up lean and strong and liked football. We trained together and had some great times. I would go to his games—often unable to leave the hospital until the second half—running up and down the sideline shouting instructions while he played with all his ability and full of glory.

I also ran on his sidelines during homework, especially during his struggle with English compositions. We did one describing a thunderstorm that his teacher read before the class as an example of a perfect essay.

"Did you get a little help on this?" she asked.

"Yes, a little."

"But is it yours?"

"Yes, it's mine," he said and made sure it stayed that way.

A final exam called for an essay describing a perfect day in spring. That was all Boetie needed. He began his composition, saying it was such a perfect day—until a thunderstorm broke loose. This time he made it something really magnificent—and really his own.

Yet the urgency of Deirdre's training inevitably rode over everything else, demanding she receive most of my time. Everything was geared to one goal: She had to be made a world champion.

This required an even more powerful boat. Basil Reed, son of one of my patients, helped me obtain an eighteen-foot, 225-horsepower Mercruiser inboard with an outboard drive. I had put a pacemaker in his mother's heart, and we christened the beautiful craft just that—*Pacemaker*. It had come as a most generous gift and something of a miracle. For finally we had the power and speed needed to train for the 1967 world championship in Canada.

At the same time, I became concerned about Deirdre ever reaching the top. She was, I feared, too nice a girl. She did not have the killer instinct needed to become a world champion. She would be beaten and laugh about it. When I am beaten, I might laugh—yet I also cry inside. But not Deirdre. She would cry if she saw an overloaded donkey, or a colored child alone in the street. If I shouted at her, she would cry, too. But if she lost, she would laugh it off.

This caused me to drive her even harder, trying to instil something of myself into her own personality. Inevitably, this caused bitter moments on the lake.

One day she needed to work on her tricks, especially the toe-hold 180 which we had practiced most of the day previous. It is done by hooking one foot onto the rope, then turning about 180 degrees on one ski—at the same time moving across the wake. She seemed to have mastered it, and we had come home happily in the evening—Deirdre up in the bow to lift the motor clear of the shallows, Louwtjie with her needlework peering at us from her attic room. If Deirdre was not crying, it was a good day—like this one. The dogs, Ringo and Sixpence, also sensed everything was fine and rushed out into the water, barking happily.

That was how it had gone the day before. But now Deirdre seemed to have forgotten all she had learned. She succeeded in doing everything incorrectly until I lost my patience.

"Listen," I said. "To do a toe-hold 180 turn, you must lift off the water first. If you turn when you're deep in the water, you'll spill. You know this—why don't you do it?"

"I am doing it."

"No, you're not."

From the water, she glared up angrily.

"Look," she said, "if you're so damn good, why don't you come and do it?"

"I'll tell you why. Because you're trained to do skiing, and I'm trained to do heart surgery. Also, when I have a problem in surgery I work on it until I've got the answer. I don't keep making the same mistakes all the time."

We started off again, and in the rear mirror I could see her sticking out her tongue at me. It was so funny, I laughed. But then she spilled again, and that was the limit.

"Jesus, Deirdre, you don't try. You're just wasting my time."

"I am trying," she said from the water.

"You're not trying. You stay out too late at night. You don't think. You don't use your head."

"I haven't been out in a week. I don't go anywhere. I'm trying as hard as I can to please you. That's why I'm trying so hard."

"Not for me. You're doing it for your own sake, because you're not pleasing me—not at this rate, anyway."

Tears began, and I felt miserable. Something had gone wrong in my calculations. Deirdre had the natural ability to become a champion. Yet it also required drive and discipline, and I had thought I could make up for any she lacked. But it was becoming clear you could not transfer that to someone else. Champions were hungry people. They were made that way, and what they had could not be transferred, especially the hunger. You had it or you did not have it.

"Come on," I said. "Get into the boat and let's go home. We just have to admit that you're not a skier. So let's forget the whole bally affair."

As we came in, Louwtjie saw the tears. So did the dogs and they stayed back on the lawn. When Deirdre finally reached her mother, she began to weep openly.

"You're mean," said Louwtjie. "This little girl can take only so much."

"She's not a little girl," I said. "Not any more."

"I don't know what I am," said Deirdre. "I just don't want to ski any more."

Louwtjie tried to comfort her.

"It'll be better tomorrow."

"No, I don't want any tomorrow. I hate it. I used to love skiing, but now I hate it."

Later that night, the wind changed to the northwest and it woke me up. I awakened Deirdre, too, and together we climbed into our wet suits over the pyjamas. My arthritis pained me so much that she had to help me into the rubber suiting. Then we waded into the dark water to move the boat away from the rising waves and into the cove of a neighbor. The water was chest high, and it was cold. On the way back, Deirdre took my hand.

"Do you think it will rain tomorrow?" she asked.

"It usually does with a northwester."

"Even if it does, we can go out—no?"

"Do you want to?"

"Yes. I want to."

"I'm glad to hear it."

She squeezed my hand to say this made her happy, too. She was ready to go again—to please me. But there were increasing signs of resentment at being driven at such a pace.

One day I decided to do a little skiing, and Deirdre sweetly offered to help.

"Yes, Dad, come on—I'll take you out."

I wanted to make one turn of the lake, but she took me round and round until I was ready to collapse. I kept signaling her to return to the shore, but this only sent her back out into the middle of the lake. Finally I let go of the line, and she left me there.

Everyone at the club thought it very funny: The slave had turned on his master. I knew it was not at all like Deirdre, and I should have taken it as a warning. I was too busy, however, looking beyond her—toward the Canadian World Championships.

One Sunday morning, a few weeks before her departure for Canada, we began early. The water was like a mirror, and Deirdre slalomed beautifully, did her tricks in great form, and I suggested some jumping.

"I don't feel like it," she said.

"Well, you must practice. It's a nice day for it."

"No, I don't feel right for it."

"That's because it's Sunday. You never like to jump on Sunday."

She did the first jump, and it was not a good one. The second one was also not in form. On the third run, she tried very hard and hit the ramp too low—slipping dangerously off to the side. As she landed there was a loud crack, and she cried out, and I knew we were in trouble. She came up without raising both hands to indicate that she was unhurt. Quickly I turned the boat and raced to her side.

"My leg is broken," she said.

I pulled her into the boat, and she was in extreme pain.

"My leg is broken. I can't move it," she said.

I was afraid it was true because of the sound it made when she hit the water. Sometimes when a leg breaks you can hear the crack as the bone snaps.

"Don't move it," I said. "We'll examine you on shore."

"No, don't take me there. Please don't take me there, now."

She was ashamed to be seen crying.

"Please, Daddy, please stay away from everybody."

After she got herself under control, we went in and she was helped from the boat. The leg did not seem broken. It was tender under the left knee at one side, and I decided it was a pulled tendon. After a bit, she began to bend the knee and said it felt better.

"Maybe it'll be all right," she said.

"Yes," I said, but I suspected it was not going to be that simple.

When we got to the house, she wanted to help dock the boat and carry in the skis. She was limping, however, and I made her stop.

"Don't move that knee any more," I said. "Go sit down."

"No, it isn't so bad," she said.

That night she could hardly move the leg. It swelled up at the knee, she had much pain, and the next day Louwtjie took her to a specialist. He confirmed my fears: She had injured the median ligament and perhaps the cartilage.

"I'll have to put it in plaster," he said. "You won't be able to move for a while."

"Not even go to Canada?" asked Deirdre.

"There is no Canada," he said. "Forget about it."

She was put in plaster, and they phoned me at the hospital.

"He said to forget about Canada," said Deirdre.

"Don't believe him," I said. "You have to go. We can't afford to miss this."

"He says I won't be well in time."

"We'll make you well. You have to be well."

In the plaster cast, she could not ski. But I made her work in the gym so that she would keep fit. I went every day to direct her exercises. Two days before she was due to leave, the plaster came off. I looked at the knee with the doctor.

"All right," he said. "She can go. She should really rest. But the championship means so much to you, let her go."

We went down to the lake and Deirdre began to ski. She did fairly well, but you could see the knee worried her. We both knew it was not right. She was very brave about it, however.

"It will loosen up," she said. "It will get better when I practice in Canada."

"I hope so," I said.

"I hope so, too," she said, "because I know you want this championship very much."

"Don't you?"

"Yes—of course. But nobody could want it as much as you, and I hope I don't disappoint you."

There it was again. I wanted it more than she did. All the years of training, all the tears in Zeekoevlei, all the trials and medals and victory cups came down to this: I had failed to transplant into her my own hunger for victory. She was still not going to beat her fists and cry if she lost. She could laugh it off. She would never make it. Even with a good knee, she would never go to the very top. She was just too damned nice.

In Canada, she tried hard. But the knee bothered her all the time, and she did not place in any event. Yet before this happened, I knew that it was over between us. The time had come to cease using my daughter to satisfy my own ambitions. So I told her when she came home: I would give all the help she needed, but I was no longer going to train her every day, nor even guide her training.

This had two immediate results. Deirdre was free to enjoy skiing once more. I also had a greater freedom. No longer compelled to transfer myself into my daughter's career, I could concentrate on a far larger transplant.

CHAPTER 20

THE BIG BATTLE in a heart transplant was not going to be in placing a new heart in a human being, but in getting it to stay there. Our experiments with animals and reports from overseas made this quite clear. We could insert a new heart and immediately it would begin to sustain life. Yet at the same time, a rejection process would begin because the host body was immune to any foreign element—even an organ sustaining it in life. This was our problem. Unless we could control this immunological rejection, there was no basis for attempting a heart transplant.

At the beginning of 1966 evidence indicated some control was possible. In kidney transplants ways had been found to prevent, or at least delay, rejection—indicating we would soon be able to transplant a heart. For if the human system could be conditioned to accept a kidney, it could take other organs, especially something as basic as a pumping muscle. Obviously we had to learn to transplant a kidney, and more important, control its rejection. The kidney had become a stepping stone to the heart. Its transplant would be a run-through for a heart transfer.

With this in mind, I applied for a training course under one of the great pioneers in this field—Dr. David Hume, formerly of Harvard and now with the Medical College of Virginia, at Richmond. Dr. Hume and his team were experienced both in kidney grafts and rejection control. He graciously accepted me for a three-month course, to begin in August.

Since my first return from Minneapolis, I had made six trips abroad—attending conferences, seminars, and visiting medical centers in Europe, the Soviet Union, India, Australia, and New Zealand. Whenever possible, I also returned to America because it was there I learned the most.

Richmond was no exception. It met all my expectations. Dr. Hume assigned me to work in a renal transplant unit, and I assisted at kidney transplant operations. With this I learned how to manage these patients in the postoperative period. I studied rejection and its control by means of drugs in rats, dogs, and people. Besides this, Dr. Hume allowed me to visit other medical centers working on the same problem. This included Denver, where they had developed the use of antilymphocyte serum as an immuno-suppressive agent.

There was a spirit of open scientific inquiry at Richmond which was stimulating. The staff included Dr. Richard Lower who had worked with Dr. Norman Shumway on the technique of heart transplant. Prodded by Dr. Hume, we never slept and the drama never ceased.

One morning during a ward round, we came across a young man suffering from jaundice and severe liver failure. He was being treated by an interesting technique, which consisted in giving fifteen pints of blood, one pint at a time, while withdrawing the same amount—an exchange transfusion. In this way, they diluted the poisons that had accumulated in the body as a result of liver failure and so obtained time for the liver to recover. Unlike other organs, the liver is self-regenerative. If given a rest, it can often repair itself.

The problem was how to do it. Machines can take over for the kidney, as well as for the heart and lungs, yet nothing has been built which can stand in for the liver—a chemical filter and factory of staggering dimension. It has been estimated that a man-made installation duplicating the liver's known functions would spread over six square miles.

The blood transfusion we were witnessing could only give brief help. A more radical approach was to remove a pig liver, quickly wash out the pig blood, and hook it up to the patient. Even though separated from a body, such a liver would function from six to eight hours. This is sufficient to relieve a serious liver paralysis in a human being, yet still not enough for sustained support.

Dr. Hume, watching his staff desperately trying to save the young man, turned to me.

"You know, it's a shame we can't hook a patient like this onto a live liver."

"Why can't we?" I asked.

"Have you ever done it?"

"No, but I don't see why it can't be done—for example, with a baboon."

Dr. Mel Williams, a staff doctor with us, said it was impossible.

"The baboon has natural antibodies in his blood against a human being."

"I'll get rid of them," I said.

"How?" asked Dr. Hume.

"I'll take a baboon and cool him down, wash out his blood with water, then fill him up with human blood of the same group as your patient. That will be your baboon with human blood."

Dr. Williams shook his head, but Dr. Hume was interested.

"You believe you can do that?"

"Yes, I can do it."

In Cape Town I had drained a patient with liver failure of all his blood and run in a fresh supply. There was no reason why we could not do the same thing with a baboon, including a washout of his whole system. It would have to be done quickly, however, since I was due to leave for Cape Town in two days.

Dr. Hume immediately agreed, and the college moved into action. We needed three heart-lung machines, or two plus a switch-over container, and this was easily obtainable. But there were no baboons, and since I was leaving, one had to be found immediately—or we would have to call off the experiment.

I discovered then that America has almost everything, but it is very low on baboons. Phone calls were made through the night, until one was finally on its way to us by air freight. It arrived the day before I was to leave—a medium-sized male—and we began the experiment before a small crowd of doctors and students with movie cameras.

I had three heart-lung machines ready to use, one after the other, and we hooked the baboon onto the first one. This did nothing more than circulate the animal's blood through the machine, but with a heat exchanger adjusted for extreme cooling. When body temperature reached five degrees centigrade—a deep enough hypothermia to prevent brain damage during the period when the animal would be without blood circulation—I cut the pump and quickly drained the baboon of all its blood.

It was then hooked onto the second machine containing Ringer's lactate solution. This washed through until it came out crystal clear, indicating no blood was left. We were then at the critical point, and I quickly attached the leads to the third machine containing human blood.

It was barely in time. For as the flow entered the bloodless body, the heart went into fibrillation.

"I knew it," said Dr. Hume. "The baboon's going to die."

"Just wait, Professor."

I rewarmed it for a while, then gave the heart an electric shock and it restarted immediately, pumping human blood through its chambers and so into the arterial system. But then it developed pulmonary edema.

"It's going to die," said Dr. Hume again.

"It won't die," I said. "The venous pressure is too high. We have to lower it, and then the lungs will clear."

The next morning, on my way to the airport, I went to see the baboon. He was sitting up in a cage, eating an orange. They had bright lights on him, and movie cameras were still recording his new existence—an animal form, living with human blood.

Dr. Hume was delighted.

"We will eventually use this on a human being," he predicted.

"Good, but there's a hidden danger we haven't considered."

"What's that?"

"You'll do this on a patient in a comatose state, due to self-intoxication?"

He nodded.

"Suppose the patient wakes up to find he's practically in bed with a baboon—what next?"

Dr. Hume laughed. Both scientist and humanist—he had that precious mixture of knowledge and faith that I had come to expect among the best of the Americans.

I returned to Cape Town, prepared to do a kidney transplant. But first we had to create a team for it—a team whose structure was most fundamental since it would also do the eventual heart transplant. In effect, it would be a permanent transplant team, with a fixed nucleus of specialists needed for any organ transplant. This included the surgeons, the nursing unit, and other basic disciplines. Tissue compatibility would be tested by Dr. "M.C." Botha. Bacteriologists, trained to detect infection at the first onslaught, would be captained by Dr. Arderne Forder. Professor Philip E. Palmer would run the X rays, Professor James Kench biochemical support, and Dr. Reuben Mibashan hematology needed for blood analysis.

Specialists would also be called in, depending upon the organ to be replaced. For the kidney transplant, we would be joined by Professor Lennox Eales and Dr. Geoffrey Thatcher, renal experts. Professor Schrire and his cardiac department would govern the selection of heart cases, while others would be called in for special problems—Drs. William Jackson and Bernard Pimstone for diabetics, Drs. Simcha Banks and Israel Marks for gastrointestinal trouble.

In all of this, there was to be one important change in accepted procedure. Normally, the specialist in medicine gave a patient to the surgeon for the period of the operation and the immediate postoperative recovery. After this, the patient returned to his original doctor or the medical specialist. This occurred with heart patients. After leaving my ward, they reverted to Professor Schrire's cardiac unit, which could better diagnose their progress.

In transplants, however, the operation would be followed by a struggle to control rejection. Here there was no established discipline. It was a new and expanding field—inextricably linked to the surgical transplant, a close and immediate consequence of the operation itself. As a result, transplant surgeons had begun to retain control of their patients and personally direct the postoperative antirejection battle.

So it was to be with us. Once the surgical team received a patient, they were to keep him under their supervision—even after his discharge, although he would be checked periodically by the cardiac clinic.

Besides a team of men and women, we also needed special equipment—treatment rooms for patients before and after the operation, a system of obtaining donors, and specific medicines such as antilymphocyte serum to combat rejection. Finally, an artificial kidney unit was required.

I had begun to structure some of this before going to Richmond—meeting first with Professor Eales and Dr. Thatcher to select the proper dialysis unit. But it was not until October 1967—a year after my return—that we were finally ready and able to receive into our ward Mrs. Edith Black, suffering with disease of both kidneys yet hopeful we could give her at least one new one.

Three weeks before the operation, I assisted Professor Louw in the first step—a bilateral nephrectomy, or removal of both kidneys. We then inserted a plastic shunt in her arm—from artery to vein—which could be attached twice weekly to an artificial kidney. This would be enough to clean her blood, and conceivably she could live for years this way—as do hundreds of others without kidneys. It is a limited and costly life, however, circumscribed around a dialysis machine. For Mrs. Black, a new kidney was infinitely preferable. So we kept her in the ward, awaiting the arrival of a proper donor.

Here again, we had to prepare a set of criteria that would apply to all future donors—including heart donors. There were three which governed acceptability. First, the organ to be transplanted had to be normal and healthy. Next, to minimize rejection, donor and recipient had to have compatible red-cell groups. As for white cells, we would do leucocyte typing and if there was too great a disparity between the antigens of donor and recipient, we would refuse the donor. Finally, the donor had to be free of infectious diseases.

We also had to clarify the rules governing our right to remove an organ from a human body. Fortunately, a basis for it already existed within our laws. Any person dying from unnatural causes—such as an auto accident or a death for noncertifiable reasons—must legally undergo a postmortem. The body is opened up, its organs examined, and it is then closed up for burial. During the postmortem, one or another organ may legally be removed for purposes of teaching or study, provided the parents or relatives give consent. We intended to operate within this law, putting the kidney or heart within a new body, rather than in a bottle on a shelf. It would thus be taken for therapeutic use rather than an educational one. In patients dying from a known cause, permission had to be obtained—both for the postmortem and for the removal of any organ.

There was only one difference: We had to do it immediately, before the organ became unserviceable. This required establishing clearly a criterion for death: no respiration, no heart beat, dilation of pupils with no response to light, no response to painful stimuli—all indicating the brain is dead.

To ensure against hasty decisions, or charges of pirating living bodies, we decided that none of the doctors involved in the transplant would pronounce on the death of a potential donor. This would be done by a separate neurological team. Finally, after clearing these legalities with Dr. Lionel S. Smith, professor of forensic medicine, we felt prepared to move into action.

The casualty department was alerted that we were ready for a kidney donor, as were my three registrars, Drs. Siebert "Bossie" Bosman, Coert Venter, and François Hitchcock. It did not begin well. One after another, six potential donors were discarded as imcompatible. The seventh—a colored youth with severe brain injury from an auto accident—was acceptable. After he had been declared dead and permission granted, we moved him into the operating room, removed the left kidney, and proceeded to put it into Mrs. Black—joining renal artery to hypogastric artery, renal vein to common iliac vein, then implanting ureter into the bladder. It proceeded with surprising ease, and the patient immediately began to secrete urine.

The South African newspapers hailed it as a major surgical event, and the foreign press gave it overtones of racial integration in a limited physiological arena: "Mrs. Black Gets Black Kidney." Three weeks later, Mrs. Black—with a kidney whose potentials of rejection or tolerance did not depend upon the color of skin—left the hospital to begin a normal life.

The machinery of the transplant team had functioned perfectly. All the elements had fused into each other: selection of donor, tissue-typing for compatibility, preoperative care of donor and recipient, coordination of two surgical teams in the theater, postoperative care, and rejection control. We had completed our run-through. As a team, we were ready to undertake a heart transplant. All elements had reached the point of readiness—including the surgical technique for doing it.

In experiments with dogs, we had done forty-eight heart transplants. In over 90 per cent of these, the new heart had begun to beat regularly. It was a technique built on that developed by Shumway and Lower who had experimented on more than three hundred dogs. The body of their work was formidable—especially in the studies of rejection. Adding their findings to ours, I could see little sense in continuing the further sacrifice of animals. Scientific inquiry consisted in this: the use of knowledge to go on to further knowledge.

I went to Professor Val Schrire to tell him we were ready. The future recipient would come from him, from the cardiac clinic he had built within the Groote Schuur—an immense and dedicated labor of fifteen years. It had already begun in 1953 when I returned from work at the City Hospital, and during those early years Professor Schrire—with a dedicated love of his work—had stimulated my interest in heart surgery. Without him, without the edifice he created, a heart transplant in South Africa was not possible. Nor was it possible to do one without giving us a patient.

"What makes you think you can now go ahead?" he asked.

"Everything is ready," I said. "We have the team, and we know how to do it."

"How do you know? Because you've done it on dogs?"

"What else do you suggest?"

"Your dogs don't live very long. You should get longer survivors before you try this."

It was going badly. He was openly hostile to the idea of an immediate transplant and clearly he did not intend to give me a patient. He sat behind his desk in a cluttered office. Before him was a fat folder of unanswered letters and a dictating machine. I had come at a bad time. My project was foundering between a fat pile of old letters and a recording tape.

"Val, let me explain it to you."

"Go ahead."

He took off his glasses to clean them. He was a short man of neat, precise habits. He wore a doctor's white coat, even sitting in his office. Wiping his glasses, he looked at me—blue-gray eyes, finely shaped nose, unsmiling lips, gray hair—all of his features once more stating his basic proposition: "Your dogs never live very long."

"I'm not trying to get longer survivors in dogs. I can't nurse a dog like a human being. I can't handle a dog on immuno-suppressive drugs as I can a human being."

"I don't know."

"Well, I know. I studied it at Richmond, and we have applied it here successfully with the kidney transplant. I know how to handle such a patient. All we need now is for you to give us one."

"We have first to consider all the risks."

"What risks are you talking about?" I asked, trying to control myself. "We're preparing to do this on a patient with irreversible disease who is beyond hope of recovery, and who has only a few days or hours of life . . . you call that a risk?"

"Some people will."

"Not the man who's about to die—and you know it, Val. He will beg you for it. He'll beg you for the chance. Because that's what it means to him—a chance, not a risk."

"I'll think about it," he said.

"As for the recipient, I have an idea. We can take a Bantu with cardiomyopathy because it is a disease common to them with no known cure. This will give us a young man with a good body who has only one defect—heart disease."

"Forget it," he said. "Our first patient will never be black or colored, because overseas they will say that we are experimenting on nonwhites."

He was right, but it did not change the immediate situation. After months of training, we were ready to go—only to discover that he was not.

"I'll think about it," he said again.

I got into my car and drove the short distance from hospital to my office at the medical school. Professor Schrire's refusal of immediate support overwhelmed me. Was he afraid that an eventual failure might reflect on his department? Or perhaps he felt this was an invasion of his territory. If so, it made little sense. He already had more work than he could handle— 19,000 cardiograms and 6,000 patients a year. Only 3 per cent of these went into surgery. If an occasional transplant never returned to him, it could hardly affect his department. Indeed, he had said he wanted no part of the rejection responsibility: "I know nothing about it and, unlike most everybody else, I admit it."

It made me sad, profoundly sad, and I sat for a while in the car parked before the office. Could it be that Val was right? Maybe we were too anxious. Maybe we still did not know enough and this was too great a risk—even to expect from a man with only a a few hours to live.

Jacques Roux came by and I asked him to sit with me in the car.

"What is it, Chris?" he asked, getting in.

"I want to talk to you."

We had remained friends since our first competitive days as housemen— the kind of friends who have enough mutual respect to say what they think.

"Jacques, I'm going to transplant a heart."

"I know."

"How do you know?"

"You've been working on it in the animal laboratory. I've seen it coming."

"I've just been to see Val. He's not very enthusiastic—in fact, he's resisting me."

"Give him time, Chris. He's a thorough sort of man. Physicians always need a little time."

"Well, that's what I don't have, Jacques. I want it now, we're ready to go now. I think he doubts we can pull it off."

"Chris, if anybody in the whole world can pull this off, it's you."

"Thank you, Jacques . . . thank you."

After he left, I felt better and went into the animal laboratory. My brother Marius and Dr. Bosman were doing one more heart transplant on a dog, to test a new antirejection serum. When I entered, they were putting in the final sutures.

"That's all, boys," I said. "After this, you can forget it. The next one will be a human being."

All through the last two weeks of October I kept after Professor Schrire —plaguing him day and night. The delay and the subsequent anxiety caused an alarming flare-up in my arthritis. Both hands and feet began to swell and with such pain I feared it would prevent me from operating when Professor Schrire finally decided to release a patient.

Finally, in the first week of November, he called me into his office. The pile of letters still lay on his desk next to the recording machine. But now he was less reserved, and I knew the moment had come.

"Look, Chris, I think we have a patient suitable for a heart transplant."

"Yes?"

"His name is Washkansky . . . Louis Washkansky."

PART VII
THE TRANSPLANT

CHAPTER 21

I DOUBT IF I ever thanked Professor Schrire for giving me Louis Washkansky. My first reaction was to know who he was.

"We offered him to you for surgery in July but you said nothing could be done."

"He must be in pretty bad shape."

"He is—worse than ever."

As we examined his folder, I remembered the case. They had made some angiograms of him and I suggested we look at them—film studies of the heart in function. Professor Schrire agreed and we left his office to go to the projection room. In the corridor, I felt like running. It was the beginning of my longest mile and almost too much to believe.

"The patient has agreed?"

"Yes—but you should talk to Dr. Kaplan about it. He has been the family doctor. I think you know him. He is a consultant in the cardiac clinic."

"Yes, I'll talk to him."

Dr. Kaplan would give me the patient and then withdraw, as would Professor Schrire. In this way, the race would be run in an ever-diminishing arena—eventually narrowing down to a donor and a recipient and a team of people holding a new heart. Yet before that happened, many others played a part. Each one in his way made it possible for us to arrive at the final act. One of these was a most human and sensitive physician, Dr. Kaplan.

Dr. Barry Kaplan, Consultant Physician

"I knew Louis Washkansky socially and in April 1966 he came to see me with his wife, Ann. He could not sleep at night because of shortness of breath, and they thought it might be his lungs. He already knew he had heart trouble but he did not realize that his trouble, medically called Cheyne-Stokes breathing, was caused by gross heart failure.

"It's rather terrifying to witness. The patient takes a short breath then a deeper one, then a still deeper one—going on like that until he stops breathing altogether, lying there with no sign of respiration. Looking at it, the observer can only conclude that the heart has ceased to function. Ann used to sit up nights, listening to this and not knowing when it was going to stop. She was already nervous about Louis' heart condition and looking at this wild sort of breathing made her think he was going to die in bed next to her. 'I'm not sleeping anymore. I know as soon as I close my eyes that he will take a real long one and never breathe anymore.'

"I told them the breathing was due to his heart and prescribed aminophylline suppositories. This helped and Louis and Ann told their friends, 'Dr. Kaplan has the greatest pills ever. You shove them up your arse and air comes in the top.'

"He was fifty-three then, a big man and a stoic type. He never told Ann anything. In fact, he lied to her about himself, saying he was fine, saying always, 'I'm on top of the world.' He was running into trouble and he knew it, but he was not going to cry about it—not to her or to anybody. He had lived in a certain way and he was set to go on living that way.

"A little bit of him kept dying all the time but he was staying with it to the end. He had already lost so much that I was never sure he would come back for the next appointment. Already he had a heart bigger than anything I've ever seen. You would never believe the last X rays. There was only one inch from the left border of the chest, and two inches from the right. It was a big bag.

"I gave him a very bad prognosis, certainly no more than a couple of months. Yet this man struggled on for two and a half years before the operation. It's one of those things you can't account for, other than to say it was a will to live. I know it's a phrase that's been used a lot these days, but when you see it happen, when you see a man struggling along with a heart two-thirds dead, you can only say you've seen something really remarkable about a human being.

"Of course those suppositories couldn't keep the whole thing going forever. In June he came back again, short of breath and with a cough. So I increased the diuretics. Three months later, the real trouble began. He developed swelling of the legs and the liver and all that went with it. The disease was extending itself—destroying his body. From the beginning, he had been in left ventricular failure. The swelling of legs and liver meant the right ventricle was also going.

"His diabetes also became worse but since I knew he had not much hope to live, I saw little point in getting heroic about the diabetes. It seemed heartless to further restrict his diet or add more pills. He was already taking fifteen a day—Lasix, digoxin, Diabinese, Dindevan, and Aldactone. His ECG showed deterioration with a P-R interval of 0.44 seconds which is the largest I have ever seen in a man who could still walk and sell groceries.

"Everyday he would somehow get into his car and drive around the Cape to his customers, taking orders for his wholesale business. About that time he began to have more anginal pains, as well as fainting attacks, breath failure, and spitting blood. Just the same, he kept at it, taking orders by telephone when he could not get to his car. And you know what? His customers all stayed loyal to him. His struggle to live, his figure as a man who would not give up existed even then—long before the agony of that transplant. There was something about him which created loyalty and friendship.

"I sent him to the cardiac clinic, hoping something could be done. They took angiograms and other tests and then sent him back to me—nothing was possible. But it did not stop Washkansky. He went on, anyway. He never missed a Friday night soccer game, and he went out to parties and had his few drinks.

"It was a matter of time before we had to return him to the hospital for the last time—if he managed to live through his next heart attack. He had suffered his biggest one in 1965 when he was talking to a customer. He felt it coming and said he needed a doctor immediately. The storekeeper said there was one nearby, but the doctor was not there, and they drove around for an hour looking for one. Finally, they went to the Rondebosch Cottage Hospital and Louis got out of the car to walk up the stairs to where he thought he should go—climbing the stairs rather than take the elevator. He got to the top and collapsed in severe failure. He had delivered himself, on his own two feet—but this destroyed most of his left ventricle.

"You could be sure he would never climb any steps the next time. Even so, nothing could keep him in bed for more than two hours a day. Normally, for anyone in heart failure, total rest is imposed until they're out of failure. But not Louis. He would say: 'This is no life to stay in bed already,' and get up to hit the road or to start telephoning his customers. So in September we sent him to the hospital—mainly to make him rest.

"In the hospital, they tried everything, but he did not respond, and the cardiac clinic said nothing could be done. We had only to wait for him to die. But that chap just could not die. He went into a coma—a diabetic coma—and they got him out of that. Then he developed a little stroke and could not move one hand. When he did try to move it, the hand would start shaking. It's called hemiballismus.

"I don't know if you know anything about cricket, but the movement was like a bowler. They throw their arms around involuntarily—that kind of movement. When this improved, we came to the terrible part. Because his heart failure would not respond to ordinary treatment, his legs became edematous and filled up with liquid. So they put in Southey's tubes to relieve it. They sat him in a chair with his feet in basins and inserted needles to physically draw off the liquid. He sat upright that way for five days and nights.

"Picture for yourself a man. Everyone had given him up. The physicians had given him up. The cardiac clinic had given him up because there was nothing else they could do. Yet this man refused to die. It's fantastic!

"I'm a member of the cardiac clinic, and we have a meeting every Monday morning. I used to go into the meeting saying, 'Why don't you chaps do something for Washkansky? You can't let him die, man, you must do something.' It got to be a sort of joke every Monday morning. Anyhow, nothing was being done because nothing could be done. Then, sometime early in November, Schrire asked me to come and see him.

" 'Look,' he said, 'we're thinking of transplanting a heart into Washkansky. How do you think he'll accept it?'

"It was in his office. I'd never heard of such a thought, but since Schrire looked rather nonchalant, I decided to look nonchalant, too—although I was a bit staggered by this, as you can imagine.

"So he said: 'How do you think Washkansky would react to it?'

"So I said: 'Well, he's quite a chap and will accept whatever it entails. He will accept anything for life.'

"Schrire than asked me to talk to him about it. There was no point in waiting, so I began to walk from the clinic to the ward. Louis was sitting up with his swollen legs dangling outside the bed, smoking a cigarette. I said to him: 'Louis, something may be able to be done for you, but it entails a tremendous gamble.'

"Then I said: 'It is such a gamble you may not come out of it alive.'

"So he says to me: 'What is it?'

"I said: 'Professor Schrire said to me that there was a possibility they might be able to transplant somebody's heart into you.'

"He sort of looked at me and said: 'If that's the only chance, I'll take it.'

"So I said: 'Louis, don't you want to think about it? Don't you want to discuss it with Ann?'

"He said: 'No, no . . . there's nothing to think about. I can't go on living like this. The way I am now is not living.'

"There and then he made up his mind that he would take the operation, whatever it meant. I said to him: 'Louis, it has never been done before. I'm not even sure whether it's been done on dogs.'

"I didn't know then, because after Schrire spoke to me I did not go and read up about it. I went straight from Schrire's office to Washkansky.

"I said again: 'Don't you want to think it over?'

"And he said: 'No, no. There is nothing to think about. I'll take the chance as soon as possible.' "

In the corridor, on the way to look at the film studies of Washkansky's heart, I recalled talking in America to Dr. Richard Lower and to Dr. Norman Shumway on what they believed would be the proper circumstances for transplanting a heart. They said we had to have a patient on the operating table and in such a condition that he could not come off the heart-lung machine. At that point, according to Lower and Shumway, we could attempt a transplant since the patient was going to die on the table without it.

It seemed to me that this was highly unrealistic. First of all, there was little possibility in having a donor ready at the moment of such a crisis. Next, it did not seem fair to make the patient wait that long—that is, until he had to have a donor immediately—or die. I therefore moved the situation back in time and decided on three basic criteria for the acceptance of a heart transplant patient. First, he had to be in a condition that was irreversible and would eventually kill him. Next, all forms of treatment must have been attempted and proven of no avail. Finally, he must be close to the point of death.

The medical report on Louis Washkansky indicated he filled all these requirements. The film study of his heart would undoubtedly confirm it even further, as well as give me an idea of what I would find when we opened him up.

Angiograms, or movies of the heart, were another dramatic advance in fighting cardiac disease. They were actually X-ray motion pictures, taken at the moment an opaque dye is injected into either side of the heart. This is done by running a catheter, or spaghetti-thin tube, up a vein to reach the right side of the heart or up an artery to enter the left side. With expert handling, the tubes can enter an upper chamber, go past its valve into the lower chamber and then continue out of that through still another valve towards the lungs or into the aorta. The patient feels no pain, other than a slight sense of discomfort from the tube being wiggled through successive valves and chambers of his heart. Besides serving to inject an opaque solution—so that the shape of the heart and its vessels will show up on an X-ray film—the catheter is also used to take blood samples and pressure readings within the heart. It can further measure the degree of valve blockage, the septal or the valve leakage, and the amount of oxygen provided by the lungs. With this technique, the heart had ceased to be an unexplored country. It was open to the sight of man, just as it was open to his touch on the operating table.

They had made two movies of Washkansky's heart—one of the left ventricle and one of the coronary vessels supplying blood to the heart's working muscles. They showed advanced disease in a most dramatic manner. The left ventricle had swollen out like a bag. Normally this chamber contracts to expel its contents of fresh blood into the body. But here it hardly moved, emitting only a little puff of the dye, like a spurt of white ink from a monstrous and insensitive jellyfish somehow lodged within a human chest. The coronary vessels were equally amazing. Two of the three were so clogged that the dye could not get through them.

It was a shattered and ruined heart, and I looked at the folder to see what forces had blown it into such a shape. The right atrial pressure was ten millimeters of mercury against a normal three or four, pulmonary artery was seventy-five against twenty-five, left atrial thirty-five against eight. Lack of blood through the coronary vessels had brought death to two-thirds of the left ventricle, causing the remainder to expand like a bag in order to meet the body's urgent demand. Yet even this was failing, and the immense chamber was now able to pump only 2.36 liters a minute into a body that could require fifteen or more liters.

No wonder we had turned him down in July. This heart was beyond the reach of medicine or surgery. It bore the waste of a battle field, strewn with many separate deaths. After the film, I turned to Professor Schrire and his assistant, Dr. Wally Beck:

"I have never seen such massive destruction—are you sure this man's still alive?"

"He's in A-1 Ward, why don't you go and see for yourself?"

"Besides the heart," said Dr. Beck, "he's got diabetes, liver failure, kidney failure, and cellulitis of his left calf following insertion of Southey's tubes."

"What makes him go on?"

"He's a fighter," said Schrire. "He was an amateur boxer, and he won't give up until he's knocked out for good. At Muizenberg there is some sort of gadget you hit with your fist. This man was the only one in his group who could hit it hard enough to ring the bell at the top."

"I think you picked the right man, Val."

"I hope so."

After this, I phoned Dr. Kaplan who said Washkansky had agreed to accept a transplant—but it would be better if I explained it to him. I thanked Dr. Kaplan and left to find Louis Washkansky in A-1 Ward.

He was propped up in bed, reading a book, and he looked up at me over the top of his glasses.

"Mr. Washkansky, I have come to introduce myself. I believe Dr. Kaplan and Professor Schrire have spoken to you about it—we intend doing a heart transplant on you, and for this you will be admitted to my ward."

"That's fine with me—I'm ready and waiting for it."

"If you like, I can tell you what we know and what we don't know about this."

He nodded and waited for me to go on. He was obviously very sick, but you could see he had once been quite strong and good-looking. There were also the features of a generous man—a large mouth with the face folds of one who smiled often. He had big ears and big hands, and his eyes, peering at me over the spectacles, were gray-green—and waiting. So, I spoke to him.

"We know you have a heart disease for which we can do nothing more. You have had all possible treatment, and you are getting no better. We can put a normal heart into you, after taking out your heart that's no longer any good, and there's a chance you can get back to normal life again."

"So they told me. So I'm ready to go ahead."

He said no more. His eyes remained on me but with no indication he wanted to know any more.

"Well, then . . . good-bye," I said.

"Good-bye."

As I turned to go, he began reading again. It was a Western. How, I wondered, could he return to pulp fiction after being suddenly cast into the greatest drama of his life? What was it about human nature that caused such a reaction? No man in the history of the world had ever met the surgeon who was going to cut out his heart and replace it with a new human one—at least, not until this moment, which was now being lost somewhere in a Western novel.

What had made him turn away? He was a realist. He carried no false illusions, no special clouds of rationale. He lived for the moment, for the hour, for the full living of all of it. And now, I had offered him just that—life. Yet he had not asked the odds, nor any details.

So they told me about it, so I am ready to go ahead.

There's nothing more you want to know?

No, I'm waiting.

Perhaps that was all that could be said. He was ready to accept it because he was at the end of the line, waiting for the transfer. What else was there to say? Either you got it, or you folded up.

Mr. Washkansky, we think we can do it.

So I'm ready—do it.

Nothing more, no words were needed. Since then, many people have said it was very brave of Louis Washkansky to accept a heart transplant. They really mean it would be brave for them to accept one—not Washkansky. For a dying man, it is not a difficult decision because he knows he is at the end. If a lion chases you to the bank of a river filled with crocodiles, you will leap into the water convinced you have a chance to swim to the other side. But you would never accept such odds if there were no lion.

Washkansky was a brave man—a hero. But he was not brave or a hero because he grabbed at a chance for life. Rather more, his special glory is because he struggled to live long enough to be there when we arrived. The man with a heart like a ruined battle field had refused to surrender—fighting on and on, until the moment came when I walked in to say he had a chance to live with a heart transplant.

So he did not ask the odds—not then. He merely looked up from his book as though this was a long-expected appointment he had known about since the beginning, perhaps since the first angina pain had grabbed him in its terrifying grip.

So they told me. So I'm ready for it.

I hurried up to my ward to make ready. This was a very special patient and worth everything we could give him.

Ann Washkansky, the Wife

"He went to the hospital in September and as soon as he got there they put him on the danger list. Only then did it hit me that he was dying. I had not known because he used to keep it away from me, you know. I used to watch him and he could not take that. 'What are you looking at?' he would say. 'What are you watching me for? I'll be all right.'

"Always he'll be all right.

"At the hospital, they used to let me come anytime I wanted. He was dying every day for two months and there was always a crisis. To get rid of water in his legs, they resorted to this old method—they drilled holes in them. Oh, that five days—if I live to be an old lady of a hundred years I'll never forget him sitting in that chair, five days and five nights, with the water dripping down his legs and his feet in those basins. His face was black from the agony and I thought he would never get out of that chair, never. After they drained the water, they put him back in bed and then he developed a twitch, which he tried to hide from us. So we pretended it was not there.

"He never complained about it—not him. But he complained about the food.

"He used to say: 'Look at this piece of fish, it died on the plate.' You know hospital food. It's dreadful. 'It died in front of me, it just dropped dead.'

"They would not let me bring anything, but I used to secretly take him a few little things, like maybe he was allowed two cherries and I'd do that. Only I'd bring him a pound of cherries and he would put the whole lot down. You see, there were no half measures with him. He took it from my hand. I said: 'Louis, the sister said you could have two or three.' So he told her what she could do in a nice way and he ate the whole lot. I couldn't handle him.

"It was like that even with the orange squash, which he wasn't allowed to drink. I would bring him a bottle in the morning, then my brother, Solly, would come in the afternoon and Louis would say that I didn't love him anymore because I had forgotten the orange drink. So Solly would go down the bottom of the road and buy some more until one day a sister saw him walking in with a bottle and took it away, saying Mr. Washkansky wasn't allowed to have it. When Solly came without it, Louis said: 'What sort of friend are you? You didn't bring me any squash.' Solly told him what had happened and Louis said: 'Don't worry, kid, Washkansky will get organized, I'll get somebody else.'

"One day after two months, I arrived there and he says: 'You know who came to see me?'

"Then he says: 'The big bugs came to see me.'

"So I said: 'Who are they?'

"So he said: 'Professor Schrire and Professor Barnard.'

"Of course I knew who Schrire was, but Professor Barnard I didn't. I'd never heard of him, although he had been years at the hospital.

"So I said: 'What are they going to do, Louis?'

"So he says: 'They are going to give me a brand new heart.'

"I just looked at him blankly, you know. His sister, Anne, was with me and I looked at her and we did not know what to think.

"So I said: 'You mean a valve.'

"He got annoyed and shook his head. Then he said: 'No, a new heart.'

"We sat there and said nothing.

"He said: 'Don't argue with me, if I tell you it's a new heart, it's a new heart.'

"His sister could see he was getting very upset, so she said: 'Don't argue, Ann. If he says it's a new heart, let it be a new heart.'

"We thought he was delirious, really. Well, if somebody had told you, would you have believed it? So, this was in the afternoon. I came back in the evening, and we got the same story from him. By then he was arguing with the whole family and nobody believed him. He had more visitors than anybody else in that hospital. Sometimes there used to be thirty people outside. He had a lot of friends and a large family and he was very popular.

"So he told everyone the same story again. We kept saying well, maybe it's just a pacemaker, or it's a valve. But he kept to his story. So we pacified him. We did not argue with him.

"He was downstairs in A-1 Ward, and he told this story for two days running. On the third day, I arrived and he was not there. Of course I thought he was dead, so I panicked. I started running to the sister and I said: 'Where is he?' She said they had moved him upstairs and I thought, for sure that's the finish.

"I thought most probably they had phoned for me while I was driving to the hospital. So I ran upstairs and there he was in a private room. Only then did I start to believe him. I was with some other relatives and when Professor Barnard came in, I didn't see him until I heard somebody say: 'Mrs. Washkansky?'

"I turned around and saw a young man. So I said to Louis in Yiddish: *'Ver is ërr?'*—Who's he?

"So he says to me: 'That's Barnard, that's him.'

"I must tell you I was quite horrified. I saw this young boy. You know, I thought he was about twenty-five. Then I had a look and thought he must be a little older and he started telling me what he was going to do.

"He said: 'Do you know what we want to do?'

"So I said: 'Yes, he told me you want to give him a new heart.'

"So he says: 'Do you know what this implies?'

"So I said: 'Obviously, from an accident.'

"I knew that much. It could not be anything else. I want to tell you, this part nearly killed me.

"So I said: 'Professor Barnard, what chance do you give him?'

"Without hesitation, he says: 'An 80 per cent chance.'

"I could only see the other 20 per cent, so I said: 'And if you don't operate on him?'

"He says: 'Then he has no chance at all. My only worry is to see him alive until the operation. I am not worried about the operation. I am worried about keeping him alive until the operation.'

"After he left, I said: 'Louis, for heaven's sake, do you know what you're doing?'

"So he said to me: 'Don't argue with me, woman. I have made up my mind.'

"So I said to him: 'Do you know what the implications are?'

"He says: 'I told you don't argue with me. They are giving me a new heart.'

"I was petrified and went home to phone Dr. Weinreich. He's been our family doctor since I was about ten years old and I told him what happened.

"He asked me: 'What chance does he give?'

"So I said: 'Dr. Weinreich, he says an 80 per cent chance.'

"So he said to me: 'My dear, if he gives him a 10 per cent chance, take it.'

"He did not have to say more than that. I realized then exactly how sick Louis was."

As soon as we had Louis Washkansky in our ward, we tried to put him in the best possible condition to receive a new heart—and then to stay alive until one came along. This meant we had to know everything about him— inside and out. In fact, it was as though we were to open him up and look at every particle through a microscope. To achieve this we used all the techniques of modern medicine to spy on the hidden interior of the human body.

Kidney function was checked by measuring its urine output and ability to get rid of creatinine, a waste product of protein metabolism. The liver was studied through urine and blood analysis. The heart pattern was plotted by an electrocardiogram, the lungs were X-rayed and sputum analyzed.

Blood chemistry was also checked in the laboratory to see that acids and alkalis were at a constant level—so that the blood retained its pH value, or acid-base equilibrium. During metabolism, acid waste materials are formed —much as ashes are left after a fire. An overaccumulation of these acids, upsetting the pH or acid-base equilibrium in the blood, can damage and even kill cells—just as too many ashes can smother a fire. Normally, this does not happen because the body has its own mechanism to sweep out the acids and keep the balance. Disease and heart trouble may upset this and so lead to further trouble—hastening the death of a dying heart or attacking a new one.

In the laboratory, we also determined Washkansky's blood group—A Rhesus-positive—and counted the leucocytes or white cells circulating in his body. An increase in these would indicate an abnormal condition—one of them being possible infection. We plotted the antigenetic pattern of the white cells so that we could match them as closely as possible to a donor. We counted the red cells, too, and measured their oxygen-bearing, hemoglobin—another basic norm to watch later. Similarly we studied the amount of enzymes in his blood serum—precious organic catalysts which start or accelerate chemical reaction in the protoplasm. We also tested the blood's electrolytes—inorganic salts which break up into ions vital to the chemistry of blood cells. The potassium level was also controlled to prevent it triggering off arrhythmias or dangerous changes in heart rhythm.

All of this and more was part of a campaign to preserve nature's balance within the patient's body. At the same time, we had to get ready for what would happen when we violently upset this balance by the trauma and injury of surgery to tissue, muscle, bone, and blood chemistry. This would inevitably follow the splitting open of his chest wall and removal of the heart while Washkansky's blood was reoxygenated within a machine ten feet away from his body rendered insensate by drugs.

It is a general rule that the fitter the patient, the better are his chances of survival. For us, however, this was almost an abstraction since a heart-transplant patient was never going to be fit. In fact, he was only accepted when near death and there was little or nothing to be done for the heart that was killing him. So we were limited. Yet we did what was possible.

Besides ensuring the balance of blood chemistry, we had other targets specific to Washkansky. We controlled his diabetes by giving Diabinese orally, and injecting insulin when the urine showed a rise in sugar content. Other medicine was given to alleviate his anemia, as well as the infection in his leg. Drugs were administered to ensure maximum cardiac output. Finally a limited physiotherapy was prescribed to see that he breathed well and that his lungs were in the best possible condition.

Besides the inescapable violence of surgery, we were preparing to upset the balance of Washkansky's body in a much more serious manner by destroying his natural resistance to infection and disease. The operation would be accompanied by the administration of drugs to prevent rejection —drugs dampening the biological mechanism that would otherwise reject a transplanted organ with "foreign" tissue. This would allow Washkansky to accept a heart—but it would also put him in the vulnerable condition of accepting other pathogenes or organisms capable of causing infection and disease.

There were quite a few available to do just this. Germs exist everywhere —in the air we breathe, in all we touch, and even on our own bodies. The average person is estimated to have 60,000 pathogenic microbes or disease germs on each square inch of his skin. They are even more concentrated in the orifices of the body. Despite their numbers and constant presence, these infectious organisms are kept at bay by the body's immunological mechanism—which we were about to block by drugs. At the onset, until we knew the extent of the rejection process to be encountered, this was going to be particularly dangerous. Eventually we would strike a delicate balance between tolerance of a foreign heart and the necessary amount of immunological intolerance to infection from the ever-present pathogenes. Until then, however, the patient would lie exposed to attack—a city without defense, surrounded by enemy forces which were even present within the city itself.

Perhaps most dangerous were the enemies within the gate—organisms harbored within the body. We took swabs from the skin, nose, throat, mouth, and rectum. Cultures were made of these to isolate the virulent types and so establish what antibiotics would be effective against them. In this way, we were preparing weapons to be used against one or another organism—if it eventually invaded Washkansky's weakened body.

The infection in the left calf, caused by the Southey's tubes during the drainage of liquid from his legs, was chronic and a real threat. It was a cellulitis, or subcutaneous infection which did not respond to treatment. X-ray therapy suggested by Professor Louw was followed by a breakdown in the area which became soft. We aspirated some of it and from this grew a virulent klebsiella organism. We injected drugs to kill the klebsiella, but

Washkansky's circulation was too poor for the blood to reach the area in sufficient amounts to clear it up.

We also washed him continually with Phisohex, an antiseptic solution—especially the chest area where we were going to operate. His mouth was treated as well with a special agent to stop any fungal growth and an antibiotic ointment was put in his nose to prevent organisms from accumulating there.

Room 270, where he was to be nursed after the operation, was fumigated. Its walls and floors, plus all cracks and corners, were washed with Phenolic disinfectant. Every utensil in the room was boiled, and every apparatus was autoclaved—sterilized in a special machine—or boiled or immersed in Phenolic disinfectant. If it could not be boiled, such as a whole bed, it was wiped down. Mattresses, blankets, and linens were autoclaved. All members of the staff who were to look after the patient had their noses, throats, and rectums also studied to determine what organisms they were carrying and the antibiotic sensitivity of these organisms. Anyone bearing especially virulent pathogenes was barred from care of the patient. In order to minimize germs being carried into the ward, we also prepared an area where the staff could scrub their hands and put on a sterile cap, mask, gown, gloves, and canvas overshoes.

When we had this all prepared, I went to neurosurgeons Dr. Jacques "Kay" de Villiers and Dr. Peter Rose-Innes, who had given me a donor for the kidney transplant. I explained that we were now ready to do a heart transplant and had a patient waiting.

"Could you provide us with another donor?" I asked.

"We'll do our best," said Dr. Rose-Innes. "When one shows up we'll let you know."

So began the long wait. Some day, we knew, one of the screaming ambulances would come up the hill, bringing a dying human being—with an uninjured heart. Some day it would happen—but would Louis Washkansky live to see that day?

CHAPTER 22

LOUIS WASHKANSKY LAY IN MY WARD three weeks waiting for a donor. Each day he became progressively weaker. Two red streaks ran up his left leg from the infected calf, further attacking a body that was slowly crumbling from its dying heart. He was going down into a valley of no return.

He knew it and I knew it, but we never spoke about it. Washkansky never admitted there was a possibility that he would die before we could find a heart for him.

Saturday morning began like any other Saturday—or any other day of the week. I shuttled around within the fixed triangle of my life—office, animal laboratory, and Groote Schuur—working on papers, overseeing surgical experiments, and checking on patients.

Shortly before noon, I dropped in to see Louis. I had come to know him in a way that had never happened with other patients. He had been there longer than usual, and our concentrated care had brought us into unusually close contact. As a result, he had become a friend as well as a patient.

He was rough, an uncut diamond—and very real. Above all else he wanted no pity. As death was closing in on him, he gave no quarter—fighting back with growing impatience, generally directed at us. Every day he gave the same ultimatum. If we did not get him a donor he was going to get up and go home. He could no longer stand on his left leg nor even breathe well lying on his back, but this did not prevent him from threatening us with a walkout.

I found him sitting up in bed with glasses raised onto his forehead. He had been reading a James Hadley Chase mystery.

"Are you going fishing, too?"

He asked it with mild disgust as though I was threatening to pull out of a poker game while ahead.

"Everybody's gone fishing or left for the weekend," he said.

"There's an alert on all of them," I said. "Nobody's far from a telephone. The whole team can be called in within a matter of minutes."

"Fishing," he said. "They go fishing and I'm stuck here. You know what I'm going to do?"

I knew what he was going to say, but shook my head to indicate I did not.

"Washkansky's getting the hell out of here," he said. "This comedy has gone on long enough."

"You have to be patient, Louis. Something is liable to happen any minute."

"Any minute, like next year . . ."

He began to cough. Occasionally now, he brought up blood and he had trouble breathing, especially when he became excited. He had lost much weight but his face and hands remained those of a big man. I looked at his hands, trembling as they held some paper tissues against his mouth—hands which had slammed that leather pad at Muizenberg with such power that it had banged the top bell. Yet now he could not even raise an arm to shave himself. He breathed in increasing drafts and began to cough again. This caused his glasses to fall down on his nose. Angrily, he pushed them back up as though this was an unwarranted invasion on his privacy.

"Where are you going now, Prof?"

"Nowhere. I'll be here."

I had planned on going to Ceres to see Deirdre water ski in an exhibition, and Louwtjie had been waiting all morning to hear from me. Yet somehow I was afraid to make the two-hour drive from Cape Town. A donor could turn up at any time.

"Do you think there'll be another one soon?"

"Maybe. I hope so . . . yes."

It was one of those lies you tell to keep courage and hope, both for yourself and the patient. I had no way of knowing when we would get a heart for him—if ever.

On Wednesday afternoon they had brought in a colored boy from Riversdale. He had fallen off a truck and suffered severe brain injury. When admitted to the hospital, he had low blood pressure, thready pulse, and very irregular breathing. The neurosurgeons put him on a respirator and his cardiocirculation rapidly improved. But there was a gradual deterioration of brain function, until there was no doubt among the neurosurgeons that his brain was dead. Tragically reduced to the status of a pithed frog, he was declared a potential donor.

The heart-transplant team was called into action. Louis Washkansky had his chest and belly shaved, and they notified him that the operation he had expected for so long was now at hand.

The blood groups were compatible. Tissue typing also revealed an acceptable compatibility. Everything was ready for removal of the donor's heart. I phoned the Riversdale Police Station, asking them to reach the relatives, but for several hours got no one. Eventually we found a doctor who located the father. Permission was granted by phone, but by that time the boy's condition had so deteriorated this his heart had also suffered damage.

Washkansky had to be told that the operation was off. I went into his room where he lay shaved and cleaned and waiting—only to tell him I was sorry but the donor's heart had faded on us. I felt very sad, and he must have seen it because he tried to comfort me. "You doctors know what you're doing. If there's no heart, there's no heart. It will come along—don't worry."

That was on Wednesday and now it was Saturday.

"You know something, Prof, I had a dream . . ."

"Who gave you that?"

It was Sister Papendieck who had come in to take his temperature and pulse rate and give him an insulin injection to control the diabetes.

"Who gave you that bottle of lemonade?" she asked.

"What bottle?" replied Washkansky, looking innocent.

"Who smuggled this one in to you?"

It was a half-finished bottle of lemonade partially hidden on his bed-stand behind a pile of James Hadley Chase thrillers. The nurse lifted it up and held it in front of Washkansky's nose. He lowered his glasses to inspect it carefully, as though seeing lemonade for the first time in his fifty-three years.

"Never saw it before in my life," he said.

"He's terrible," said Sister Papendieck, trying to sound angry. "People smuggle him everything. The other day I caught him with an empty bag of cherries. I asked him: 'Where'd you get this and where'd all the cherries go?' He looked at me innocent-like. 'What cherries?' he asked. Now is that true or not?"

She stuck a thermometer into Washkansky's mouth before he could do other than mumble. Then she laughed and stroked his hair. Everyone loved him—and it was only the beginning.

I went out to my car and started home. On the way, I began to think nothing would happen this weekend. The transplant would not come off. Perhaps it was worth running over to Ceres. It was a hot summer afternoon —perfect for water skiing. If we left immediately, we could make it in time to see Deirdre. And she did need help with the one ski step-over, especially in crossing the wake.

I stopped at my office in the medical school to phone Louwtjie. Lizzie, the maid, answered.

"Madam has gone shopping," said Lizzie.

"When she comes back, tell her to get ready. Tell her we're going to Ceres."

"Yes, I'll do that, Doctor."

When I arrived, Louwtjie was still not home. Our two dogs, who think they are people, told me about it as I got out of the car. Ringo, a Dutch Keeshond resembling a small Alaskan Husky, barked from the kitchen door —glad to be relieved of his watch. Sixpence, a low-slung, white mongrel the children had smuggled home from the animal laboratory, leaped all over me as though eternally happy to never be in a cage again.

Inside, Lizzie said Louwtjie would be back any minute. I went into the living room and put on an Ink Spots record. From the bay window, you could see the sun slanting through the blue gum trees, flooding the lawn with yellow and green. Beyond it, the lake was wrinkled by a light wind, yet beautifully flat. It would be like that at Ceres.

I went outside onto the lawn, walking toward the lake. You could hear the southeaster going tick-tock through the blue gum leaves. There was a feel in the air that it might change around to a northwest wind and bring rain—but no, the sky was clear and it would probably hold for several more days.

Far out on the water, a giant white pelican coasted in for a landing. Beyond that, from the distant shore, there came the thousand-throated sound of feeding starlings. And then a sea gull screamed overhead.

The lake and its shoreline abounded with birds and animals—pink flamingo, otter, pheasants, duck, coots, guinea fowl, and even small buck. They called it Zeekoevlei, or Lake Hippopotamus, because it once also held their great forms. I loved the lake and the house. Perhaps it was the greatest trophy from Deirdre's skiing. Her boat was there, docked within its shed next to the red awl tree. It rocked with the lapping water like a fading heart. I counted thirty-five beats a minute—much too slow for a creature called "Pacemaker."

There was the sound of Louwtjie's car coming onto the drive, and I hurried back to the house to suggest we leave immediately for Ceres. Louwtjie, however, was upset and said no.

"You waited too long."

"I had a lot to do."

"You always have."

"I know, but now I am free. We can go now. We still have time and I'd like to see Deirdre go through her tricks."

"I'm not going," she said, leaving the room.

On the record the Ink Spots had reached an old favorite:

> Some early morn a fool is born
> A fool is born
> For aren't we all . . .
> But little by little, a fool grows wise.
> Suppose he laughs at dreams
> And skies are blue
> And captures all the world—
> Fools sometimes do . . .

Louwtjie had locked herself in Boetie's room. I called to her to come out.

"Please Louwtjie, I would like to go very much . . ."

"No, the answer is NO!"

> What good's the world he calls his own
> What good's the world if he walks alone?
> That's how he learns
> For what he yearns
> He yearns for love
> For don't we all . . .

So true, so damn true, I thought, and stretched out on the bed. Outside the window, the blue gum went tick-tock. On the lake, a speedboat raced over the flat water, its motor sounding like a dentist drill—hmm, hummm, hueeeEEEE-ummmmmm. How would that sound to the fish at twenty-eight feet—or at a hundred feet? Of course they could hear it. We could hear carp spawning near the shore in the spring. They went choo-choo, choo-choo, like faraway freight trains.

I slept a little. Then I awakened and remembered Washkansky had started to tell me about a dream—only to be interrupted by Sister Papendieck. I tried to imagine what sort of dream it could have been, and dozed off again.

Some time after that I woke up. This time I lay there and began to think about the operation. I began with Washkansky's chest opened up and proceeded to go from there—step by step. Suddenly, as I was removing the donor's heart, it occurred to me that the transplant could be done without incising the donor's interatrial septum. This would eliminate completely the danger of damaging the atrioventricular node. It differed from techniques we had so widely exploited in animal laboratories for many years. It also differed from techniques reported from laboratories in other parts of the world.

Were we entitled to make a change at this critical moment? The more I thought about it, the more I became convinced it would add no real risk, while having real advantages—yet not change the operation so much that it would be unfamiliar to me. It would not put me out of touch with the technique I had practiced so long. Definitely, the change was a safe one.

Yet was it? I had never done this before in the laboratory. Maybe it would not work. Perhaps it would be better to try it first on dogs—postponing the transplant a little longer. Or was this only one more excuse for delay, one more beachhead for my oldest enemy—doubt?

Disturbed and excited, I arose and had some tea. Then I called the hospital, asking for C-2 Ward. Dr. Venter was on duty, but Sister Papendieck said he had gone down to the casualty department—probably to inquire about a possible donor. Washkansky's wife had come for a visit and after her departure Washkansky had complained of nausea. Also, the infection in his leg seemed worse. But he had no temperature. No, Mrs. Washkansky had not smuggled in any Jewish cooking. She had stopped that. It was now the brother-in-law who did most of the smuggling.

I hung up and had a light supper. After that, I went back to bed and shortly after eight o'clock the phone rang. It was Dr. Venter.

"Prof, I think we have a donor."

"Who is it?"

"It's a young girl who was run over by a car. She has severe brain damage."

"Is she colored?"

"No—why?"

"What do the neurosurgeons say?"

"Dr. Rose-Innes is examining her now, I think."

"Well, ask him to phone me as soon as possible."

I waited an hour—an hour of unexpected conflict. I sensed this was going to be the real thing and I wanted it to happen. At the same time, I hoped it would not happen—that the donor would not prove suitable and so I would not have to take this final leap. I was about to close in on it—the final breach, the untouched ten yards, only to be suddenly seized with doubt.

It went like that, until I could wait no longer and called the hospital. Sister Papendieck said nobody knew anything but she would get Dr. Venter to call me. After ten minutes, he called and I knew from the sound of his voice that we had something.

"I've got the donor in our ward," he said.

"Already—in C-2 Ward?"

"Yes."

"What's her blood group?"

"It's all right. It's O Rh-Negative."

"What about consent."

"No, I haven't got consent."

"How can you take in a patient without getting consent—we're not running a multiple injuries ward!"

Dr. Venter remained calm.

"Well, we will find out whether we can get consent. And I think it will be a good donor."

"I'm coming immediately," I said, and hung up.

Going out, I called into Louwtjie who was still locked in Boetie's room: "Louwtjie—I'm probably going to do the heart transplant tonight!"

There was no reply from behind the closed door. I ran through the kitchen and out to my car for the nine-mile drive to the hospital. Only later did I learn the details of the event which had led up to this moment, the blind and monstrous accident that destroyed a family and brought a young girl into my ward—and her heart into Louis Washkansky.

Edward George Darvall, the Father

"Denise had this new car and she liked to go places in it. So we decided to drive over and see some friends. My wife and I were in the back seat, with Denise and Keith up front. All the way down Kloof Nek, they sang that 'Doctor Zhivago' song. She had been teaching her brother to play it on the piano, and they kept at it till we got to Main Road. You know, I can't remember the name of that song, but it's still under the piano seat where she left it.

"My wife wanted a cake for our friends, so we stopped opposite that bakery at Salt River. She got out with Denise and because she liked so much the cream doughnuts they make at that bakery, I told her to get some of them, too.

" 'No,' she said. 'We'll just get the cake—won't be a minute.'

"My son and I waited in the car and after a while he said to me: 'Dad, Mom and Denny are sure taking a long time to come.'

" 'Yes,' I said, 'I suppose the place is busy and they have to wait their turn.'

"We were parked facing Simonstown way, about a hundred yards down from the bakery. I was sitting on the side next to the sidewalk, but Keith was next to the road and could see better. So he turned to look for them.

" 'Oh,' he said, 'There's Mom and Denny coming now.'

"After a few seconds we heard a thud and a bang and a screech of tires. Keith turned around again and this time he said: 'Oh Lord, there's been an accident.'

"Instead of turning around, I looked straight ahead because I thought it was in front of us.

" 'Where, where?' I said.

"Keith did not answer.

"He opened the door and looked back, so I thought: 'Oh! it must be that way.'

" 'Dad!' he shouted. 'It's Mom and Denise!'

"Gosh, it stopped me right here. You see, I had a big operation on my stomach and it hit me right in here. I got out of the car, anyway, but I couldn't run like he could. He got there first and I struggled along by myself.

"When I got to the scene, I saw them lying in the road and everything seemed to go black in front of me.

"Somebody must have pulled me off the roadway, because I next found myself sitting down on the sidewalk.

"Then all of a sudden it came back to me and I got up to look around for my son. But he was gone, looking for my daughter's keys—the car keys she had in her hand when she had gone into the shop.

"I got to the place again in the middle of the road but there were so many people I couldn't get near my wife. She looked so still and not moving at all that I was suddenly scared she was hurt real bad. So I tried to get closer, but they pulled me away.

"Stand back, and give the lady air."

"I didn't know my wife was dead at the time. I didn't know anything. I went over to my daughter and started to pick her up, but a chap said: 'No, leave her alone.'

"I could see he was a doctor, because he lifted away her hair and looked at her head. He had some bandage and began wiping her face. Her nose was bleeding, her mouth was bleeding and her ears were bleeding. Oh God, to see her so fallen.

" 'Don't touch her,' he said to me again.

Since I could touch neither my wife nor my daughter, I waited on the sidewalk until a policeman came to me.

" 'Are you the husband?' " he asked.

" 'Yes,' I said, 'I was the husband.' "

Ann Washkansky, the Wife

"When we went for the afternoon visit, he was livid. I've never seen him so cross. Apparently, they all came and said good-bye as they were going fishing for the weekend. *Veh,* I could not pacify him. He said: 'They can go to hell because I'm getting out of here.' Shame, and he could not even walk with his heart and that terrible infection.

"I left and drove along Main Road. My sister-in-law, Anne Taibel, was in the car with me. We saw this enormous crowd and I said: 'Oh my God, I think there's been an accident.'

"As we drove up, the police were waving us on. You know, they did not even allow us to stop.

"Then I said: 'Oh my God there's a woman in the road.'

"Anne said to me: 'There are two women.'

"When we slowed down, we saw one of them was covered. I wondered what she looked like and if I knew her. You never know how lucky you are sometimes. Pity that poor woman. At least my Louis was still alive.

"Then Anne said: 'There's Louis Ehrlich.'

"Dr. Louis Ehrlich is a doctor we both know. He was bending over the second one. Later I learned it was Denise Darvall. I don't know how Louis Ehrlich got there. Maybe he just happened to pass by."

Dr. Louis Ehrlich, Physician

"It was a very hot afternoon and I had been to a bar mitzvah for the son of a colleague. So I was taking a shower to cool off when there was this pounding at the door, someone pounding and banging like crazy until my wife went to see what it was. Then she came to the bathroom, saying there was an accident and a doctor must come.

"I got dressed quickly in a pair of pants, slippers, and a shirt. I wasn't dressed properly, but I hurried out just the same, to see what it was.

"When I got there, I found Mrs. Darvall crumpled up and dead. She was lying in the middle of the road, near the traffic island. Then I saw there was another one, lying near the gutter, bleeding from the ears. She was badly injured and deeply unconscious.

"There was a crowd and a little gray-haired man on his knees next to her. I thought at first he was a doctor, but when he began to lift her up, I knew he was no doctor. Later, I realized this must have been her father, but I did not know it at the time.

" 'Don't touch her,' I said.

" 'She doesn't speak,' he said. 'She doesn't say anything anymore, nothing at all.'

" 'Leave her alone,' I said, and began my examination. Almost immediately it was apparent that nothing could be done—nothing in the street, anyhow.

"Soon after that the ambulance pitched up. Somebody must have called it from the bakery. There were people everywhere."

Fred Jones Munnik, Ambulance Driver

"I was at the depot in Pinelands when the call came in. It was three-forty in the afternoon and my ambulance for the day was Number 16—one of our standard jobs with the Morris motor, top red flasher, and four red lights on each end. By the time I had swung out of the depot and gone a hundred yards down Alexander Road, I was doing sixty. I put on the siren as we came into the first junction and kept it going on and off until we got to the scene, about four minutes later.

"There was the usual mob all over the place, blokes who only make matters worse poking around at the victims and getting in the way. They scattered as I came up—they always do.

"I found Mrs. Darvall in the middle of the pedestrian crossing, quite obviously dead. Denise was not there. She lay next to a parked automobile, her head just below the hub cap. From a dent in the hub, I could see immediately what had happened. The speeding car had hit the mother first and she had slammed against her daughter. This left the mother dead where she was, but sent Denise flying through the air, going head first until she hit against the car hub cap. If this hadn't happened, if she had had a free fall, she might have hit with her shoulder first—rather than her skull—and be alive today.

"She was lying on her back. Blood was coming from her mouth, her nose and her ears. She was breathing heavily, but she made no sound and occasionally turned her head from side to side, like she was trying to adjust to the terrible pain and concussion in her brain.

"A doctor was there and confirmed my fears that this was a compound skull fracture and needed treatment as fast as possible.

"With my assistant that day, Jan Marais, we loaded up the two women and also the husband, who kept calling both women by their names and asking them to speak to him—the usual shock case.

"At the wheel, I put on the siren and dug out as fast as I could, calling in over the radio phone.

" 'Sixteen to control—over.'

" 'Control to sixteen, we're listening, come in—over.'

" 'Have two European women, both seriously injured, please inform Groote Schuur emergency am en route—over.'

" 'We're acting—over.'

"It had taken four minutes at the scene to load them up and get moving. It took three more to make it to Groote Schuur. We unloaded the girl first, wheeling her into emergency. Then the duty doctor came out with a stethoscope and climbed aboard to look at the mother.

"Mr. Darvall had followed his daughter into emergency and now he came back out and was hanging on the ambulance door as if he was going to collapse any minute. The doctor stepped down from the ambulance.

" 'Are you the husband?' he asked.

" 'Yes.'

" 'Well, I'm sorry to tell you that your wife is absolutely dead.'

"Mr. Darvall's knees gave way then. So we put him on a stretcher, too, and wheeled him into the corridor outside the emergency room where they had his daughter.

"After that, we continued as required by law—taking Mrs. Darvall to the city morgue where they undressed her and put her into refrigeration pending an autopsy and police investigation."

CHAPTER 23

I ALWAYS PRAY before any major operation—usually in the car on the way to the hospital because I am alone then. And now, as I drove through the night, I felt more than ever the need for it. Yet I could not pray. Each time I began, my thoughts broke in upon me.

Dear Lord, help me with this operation. . . .

No, there were two operations—not one. We needed two teams of men and women. One would hold in life some vital organs of the donor while the other prepared the recipient, Louis Washkansky. They had to be timed so that neither would excise the heart too soon, or too late—causing the loss of precious minutes. A heart, a life, could be lost in a few seconds.

Both teams had to work together as one. Even then, a single error on either side could collapse the entire operation. Any team was as strong as its weakest link and here there were twice as many links—all of them tense and nervous human beings. Many had worked all day in the hospital and now, without rest needed for such precision work, they would be ordered from their sleep to labor all night and perhaps into the next day. It was impossible to say how long it would take. For who had ever seen the end of such a tunnel?

Lord, I ask only to be free of error, to do it as I know it must be done. . .

Some of it, however, was beyond my doing. In fact, many of the problems were beyond anyone's control. Who was this girl they had picked up off the highway? Maybe her heart was injured. Maybe she carried an infectious disease. Maybe her cell makeup was so different that Washkansky's body would reject the young heart it so desperately needed to stay alive. Maybe the neurosurgeons were wrong, and she could be saved. Maybe her family would not allow us to remove her heart. Maybe . . .

All of these were hurdles before me. Each one had to be crossed before I could order the two surgical teams into action, before we could ever move the girl into the theater. It was these which made it impossible to pray—at least so I told myself in the car. Yet I knew there was something else. The hurdles were also a secret source of comfort—barriers of delay. As long as they remained, I did not have to make the final leap over a frontier never before breached by man.

Yet I was not to be alone—that is, not until the final moment of removing the heart. For some hurdles were being crossed by other members of my team, even as I raced past red lights toward the hospital. Indeed, one of the major ones was at the moment being cleared by two doctors in my ward.

Edward George Darvall, the Father

"When I got to the hospital, they told me my wife was dead, killed outright. It was a terrible blow. I didn't know she was dead with me in the ambulance.

"My daughter was moaning so I thought perhaps they could save her. At first I lay on a stretcher in the corridor of the emergency ward. Then I sat on a bench while they worked on her in another room. Finally they brought her out to take her upstairs, and when I saw her it was another kick in the stomach.

"They'd put a tube in her nose and a doctor was pumping air into her with a black bag while they moved her along on a stretcher with wheels. I went along, too, and when we got to the elevator, there was no room for me—only the doctor squeezing the bag, a nurse holding some empty bottles, and another man pushing the stretcher with Denise. So I took the next elevator with my son, Keith, and when we got out they'd already moved her into a room. I went there and saw a lot of people around the bed, putting up bottles and tubes.

"Dr. Bosman said I could not stay there and took me into the doctor's office where there was a couch. I could hardly walk and he said I'd better lie down. I was so ill my son thought I ought to go home. Two of our cousins came to see us and he said they could take me along.

" 'Dad,' he said, 'you'd better go home. I can wait here.'

" 'What home?' I asked him. 'There's nobody in it. How can you go home with nobody in it?'

"About ten o'clock Dr. Bosman came with another doctor, Dr. Venter, and I got up because I thought they wanted me to see my daughter. But he asked me to lie down again on the couch. He said he wanted to talk to me and I knew it was not good.

" 'Look,' he said. 'We've done everything we can. We can't do any more now, and I'm afraid the brain specialists say there's no hope for your daughter.'

" 'That's pretty hard luck,' I said.

" 'I tell you what,' he said, 'I'd like to ask you a question. Do you mind asking your cousins and son to go out?'

" 'No,' I said, and asked them to go out.

" 'Look,' he said, 'we can't save your daughter—her injuries are too bad. But I tell you, we have a man in the hospital here, and we can save his life if you give us permission to use your daughter's heart and her kidney.'

"It took me about four minutes to make up my mind. I thought of what I would do if he hadn't asked me that question and realized I didn't know what I was going to do with my daughter. You see, my wife always said—she had it done to her mother—that if anything ever happened to her, she wanted to be cremated. My daughter never said anything, but now I had to decide for her about that—and about her heart as well. I remembered a birthday cake she once had made for me with a heart on it and the words DADDY WE LOVE YOU. I remembered a bathrobe she bought me, too, with her first week's salary in the bank and I thought she was always like that—giving away things to other people. So I decided she would have said yes to Dr. Bosman if he had asked her, instead of me.

"I looked at him and he has very kind eyes. He was sad because my daughter was dying and he could do nothing for her. He wanted her to live, but she couldn't, so he wanted another man to live with her heart and her kidney. Only later did I realize the kidney was for someone else—a colored boy. But it didn't matter. If they could take my daughter's heart or kidney and put it into someone else, it was better to do that than to let it die with her and then bury it or burn it up into a pile of ashes. So I told him:

" 'Well, doctor, if you can't save my daughter, try and save this man.'

"Then he brought a form, a red card, and I had to sign it.

" 'You'd best go home and rest,' he said, 'you look absolutely worn out.'

"So I shook hands with him and the other doctor and off I went. He said he would get in touch with me by phone and let me know how they were getting on.

"It's a business, that was, the biggest shock of my life. I just can't get over it. I do what I can to forget it, but I just can't. Just the same, I don't regret giving Denny's heart. I could never have lived with myself if I hadn't done that. Maybe I would have been haunted by her voice asking me, 'Why, Daddy, why didn't you do it—why didn't you want to help that man to live?' "

So I drove, with broken bits of prayer, through the dark to the hospital —until its lights suddenly loomed before me. Parking in front, I ran immediately into the Casualty Department where I met a Sister.

"Do you know anything about a potential donor?"

"Yes, Professor, she's already in your ward."

"What neurosurgeon saw her?"

"Dr. Rose-Innes, but I think he's left."

All around us in the corridor was the usual Saturday night wreckage of humanity. A stretcher rolled past, bearing an old man, frothing blood at the mouth. Nearby, a youth sat alone on a bench, his head wrapped in bandages excepting for one bloodshot eye trapped and terror-stricken within white folds. A door opened briefly into an emergency room, revealing a woman on an operating table, her handbag on the floor. From somewhere, a child screamed.

It never ceased to sadden me that such a potentially happy event as a weekly shower of pay checks on the city inevitably resulted in this tidal wave of injured human beings, bleeding from car wreck and knife wound, drunk from cheap wine and brandy, sobbing from loss of life and love—all of it spilling into this one hospital corridor where whites and nonwhites came in by separate doors but, once inside, were treated by the same people.

Here Denise Darvall had come—broken of leg, pelvis, and skull. So had come Dr. Peter Rose-Innes, to witness her appointment with death. Yet neither of them were here now and I hurried down the corridor to the stairs, climbing them two at a time to the third floor—and C-2 Ward for heart surgery.

Denise Darvall was in Room 283, with Dr. Coert Venter at the side of her bed, doing a cutdown in the right groin to expose the saphenous vein. The girl's bare leg was distorted and bent in a way which indicated the right femur and tibia were broken. The left leg was twisted oddly, too, probably from a break at the knee. It was these—the broken and untended legs from the young body—that disturbed me.

"Can't you do something for that girl before you make your cutdown?"

Dr. Bosman was with Venter, and he spoke for them.

"We called Ozzie and he's coming any minute."

Dr. Joseph Ozinsky, the anesthesiologist, was vital to us in any heart operation as well as in preparing patients for the theater.

"I'm not talking about that, man. Where are the orthopedic surgeons? Why haven't they put this girl's leg in a splint?"

"They haven't come yet."

"Go call them immediately, Bossie. I'll help Coert."

Both men looked surprised.

"We can't stop halfway. As long as she's alive—or at least until the neurosurgeons say there's nothing to do—we have to treat her as though she was going to live."

"They've already said that."

"What?"

"That nothing can be done to save her."

"Not to me they haven't, not in this ward yet. Call Rose-Innes and say we need a final examination. What about permission from her family—do we have that?"

"Yes," said Bossie, going out of the room. "The kidney too."

I washed up and put on gloves and helped Coert insert the catheter into the vein. We ran it—a flexible plastic tube—from the groin up to the level of the abdomen. This would allow us to measure her venous pressure, take blood samples, and provide a route for transfusions and drugs.

With that done, I had a chance to examine the girl more closely. She was rather pretty, with dark hair and soft features. But her death was there, visible to the eye in brain tissue oozing from her right ear. It was this brain death that made clear there was no way to save her, though life could be sustained in the rest of the body by artificial means—as was already being done.

A tube had been passed through her nose into her lungs and connected to the ventilator—an automatic machine that could breathe for her. Other tubes had been attached. In the left arm an Isoprenaline drip ran at twenty to thirty minidrops a minute to stimulate the heart. In the right arm a blood drip compensated for blood loss resulting from internal bleeding—her waist had increased an inch since the accident. A catheter had also been inserted into her bladder to help measure the urine output—an index of kidney function and circulation.

Other connections ran from electrodes on her arms and chest to an electrocardiograph machine. This flashed the beat of her heart on a monitor above the bed: a bouncing yellow dot crossing a circular orange screen

—*beep, beep, beep, beep*. With the stethoscope, her heart sounded normal, though some fluid was gathering in her lungs. Rather than a nasal tube, we needed a larger one through her mouth to drain the lungs. I spoke to Coert Venter.

"I think you should get Ozzie, because we need a larger intratracheal to suck her lungs."

"He's coming any minute, Prof."

"We also need to test the acid-base balance. She probably needs sodium bicarbonate and potassium. Also we need white cell typing and cross matching with Washkansky. You say she's O-Negative?"

"Yes."

"That's something . . ."

But it was not everything. There had to also be some compatibility of tissues, otherwise the danger of rejection of the new heart would be greatly increased.

"They can't do the tissue matching in less than two hours. So we have to start it right away."

" 'M.C.' has already sent his girls to the lab."

"Then get some blood to them immediately. This chart says her pressure is sixty."

"No, Prof, it's over seventy now, after the last infusion."

"Get it up to ninety at least, and try to keep it there."

Other reports in her folder showed she was free from disease. Her chest X ray revealed no signs of pulmonary tuberculosis. There were also notes by the various neurosurgeons tracing her progressive decline with the dying of the brain.

Bossie returned, bringing the cardiographic strip which had just come up from the clinic. There was a dip in the Q-R-S complex that I did not like at all.

"Has Professor Schrire seen this?"

"I don't know."

"He has to examine this. Maybe it's due to her brain damage, but I want him to see it. I'm not going to take out a bad heart and put in another injured one."

We needed Professor Schrire immediately. If this irregular dip meant the heart was undergoing damage, we had to call everything off—just as we had done with the other donor.

"I'll get Val," I said. "You get Dr. Rose-Innes."

"I called," said Bossie. "He's out, but they'll send him over soon as they locate him."

Then he said: "So maybe I'd better call in the rest of the team."

I hesitated. We had not yet crossed all the hurdles. Until I got final clearance from the neurosurgeons, we had no donor. Unless Professor Schrire passed the cardiograph, we had no heart. Yet the team of technicians, sisters, and doctors was scattered all over the city. They had to be found, wherever they were, and told to come immediately.

"All right," I said. "Call them all in."

Bossie left to phone. Dr. Venter also left, taking a nurse with him to start preparing Washkansky for the operation. I started to leave, too, but an extended *beep* on the heart monitor turned me back to the bed—nothing serious.

Then I saw the flowers by her bed—a little bunch of violets in a glass—and I spoke to Sister Papendieck who was filling in the charts.

"Where'd these flowers come from?"

"Sister Hall brought them in."

"From where?"

"I don't know—shall I find out?"

"No, no—it doesn't matter."

What mattered, of course, was that somebody had sent them. Somebody had cared enough. Somebody was clinging to a hope that this young woman would live, would wake up and find these little flowers within her reach.

Her skull was cracked, her brain destroyed forever, and the pupils of her eyes would never again focus on anything, not even a purple flower. Yet somebody had not given up. What mattered now in our lives was no longer whether people believed or did not believe. The issue was whether they cared—or did not care. The flowers were there, speaking for those who did care, saying, "Don't die, Denise Darvall, don't let go of life—cling to us, touch us, take us to yourself for what we can give you."

I looked again at her face, the dark hair, the young shoulders, and wondered if she was in love, if she had a young man somewhere who would weep when he learned of her end—learned that she was leaving this world with only a little glass of violets sent by Somebody.

Yet would he weep if he knew that some part of her had given life to someone else? What had her father thought, if not that, when he gave permission? It gave her meaningless death a measure of dignity and worth.

The walk in the evening, the whisper, the laughing voice, the sound of her feet on the stairs—all of it was gone now because the control center had been destroyed and all the pieces were falling apart. So there was nothing to be done, except one remaining gesture before all the pieces died their separate deaths: give them away.

Horatio had asked about the last exit:

> How can man die better
> Than facing fearful odds,
> For the ashes of his fathers,
> And the temples of his gods?

Well, there was a better way. There was a gesture worthy of so great an exit. You could give part of yourself to hold someone in life.

"You know," I said, "I would die a wonderful death if I could feel that as a result of my death, somebody else would be able to live. It's better than just dying for your country or your flag, no?"

"Maybe," said Sister Papendieck, who was on her knees under the bed, reading the urine output.

Christ on the Cross would have done it, too. If there had been a possibility of doing a transplant, of using one of his organs, he would have given it immediately. He had given his whole life for mankind. So he would have given part of it for part of mankind. He worried about the criminals next to him, about their suffering and death. If he could have given his heart and kidneys to save either of them, he would have done that, too.

Sister Papendieck stood up with the bottle.

"Good output," she said.

Yet Christ was not alone. All men wanted to give. This girl's father had given away her heart. She would probably have done it, also, and I wanted to give the world an operation which would save many lives. These were not heroic acts, nor even singularly Christian ones. They were part of the natural instinct of man—of all men, for human beings were essentially good. The harm we suffer, the badness we draw out, comes from our turning man into an artificial creature. Divorce him from his true self and he turns bitter—killing others or killing himself with the same desperate gesture. Drunken with defeat, he slaughters two women on the highway who might be his own wife and daughter. Yet then from somewhere, from somebody, comes a little bunch of violets . . .

"I've done the charts and checked the drips," said Sister Papendieck. "What do you need now?"

"Nothing," I said, taking one violet from the glass and leaving the room to see Washkansky.

I put it in my pocket, for it was more than a flower. It was for me, at that moment, proof that man lived to give—to give of mind and body. It was proof that man cared. And it was an extended hand through Darvall to me. It meant we had a heart offered for transplant. All that remained was Dr. Rose-Innes to give his clearance and Professor Schrire to say there was no cardiac damage.

Perhaps I had looked for this, seeking some approval from God and man for what I was about to do. And perhaps it was to complete the second half of this projected odyssey that I began to walk down the corridor toward the room of the man who was about to receive this girl's offered heart.

The C-2 Ward extends along a fifty-yard corridor, flanked by eleven rooms for patients facing toward the front of the hospital. Opposite them, on the other side of the corridor, are the service rooms, an office for the sisters, and the Doctors' Office where I met the staff each day to discuss pending operations and the condition of patients. The office is located midway in the corridor between the room of Denise Darvall and that of Louis Washkansky.

I went into it for a moment to call Professor Schrire who said he would come immediately. As I hung up, Sister Papendieck came to say Dr. Rose-Innes was with Miss Darvall and had already begun his examination. I started to go to him, but was called back to the phone twice. After that Dr. Ozinsky came in, saying he had inserted a larger intratracheal tube through the mouth. After we discussed further handling of both donor and recipient, he went to see Washkansky, and I returned to Denise Darvall.

When I arrived, I found Dr. Rose-Innes bent over with an ophthalmoscope, studying the pupils of her eyes.

"What does it show?"

"Same as it's been since five-thirty this afternoon. They're fixed and dilated."

"What else?"

"No reaction to painful stimuli, no reflexes, and the brain registers no activity."

He held up an X ray of the skull. It showed the brain had shifted, with fractures extending across the base to both ears, revealing why brain tissue had exuded from the right ear. The skull was also fractured into the nose which had caused bleeding there.

"The pineal is calcified and has shifted to the right," said the neurosurgeon. "From the start, there was nothing to be done. This brain was dying when we received it and now every test shows that it is dead."

"That means," I said, "that we can go ahead."

"Yes," he said, "you may go ahead."

For a moment we said nothing. There was the sound of the Bird ventilator clicking on and off, with its muffled thrust of air and oxygen into the girl's lungs. Her chest rose and fell every three seconds—showing no sign that this moment was different from any before it. Yet something had happened which radically altered the immediate handling of her destiny.

Dr. Peter Rose-Innes, senior neurosurgeon of the Groote Schuur hospital, had finally confirmed the findings of two previous examinations. He had decided that Denise Darvall, 24, of 2 Marine Flats, Tamboers Kloof, Cape Town, no longer had any hope for life.

Patient Number 226-070 was, in effect, medically dead. Formally, she had been handed over to the transplant team. From that moment onward, our duty was to use every means possible to maintain life artificially in a body having a dead brain, in order to take her heart in as perfect a condition as possible.

The violets in a little glass at her bedside no longer served as a bright hope for an awakening at dawn. They became, instead, the first of many flowers destined to be sprinkled on her grave. For she had passed from the living and was in that moment joining the dead.

It was a moment of immense importance for without it the first heart transplant would not have been possible. I felt it profoundly and realized the enormity of its implications. Later, thousands of people would seek to also crowd into that same moment, giving to it their own particular interpretations—some critical. These included many well-meaning people who knew little, as well as some who should have known better. Among them was the German heart specialist, Dr. Werner Forssmann, winner in 1956 of a Nobel Prize for medicine.

"Is it not a macabre scene," he asked shortly afterward, "when doctors place a patient on the heart-lung machine in one operating room while, simultaneously in a similar room next door, a second team waits, forceps in hand, around a young person fighting against death? These people are not there to help the patient. With feverish eagerness, they are waiting to open his defenseless body in order to save someone else."

Since this sort of nonsense can be uttered by an otherwise respectable figure—and a courageous pioneer of medicine who inserted an experimental catheter into his own heart nine different times—it appears necessary to examine what happened to both the patient and ourselves at that historic moment. Otherwise, much of what is to follow will not be understood.

Denise Darvall had entered a no-man's land between life and death—an area created by modern science and medicine. She was being held there by drug stimulants, blood transfusions, and, most important, artificial breathing provided by the automatic ventilator. How long it would take her to cross over to total death depended mainly upon how long we continued to run the ventilator. A flip of the switch, turning it off, would result in immediate cessation of breathing. Her heart would continue to beat for three, four, maybe five minutes—and then stop.

At that point we would have the three criteria that doctors have used for centuries to determine death: no heart beat, no respiration, and no brain function. Denise Darvall, who had been medically dead, would then be legally dead. We could consign her for burial—or, as we intended, open her chest and remove her heart. On the other hand, if we restarted the ventilator immediately, and at the same instant gave her heart an electric shock, we could in all likelihood set again in motion the twilight existence we had just terminated. From being legally dead, the patient would be returned to the same no-man's land she had just left—and where she could continue to exist for an indeterminate length of time as a biological vegetable.

There is no fixed limit to the length of such an existence—a few hours, days, weeks, and even longer. In an auto wreck in 1957, a Canadian— known medically as Mr. R.—suffered severe brain injuries similar to

Denise Darvall's. Doctors ventilated him through the windpipe and fed him through a tube directly into his stomach. So provided with air and food, the remainder of the body continued to exist—the word "live" can hardly be used. Mr. R. lay in permanent coma. He recognized no one, food was shoved into him through an abdominal opening and routinely collected as he expelled it—since he was unable to take care of himself. This vegetable existence of a human being endured eight years, eight months and nineteen days—after which he died. Autopsy revealed no cause of death, other than brain injury.

So there is evidence that a person with "brain death" can still exist for years—that is, the death of the remainder of the body can be held off until someone pulls the switch. And conceivably, Denise Darvall could have been held much longer in her no-man's land—her heart beating away in her own body, her brain destroyed—if we had not turned off the ventilator that kept her from crossing over to total death.

There are a few people who believe that we have no right to so terminate the vegetable existence of a human being. They advance it as a moral and ethical point rather than a practical one since the maintenance of such "life" would cost from $30,000 to $50,000 a year, as well as require trained nurses, medical personnel, and hospital space otherwise needed to save real lives rather than hold a person in a state of arrested death.

Yet how can we assume to have the right to place a human being in such an artificial existence and keep him there—creature of our making, prisoner of our tubes and machines, held in life by an electric switch? How dare we take a girl such as Denise Darvall who once raced over fields, who laughed with children, who whispered words of love, who prayed to God—how can we condemn her to an insentient existence where she is unable to see or speak or feel the world around her? Even worse, suppose one small remote area of the brain lived on, undetected and suffering pain—or at some thin edge was mutely aware of the indignities heaped upon the body, of food being shoved in through a hole in the abdomen?

Even without such a nightmare, the reduction of this girl to a vegetable would be equal to thrusting her into a limbo, into a hell on earth. It was a desecration of the body, the Temple of the Holy Ghost. Also, would her soul stay locked inside the headless body—or would it leave its temple? If not, how much could you cut away and still have space to house the soul? If we accept a body without a head—seat of man's reason and consciousness, highest of his attributes—then we logically should accept the head without a body. This, too, could be done. A human head could be connected to a heart-lung machine, provided with fresh blood, and kept alive for days. Obviously, there had to be a cutoff point.

The majority of the world's major heart surgeons agree with Pope Pius XII who told a group of physicians in 1957 that artificial and extraordinary means of resuscitation are not morally required—provided there is no hope of recovery. This was true of Denise Darvall whose brain was destroyed. Her passage across no-man's land was a one-way trip with no hope of return to the conscious world.

So we were prepared to turn off the switch, which would halt her breathing and bring her heart to a stop. Yet even then she would not be totally dead, for the separate organs and tissues of her body would die their own particular deaths at separate intervals. Her brain, had it been alive, would go first.

Her liver and adrenals would die next, within an hour. The heart would take anywhere from one to two hours—depending a great deal upon its temperature. Tissues such as bone, skin, arteries and cornea could be used several hours after death and kept alive much longer under certain conditions—such as freezing.

This extra life span of organs and tissues was vital in doing a transplant. It allowed time to take the heart—the liver or kidney—from one body and place it in another. It was an extra margin of time that made organ transplants possible. To insure this margin, the donor had to be kept "alive" until the last moment.

For this reason, I intended to hold Denise Darvall artificially in life until I needed her heart. She would be brought to the operating table while being automatically ventilated, with her heart still beating in her body. At that point, we could take it at any time. Indeed, since brain death had been established, and her heart was kept in life by us, there was no reason why it could not be removed while still beating.

Such was the substance of that vital moment when Dr. Rose-Innes confirmed the findings of two other neurosurgeons that Denise Darvall was beyond recovery—converting her into the first human heart transplant donor in history.

There remained, however, one final hurdle. We had to know the quality of her heart and the extent of any possible damage. This was an assessment that had to be made by Professor Schrire—who arrived almost immediately.

He examined the donor, studied her cardiograph tracing, and looked at her X rays. The heart, he decided, appeared to be normal and fit for transplant. The dip that I had feared was caused by brain damage. It did not indicate the heart had been injured.

"So we can use it—it's healthy?"

"Right now it is. But some damage is going to be inevitable, the longer you wait."

"All right," I said. "We'll wait no more."

I hurried down the corridor to Louis Washkansky's room. He was on his back with an orderly shaving his chest.

"This is it, eh Doc?"

I nodded. "How do you feel?"

"Great."

There was a silence. Then he said the truth.

"Actually, I feel kind of shaky. Like going into the ring when you don't know who you're up against."

I said nothing.

"You're my manager, Doc. What's he look like?"

I knew what he looked like. He was the *Skoppensboer*—the wild Jack of Spades. He was death and against him I had only the King of Hearts.

> *Want swart en droef,*
> *die hoogste troef*
> *oor al wat roer,*
> *is Skoppensboer.*
>
> (Yet black and tragic,
> The highest trump,
> Over all that moves
> Is the Jack of Spades.)
>
> —*Skoppensboer*,
> Eugene Marais

When we first met and talked about doing the transplant, Louis had not asked the odds. Then his wife had asked me, and I had told her it was 80 per cent. Louis had translated this into betting terms.

"You figured four to one."

"That's right."

"The odds always change at the last minute. Are they going my way— or against me?"

"Your way," I said.

The orderly began to shave his belly.

"Tell Ann," he said. "Tell her it's in the bag, so she won't worry."

"All right," I said, and prepared to leave.

"Will I see you again . . . before it happens?"

I looked into his eyes, trying to see some trace of fear, and saw nothing other than his looking into mine—perhaps for the same thing.

"Yes," I said. "I'll come and see you beforehand."

I phoned his wife from the doctors' office in the ward.

"Mrs. Washkansky, this is Doctor Barnard. We have a donor and will probably go ahead with your husband's transplant."

"Oh, thank God."

"I just wanted you to know."

"Thank God. When the phone rang, I thought it was worse."

"He says you should not worry about him."

"If it helps, say I'm not worrying."

"All right," I said and prepared to hang up.

"Please," she said, "can you tell me what his chances are?"

"I told you, 80 per cent. But remember, it's something completely new ... we'll try our best."

"Yes . . . yes."

Then she said: "Go ahead, Professor Barnard. I'm sitting here."

"You're what?"

"I'm sitting here and waiting all the time."

"All right, good-bye."

I told myself everything was now in order. We had cleared all the hurdles. Nothing remained, other than to proceed with the operation.

I was wrong, however, for I found another hurdle. Last and most formidable of all, it was inside myself.

CHAPTER 24

ON THE WAY to the operating theater, I felt for the first time that the transplant was actually going to happen. Until that moment, there had been so much to do, so many hurdles to cross, that the reality of the event had been lost in getting ready for it. Only now did it seem possible. And only now, alone in the passage leading to the theater, was I aware that I was walking forward with the hope that I would never get there, that something would still block my way.

The further I went, the worse it became. With each step, the weight of my doubt grew until it seemed almost unbearable. I wanted to turn back, but there was no turning. Two people—a girl and a man—were now being moved into adjacent theaters. Both of them had living hearts that could not continue to beat for much longer. We were approaching the moment when there would be nothing else to do other than cut out both their hearts, and place one of them—the girl's—within an empty chest of the man who would otherwise never leave the operating table alive.

If we succeeded, it would be more than the grafting of a heart. It would be the conjoining of many disciplines of medicine and science. It would also be the crowning effort of a team of men and women who would bring to bear upon that moment the training of a lifetime, structured with the inherited technique and skill of a millennium. All of it would be fused into one objective—to replace a dying heart with a new one, to save one life.

In that instant, would be realized a dream as old as the heart of man. Certainly it was within Moses as he fell in a valley before seeing the Promised Land—of Alexander before he reached the Ganges, of Columbus before the Indies, and Einstein before he could harness the Unified Field Theory. It lay in the heart of kings and popes and shoemakers, forced to quit before their time. It was sewn into the pattern of life itself for no one was born with the belief that he came into the world to quit it. He came to stay, with the hope that the leaving of life would never be a simple mechanical failure, but rather the arrival at a time when he could say that he had completed the circle, he had done his best, he had lived his promise and made it—or had failed it. Above all, he should not be forced to withdraw because the central pump of his existence had failed him.

So I had thought, using this as an orientating peak in my attempt to scale cliffs of indifference, jealousy, and ignorance, using it to guide me through blind hours in the laboratory—arriving finally at this moment of chance. Yet now, walking in the corridor to the operating theater, I was not so sure that this was the right moment. Maybe it was too soon. Maybe we were not ready for this.

It was not a new emotion. Doubt was my oldest enemy. I knew it well. Yet I had never expected it to come this way, to arrive so suddenly and with such force at this crucial time. It was this that was most confusing. If I had become accustomed to its presence in my being, why could I not keep it within bounds? How did it sneak past the high walls of hope to appear now where it could do such terrible damage?

Before going into an operation, we took showers, we scrubbed our arms and hands, we poured on an antiseptic solution to kill germs. We applied antibiotic ointment to our nostrils, we covered our face and hair, and we clothed ourselves in germ-free linen and rubber. Yet I was bringing with me something which could not be scrubbed away or covered up. It was within me, a beachhead of doubt which had split my camp in two— one half pulling me back, the other moving me on.

So I went down the corridor, arriving finally at the dressing room door: MEDICAL STAFF ONLY. I pushed it open and entered the first locker room for registrars and junior surgeons. Some of the team had already arrived and were stripping for the shower—Marius, my brother, and Doctors Bosman, Terry O'Donovan, and François Hitchcock. As I came in, they all turned toward me. Everyone knew his role and where to go, but inevitably there were some last-minute questions. Marius, who would be with the team removing the donor heart, wanted to make sure of the timing between the two theaters.

"We'll get the donor ready for bypass, in case the heart starts to fail. But we will not open her up until you say so—right, Chris?"

"Right."

"Then when it's ready you can come in and excise the heart."

"Don't you and Terry want to do it?"

"No."

"Why not?"

"Because it's like with dogs," said Marius. "Unless you cut it out yourself, it's not going to be familiar. If we do it, you'll receive an unfamiliar heart. It's better you get acquainted with it from the beginning."

He was right, and only later did I realize how grateful I should have been to him. But I had no room for gratitude, no desire even at that moment to talk about vital matters of procedure. I wanted to be alone, to become familiar with something nearer than a stranger's heart—my own, perhaps. I had to know which part of me was right: that which said go ahead, or the other part which said to stop before it was too late.

"Okay, Chris?"

"Okay."

I went on, opening the second door marked: SENIOR SURGEONS. Here I was alone. Rodney Hewitson, who would be my first assistant, had not yet arrived. For a moment I paused before my locker, looking at the name: PROF. BARNARD.

Your dogs don't live long enough. You're not ready for this.

This isn't a dog. It's a man.

That's just it. You haven't any right to experiment on a human being. It isn't a dog.

I'm not experimenting. I know what I can do. We've proven we can transplant a heart and make it work.

It'll work, will it? For how long?

I don't know.

You see what I mean? How can you go into such an undertaking if you don't have some idea of how long it'll work?

That's not a fair question. How many times have others tried to cure a patient without knowing whether or not it'll work?

But in treating a patient, we don't cut out his heart. We don't terminate his life. Whatever life is left, we leave to him. You're going to take life away from a man with the belief that you can sew it back. That is an enormous step. You'd better be damned sure you know what you're doing. Otherwise, it'll simply mean you've transformed two operating theaters into laboratories and substituted human beings for dogs.

No, it's different. We use healthy dogs for experiments and they don't need a transplant. This is a dying man and something must be done. We must act. We must save his life if we have the means for it. And we have them, including a waiting donor and a waiting team.

But for how long, Chris? How long will he live?

Suppose I say a year, would you say it was worth it?

Yes.

And if it's only a month?

I don't know.

A week?

Certainly not.

How can you say that? Have you the right to decide on how long a man can live?

You're doing that, man. You're going to cut out Washkansky's heart. That's a decision on how long someone can live—if ever there was one.

No, because he's not living. He's dying. He wants to live again. He wants his life extended. Suppose it is only a few days—but in those few days he can walk and see the sky and feel alive again. Do you have the right to say: 'No, Mr. Washkansky, you can't have those few precious days.' Who are you to hold back such a promise? How can the length of an added life be measured against its death? There is no way to measure the promise against the refusal.

You should never have made the promise, until you were sure you could deliver.

I promised him nothing more than an 80 per cent chance he would come out of the operation alive.

Yes, but Washkansky interprets this to mean he has an 80 per cent chance to get well. You falsely raised his hopes because you know that coming off the table alive is one thing—and living with a transplant is another.

I offered a chance, and he grabbed it, without asking any questions. At the South Pole, the wind can blow in one direction only—north. At the point of death, any promise of help can go in one direction only—toward hope. So I offered him hope, believing this was my duty. To have refused it would be a betrayal of myself and my profession. In a way, we share the same hope. We're in this together.

Except if you fail, he will die and you will live.

He will complete the act of dying, while I will try and complete the act of living.

By doing it again?

Why do you ask?

Because if you fail now, you will have to do it again. Otherwise, your first act will appear to be a reckless experiment, rather than what you claim it to be: an ethically and medically acceptable act to save a man's life. So you try it again—and again you fail. Then you will be in real trouble. It will seriously damage your career. Are you prepared for this?

What else is there to do?

Wait, man, wait a little longer. Other surgeons are preparing to do this, too. Let them go first—let them risk their careers. After all, is it worth it? If you succeed, it will be only the projection of the thinking, the experi-

ments, and the plans of other surgeons around the world. But if you fail, it will be all yours, Professor Barnard—no one will share your failure. Can you take that?

"Professor Barnard, may I come through?"

It was Sister Tollie Lambrechts. She stood at the rear door to the dressing room, looking at me. I was sitting in an armchair, wearing nothing more than a pair of tartan underpants.

"I have the second pump to take through," she said.

It was the heart-lung machine to be used on Denise Darvall—the old one of many memories which I had brought back from Minneapolis. To reach the theater, it had to be pushed through both locker rooms, beginning with the one where I sat in my underpants. If a moment remained to call off the operation, it was now. I looked at Sister Lambrechts in the door and beyond her at the machine with which I had done my first open-heart surgery. At that moment, all doubt left me.

"Bring it through, Sister."

Standing up, I opened the door to the first dressing room. Dr. Bosman was there, with a towel around his waist.

"Bossie, can you or somebody help Sister Lambrechts pull the heart-lung machine through here. What are we waiting for, boys?"

In the shower I was finally able to pray:

> Oh Lord, please guide my hands tonight—
> Keep them free from error
> As you have freed me from doubt,
> And shown me the way
> To do this as well as I can,
> To do it for this man
> Who has placed his life
> In my hands . . .
> And for all other men
> Like him.
> And for all others on the team,
> That they may also be with us—
> Every minute of the way.

After the shower, I got into the white undergarments for surgery—pants and sleeveless shirt—and a pair of sterile rubber boots. I then crossed the corridor and entered the operating suite, where a sister told me that Dr. Ozinsky had already brought Washkansky into the theater for induction of anesthesia.

This was out of the ordinary. Normally we induce the patients in a small room off the central corridor of the two theaters. It is less disturbing to do it this way, in a small room where they cannot see the operating table and lamp and amphitheater. Patients are put to sleep within the theater only when we fear complications may arise during induction of anesthesia— where there is a possibility that the heart might give way before the patient has been placed on the heart-lung bypass.

I quickly prepared myself—putting neomycin ointment in both nostrils, then grabbing a cap and face mask—and entered through the double doors into A Theater, which would soon be closed to further entry.

Washkansky was sitting on the table with some pillows behind him, as though this was simply one more bed in the hospital.

"Where you been?" he asked.

He said it as though it was all over and he already had his new heart and was ready to go home. But it was not very convincing. He was very sick and could hardly talk. He looked at Sister Fox-Smith and then at Dr. Ozinsky who was returning from Denise Darvall in the adjoining theater.

"I kept telling them that I didn't want any Mickey Finns until you came to say good-bye."

"Good-bye?"

"Good-bye to the old Washkansky . . ."

He paused to get his breath.

"Aren't you going to give me a new heart?"

"Yes."

"So it's out with the old and in with the new . . . *Auld Lang Syne*."

He wore a white gown open at the back. They allowed him to sit up in order to aid his breathing while being prepared for induction. Already, they had fastened green blood pressure cuffs around the right and left upper arms. There were also silver electrodes strapped to both lower arms and onto his left calf, with leads going to the electrocardiograph monitor.

He was ready to be put to sleep and Sister Fox-Smith suggested he now lie back on the table.

"Can't you do it while I'm sitting up?"

"No," she said.

"You have to recline," said Dr. Ozinsky. "These surgeons are worse than movie stars. They don't like anyone stealing their limelight."

That was Ozzie, whose broad knowledge of modern anesthesiology was coupled with a deep understanding of both patient and surgeon. He had brought Washkansky down from the ward, talking to him in a way that helped him remain calm and ready for this moment—doing all this, while also supervising Denise Darvall's entry into the adjoining theater.

The anesthetist had become a major figure in modern surgery. He protected the patient from surgical trauma and damage, using as few drugs as possible—checking blood pressure, venous pressure, control of respiration, acid level, pulse rate, urine output, cerebral reflexes. In effect, he was both caretaker of the sleeping body and its physiological bookkeeper.

Without an anesthesiologist such as Dr. Ozinsky, no transplant or major heart operation would be possible. Besides all this, Ozzie had a sense of humor and a feeling for people that made him invaluable.

"Can I help you lie back?" he asked Washkansky.

"No, I can do it myself."

Sister Fox-Smith removed the pillows, and Louis Washkansky lay back to accept whatever they were going to give him. Dr. Ozinsky held up a black oxygen mask.

"This isn't going to put you to sleep," he said. "It's pure oxygen. They give it to athletes to make them break records."

Washkansky nodded and accepted it, looking at me.

"Just breathe normally," said Ozzie.

Washkansky did that, his eyes remaining fixed on me. Suddenly they seemed to indicate he wanted to say something. I could only think of Ann Washkansky and perhaps him asking me: "Did you tell Ann it's in the bag?"

I nodded to him and said: "Yes, I told her."

He understood and blinked his thanks. Dear God, I thought, please keep me that close to every other part of him. Please let me deliver this man back into the arms of the woman who loves him.

Dr. Ozinsky gave an injection of thiopentone and the barbiturate took effect almost immediately.

I watched his eyes close and wondered if I would ever see them open again. He had gone under in a special way, hiding any fears with an extraordinary display of courage—even trying to give some of it to me: *Auld Lang Syne.* What else went on inside him at that moment? What memories, what part of his life did he take with him?

He had a great deal in his favor. There was a team of men and women who had been trained for this sudden moment at midnight. They were going to begin work without sufficient rest. But they would be driven on, beyond the demands of sleep, to save this life—their routine work inspired by a special respect, perhaps even a love, for this singular man. He was a fighter, too, and his will to live would help us greatly.

Against all this, there were unknown dangers we would meet along the way, perhaps even the *Skoppensboer,* the Jack of Spades. He was always there, waiting his turn.

> The one who through the night
> Watches our fun
> And who laughs the last
> Is *Skoppensboer.* . . .
>
> Only tenants we
> Of dust and down
> To be handed over

To *Skoppensboer.* . . .
The violin and the flute make their sound,
But long is the night that lies ahead. . . .

The barbiturate was followed by an injection of a relaxant, Scoline, which would paralyze the muscles—including the patient's ability to breathe. The extra oxygen in his system would now help to maintain him in life for the time that Dr. Ozinsky needed to slip an endotracheal tube through Washkansky's mouth and down his throat. It stopped three inches above the carina, or the point where the windpipe separates for the two lungs. With this in place, he quickly hooked the tube onto a black bag and began to breathe for the patient, pumping pure oxygen into him, squeezing the bag at a rate he considered best at this moment—about forty times a minute.

This had taken less than one minute. The paralyzing effect of the Scoline would last another two minutes—enough time for Dr. Ozinsky to now insert a transparent nasal-gastric tube into Washkansky's left nostril, threading it down into the stomach. This would be an air vent to prevent overinflation and also to draw off accumulated secretions—preventing the patient from burping up liquids that could be inhaled into the lungs.

Dr. Ozinsky then ran two other leads through the mouth—electric thermometers which remained in the esophagus on a level with the heart. At that point, the thermometers were about one-quarter inch from the heart's right atrium, separated only by the wall of the windpipe, some tissue and the heart's pericardial sac—giving an approximate reading of heart temperature. Two were needed: one for the anesthetist and the other for the heart-lung technician, to be used as a guide during cooling and rewarming of the patient.

By now the paralyzing effect of the Scoline had worn off. Dr. Ozinsky continued ventilating with a mixture of oxygen, nitrous oxide, and halothane, which would keep the patient asleep. He then ceased pumping the bag by hand, hooking its tube onto an automatic Bird respirator—freeing himself for other duties.

Dr. Hitchcock arrived, gowned and gloved, to insert a thin catheter, or tube, up the urethra into the bladder. This was joined by rubber tube to a bottle on the floor next to Dr. Ozinsky, allowing him a constant check on the urine flow—important parameter of blood perfusion to the body.

A needle with tube attached was inserted into each forearm, providing intravenous entry into the body for plasmalyte—a balanced salt solution to keep the veins open—as well as for drugs and blood.

A metal cuff was applied to the left leg and connected by electric line to the diathermy machine, grounding Washkansky's body. This made it possible to run a low charge of electrical current through surgical instruments severing his blood vessels—cauterizing them, and so stopping the flow of blood.

Sister Fox-Smith ran a bandage under his waist, securing both arms to prevent them from slipping off the table. A leather strap was placed over his knees, stabilizing his body in event the table was to be tilted. The operating lamp was turned on and under its glare Dr. Hitchcock and Sister Jordaan prepared the operating field by painting chest, belly, and thighs with an iodine solution until his torso was a golden brown. This was then covered with Steridrape—a sterile transparent adhesive plastic sheet. Finally, his entire body was draped with green toweling so that only the chest and right groin would be exposed for surgery.

I left then to see what was happening to the donor in B Theater. She was still not toweled, and Sister Sannie Rossouw was painting her. Dr. Cecil Moss, the assistant anesthetist, was checking ECG leads to her arms, which also had been connected to intravenous feed lines. To facilitate this, they had inserted two arm rests onto the operating table, extending out from it so that Denise Darvall lay with her arms outstretched—as on a cross. Dr. Moss had already raised up a green curtain that came down over her head, leaving the body with its extended arms exposed to the operating light and to the doctors—Marius and Terry O'Donovan—as they prepared the surgical field, prior to opening the chest.

The recording of her heart action appeared on the ECG monitor—and I did not like the look of it. Neither did Dr. Coert Venter who was in charge of the intravenous drips which were to sustain the heart.

"There's deterioration of the patient's condition," he said.

"What's the reading?"

"Blood pressure ninety-five, pulse one hundred. But there's no urine output and the temperature is thirty-nine."

This was not good. Her heart could fail and damage the myocardium before we had Washkansky ready. There was, I knew, a way to avoid it: Open the chest and connect the circulation to a heart-lung machine. This take-over, with an immediate cooling of the bloodstream, would slow down the body's metabolism and so help preserve the heart until we were ready for it.

Subsequently, I concluded this was the best method. At that time, however, I did not want to touch this girl until she was conventionally dead—a corpse. Brain death had already been established, but I felt we could not put a knife into her until she was truly a cadaver. That meant eventually turning off the respirator which was breathing for her, then waiting for the heart to stop beating.

When that occurred, the muscles of the donor's heart would slowly die. This had to be delayed until the last moment—until Washkansky was ready to receive his new heart. At the same time, we could not remove his heart until we had seen Denise Darvall's, and so determine that it was normal and could sustain life. It was a question of timing: Two people, both with dying hearts, had to be held in position until we were ready to remove one, then replace the other.

It was necessary, however, to be prepared at any moment for cardiac failure. We had to be ready to put this girl immediately on the machine, perfusing her with blood to save not only the heart, but also the kidneys, which were to be taken across town to the Karl Bremer Hospital for transplanting into a colored boy. Dr. Johan "Guy" de Klerk, from the Karl Bremer, was standing by with a plastic bag to do just this.

I spoke to Terry O'Donovan who was going to expose the heart of the donor.

"Terry, get ready to open the chest and go on the pump as fast as possible."

"We're ready," he said. "I plan to make it a total midline incision, so Dr. de Klerk can also get to the kidneys."

I was very pleased that a kidney would be used, but I wanted no confusion about who went first.

"Listen, Terry, you cut for the heart and let de Klerk worry about his kidneys afterwards."

Terry smiled. Of all our young surgeons, he had real promise. And with him was Marius, whose experience in the animal laboratory and instinctive knowledge of what I wanted made him an ideal catalyst. This was important.

If we could not control events in both theaters, we were going to lose either donor or recipient—or both. For this reason, I had not yet scrubbed. It would be necessary to move constantly between the two theaters. A chain was only as strong as its weakest link—a link that had to be strengthened before it gave way. This would mean issuing orders which were often only checking commands, ensuring us against the invisible point of breakage.

Two connecting rooms separate A and B Theaters. One is the "setting-up room" where instruments are sterilized and set out on trays. The other, nearest the corridor, is the scrub room, where surgeons do the final act of washing and then putting on operating gown and gloves. Here I met my chief assistant, Rodney Hewitson, who had finally arrived from his summer home at Hermanus, after being summoned by police radio. Sister Kingsley was helping him dress, holding the tapes of his gown with sterilized Cheatle forceps.

"Hello, Rodney—I'm glad to see you."

"Hello," he said.

"The donor's going downhill," I said. "We must get a move on with the recipient as soon as possible."

Mr. Hewitson nodded. (As a Fellow of the Royal College of Surgeons, he was called Mister.) He was a tireless and precise surgeon. But he was not much of a talker, and even now he said no more.

We went into the theater together, where Washkansky and Dr. Hitch-cock were waiting. Not being scrubbed and in my gown, I stood behind the green anesthetist's curtain, which Ozzie had raised between himself and the patient. Rodney took his place on the left side of the table, with Dr. Hitchcock on the right, to begin the cutdown—an opening into the right groin where they would insert two lines.

One would enter a vein, to be threaded up to a juncture near the inferior vena cava. This was to measure the pressure of venous blood returning to the right side of the heart. The venous pressure is a vital index, especially important in operating the heart-lung machine, since it indicates the volume of blood inside the body.

A second catheter would be inserted in the femoral artery exposed by the same incision in the groin, enabling a connection to be made between the arterial system and the heart-lung machine. Since both heart and lungs were soon to be bypassed, this was to serve as the point of entry into the body for cleansed blood from the machine. From here the pump-driven bloodstream would flow up to the heart, encountering a blocking clamp and so be shunted off to the rest of the body. The venous blood, returning from the tissues, would be channeled back to the heart-lung machine by two tubes inserted into the superior and inferior venae cavae where they enter the heart. In this way, the body was to be perfused with blood while the heart and lungs would be taken out of function—that is, on total cardiopulmonary bypass.

As Rodney Hewitson, assisted by François Hitchcock, began the cut-down, I left them to return to B Theater. There, all was finally ready, except that both Marius and Terry were worried about further deteriora-tion in the donor.

"I don't like the looks of her," said Marius.

"There's internal bleeding," said Terry.

"What have you now?" I asked Coert Venter.

"Pressure seventy-eight, pulse eighty. Temperature's 39.8."

"What's the last potassium reading?"

"Three point four."

"Give another gram . . . and the isoprenaline?"

"It's running at twenty."

"Raise it to thirty."

Added isoprenaline would help stimulate the heart, but it was not certain how much more time this would give us. Marius wanted to proceed imme-diately toward bypass—turning off the respirator to stop the breathing and so bring on heart arrest.

"The neurosurgeons say we can pull the switch at any time," argued Marius. "So let's do it and get going. As soon as we have her on bypass, we'll be in a safer position."

Terry was also ready to do this, but for another reason.

"After stopping respiration," he said, "we'll have to wait until the heart stops. It might take a few minutes—but what if it takes fifteen or twenty minutes? What will you do with Washkansky in that time?"

It meant we would have Washkansky's heart exposed while Darvall's heart continued to beat in a body that had ceased to breathe. On the other hand, if we cut the respirator now, we would create a larger time gap between the death of the heart and its eventual transplant. If there were an unexpected delay in getting Washkansky ready for bypass, the chances of damage to the donor heart would be increased. This had to be avoided. My responsibility lay with the waiting patient—not with a dead donor.

"No," I said. "We can't stop the respirator until Washkansky is open and ready for bypass. Then you boys will really have to move fast. As soon as you have her on bypass I'll come in and remove the heart."

Time was now measured by heart beats, and it seemed to be racing on, beyond our grasp. Was Rodney moving fast enough with Washkansky? I returned to A Theater, where he was making the skin incision—a straight cut down the center of the chest, cauterizing blood vessels along the line of the cut. The breastbone was exposed, and this was split in half by an electrical saw, its blades oscillating back and forth, their friction with the bone creating a nimbus of rising smoke. Wax was rubbed along the bone edge to halt further bleeding from its raw, spongy surface. A retractor was inserted between the two halves and cranked open, drawing apart the rib cage.

This exposed the area between the lungs, revealing the pericardial sac streaked with red blood vessels—its glistening surface slowly fluttering from contractions of the hidden heart. Sister Jordaan handed Rodney a pair of scissors with which he opened the thin sac, its edges retracted with stay sutures.

Louis Washkansky's heart came into full view—rolling in a rhythm of its own like a separate and angry sea, yellow from the storms of half a century, yet streaked with blue currents from its depths—blue veins drifting across the heaving waste and ruin of a ravaged heart. On the right, its purple atrium slid back and forth with each contraction—struggling as would a monstrous fish tied to the shoreline of the yellow sea.

The split chest cage hung open, motionless as sundered rock. Separate and alone within the hush of its dark cavity, the great heart twisted on itself as though seeking some exit, only to return with a sudden shudder as the left ventricle once more—how many millions of times had it happened?—sought to expel its own private lake of blood, its scarred and ruined muscles closing in sudden spasm, then collapsing in a moment of exhaustion, a moment seized by the upper atrium to send down still more blood into the unemptied lake below where the life of Louis Washkansky lay trapped, beyond the reach of knife or prayer.

From his position at the table, Rodney looked at me on the other side of the anesthetist's curtain—brown eyes over the pale blue mask, bushy eyebrows lifting in amazement at what lay below us.

"Did you ever see anything like it?" I asked.

"Hardly."

"Let's see more of that left ventricle."

He lifted it up. The chamber was larger than any I had ever known —its walls scarred as the humps of ancient whales, bloated and extended from coronary attacks and muscle death. The ability of the human body to continue life was an unending miracle.

"One thing is certain. He'll never leave this table without a transplant."

Rodney nodded—and that was it.

"Get him ready for bypass as fast as possible. I'm going to start the donor."

As I entered B Theater, Terry saw me first and then Marius turned around.

"Now?" asked Marius.

"Now," I said, turning off the respirator.

I looked at the heart's monitor—unchanged. Dr. Venter closed the taps of the intravenous lines: There was no need to further support her. But we would need Heparin to prevent clotting in arteries of the heart.

"Coert, let's put in the Heparin."

He already had it up, and it began to drip into a tube leading to her left arm. I watched it start, then looked at the ECG machine. A waving green line registered the life of Denise Darvall's heart, in the classic trajectory of a heart beat, making six-second trips across the screen. I counted eight ventricular peaks—eight times ten meant a pulse of eighty—of a heart going faithfully into each of its phases.

Soon, I knew, the tragedy would begin. The heart would find its life fluid returning from lungs which no longer breathed the oxygen of life. It would begin then to struggle against its death, reacting at first as if meeting only a small inconvenience. Unaware of what was about to happen, it would simply pump more excitedly—expecting some relief. Yet this would never come, and it would fall back in the first wave of confusion and fatigue.

This would lead to a final thrashing for survival—from its strangulation. The ventricular peaks would shoot up in wild flight and their intermediate planes would begin to jumble against one another like the sudden crashing of cars on a freight train. The heart's beautiful symmetry would then be reduced to an erratic green line of wild jerks, struggling along until it entered the final isoelectric phase resembling a sawtooth—jagged lines of the heart seeking to rise like a dying bird, fluttering upward, only to fall once again onto its flat plane of death.

This was to come. Yet it did not happen as soon as expected. The heart of Denise Darvall continued to beat on. The body lay inert, its brain destroyed, the lungs without life, the blood without relief in its unending cycle—returning with carbon dioxide from the cells, pulsing into the right side of the heart which pumped it on to the lungs where it found no aid, returning then to the left chambers which expelled it back into the body, only to pick up still more waste material—returning once again to the unmoving lungs. So the blood went, around and around in the system, driven by a heart that refused to give up, beating on as though it had found a secret supply of oxygen or power from a source outside the body. It would not die.

"What a shame," said Marius. "We're killing a heart."

No one answered him, but I knew he was right. If the donor was dead, and we wanted to put her living heart into a patient, our duty was clearly with the patient. To provide a donor heart in the best condition, we should act now—cutting it out while it was still beating. Waiting for it to collapse, would only cause the heart to be less perfect when we finally took it. We were manifestly acting against the patient and our duty to save him—why? What intermingling of mythology and ritual prevented us from touching a beating heart in a body that had been declared clinically dead? If this was forbidden, we should not even be making the transplant.

"I'll not lift an instrument until the ECG line is flat," said Terry O'Donovan.

I nodded, knowing how he felt.

All the years of our training, all the structures of our belief rested on one concept—to protect life, not to take it. Yet what life were we protecting in waiting for this heart to die—and perhaps injure itself? Certainly not Washkansky's. Nor could we take away the life of Denise Darvall, for it had already been removed from her. So this was not another temptation to commit the Great Transgression—to cross the line and play God, to decide when a life should be terminated. Here there was no decision to be made by us. It had already been made. Unlike Maria, who had asked to be removed from life, Denise Darvall was beyond the possibility of living. Clinically, she was dead. Her heart lived on, yes—but it had been supported by us, to reach this moment when we could take it to a man waiting in another room.

"What do you say, Chris?"

Marius spoke as though he knew my thoughts—and believed we should take the heart now.

"No, we must wait until it stops."

So we waited, while the heart struggled on—five, ten, fifteen minutes. Finally, it began to go into the last phases, its wild peaks slowly sinking into exhausted rolls that became longer and longer until it finally revealed itself in a straight green line across the screen—death.

"Now?" asked Marius.

"No," I said. "Let's make sure there is no heart beat coming back."

So we waited—one, two, three minutes. The esophageal temperature was 37.4. Without cooling, the heart and kidneys were deteriorating rapidly.

"All right," I said. "Start cutting, Terry."

I hurried into A Theater.

"Rodney, hook on to bypass!"

I returned to the scrub room and began to prepare myself—carefully going through a ritual that never changed. Even the sink had to be the same—the first on the left. My arms covered with soap, I went to the door of the theater.

"Rod, don't forget to put the venous catheter through the atrial appendage"—getting a nod from the back of his head.

"Ozzie, don't forget the cortisone—we have to start antirejection treatment now . . . also raise that curtain more. There'll be extra people looking over and we can't afford the risk of infection."

He nodded, bending down to read the urine output. It had been a useless reminder. He had done it a thousand times. I spoke to Johan van Heerden, who ran the heart-lung machine.

"Are you ready to go on bypass?"

Again a nod in return. They were used to me—but they were not used to a night such as this. A small error could destroy a life.

Once again at the wash basin, I heard the saw cutting through Denise Darvall's chest and thought that Terry O'Donovan was making record time. He did not need to cauterize or tie off the blood vessels. All he had to do was cut. He had probably already reached the heart.

At least five minutes scrub is mandatory before surgery, and I was still at it when I looked in at them.

"Is it all right?"

"Fine—we've exposed the heart and are preparing for bypass."

"What does it look like?" I asked, entering the theater.

It was a tiny little heart. Later I realized it seemed especially small because I seldom ever saw a normal one. It lay there, blue and limp and half empty, and its stillness chilled me. Had we waited too long? Had this tiny heart gone beyond the point of life?

"Terry, how does it look to you?" I asked, feeling the need for some assurance.

"A little blue, but at least there was not a single beat when we opened it."

"Thank God," I said.

Then I said: "All right, let's get it onto the pump fast."

Terry and Marius made the connections quickly—a catheter into the right atrium for venous drainage and another into the ascending aorta for return of the blood from the machine—completing the circuit for perfusion of both body and heart. Terry also put a vent with a catheter in the left ventricle to release any excess blood rushing into the heart—preventing dangerous expansion of the muscles. With this in place, Marius turned to Alastair Hope and Nic Vermaak at the heart-lung machine.

"Ready, Alastair?"

"Ready."

"Pump on."

Almost immediately the little blue heart became beautifully pink—tense and firm. Yet there was nothing more from the impassive muscle. No responsive beat arose to help it along its way. Desperately, I told myself this was not a damaged heart. It had not begun to beat because of cold blood being sent into it.

"Alastair—are we cooling as fast as possible?"

"The water tank is at two degrees."

"We've got to cool the donor below twenty-eight. How fast are you flowing?"

"Three liters."

Three liters a minute, flowing through a heat exchanger set at two degrees centigrade, would rapidly cool the donor. Alastair confirmed it.

"Temperature now down to thirty-two," he said.

Good. The donor was almost ready.

"Okay, boys—I'll be back in a minute."

I finished scrubbing, and a nurse poured antiseptic solution over my hands. I let it run down to the elbows and she passed a towel, using sterilized Cheatle forceps. Then she gave me another one, to make sure there was no dampness to carry germs. After that, I pulled on a green gown, then rubber gloves—white, thin ones because the heavier rubber increased the arthritic pain in my hands.

I went quickly into A Theater, ducked under the heart-lung line connected to Washkansky's femoral artery, and took my place at the right side of the table.

The tubes were all connected—the arterial line to the femoral artery and the venous line from the two venae caval catheters. We were ready to start the pump on the heart-lung machine, putting Washkansky on bypass.

In the operating theater there were fourteen people: sisters, doctors, technicians—all in masks. Behind us, the open amphitheater was filled with doctors and specialists—the watching world, also in masks.

"All set, Rodney?"

He nodded.

"Johan, all set?"

"Yes, Professor."

"Pump on!"

Immediately there was the hum of five motors. Blood began to move through pulsating tubes, going through the femoral artery, then surging up to the heart where the closed aortic valve shunted it off into the body's cardiovascular system that flushed it out to millions of cells. After this, the blood came back—bearing carbon dioxide, and a darker red, almost blue —returning through a network of veins. These poured it into two big vessels—the superior vena cava and the inferior vena cava—which normally spilled their venous blood into the heart's first chamber, the right atrium. Before the blood could reach the atrium, however, it was caught by catheters, channeling it off to the heart-lung machine. This completed the circular flow of blood—from machine, through patient, and back to the machine—bypassing the heart and lungs.

Dene Friedmann, Johan's assistant, began to call off the pressure readings that would indicate whether or not the circuit of blood was flowing freely. The first words we heard from her were alarming.

"Line pressure's just over two hundred."

It was not possible. The pressure in the line from machine to patient should be one-half that.

"What's the venous pressure?"

"It's twenty," said Dene.

"I get eighteen," said Ozzie.

"Yes, it's dropping," said Dene. "But the line pressure is now 240."

The venous pressure—or flow of venous blood returning to the heart—normally was between five and ten millimeters of mercury. Washkansky's initial 27.5 had been expected, indicating failure of the right side of his heart. With the help of the machine, it was dropping. Yet the line pressure was going sky-high.

"Line pressure 250," said Dene.

She said it to a silent theater—broken only by a slow *beep-beep* from the ECG machine and an even slower *whissh* in the Bird respirator. Johan, sitting at the machine's control panel barely four feet from Dene, spoke to us in disbelief.

"But I'm not on full bypass yet, I'm not giving the patient all the blood he needs."

He said it with the shame of a man suddenly discovering his horse was lame. Johan knew that pump as one who had created it with his own hands.

"Pressure's 260," said Dene. "Now 265, 275 . . ."

"But I'm only on half flow," said Johan, in further disbelief.

"Ozzie—what are you getting?"

"I'm afraid it's now . . . let me see . . . yes it's 290."

At this rate we would blow the lines.

"It's got to be the femoral artery," I said.

"It's very poor," said Rodney, who had put in the metal cannula. "Very sclerotic."

A narrowed artery was blocking the fresh blood. Without sufficient flow to ensure perfusion of the entire body, we would never keep Washkansky alive long enough to do the transplant. There was only one answer: Remove the arterial line inserted through the groin, and connect it directly into the aorta as it left the heart.

In the silence, a metal bucket was suddenly kicked. The high walls and tile and glass of the theater echoed back every sound—like working inside a drum. Within the racket caused by the bucket, I detected Dene's voice.

"Jesus! I can't hear a damn thing!"

"Line pressure three hundred!" said Dene again.

"It seems to be holding at three hundred," said Ozzie.

"We've got to stop it there," I said. "Johan, don't increase your flow. We've got to cool this patient fast, so I can interrupt the circulation for a while. What's the temperature now?"

"Temperature 29.5" said Johan and Ozzie together—reading from their separate temperature leads that lay parallel in Washkansky's esophagus, next to the heart.

"Get him down to twenty-six, Johan."

"Yes, sir."

"Give me a 2-0 suture," I said to Sister Peggy Jordaan.

She was opposite me, between Rodney and the swab sister, Tollie Lambrechts, who stood before an assembly of surgical tools on three trolleys. Sister Jordaan was a veteran of the operating theater. As instrument sister, she could anticipate every move and instinctively knew better than anyone else what I needed—even before it was requested. She gave me the size 2-0 silk suture, fixed to its needle and clamped in a needleholder, almost as soon as I asked for it.

I made a purse-string or circular stitch in the wall of the aorta—then stabbed a hole into its center and plunged in a catheter. After that, we slipped a rubber snare over the tough silk thread, sliding it down to tighten the stitch. This caused the wall of the great vessel to draw securely around the inserted tube. The channel into the aorta was fixed—blood-tight. It was now ready to be hooked onto the arterial line of the heart-lung machine.

"Now, clamp the line," I said—speaking more to myself than to anyone else.

It was received as an order by Sister Jordaan, who clamped it. Within two seconds, there was a sudden swissSHH!—followed by the sound of blood spilling onto the floor. With horror, I realized we had clamped the line without turning off the heart-lung machine, causing it to blow at its weakest point—the connection at the heat exchanger.

"Turn off the pump!"

The motor hum faded away like a distant boat in the wind—silence.

"Is there air on the arterial side?"

"Yes, it's full of air."

Lord, I thought, we're really going to kill this patient before we can even attempt a transplant. We were going to put air bubbles into his brain and turn him into a vegetable.

"Who made this stupid mistake?"

I looked at Dr. Hitchcock on my right, then at Sister Jordaan across the table—brown eyes blinking over a blue mask.

"Dammit, keep your hands off if you don't know what you're doing!"

"But you said to clamp it."

"I said nothing like that," I replied, knowing at that moment that I had said it.

Inside myself, I fought for control. It was useless to shout. We were in real trouble. With air in the heart-lung machine, there was no way to keep Washkansky alive. After a thousand open-heart operations, we were about to kill a man through a technical error that had never happened before—an error caused by my own lack of clear command. Somehow, we had to correct it immediately, or lose the patient.

"Johan, can you get the air out?"

Before he could answer, I knew what to do—take the ends of the two lines out of Washkansky, connect them, and restart the machine. Its own debubbling process would clear the arterial circuit.

I removed the leads, connected them, and turned to Johan and Dene.

"Turn on the pump."

The circulation began, while Ozzie's voice came constantly over the curtain—giving us courage.

"It's going well, don't worry. The heart is still beating at thirty—and that's something from this old boy . . . besides, the temperature is down to 26.8 . . . so there's plenty of time."

How much time did we really have? How long could this continue without destroying the brain of this man, wiping away forever the image of his wife, his dream of a new life—the dream he had started to describe when Sister Papendieck had interrupted us. And then he had said: "Tell Annie it's in the bag."

Well, it was in the bag all right—a busted one, with his blood spilled out onto the floor where Dene was laying down green towels—green that turned black with red blood.

"The venous pressure had almost reached twelve when the line blew," said Ozzie, trying to cheer us with the best figure he could throw out from the jumbled wreckage of statistics in his lap. Later, I recalled this and how important had been his moral support at that moment. Every team had its heart, and Ozzie was very much part of ours.

I felt grateful, yet there was no time for anything except the next moment. I looked back over the curtain to follow the pattern of Washkansky's heart on the ECG. It barely made three beats crossing the screen—a pulse of thirty. Then we saw the first signs of ventricular collapse which would lead to fibrillation.

"Dammit, Johan, how much time do you need?"

"Just a bit more, Professor—the line's clearing fine."

"Hurry, man, we can't stand here forever!"

We could stand there, of course. There was nothing else to do, except wait for a mechanical process that would take at least two, maybe three minutes. We waited in a silence, broken only by the hum of the motors, the beeping of the ECG and Johan and Dene thumping helix and heat exchangers with hard-rubber hammers—knocking out any remaining bubbles. After two minutes, Johan was satisfied.

"All right, Professor—all clear."

I separated the line—reconnecting one end to the venae caval catheters, and the other to the new lead into the aorta.

"Pump on!"

"Line pressure one hundred—venous eleven," said Ozzie. That was more like it. Then he reported the first indications that Washkansky's heart was about to collapse.

"The ventricles are fibrillating."

We could see it with our eyes. The slow roll of the heart, caused by its chambers working together, began to falter and then its unity dramatically broke apart. The rhythm of contracting ventricles, responding to the pulse of the upper atria, suddenly ceased—causing the muscle fibers to jerk in separate spasms. Each fiber went into its own rhythm—tiny spasms within spasms. What had been a rolling sea became a lake of worms.

The incredible heart of Louis Washkansky had endured long enough to reach the operating table—and go beyond it. With catheters through its upper chamber, it had continued to beat on, even during the three-minute breakdown of the heart-lung machine—refusing to give up though chilled with cold blood. And now, when the crisis was over and the pump again able to return its blood, the destroyed heart was finally collapsing.

This was a heart for history—equal to the man who carried it, the man who refused to lie down and give up. And now, there was little left—other than to watch it die. The fibrillation, tragic spasms heralding the end, became more aggravated. The heart which God had given to Louis Washkansky was approaching its moment of death.

It was also the moment to return to B Theater for the heart of the donor.

"Johan—everything okay?"

"Okay, Professor."

"Ozzie?"

"Just fine. Maybe you should go get that other heart, before someone else claims it."

CHAPTER 25

I ENTERED B THEATER telling myself I had to be very careful. One accident was enough. There could be no more, especially in the removal of the donor heart. A wrong incision, and I would ruin everything. A heart may be opened in many places without serious damage. Yet there are some areas that cannot be cut without destroying its ability to function, such as coronary arteries nourishing its muscles, or the sinoatrial node—a collection of cells near the superior vena cava, serving as a pacemaker and giving the heart its rhythm.

"All yours," said Terry, stepping aside.

I looked once more at the little heart. This time, it was more clearly defined. Terry had isolated all the main vessels, clearing them from the surrounding fat.

"Thank you, Terry. You might as well have taken it out."

"No, Marius is right. It's better you do it, so that you're familiar with all of it from the start."

"All right—let's turn off the pump."

Alastair Hope switched off the heart-lung machine, and I removed the catheter in the right atrium, which had been channeling off the return of venous blood. From that moment, the blood of Denise Darvall would never circulate again. Two more catheters remained and I left them there. One, in the aorta, would be used for the entry of blood into the limp heart when we began to perfuse it in A Theater. The other, the vent in the left ventricle, was to continue serving as an escape for excessive blood and air.

We were ready. Sister Rossouw handed me a small pair of scissors and when I started to make the first cut, my hand was shaking. I tried to steady it, but it continued to tremble. I was far too tense to work well, but hoped for more control as I went along.

There are eight vessels into the heart. I cut the two easiest ones first—the superior vena cava and the inferior vena cava—telling myself: "Cut them high up, leave as much as you can. You can always trim down, but you can't ever put any of this back again."

The aorta was divided next, leaving plenty of length—necessary because this vessel was much smaller in diameter than Washkansky's. Its size would have to be increased to make a proper anastomosis—joining. This could be done by cutting it on the bias—similar to cutting a loaf of bread at an angle to get a bigger slice.

The pulmonary artery presented the same problem. It was too small, yet could also be enlarged in another way. Upon leaving the heart, the artery branches out to the right and left lungs. At this fork—or bifurcation—the vessel broadens out. Here it would match Washkansky's larger vessel. I dissected it free beyond the fork, cutting first the left, then right branch of the artery.

All that remained were the four pulmonary veins which enter the left atrium. This is located in the back and to reach it, Terry lifted up the heart, exposing the four veins—two from the right lung, two from the left. After they had been cut, the heart was free.

Marius held out a round basin filled with ice-cold Ringer's lactate solution. I lifted the heart with my hands and placed it in the basin. Immediately, the blood turned the salt solution pink, causing the heart to disappear, excepting for the catheters that dangled over the edge.

"Okay, here goes," I said beginning the journey from one operating table to the other—thirty-one steps.

It was a walk through total silence—from B Theater, into the scrub room and then into A Theater—everyone motionless before the vision of the metal basin, its two dangling catheters the only evidence that within the pink liquid lay the hidden heart, the unwitnessed miracle.

Sister Jordaan stood waiting at her place near the end of the table and I gave it to her.

"Here—you keep it."

She put it on the green toweling over Washkansky's legs. Still holding it, she spoke to Dr. Bosman who had now joined the table, after helping Dr. de Klerk prepare for the preservation of the donor kidney. Her husky voice boomed in the theater:

"Here, you keep it, and don't let it fall off!"

Bossie, who would control the coronary perfusion, took the heart and helped Dr. Hitchcock shift it to an empty basin. They then attached the catheter we had left in the aorta to a line from the coronary perfusion pump. This was a smaller, separate pump, but drew its blood from the heart-lung machine. In this way, a small flow of Washkansky's own blood —300-400 cubic centimeters a minute—began for the first time to perfuse his future heart. The vent opening into the left ventricle again served as an escape valve to prevent machine-driven blood from causing overexpansion of the muscles. A sucker returned the flow of blood leaving the heart muscle at the coronary sinus, returning it all back to the heart-lung machine where it again joined the circulating stream.

I rinsed my hands in a fresh basin and took my place on the right side of the table. The first frantic fibrillation of Washkansky's heart had diminished to an occasional quiver of its muscles—the tremor of clinging leaves. And now even this would be gone. I extended my hand towards Sister Jordaan.

"Give me an aortic clamp."

The aorta was clamped just below the catheter leading to the heart-lung machine—stopping the blood supply to the heart. Once again, I extended my hand, and Sister Jordaan gave me what I wanted without speaking—a small pair of Stille scissors.

My hand was no longer shaking as I cut the aorta close to the heart, where the coronary arteries begin. Once again I told myself: "Take out the heart but leave behind more than you need because there's no way to put any of this back again."

The pulmonary artery was cut in the same way, close to the heart. This left too much vessel since we already had the extra length of artery from the donor's heart, including its branches to the lungs. Yet it did not matter. We could trim away the extra length when the donor heart was in its new cavity and we could see exactly how much to take off—similar to matching two halves of a sleeve while fitting a jacket.

After the two great vessels, there remained six lesser ones, entering the upper chambers of the heart—two venae cavae from the body into the right atrium, and four pulmonary veins from the lungs into the left atrium. These had to be left in place. I would cut below them, around the top of the heart, leaving the "lid" with all its veins in place. It would be like carving a jack-o'-lantern from a pumpkin. The stump to be left behind would be the lid of the pumpkin.

To understand what this lid would look like, imagine the pumpkin being divided by a septum, or a vertical wall, separating it down the middle. Then imagine another division, a horizontal floor cutting across the center, making four rooms—one atop the other on the right, and a similar upper-lower arrangement on the left. The two top rooms, or atria, are the receiving chambers which pass blood down to the lower ones, the ventricles. These pump it out again to the lungs and body.

We were about to cut horizontally across the two top rooms, removing their floor and both lower rooms, yet leaving the wall receiving the two venae cavae on the right and the four pulmonary veins on the left. That meant cutting it low, where the atria join the ventricles—the atrioventricular groove—keeping as much of the atria as possible. The prime purpose of the heart transplant is to replace the pumping chambers, the ventricles—the atria being merely receiving chambers.

So I began, but upon reaching the level of the inferior vena cava, I found there was not much space between its opening and the "floor." This required cutting as close as possible to the ventricle. From our work on dogs, we had learned to be careful here—otherwise there would be very little tissue on which to stitch, or anastomose, the new heart. In making this dip, I inadvertently cut away part of the lower right ventricle, entering the coronary sinus—a vital vein which returns used blood from the heart muscle. When this happened, I halted with fear, thinking: "God, you've cut the coronary sinus . . . what's going to happen now?"—realizing then this heart would not need a coronary sinus because it would have a new one with the donor heart.

Yet my own heart continued to pound on with excitement, for here we were cutting something big—something I had never before destroyed in a living heart. Finally the chambers were opened and all that remained was to cut down through their common central wall, or septum—incising near the floor where it joined the lower ventricles.

The heart then fell back into its cavity, severed from its moorings. Supported by its veins, the atrial lid hung down, its two floorless rooms sharing one septal wall—their interiors gray as old bone, streaked with red veins and splotches of yellow fat.

The fallen heart lay in a red pool at the bottom of the cavity. Once it had roared in that chamber. It had risen to every challenge. It had vibrated to the first thrill of being alive and it had beat on in continuum within the body that held it—a house without windows open to the light of the sun, the touch of lips, the sound of prayer.

Every season had affected it—and every emotion of man. It had hidden nothing, and it had responded to all the climaxes of the human experience —the heat of passion, the sudden paralysis of doubt, the long march of faith. It had been carried by sleigh through Lithuanian winter, by cattle car into a Jew's exile in Crimea—and then by ship to its final home on the extreme tip of the African continent.

Man was a wanderer—Jew or not—and he walked through the dark feeling the beat of his heart, knowing he had this at least in his search for light. Jason could fall, but he rose again, feeling it. No man died as long as it beat on, this miracle of God, this incredible system of chambers, this harmonious creation of muscles born in dialogue, this unity of continual disunity, this little theater of life where every contraction led to its opposite —constant as the tides, inevitable as the seasons, enduring forever—until now, when it had fallen into a quivering mass at the bottom of its own dark cavity.

Inserting my hand, I removed Washkansky's heart from his body and placed it in a basin held by Sister Jordaan. With a slight roll, the empty heart spread out in the metal bowl. Incredibly, there was a slight tremor in its ventricles, as though they had been suddenly invested with a still smaller heart of their own at the moment of separation from the parent body. It was also a final reminder that we had taken away the last moments of life in this man and now had to return them—plus much more.

The *caw-caw* of the sucker turned me back to see Rodney draining the pericardium until there was nothing else, other than a yawning cavity with some tiny pools of blood. The stumps of the aorta and pulmonary artery hung down in disuse. The atrial lid with its gray-walled rooms flabbily clung to its supporting veins.

Below this was the hole and it seemed immense. I had never seen a chest without a heart or with such a hole—as though the hole itself was fixed and permanent, while the man, with his chest split open, was merely a temporary object, existing briefly around the hole. And in fact, it was just that—something few men had ever seen: a human being without a heart, held in life by a machine eight feet away. I spoke to Rodney.

"Boy, this is really the bottom point of no return. Now we have to do something."

Bossie moved the bowl with its heart up onto the groin of Washkansky, and I took Denise Darvall's little heart in my hands—pink and firm and cold.

We now began, for the first time, to cut into the donor heart, rather than across its connecting vessels. At that moment, the operation became increasingly dangerous, allowing more chance for innovation and error.

The accepted technique for a heart transplant, patterned upon that developed by Shumway and Lower, was to cut away the "lid" of the donor heart so that what remained would match the waiting "lid" of the recipient. Yet to do this, it was necessary to cut across the central wall, or septum, in the upper chambers of both hearts. It did not matter with the recipient, but it could be dangerous to do this in the donor heart because there was the possibility of cutting the coronary sinus or of harming the heart's conduction system—causing a slow heart rate and requiring the insertion of a permanent electric pacemaker into the heart cavity.

The solution I had conceived in bed that afternoon was to leave the donor's septum intact and not cut off the entire lid, but rather two smaller patches of the roof—that is, only those two areas where the veins came into the two separate chambers. After cutting this away, I would be left with a heart having two holes at the top: one where the two venae cavae had entered and another where the four pulmonary veins joined the heart. I could then stitch these holes onto the waiting lid of Washkansky's heart. If there was a difference in size, it would not create a problem: We could enlarge the openings in the donor heart to match the lid of the recipient. It had one great advantage: The septum of the donor heart would not be injured.

So I began, explaining it to Rodney, who appeared somewhat amazed.

"This idea came to me in bed today," I said, without realizing this would startle him even more.

Slowly, I cut as planned—leaving two openings in the top of the heart and two vessels coming from its ventricles: the pulmonary artery with its branch and the aorta, which contained the catheter attached to the line bringing blood from the little coronary pump.

We were ready to place the heart in its future home. Gently, Rodney lifted it into the empty chest of Washkansky. For a moment, I stared at it, wondering how it would ever work. It seemed so small and insignificant—too tiny to ever handle all the demands that would be put upon it. The heart of a woman is 20 per cent smaller than a man's, and the heart of Washkansky had created a cavity twice normal size. All alone, in so much space, the little heart looked much too small—and very lonely.

Then we began the first step, which was to sew the two openings in the top of the donor heart onto the two halves of the waiting lid—sewing around the edge and then onto the central septal wall.

The left atrium had to be completed first. It lay at the back of the heart and, once closed, would be difficult to reach again. More than anywhere else, this meant we had to make sure there were no leaks in our suture line. I therefore ran two continuous sutures, stitching from the inside of the heart while Rodney retracted the right atrial opening to enable me to reach the area. Bossie and François also helped with retractors and suckers, anticipating each movement.

I worked with 4-0 silk and two needles, stitching one way, then the other, and then back again to the center. When the far side was done, Rodney let the heart fall back, to complete the remainder of the left atrium from the outside. The suture line was carefully inspected.

"We have to be sure here," I said, "because this is one place we can never return to."

Rodney pointed to a gap in the stitching on the left side of the atrium. I oversewed it again, relieved.

"That could have cost the patient his life."

The right atrial connection was then joined in a similar manner.

"We're halfway there," I said.

The body of the heart was now complete with six of its vessels in place. Two giant arteries remained: the pulmonary and the aorta. The pulmonary —cut at its point of bifurcation to match the recipient—was no trouble, and we closed it without difficulty.

The aorta presented a different problem, however—related to the perfusion of the heart. Since bringing it into the theater at 3:01 A.M., the donor heart had been perfused continually with Washkansky's own blood, cooled down to thirty-two degrees centigrade. It came from the coronary perfusion pump, entering the clamped aortic stump, then plunging down toward the heart—only to meet the closed aortic valve. This forced the blood into its only remaining outlets—coronary arteries in the aorta just above the heart —and so perfused the heart muscle.

The stump of the donor aorta, containing the catheter, had to be sewn onto the hanging aorta of Washkansky, which also held the catheter allowing fresh blood to enter his body from the heart-lung machine. Was it possible to successfully join the two ends of the vessels while the catheters and clamps remained on either side? Rodney felt we could do it, even though we would have a very small area in which to join an artery receiving the heart's greatest pressure. I was not sure and had to decide between two methods: continue to perfuse the heart while attempting to join the great vessel in a severely limited area, or else cut the coronary blood supply and so obtain more space.

"Rodney, I think we had better do it without perfusion. I'll do the half on my side and you do your half."

He nodded.

"Cut the coronary pump!"

Johan flipped the switch and immediately the heart lost its pink color and tone—slowly turning blue. It was now without any support in life and inevitably would begin once more to deteriorate. I looked at the clock: five-fifteen. Every minute counted.

We removed the catheter: It would never be needed again. Once the aorta was joined, and the clamps removed, the heart could be perfused directly with warmer blood flowing into Washkansky's body.

"Start warming."

"Warming on," replied Johan, who knew he was slowly to run the temperature up to thirty-four degrees, rather than to the usual thirty-seven.

At the same time, Ozzie began to run warm water through a rubber mattress beneath Washkansky's body.

I trimmed the donor aorta back at an angle, creating a larger opening—to match Washkansky's dilated vessel. As Rodney brought the vessels together, there was still too much play and more had to be cut away from either donor or recipient. I chose to remove two centimeters from Washkansky's vessel because it became narrower, and also I wanted as much of the new and as little of the old as possible. We began then to sew, using finer 5-o sutures which left smaller holes. I did my side, and then Rodney took over from his side to complete the anastomosis.

As he worked, I looked at the blue heart and then at the clock: five-thirty. Already it had gone without oxygen or blood for a quarter of an hour and still we were not finished. Slowly the minutes dragged on, as Rodney stitched quickly and well—until the final suture was tied: five-thirty-four.

I released the venous snares and allowed some blood to run past the catheters, filling up the spaces. Suddenly we ran into more trouble. Trapped air began to bubble through the suture line in the pulmonary artery—a sign of real danger, indicating air was about to be forced into the arterial system of the lungs. This had to be prevented immediately.

"Give me a stiletto blade knife!"

There was a delay and I looked up to see Sister Jordaan trying to fit an awkward blade.

"Hurry, man!"

She slapped the handle into my hand, and quickly I jabbed a hole into the pulmonary artery. More air bubbled out, and I inserted a sucker to insure that all remaining air would be removed. On the left side the air was allowed to escape through the vent in the ventricle by tilting it upward.

Satisfied that the heart was finally free of air, I closed the hole in the pulmonary artery and released the clamp on the aorta. The heart became tense as blood rushed into the muscle—warm blood.

This had an immediate and startling effect: The heart began to fibrillate. Where this movement had been a presage of death in Washkansky, it was here a sign of life—the first sign since its last beat in Denise Darvall three hours previously. The heart wanted to live—perhaps. Most certainly, we wanted it to live, and our emotion was echoed in Ozzie's voice—consciously underplayed, yet betraying our hope.

"I'm getting some fibrillation and it looks . . . yes, it looks like it's becoming more active."

Perhaps it would start to beat on its own, and we waited for this to happen while the tension increased in the silent theater. This was the moment we had been trying to reach all night. This was the peak we had struggled to find, climbing over two great barriers: coordinating the death of two hearts, and then joining them. A third barrier remained: Would the conjoined heart begin to once more pump as a unit—or would it pull against itself and so die of disunity? It could go either way. Often in the dog laboratory, we reached this point—only to find the new heart refusing to take over, doing little more than fibrillate briefly and then die.

That happened with dogs we had deliberately sacrificed—removing a living heart. This heart did not even have that advantage. It was not alive when we took it. We had waited for it to die. We had waited twenty minutes until it ceased beating. Perhaps we had waited too long. Perhaps it would never start again.

If so, we would know it as soon as we stopped the fibrillation—or failed to stop it. The muscles, which were now contracting separately out of rhythm, had to be brought to a total standstill by electric shock. After that, there was a chance that they would begin to contract together in their natural rhythm.

"Ozzie, are you ready to defibrillate?"

"Just a minute."

He left the little area where he worked behind his curtain—between the ECG machine, the water heater for the blanket, and the electric diathermy box. At the heart-lung machine, he injected into the blood supply a hundred milligrams of Scoline, a relaxant drug to help prevent Washkansky's body from jerking violently with the voltage we were about to administer to his heart.

"All set," said Ozzie, returning to his narrow compound.

"The paddles, please."

Sister Jordaan passed them—two gray circular discs on plastic arms with wires running to the defibrillating machine. I inserted them into the open cavity, cupping them on each side of the heart. At the same time, Rodney inserted a sucker into the pericardial sac, withdrawing all blood from around the heart. Then he pulled out, and we were ready to release the charge.

"Go ahead, shock it!"

Ozzie quickly switched on a twenty-joules charge. It shot through the squirming muscles, causing the body of Louis Washkansky to arch upwards as though kicked in the back. For a moment, the heart lay paralyzed, without any sign of life. We waited—it seemed like hours—until it slowly began to relax. Then it came, like a bolt of light. There was a sudden contraction of the atria, followed quickly by the ventricles in obedient response—then the atria, and again the ventricles. Little by little, it began to roll with the lovely rhythm of life, the heart beat of the world.

"Give me some readings!"

"Pressure ninety, pulse 120."

"And the temperature?"

"Esophagus 35.4, rectal 28.1."

"Raise it . . . start the isoprenaline. What's the serum potassium?"

"It's 4.5."

"Give another half gram, and ten cubic centimeters of calcium."

We waited, our arms folded, looking into the open chest as the heart continued to pick up strength. Each contraction seemed more vigorous, expelling its contents, then rolling back for more.

We had reached the moment that would determine whether or not Washkansky would come off the table alive. Was the heart able to take over the circulation without help from the heart-lung machine?

With Rodney, I inspected the suture lines in the heart for abnormal bleeding. It was perfect—no leaks. I removed the vent from the left ventricle and closed the opening with a 2-0 pursestring suture.

"Ozzie, all ready?"

"Yes."

"Johan?"

"Yes, Professor."

I had already loosened the tapes around the catheters in the venae cavae to allow fuller flow into the heart. Now I pulled out the upper one and withdrew the lower one, so that its end lay in the right atrial cavity—to be used in event we had to go back on bypass. The heart was now taking a greater load of circulation and behaving beautifully.

We were ready.

"Pump off!"

Immediately Dene began to call off the pressure reading—index of the heart's ability to sustain the circulation.

"Pressure ninety . . . eighty-five . . . eighty . . . seventy-five . . ."

As it dropped, the heart distended and began to labor under its load, the muscles swelling under the strain.

"Pressure seventy . . . sixty-five . . ."

"Start the pump!"

The first brief flight had lasted only twenty-five seconds—collapsing without support from the heart-lung machine. It was, I told myself, only a question of time. The little heart was not yet ready. It needed only a few more minutes to become accustomed to its new world.

"Ozzie, how fast is the isoprenaline going?"

"Forty."

"Increase it to sixty. Did you give the potassium?"

"Yes."

"Have you got the electrolytes back yet?"

"All normal."

Again with help from the machine, the heart seemed to gather strength. And this time it could manage with only one catheter. At least that was something.

"Okay, Johan, pump off."

Once more, the motor hum ceased and once more the heart hesitated, as though uncertain and frightened of what lay before it, suddenly halting, then struggling to catch up—yet too late and without enough strength. Dene read off the figures, confirming what was visible before us in the open chest as the little heart failed in its struggle to hold onto life.

"Pressure eighty . . . seventy-five . . . seventy . . ."

"All right, start the pump."

This had happened with dogs. You could not get off the pump. You could get half-way off—but not all the way. For some reason, the heart would not take over. Rodney and I again checked all the suture lines—still no leaks. I did not know what to think and turned to Bossie, who had stood by me through so many days and nights in the dog laboratory.

"Bossie, it seems this heart just doesn't want to carry the circulation."

"I think it will," he said. "It just has to get used to being alive again."

Yes, I thought, it had been dead. It had taken twenty minutes to die. Perhaps it needed that much time to come back—a little more help until it realized that it was again alive.

"Pressure gaining nicely," said Ozzie ". . . ninety over sixty-five, venous is five."

The heart showed it, giving every sign that it no longer needed help— that it was now in possession of itself and all its vessels. Dene confirmed it.

"Still going up . . . ninety-five over seventy . . . venous five."

"Johan, raise the venous pressure."

I looked at the clock: six-twelve. When it reached six-thirteen, I felt we were ready to turn off the motor and try it for the third time.

"Johan, how does it look?"

"Fine, Professor."

"All right, stop the pump again."

This time there was again a hesitation—but only for a moment as the heart suddenly accepted the added load, then plunged on, strong and sure of itself.

". . . eighty-five over sixty, eighty, eighty, eighty, ninety, ninety, ninety . . . it's holding fine, Professor . . . ninety, ninety-five, ninety-five . . ."

I turned around to look at Johan and Dene and spoke in the language of my childhood: *"Dit lyk of dit gaan werk!"*

Eyes over masks blinked back—moist with joy and wonder. In the theater, the tension of silence broke with mixed sighs, mumbled words, and even a little laugh. All of us, like the heart itself, were once again sure of ourselves.

The pressure continued to hold at ninety-five until we seemed to have reached the time to give protamine to counteract the anticlotting of the heparin. This was necessary in order to return to the patient his ability to form blood clots and so seal his wounds. Once this was done, however, we could not go back onto bypass without again giving heparin. It was therefore only given when it was considered safe to take the patient off bypass. I looked at the clock one last time: six-twenty-four.

"Ozzie, let's put in the protamine."

"Right."

I pulled out the last catheter, tying the pursestring suture, and with Rodney again checked for air in the heart. The heart took all this handling without losing its control. The *beep* on the ECG was steady and the green line rode up and down in perfect sinus rhythm.

I reached my hand across the open chest to take that of Rodney.

"We made it, Rodney."

We shook, glove in glove, but he was not too sure.

"It's still a bit early," he said.

I left him to close up the patient and walked out, ducking under the arterial line as I took off my gloves. In the tearoom, my brother Marius said François had counted the heart beats in my neck at 130.

"Let me see," he said, taking my pulse.

It was 140. I had a cup of tea and began to feel better. Bossie came in and joined us. We were all too exhausted to talk.

After a few minutes, I grabbed my mask and headed back to the theater. Rodney had begun to put wires through the sternum to pull the chest together, closing it over a drainage tube inserted into the pericardial sac and another in the mediastinum outside the sac. Ozzie said the urine output was good and the brain was fine—Washkansky had opened his eyes and responded to light. The ECG showed the heart was steady and carrying the circulation at 120 beats a minute. The antirejection treatment was now really underway.

"Ozzie, don't forget to give another hundred of cortisone."

I returned to the tearoom, and Dr. "M.C." Botha suggested we should let the hospital know what had happened. So I called Dr. Jacobus Burger, medical superintendent of the Groote Schuur.

"Dr. Burger?"

"Who's this?"

"Professor Barnard."

"What do you want?"

"We have just done a heart transplant and thought you should know . . . no, it wasn't dogs. It was human beings . . . two human beings."

CHAPTER 26

WHEN WE WERE READY to move Washkansky back to the ward, his bed was wheeled into the theater next to the operating table. He did not have a long ride before him: up one floor and twenty yards down a corridor. But it was a potentially dangerous one.

This was a different man from the one that had sat up on the table nine hours earlier, recalling *Auld Lang Syne*. He had been subjected to the massive trauma of open-heart surgery. His chest had been split open by knife, cleaver, and saw—cutting through tissue, muscle, nerve, and bone. Its ragged gap had been pulled still farther apart by steel retractors, exposing an operating area large enough for the entry of eight different hands.

After that, his blood had been driven for three and a half hours through a machine that damaged its cells without providing adequate peripheral circulation—an unnatural action causing metabolic acidosis that Ozzie had corrected by injections of sodium bicarbonate while also administering a dozen other drugs and stimulants to protect and tranquilize a body undergoing such an experience.

All of this was to be expected in any major heart operation. Yet something more had been given to the patient that delivered a special blow to the normal functioning of his body and prepared it for survival—or possibly for death. These were special drugs, imuran and hydrocortisone, aimed at blocking rejection of the foreign heart. Their effect was to lower resistance not only to the acceptance of a new organ, but also to germs that would now find little to halt their invasion of a defenseless body.

That was the big difference. Upon entering the operating room, Louis

Washkansky had been comparable to a walled city where the population was dying from lack of nourishment. He was leaving it as one now possessing the means of life—yet without walls necessary to protect it from outside attack. The same drugs that now made it possible for him to accept life from a foreign heart, also left him open to diseases that could remove it.

Until the new heart had survived its first critical stage and reached a point of partial acceptance of its new surroundings, large amounts of immunosuppressive drugs would be needed to dampen the body's rejection mechanism. During that period, the patient had to be shielded against contact with harmful bacteria. This required the erection of artificial walls, creating around him a world that contained as few germs as possible.

For this reason, the bed had arrived with a sterile plastic tent to shield the patient from bacteria—more prevalent in a hospital than in a normal home—during his trip from the operating theater to the specially prepared room.

It further meant he would awaken to find himself treated by nurses in sterile gowns and masks, while his doctors would also appear the same way, speaking through a mask, touching him only with gloves. No human flesh would come in contact with his own. When his wife came, she would have to wear similar covering and stand apart from the bed, without touching her husband. So he would exist, suspended in a void of sterilized objects and insulated flesh, until gaining sufficient strength to permit a reduction in the antirejection drugs with a simultaneous build-up of his own resistance—a tenuous balance that would allow him to hold onto the borrowed heart.

At this moment, he needed even more. Besides multiple insulation against the world of microbes, Washkansky also required many lifelines. They became visible when the towels were removed and he lay for a moment nude on the table, a wide strip of adhesive tape down the center of his chest—stark white against the golden tincture of his body.

Eighteen lines, tubes, cuffs, and leads ran either into his body or otherwise connected it to bottles, machines, and instruments. Nine of them were quickly removed—blood pressure and diathermy cuffs, electrodes to the ECG, and thermometer leads through mouth and rectum. This left nine others that would remain in place while the bed was rolled onto an elevator and down a corridor to his room in the ward.

These were essential lines to either feed the body, relieve it of waste, or monitor its interior. Three lines into the veins allowed blood and drugs to drip from hanging bottles, while the endotracheal tube into his windpipe was now connected to an oxygen bag for hand pumping. To decompress the stomach, a thin tube remained through the nose. For draining the operation area, two others emerged from beneath the adhesive strip—one in the heart sac, the other beneath the breast bone. Another catheter went up the urethra into the bladder, and one more entered the saphenous vein at the groin, measuring venous pressure and blood volume.

Lifting Washkansky off the table, with the consequent uprooting of so many lines, required six people. Four held his body, now gowned and wrapped in a bunny blanket, while Sister Fox-Smith placed the drainage bottles in racks under the bed. Dr. Moss hooked other bottles for the intravenous lines onto stands, or fixed racks, above the bed, allowing them to continue to drip into the arms and right leg of Washkansky—1.2 milligrams a minute of lignacaine to dampen heart irritability, blood at sixty drops a minute to replace blood loss, and isoprenaline at twenty minidrops to stimulate a heart whose nerve connections had been cut. The brain could no longer speak to this heart that was beating on impulses from its separate nerve system. Until the graft adapted itself, the new heart had to be informed of its extra work load.

As they put him onto the bed, Washkansky lifted up one arm and moved his head. He was surfacing rapidly and, until hooked up in the ward, we would not be able to check the heart action with a monitor.

"Let's get going," said Ozzie pumping the black bag at the bedside.

The plastic tent was extended and tucked under the mattress and the bed wheeled off towards the elevator, which had been washed down with antiseptic solution. There was barely room in the elevator for the bed and all the people—two orderlies, Ozzie pumping the black bag, Cecil Moss holding the portable oxygen tank in his arms like a baby, and Bossie watching the drips as their bottles jangled against the metal stands.

"Go on," I said, "I'll walk up."

The door closed and they were gone. I returned to the dressing room, quickly changed clothes, and went up to the ward.

When I arrived, Ozzie had already removed the endotracheal tube and inserted another, smaller one through the left nostril. This was attached to a Bird respirator and set to automatically ventilate the lungs twenty times a minute. The gastric tube entering the right nostril was connected to a Wangensteen suction apparatus. The two chest drainage lines were attached through airtight bottles, to a yellow suction pipe on the wall of the pea-green room, and the bladder catheter was connected to a urine bottle by Sister Georgie Hall who also inserted a rectal thermometer.

Dr. Moss and Sister de Villiers had quickly secured silver electrodes on upper arms and left leg, allowing us once more to monitor the heart on the gray ECG machine—beeping now at 110 a minute. The venous pressure line, linked to the manometer, showed 5.5—indicating normal pressure in the right chambers of the heart.

Dr. Venter, who would watch over the patient, for the first period, began to time the intravenous drips.

"Let's put up the potassium," I said. "Run in one gram over half an hour."

He nodded. "How about the insulin?"

"He had forty units just after seven o'clock," said Ozzie, "which ought to hold him until you get the next report."

"And the cortisone?"

"Three hundred milligrams," said Ozzie.

"That leaves two hundred more," I said, "to be administered over twelve hours."

By that time Washkansky's immunological defenses would be flattened out—rendering him more than ever vulnerable to infection. We had come to the moment when the room would have to be kept as sterile as possible. Outside the door, a screened-off area held a washbasin, sterile gowns, caps, gloves, and canvas boots. No one could enter without scrubbing and going through the same procedure required for admission to an operating theater.

"Coert, get the bed washed down again, especially the rollers and this floor. No one is to enter here, unless absolutely necessary. Put some gentamycin ointment in the patient's nose and also on his leg wound. And let's keep sending swabs from mouth and rectum to Dr. Forder."

Arderne Forder, the bacteriologist, was to culture all organisms found on Washkansky and test their sensitivity to determine which antibiotic would be most effective in the event a dangerous one invaded Washkansky's defenseless system. They could come from most anywhere. Besides the risk of infection from outside, there was also a constant threat of autoinfection. Organisms normally held at bay by the body's own resistance were now actively dangerous. With Washkansky, one source of sepsis was the infection in his left calf.

"Sister, we have to prevent crossinfection, especially in dressing his leg. Make sure he is kept clean in all parts."

"Yes, Professor."

The monitor showed no change in heart rhythm—though there were some nodal extrasystoles.

"I'll be happier when this settles down," I said to Bossie, taking an ECG reading from the machine.

"There's a partial heart block," he said.

It was there, in the PR interval. The voltage was also low—only fifteen millivolts. Further readings of the strip worried me more. There were now periods of atrial flutter and I knew the next twelve or twenty-four hours could be crucial.

"Where are the X-ray people?"

"We finally got them, they're moving now," said Bossie.

We always took a picture of the chest in the theater before moving the patient off the table. But this morning—it was early Sunday—we had been unable to find any of the technicians. Not only was it important to see the size of the heart but also the condition of the lungs.

I also wanted to have an evaluation of the heart function from Val Schrire and left the room to call him. In the corridor I saw Ann Washkansky with two men and another woman.

"Hello," I said.

She took a few steps towards me, then stopped—a little smile beginning, then fading away as she waited for some response in return.

"So, Professor—how is he?"

"We've won a 75 per cent victory. Now we must fight for the other 25 per cent."

She looked at the two men and the woman with her, but they said nothing. So she spoke again.

"This is my brother-in-law, Tevia, who is Louis' brother, and also here is Solly and Lilly Cammerman, who are very good friends of the family."

"So he has a chance?" asked the brother.

"Yes, if we can hold on to what we have."

"That's good."

"Is he awake?" asked Ann. "Is he speaking anything yet?"

"He's just waking up, but not speaking. That will come later."

He had opened his eyes, and we had told him he was doing fine. With an endotracheal tube, it was not possible to speak, and there had been little in return, other than a dull nod and a grimace—probably from pain. Then he had drifted off to sleep again.

"You say he is not speaking yet?"

"No, not yet."

"We don't want to be in your way," she said. "We only came because maybe you wanted to say something to us."

"He said it," said the brother.

"And it's good news," said the friend's wife.

"Yes," said Ann, smiling finally, yet with eyes that seemed to ask: Is it really true?

"Yes," she said again, "so we'll go away. I know I'm not clean enough to see him."

"What?"

"I mean I might infect him if I go in. That's what Dr. Bosman told us."

"You'll be able to see him, but you must be patient and wait a few days. I'll let you know as soon as it's possible."

"Thank you, Dr. Barnard."

She stepped back and for a moment they stood in silence, the two women and the two men in a little group, looking at me for more news.

"I think we can be grateful for what's happened so far," I said.

"Yes," said the brother, "I just came from the synagogue."

"Thank God," said Ann, as though she had waited all night and only now would allow herself to say it.

One of the girls from the laboratory came by with the last blood analysis from the theater. I took it and glanced down the column of figures: PH—7.35, PCO_2—40, BE—5. There had been an increase of acid in the blood. He would need more bicarbonate—about 50 cubic centimeters.

"We'll be going now," said Ann.

"What—I'm sorry?"

"We only wanted to be here in case you wanted us."

"All right—good-bye. We'll call when you can come."

"I'll wait. If it's good to wait, then I'll keep waiting."

I watched the little group go down the corridor and turn the corner. Then I returned to the doctors' office to call Val Schrire—and also Louwtjie, who was deeply touched and pleased. Shortly after that the X-ray unit arrived, and we obtained a picture showing Washkansky's lungs fully expanded with the new heart quite small in its expanded cavity.

The heart rate began to drop, stabilizing at ninety. Val Schrire arrived and was quite optimistic. Washkansky again opened his eyes, and I told him he was doing well. Soon after that he drifted off again. The drains from his chest showed little bleeding and circulation to the periphery of his body improved.

When everything appeared under control, I suddenly felt the weight of the long night coupled onto half of the next day. It was time to go home and I got into my car. On the way, the radio carried the twelve o'clock news:

The first human-to-human heart transplant in history was done last night by a team of doctors at the Groote Schuur hospital. The name of the patient, as well as the donor, are being withheld by hospital authorities . . ."

After the kidney transplant, I had stopped off to see our good friends, Captain Bert Friedmann and his wife, Dolly. It had been a successful operation and now, as I approached the Friedmann home, there was no reason not to do it again. Dene Friedmann had already arrived and told her parents we had done the transplant. I gave them the latest news, then hurried on home.

Louwtjie rushed out to meet me.

"I phoned Deirdre in Ceres," she said, giving me a big hug, her eyes bright with excitement."

"And Boetie," I said. "Did you tell him?"

"I placed a call, but it hasn't come through yet."

Our son was in school at Pretoria, and when the phone rang I thought it would be him—or the hospital. It was London. A newspaper wanted to know if we had really transplanted a human heart.

"Yes?"

"Was it a white heart—that is, a white person?"

Val Schrire had been right—so right. Yet this was irritating. What difference did it really make? We had struggled to save one life. It had nothing to do with color of the skin.

"Can you tell us the name and some details of the donor?"

"No, I'm sorry I can't do that. You must speak to Dr. Burger, the medical superintendent of Groote Schuur."

"We understand the recipient is Louis Washkansky—is that correct?"

"Who told you that?"

"It's in the news bulletin."

"Yes, it's Louis Washkansky."

At this rate they would soon know the name of the donor.

"What sort of man is Mr. Washkansky?"

"A well one, I hope—with his new heart."

Two other calls came in. From Berlin, a German magazine had a cardiac specialist with some highly technical questions. From New York, a television network also requested details of the operation, then asked if Washkansky was Jewish and what had been the religion of the donor? I said I did not know but was certain that different religious faiths would not complicate the rejection problem.

When the phone rang again, it was Boetie. I told him what happened and there was a silence.

"*Ag nee pappa,*" he said over and over—"Oh no, daddy."

Then with the wondrous father-faith of a sixteen-year-old, he asked: "Do you think they will give you the Nobel Prize?"

I got into bed, but my mind would not stop. It was almost two hours since I had left the hospital and had heard nothing. Maybe they had tried to phone and could not get through. I dialed Groote Schuur—551111. As usual, it rang on and on with no answer. A man could die or a woman have a baby, waiting for that switchboard. Eventually Dr. Venter came on the line. He had tried to phone me but had found the line busy.

"The pulse rate is up to 120," he said.

It had been ninety when I left. An increase to 120 was not abnormal after open-heart surgery. Yet this was not a normal case. Washkansky was receiving immunosuppressive drugs, and he had a transplanted heart. There was no previous pattern to establish what was normal or abnormal.

In every open-heart operation, there was an initial period similar to going through a jungle. The vision was limited to the immediate moment, and the smallest detail of sight or sound was immensely important. After a while, one learned to read these signs and to rely upon them. Yet here nothing could be counted as certain. A snapped twig—an extrasystole— could signify a threat of any size.

"The temperature is now normal," said Coert.

Even this was no comfort. It had been subnormal. Maybe it was going to now shoot up above normal.

"Is it holding there?"

"Yes, and the urine is very good—200 cubic centimeters in the last hour."

That was a lot—maybe we were not giving him enough fluids.

"How fast are you running the plasmalyte?"

"I've written him up for 1,500 cubic centimeters until tomorrow at eight o'clock."

After that, it was impossible to sleep. Every time the phone rang, I grabbed it, expecting Coert Venter. Instead, it was only the beginning of an avalanche of phone calls from around the world. After forty minutes of them, I called Coert again.

"The pulse is now 140," he said. "The urine output has diminished to fifty cubic centimeters in the last hour, but everything else seems all right."

"Now it's only fifty?"

Before it had seemed too much. Now I felt it was too little.

"I'm coming in," I said.

On the way to the car, the phone rang again. Louwtjie answered it and called to me from the kitchen door.

"It's Paris. France!"

"I've left."

"What'll I say?"

"Nothing. Tell them to call Dr. Burger. If they ask, tell them the donor was neither a black man—nor a Frenchman."

Driving to the hospital there was more news on the car radio—naming Washkansky and Denise Darvall who had been killed by an automobile.

The heart-transplant team was led by Professor Chris Barnard in a dramatic all-night operation—the first of its kind in medical history. Messages of congratulation are pouring in from around the world . . .

This was amazing. Who would have expected such an immediate reaction from so many countries? What was it about the human heart that so excited people?

. . . meanwhile, secluded behind no-entry signs in Ward C-2 of the Groote Schuur hospital, Louis Washkansky has awakened from his operation to feel the beat of his new heart and know that he is alive—thanks to another human being . . .

How in the hell could anybody know what he felt—or knew? I turned off the radio. We were alone with him in the jungle of his recovery—and what did we know? Too little. Was an increase in the pulse from ninety to 140 a sign of atrial flutter? Was it a warning from either of his two greatest dangers—rejection or infection?

When I reached the ward,the pulse rate had returned to eighty-five. This was more like it, and after some minor changes in his treatment, I returned home.

It was, I knew, only the beginning. Each day would be an extension of this one, as we struggled to bring Louis Washkansky to the open plain of safety. And each day a little bit more of the man himself would emerge increasingly conscious of his new life, more and more secure that he would live once more to say: "I told you, Ann . . . I told you we would make it."

So it would be—if we were able to protect him from disease and prevent him from casting away the heart that held him in life.

MONDAY, *December 4: First Day*

I awakened early, realizing that today he would speak. Today we would be able to say: "Louis, you have a new heart"—and hear his reaction.

It would happen if nothing had gone wrong during the night and we could therefore remove the endotracheal tube. I called the hospital. It was 6:50 A.M. and Sister Papendieck was coming off duty.

"Dr. Venter is with the patient . . . shall I call him?"

That meant Coert would have to unscrub—come out of the sterile room, answer the phone, then rescrub with a change of gown, mask, and boots.

"No—tell me, how's the patient?"

"He looks nice and pink and in good condition."

"Nothing abnormal? Dr. Venter is not worried?"

"No. He says everything's fine."

"Good—tell him I'm coming now."

When I arrived, Dr. Bosman met me in the corridor with a big smile. That was a report in itself. Bossie does not smile unless it is a major event. I looked over the top of the sterile curtain before the entrance to the room. Coert Venter, in mask and gown, looked back.

"How's the patient?"

"Nee, goed," he said, meaning he was well.

Hurriedly I scrubbed, putting on mask, gloves, cap, and sterile boots to enter the room. Washkansky looked at me—gray eyes with flecks of green. His face seemed to have been softened by drugs and the trauma of surgery.

"Hello, Louis—they say you're doing fine."

He nodded and made a feeble motion to indicate he would like the tube removed so that he could say something about it himself.

"All right, just hold on. We'll see what we can do about it."

He blinked sleepily and dozed off. Dr. Ozinsky came at 9 A.M. and we decided to put the patient under an oxygen tent, then disconnect the respirator—but not remove the tube into his windpipe until certain that he could breathe for himself. He managed well, and after an hour and a half,

Ozzie withdrew the tube as well as the gastric line to his stomach. Washkansky—under the oxygen tent—was able to speak for the first time.

"How are you, Louis?"

"Fine . . . I'm feeling okay."

"Do you know what we have done?"

"You promised me a new heart . . . I suppose you gave it to me."

"Yes, we did."

He nodded and looked at me without saying any more. Did he wonder whose heart now lay in his chest—who had died and so made it possible for him to live? He did not ask me, at least not then. He only smiled and weakly lifted up his fist, thumb upright, to indicate he was still in there giving all he could.

"We're going to move you every two hours, so that you will lie on one side, then on the other—to help clear your lungs and assist your breathing."

"Okay," he said.

"They'll also have to waken you every so often for blood samples and give various medicines—so try and sleep as much as possible in between."

He nodded but did not close his eyes. After checking his record, the monitor, and intravenous drips, I left the room.

In the corridor I found an American television team arguing with some nurses and Bossie—the first of a flood to descend upon us. We had blocked off the ward in an effort to keep them out, but throughout that day and all that followed they were to infiltrate in every way possible—masquerading as doctors and orderlies and even climbing trees outside the hospital window.

We had our first press conference in the medical school and sought to answer all that was asked of us. But the questions and requests to appear before television cameras were never exhausted. We lacked experience in this, and before we knew it, the press was taking too much of our time.

The afternoon report contained some disturbing information—more twigs cracking in the jungle. The venous pressure had risen, causing me to fear the heart had begun to dam back blood it should be pumping onward. The blood urea was up, suggesting poor circulation to the kidneys. And the enzymes—a measure of cell damage—had also gone up. Enzymes normally increased after all forms of heart surgery. Yet their continued rise here could be an indication of heart destruction—rejection.

I phoned Dr. Geoffrey Thatcher, to learn if he had a report on the creatinine clearance—another index to kidney function.

"It's just coming through," he said, "and doesn't look too good—about thirty-nine."

"That's good compared to what it was," I said. "Don't forget this man had bad renal function to start with."

"Yes, but look Chris, we want more than just urine samples. To properly assess kidney function in relation to the heart, we need the total output."

"All right."

Dr. Thatcher was an especially brilliant nephrologist. He worked under Professor Lennox Eales, head of the hospital's renal unit, and I intended to use his counsel in the days ahead. I also had to work closely with Dr. Bernard Pimstone, the endocrinologist, on treatment of Washkansky's diabetes, which, uncontrolled, could render him more vulnerable to infection.

We were to meet the next morning in the doctors' office of C2 Ward. Why not also ask Dr. Thatcher to sit in with us? Indeed, we could invite all the other necessary specialists to a daily meeting.

Dr. Thatcher agreed to come and I also asked Professor Eales. After that, I invited Dr. Gideon Potgieter and Professor James Kench, the biochemists; Dr. Simcha Banks, the gastroenterologist; Dr. Leslie Werbeloff, radiologist; Dr. Arderne Forder, bacteriologist; Val Schrire, cardiologist—and all the members of my own team. After arranging this, I checked the evening report, prescribed a diuretic to increase the urine output, and returned home. At ten o'clock the phone rang.

It was Dr. Hitchcock who had taken over from Dr. Venter.

"There are some ventricular extrasystoles. We just had three in a row, then nothing more, but I thought you'd like to know."

"What's the potassium level?"

"Okay."

"Then I'm coming in."

If the potassium was not low, an irritability of the heart could mean it was being attacked by the body. I raced through more red lights—a common practice now.

After I arrived, there were more extra ventricular beats. Despite the report, I felt he lacked potassium, and we gave him an additional amount. The heart settled down. I waited an hour, then went home.

More than ever, I looked forward to the team meeting tomorrow. From now on, it would have to be a daily event—better, we could meet twice a day.

TUESDAY, *December 5: Second Day*

It was a pleasure to see Louis Washkansky this morning—awake and smiling as I entered.

"Good morning," he said.

"Good morning, Louis—how are you?"

"Fine, I think."

"Don't you know?"

"How can I know anything? They never let me alone long enough to know who I am."

I turned to Sister Georgie Hall. You could tell from her eyes that she was smiling behind the mask.

"Sister Hall, what are you doing to Mr. Washkansky?"

"Nothing at all, we love him dearly."

Washkansky shook his head.

"They keep rolling me back and forth," he said. "It's like trying to sleep in a barrel."

Georgie Hall laughed.

"He says if we let him go home and sleep one night, he'll come back and be ready to start all over again."

"Doc, I'm not in training for this sort of thing. There's no rest in between rounds."

"I explained it to you, Louis. They turn you from one side to the other to help your lungs and the breathing."

"Also those needles," he said. "Every time I close my eyes they sneak up and stick another needle in me. This is a dangerous place."

Dr. Bosman, who had scrubbed after me, came in. Louis saw him and closed his eyes.

"So here comes Dracula," he said, and we all laughed.

His chart showed there had been some ventricular extrasystoles during the early part of the night—then nothing more to worry about. His venous pressure had dropped from fourteen to twelve, indicating the heart was functioning better. At this rate, we should be able to remove his remaining tubes—chest drains, venous line, and urinary catheter—provided no adverse reports turned up at the first team meeting.

They gathered at ten o'clock, crowding into the doctors' office, and immediately it proved to be very valuable. Each of the specialists examined the patient from his particular point of view. In effect, they cast Washkansky through a prism, exposing the entire spectrum of his physiology.

I began by reporting the patient was talking and feeling much better—though still quite tired. Also his venous pressure had dropped, and with Lassix his urine output had improved. There had been some extra ventricular beats, but these had disappeared. So from the bedside the picture looked better.

Dr. Potgieter, analyzing the blood report, found good and bad signs. The hemoglobin had gone up, revealing a better concentration of red cells in the blood. And the immunosuppressive drugs had knocked the lymphocytes down to 1 per cent—another good sign, since these cells carry the antibodies causing rejection. We were thus effectively blocking part of the rejection mechanism. On the other hand, Pottie noted the blood urea had risen from 82 to 105, indicating accumulating poison that should not be there if the kidneys were functioning properly. And the enzymes had risen still farther.

"This could be significant," he said, "though it is too soon after surgery to be sure."

Besides being an index of muscle damage—and rejection—the enzymes could also indicate the second of two threats in our transplant jungle—infection. Yet which one was it—if either? We were on a path no one had ever taken. A snapping twig could indicate either rejection or infection since both announced themselves in similar ways. Yet before either one appeared, we had to identify it, because both required different treatment. If rejection was treated as an infection—or the other way around—it would, in fact, help kill the patient.

The enzyme rise had a possible explanation. At Minneapolis with Dr. Dave Snyder, I had studied enzyme behavior after open-heart surgery and found that an early increase was part of the predictable pattern.

"I think these enzymes are a result of the damage of surgery and will drop," I said. "As for the blood urea, this man had bad renal function to start with, so this is an improvement."

Dr. Thatcher and Professor Eales accepted this—with reservations.

"We cannot get a picture from one day's reading," said Professor Eales, with a frown.

"I agree with Chris," said Dr. Thatcher. "We might expect some improvement here. Also, the creatinine clearance is up a bit and we will probably find it even higher this afternoon."

As they agreed and others nodded their heads, I felt a moment of uncertainty. Was I looking for easy answers to obvious trouble—giving reasons on which I could predict the outcome and so feel in touch with the situation? This was one more danger in dealing with the unknown—to identify it with something already known and therefore capable of being handled. It was a form of self-inflicted blindness and particularly dangerous.

In reply to other questions, I reviewed our plans for the antirejection treatment. The first massive dose of hydrocortisone—five hundred milligrams, given the day of the operation—was being diminished by one hundred milligrams on each successive day with a view to stopping it on the fifth postoperative day. In its place, we were giving sixty milligrams daily of another corticosteroid—prednisone. In addition, we were protecting the graft by giving 150 milligrams of Imuran daily. Further, we contemplated irradiating the heart to destroy lymphocytes which were now invading it.

"Perhaps," said Dr. Thatcher, "the total picture will become clearer as you diminish the cortisone. At any rate, we should have a better idea of the kidney function within the next twenty-four hours."

The meeting ended with agreement that there was no evidence to indicate the approach of either infection or rejection. Treatment was to continue as planned.

The radiotherapy department wheeled in a mobile apparatus that they had built to avoid the risk of moving Washkansky through long corridors to the hospital's cobalt bomb. It had been constructed around a one-curie source of cobalt—a brilliant creation of Dr. D. L. P. leRoux. Unfortunately, its low potential required that Washkansky lie perfectly still for two hours, which proved difficult for him.

During the day, his drains were removed, his appetite improved, and he was allowed to have soup and a soft-boiled egg.

The team met that afternoon and reviewed the latest reports, in light of a further drop in the pulse rate of the transplanted heart. From 120 on operating day, it had fallen to ninety-six yesterday, and was now at ninety-two—indicating a possible edema of its conduction system. We agreed to increase the isoprenoline drip, hoping this would stimulate it.

Shortly after midnight, Dr. Venter phoned to say an atrial flutter at three hundred per minute had begun, but the ventricles were still responding at eighty-five. While we talked, he got another reading and the atria were down further—to 240, with no change in the ventricles.

"Call me back if the ventricular rate goes up."

"Yes, Professor."

He did not call. I awakened at 3 A.M., and phoned him. Sister Papendieck said Dr. Venter was resting in a chair at the patient's bedside, and all was well.

"Thank you, Sister . . . good night."

WEDNESDAY, *December 6: Third Day*

When I called the next morning, Dr. Venter told me there was still an atrial flutter but the ventricles were now responding at 130—just what I had feared.

"Let's cut the isoprenaline to ten minidrops. . . . How's the urine output?"

"Good, Professor."

"And the color?"

"Brick—but no ketones."

"We've agreed with Dr. Pimstone that this indicates thirty units of insulin."

"I've already given it."

At least we were keeping the diabetes under control—if not the heart.

"I'll be in soon."

The atrial flutter, at a rate different from the ventricles, was not too serious—provided the ventricular response could be kept down. A rise in the ventricular rate, however, was something else. I called Val Schrire, asking him if he could come by earlier than usual today, and he agreed.

When I arrived at 8 A.M., the heart was still going at 130. The venous pressure was down to six, however, indicating improved pumping capacity. This was encouraging.

Scrubbing up, I could hear Washkansky joking with Sister Hall. Upon entering, she was still laughing.

"He says he's a new Frankenstein," she said.

"That's me," said Louis. "I'm going to scare people off the streets."

"You're no Frankenstein. You're an angel," she said.

"Yes," he said. "Full of needle holes."

"Are they still puncturing you, Louis?"

"I'll tell you, Doc. They're taking more blood out of me than is going in."

His high spirits were a good sign. And Professor Schrire, after examining the patient, was also encouraging.

"Sure, there's an atrial flutter, but it's unimportant, Chris. The heart is in good condition, the systolic murmur has disappeared, there is no enlargement of the liver that I can feel and no gallop rhythm. He's clinically well—so stop worrying."

"I wish I could."

The team had begun to arrive for the morning meeting. Val started to leave, but I asked him to stay with us.

"No thanks," he said, "I'm not the type."

"Come on, anyway."

"I've got patients waiting."

"Stay a little bit. I need your opinion."

I began by reporting the patient looked much better—even though he thought he was a new Frankenstein. Amid the laughter, Bossie noted Dr. Frankenstein was the man who created the monster—which meant I was the Frankenstein of Ward C-2. This led to more laughter.

Val Schrire gave a brief but optimistic report on the heart's condition. Dr. Werbeloff produced the latest X rays, confirming the patient's progress. Dr. Pimstone, looking after Washkansky's diabetes, urged that he get more food.

"This man's not getting enough calories. It's very well to treat diabetes by reducing the intake, but we've come to the time when it's more important to give him unlimited calories and push glucose into his cells by injecting whatever insulin he needs. Otherwise, he's going to begin burning up his own indigenous proteins."

This seemed valid. Anybody undergoing an operation is in a state of catabolism, during which he consumes basic proteins of his own body. Steroid drugs increased this destructive process. And a reduced diet would further it even more. Proteins needed to form muscle and scar tissue would be converted into blood sugar for energy.

"So what do you suggest, Bernard?"

"Let him have steak or whatever he wants," he said. "Push calories into him, ad lib."

"All right," I said, turning then to the blood and urine reports which were somewhat disturbing.

Dr. Potgieter noted the blood urea had risen still further, from 105 to 128—more waste products in the blood that the kidneys had failed to eliminate.

"But there is also an increase of urea in the urine," he said. "And the creatinine clearance is up."

That seemed to balance it off. The rise in the clearance of creatinine— an index of filtration rate from blood into urine through the kidneys— showed improved function, as did the ability of the kidneys to put more urea into the urine.

"Perhaps," I said, "we're still dealing with a postoperative response."

Professor Eales and Dr. Thatcher agreed this was possible. But Dr. Potgieter said he did not like the continued rise in enzymes.

"They keep mounting," he said. "They've almost doubled."

"What's your feeling, Pottie?"

He leaned against the wall, drawing on his pipe, which had gone out long ago.

"You started irradiating the heart yesterday?"

"Yes."

"It could be that. Or else, the aftereffects of surgical tissue damage which would tie in with the high blood urea. Or else . . ."

His voice trailed off and I finished it for him.

"Or else it might be the beginning of the destruction of the heart by rejection. But I am not convinced of it—not yet."

No one replied to this. There remained one other point. The platelet count had fallen from 120,000 to 84,000—quite a low figure for cell fragments essential for the clotting of blood. We discussed it, and some members of the team felt this was also in keeping with rejection. Others said just the opposite. So I was not sure what was happening there.

After the meeting, Val Schrire shook his head. We were alone in the corridor, and I asked him what was wrong.

"What do you accomplish by listening to ten experts give ten views limited to their own special interest?"

"It gives us a broader spectrum, Val, and we need it because we're working in unknown territory. We have to anticipate rejection or infection before it takes hold of the patient."

"How can you do that by looking at enzymes or creatinine clearance?"

"Because an indication of kidney failure . . ."

"Rubbish. The function of the kidney is to put out urine. In the last twenty-four hours Washkansky has given off one-third more fluid than he has taken in. That's damn good. You don't have to look for creatinine clearance to see it. You can measure it in quart jars."

"Val, we have to look for every reading in order to determine . . ."

"Then look at the heart, man, not at enzymes or creatinine clearance. You have transplanted a heart—not a kidney."

"What I'm trying to say is that a rise in the blood urea or serum creatinine is an index of developing kidney failure, which can warn us of trouble in the heart's pumping ability."

"How? Listen, Chris, if a heart has trouble and puts out only three liters, instead of five, there'll be less blood to the peripheral areas—but not to priority organs such as the brain or liver or kidneys. So where does that leave you?"

"Probably listening to you tell me that you were right."

He smiled and we said good-bye. Val was both right and wrong. We should never overlook clinical evidence nor forego proven procedure. But we would be fools to not monitor Washkansky's entire body for any warning, however small, to help us plan our campaign. Val was suggesting we hold our fire until we saw the whites of the eyes. Yet if we did that, it would be too late. With the big guns of immunosuppression, we were firing at distant targets beyond our direct vision. They would be useless at close range.

The rest of the day passed without further crises. We increased Washkansky's diet to include minced chicken and mashed potatoes, which he ate with pleasure. He received his second cobalt treatment and once more found it difficult to remain still for two hours. So I decided to give this up and move him to the larger cobalt source in the radiotherapy department where treatment would require only a minute or two. It meant rolling his bed through a quarter-mile of hospital corridors, and, even though covered with a plastic tent, this involved a risk. Yet everything had a risk to it, and we had to weigh this against the advantages. If we made the move early in the morning, when there was less hospital traffic and thus fewer germs in the air, the danger would be minimized.

Outside the ward we were under constant barrage from the news media. Special correspondents and television teams had flown in from around the world. It was impossible not to be civil to these men and women. It was also flattering to be the center of such attention. I accepted an invitation to the United States to appear on "Face the Nation"—a nationwide news panel show. Yet it was equally impossible to accept all invitations or to satisfy all the demands of the press, without stealing time from our work.

This was accompanied by a sense of impending trouble that never completely left me. When I called Coert Venter at midnight, the pulse rate had risen to 140. The temperature was normal however, and Washkansky was šleeping well. I went back to sleep telling myself the heart rate would settle down during the night.

THURSDAY, *December 7: Fourth Day*

When I called at 7 A.M., Dr. Venter said the pulse had increased to 150, with persistent atrial flutter. Something was wrong—but what?

"How does he look?"

"Fine, Prof. He slept well and the urine output is satisfactory. There's no temperature, and he had a good breakfast."

Everything was fine, except for Denise Darvall's heart which would not settle down—as though its removal from the body in which it was born had also freed it from nature's laws governing its behavior, allowing it to become a lawless heart.

"We're about to take him down for the cobalt treatment," said Coert.

"Keep him well covered with the tent . . . has the elevator been washed?"

"Yes, Professor."

"Stay with him every minute."

"Yes, I will."

When I arrived, Washkansky had already returned to his room and was anxious to know when he could make another, longer trip.

"When do you think I can go home?"

"If you keep improving, it won't be too long."

"Like maybe by Christmas?"

"I hope so, Louis."

"That'd be a real Christmas present, I'll tell you."

"We'll try and make it," I said.

" 'I'll Be Home by Christmas' . . . remember that one?"

"Yes."

"Good old Bing Crosby," he said.

I looked at the monitor. The pulse was 144—a small but encouraging drop.

At the team meeting, we sought to determine whether or not the increased heart rate was part of rejection and again found nothing to support this, especially since there was improvement elsewhere.

Blood urea was down from 128—seventy milligrams with an increased urine which allowed us to raise the antirejection drug, Imuran, to the normal dosage of 200 milligrams. Platelet count was up, too. The white cell count was not good—rising still more from 18,000 to 28,000—but this had occurred also with kidney transplants at Richmond. So the only disturbing factor was the heart rate—and it seemed to be settling slowly.

At 2:30 P.M., however, it rose up to 150 and an hour later reached 160.

This was becoming dangerous and I called Val Schrire, who arrived immediately. After examining the patient, we met in the office with Dr. Bosman.

"It's not good," said Val. "We must slow it down."

"With what?"

"Digoxin."

"Shumway and Lower have found that transplanted hearts are very sensitive to that drug. It can be dangerous."

"All right, try some strophanthin first. Let him have 0.1 milligrams in three doses at half-hour intervals, and you'll see where you are."

Strophanthin was a related drug—quick-acting but of briefer duration, Used in small doses, it could test the heart's tolerance of, and need for, longer-acting digitalis or digoxin.

"It's a safer approach," said Val, "though I'm not sure it's required here."

"Why not?"

"Like I told you before, Shumway and Lower are talking about dogs. This is a human being. I think you can proceed with digoxin straight away. But if you want to go slower, then do it."

Once more, Val was using his experience to expertly move from the known toward the unknown. For a moment, I envied his quick grasp and certainty. I was not all that certain. It was better, I thought, to try the shorter-acting strophanthin and then use digoxin after it had been shown to have no ill effects.

After he left, I discovered a unit from the South African Broadcasting Corporation in the corridor. Bossie reminded me we had agreed to allow them a half-minute interview with Washkansky. A sterilized wire and microphone had been placed in his room.

"How can you do it? I don't want anybody in there with the patient."

"I'll hold the mike," said Bossie, "and ask him a couple of questions."

"All right."

"After that, Mrs. Washkansky is to see him for a little bit."

"Good . . . maybe she'll help him relax. But let's test the strophanthin first."

Bossie blinked slowly and nodded. He did not move fast, like most long-distance runners. But he had something else: He believed in his work and gave everything to it. We owe a lot to both Bossie and Coert Venter for the days and nights they spent with Louis Washkansky.

Ann Washkansky, the Wife

"I didn't know my talk with Louis was being recorded. I thought we said a lot more than we did and maybe what we didn't say is more important.

"I know I was frightened and wondered what I was going to say. I can't tell you what went through my mind. I was petrified at what I'd find. Like everyone else, I thought the heart controls all your emotions and your personality—you know?

"Also, I was frightened I might give him some germs. They made me wash my hands and put on rubber gloves, also a cap on my hair and a green gown with washable overshoes, and then a white paper mask. Wrapped up like that, you feel like a stranger to yourself, which made it worse because I didn't know what I was going to find. Maybe Louis would be a stranger, too.

"When I went in, he was still flat on the bed, looking at me.

" 'Louis,' I said. 'It's me.'

" 'Hello, kid,' he said, and I saw it was the same old Louis. You know, the twinkle in his eye and the way he said it. He always called me 'kid.' I don't know why.

"I was standing next to the door and Georgie Hall said I could come closer, but I was afraid I might infect him. Then Dr. Bosman said to come nearer to the bed but not to touch him. This reminded Louis of the old joke and he said: 'All right, I'll do it—but no kissing.'

"We both laughed and I knew it was my old Louis, especially when I asked him how he felt and he said he was back on top of the world.

" 'Don't worry, Ann, I've got it under control.'

" 'I won't worry. I know you'll pull through. It's wonderful.'

"He asked me about the family. We did not talk about the operation. At that time I don't think they let him know everything—that is, everything about the girl. I mean, he didn't know where the heart came from. Not really. They only let him know that he had become world famous. But he did not believe it.

"I said: 'You know, Louis, your name is even on the Sanlam Building?'

"He said: 'Are you serious?'

"I said: 'Yes, it's running around the top of the Sanlam with the news, and it's in the papers. Everybody is talking about you.'

"He said: 'You mean it?'

" 'Everybody is listening to every word you say. You're a very famous person now, you know.'

" 'I'm not famous. The doctor is famous. What have I done?—nothing.'

" 'Well, you've been very brave.'

" 'I took a chance in my favor.'

" 'It is in your favor, Louis, you'll see it'll be in your favor.'

" 'So for what am I brave?'

" 'Anyway, your words came true, hey? You always used to say: stick around, kid, I'll make you famous . . . remember, Louis?'

"Sister Hall laughed. 'Little did he know,' she said, 'that it would happen.'

" 'Naah, cut it out,' he said.

"That was like him. All his life he was going to be famous. Then when it happened, he did not want to believe it.

" 'Is your photo in the paper, too?' he asked.

" 'Yes and I look just as beautiful as I do now with this on, do you see?'

" 'I haven't seen.'

" 'No, I'm keeping it all for you when you come home.'

"He gave me a wink like in the old days, and I wanted to touch him a little bit. But I knew I couldn't, so I just stood there with the mask on, feeling like I was hiding from him.

"I thought I must look terrible, but he did not make me feel that way. He made me feel like it was going to be the same as it was before, and when we had to say good-bye I was glad to go because I was going to cry if I stayed one minute longer.

" 'Good-bye, kid. Don't start any of your old tricks until I get home.'

" 'Oh, Louis, I'm so happy I could cry.'

" 'No, don't do that.'

" 'Good-bye, Louis.'

" 'Good-bye.'

"Afterward, the newspapers quoted me as saying Louis looked beautiful. I meant it was beautiful . . . just beautiful being with him."

FRIDAY, *December 8: Fifth Day*

I awakened, expecting to have good news from the ward. The previous night Washkansky's heart had proven to be tolerant to digoxin and after three doses of 0.25 milligrams, the pulse rate had gradually dropped, reaching 110 shortly after midnight. I had gone to bed then, believing we finally had control of the lawless heart.

Dr. Venter told me otherwise in our early morning phone call.

"The pulse rate is now back to 130," he said.

"Have you given more digoxin?"

"Yes, at one o'clock and then again at two. But it had no effect. Also, the patient is very irritable. He has no temperature, but he's sluggish."

"What do you think it is?"

"I don't know, Prof."

"How's the urine output?"

"It's down a bit, too."

"Haven't you got any good news?"

Driving to the hospital, I tried to decide if these were signs of the heart being rejected. If so, then we should act immediately. Including the post-operative period, the transplant was actually in its sixth day. We could expect rejection to set in at any time. So could everyone else listening to the news. It came in over the car radio:

Today Louis Washkansky enters the most critical phase of his new life. The first attempt of his body to reject the heart of Denise Darvall is expected today or tomorrow, according to Professor Jannie Louw, chief of the Groote Schuur Department of Surgery . . .

Despite this, Professor Barnard and his team have so far detected no sign of rejection and they hope to have their famous patient out of bed by next week . . .

Meanwhile, Mr. Washkansky, in his first bedside radio interview, has described Professor Barnard as "the man with the golden hands."

I looked at my hands on the wheel of the car and thought: the man with the swollen hands. The arthritis was leaving its mark, but so far they were not deformed. Sometimes I did not have the strength to force the mayon tubing onto the metal connectors. But there was still some time left—time to do a few more transplants before it was too late, time to even give Washkansky another heart if he rejected this one.

At the ward I scrubbed quickly and went into the room. Washkansky lay on his side, turned away from the door, and I went around the bed to say good morning. He looked at me without replying.

"How's it going, Louis?"

"I've had enough. Leave me alone."

"Enough of what?"

"They're killing me. I can't sleep, I can't eat, I can't do anything. They're at me all the time with pins and needles, pins and needles . . . all day and all night. It's driving me crazy."

"All right, Louis, be patient. We'll see what we can do."

Bossie had arrived and taken a cardiograph reading. He passed the paper strip to me, and from the look in his eyes I knew something was wrong. It was visible on the strip—a drop in the heart voltage. I looked again at the monitor; the pulse rate had risen to 150. Clearly, we were heading for trouble.

"All right, Louis, we'll arrange for them not to disturb you, so you can get some sleep."

"Thanks," he said without moving.

In the office, we went over the patient's flow sheet and again looked at the electrocardiogram tracing. It showed a voltage drop from fifteen to eleven millivolts. Bossie was quite disturbed.

"I don't like it, Prof. It's not good."

"You figure it's rejection, hey?"

He nodded. "For me, a drop in voltage means rejection. Shumway and Lower have a paper on this. Also, we've seen it with dogs. And you've always said this was one of the first signs."

"What bothers me most," I said, "is how tired and irritable he seems. He's never been like that. He's not well, Bossie. But I wonder—is it rejection, or is it maybe because we disturb him so much?"

"I'll say this—the poor bugger is never allowed more than two hours sleep. That could get on anybody's nerves."

"I think we should give him a good rest—then see where we are."

With this in mind, we gave him twenty milligrams of pethidine at 9:30 A.M. and he quickly went to sleep. At the ten o'clock team meeting, we reviewed all the factors suggesting rejection and agreed to hold off any decision until the patient had awakened from his induced sleep.

After four hours, Washkansky woke up feeling refreshed and in a better humor. His pulse was down a bit, and we gave him additional digoxin to lower it still more. He also had a good appetite.

But this did not last long. In the afternoon his pulse went up again to 150. More disturbing, the voltage sank even lower—to nine millivolts. Bossie then produced the Shumway and Lower paper, describing a link between voltage drop and rejection. After discussing it with Val Schrire, I became convinced that this was truly a rejection episode.

Reporting to the evening gathering of the team, I said there seemed to be only one course open to us: Start treatment for threatened rejection—or risk losing the patient.

Besides continuing the two hundred milligrams daily of Imuran, I proposed we raise the prednisone to two hundred milligrams a day and also give two hundred milligrams daily of actinomycin C for three days. The combined effect, I thought, would attack the rejection process both at its origin and also at the graft site.

Dr. Banks expressed fear that a high dose of steroids would cause an acute stomach ulcer with bleeding. He urged we continually neutralize the stomach acids with alkalis.

Dr. Pimstone pointed out that the proposed dose of prednisone would also aggravate the diabetes.

"We'll have to monitor the urine constantly," he said. "Steroids in the amount you're proposing can induce a diabetic condition in a normal patient. This man is already a diabetic. On top of that, he's eating sporadically, so that we never know where we are with him."

"Neither do we," I said frankly. "But you're right. Bossie, make sure the nurses realize the importance of antacids. Also that they do bedside tests for sugar with every urine sample."

Dr. Forder, the bacteriologist, reported finding a dangerous organism in Washkansky's left nostril: klebsiella.

"I don't like to sound pessimistic," he said, placing his hand before his mouth. "But we should note that this unpleasant pathogen was also found two days ago in a rectal swab and in the patient's mouth."

I felt a chill, thinking, "Oh God, everything's going wrong now."

Forder continued: "It's sensitive to colistin and gentamycin"—meaning the klebsiella harbored by Washkansky could be killed by either of these two antibiotics.

Dr. Thatcher broke in to recommend we cease using tetracyline, an antibiotic normally given to patients after open-heart surgery.

"Tetracyline is known to increase sensibility to fungal invasions," he said.

"What do you suggest, Jeff?" I asked.

"Gentamycin, which Dr. Forder says is indicated here against klebsiella. Also it's about the broadest-spectrum antibiotic you can get."

"What amounts?"

"About forty milligrams."

"All right, I agree."

Immediately after the meeting, we instituted treatment against rejection—increasing the prednisone, as well as starting actinomycin C. Later I was to question whether or not we acted correctly at this point. A drop in electrocardiogram voltage around the fifth day appeared in subsequent experience to be part of the resettling pattern of any transplanted heart.

This suggests that the process of rejection in Washkansky—immediate and unremitting from the moment of the operation—was not as advanced as we imagined. Therefore, he should not have been hit with such a strong barrage of repressive drugs—leaving him even more defenseless to dangerous organisms lurking in the orifices of his body. If so, there is the possibility that we lost this man because of my decision that day. Yet this is not certain. We might have lost him earlier if we had not acted. There is no evidence to prove it either way.

Indeed, the immediate effect of our treatment was to give Washkansky a remarkable state of well-being that lasted five days—five glorious days of new life for a man who had been dying. It was as though we had climbed out of the jungle onto an open plateau that extended without limit—without ever terminating in a cliff that would plunge us back into the jungle.

CHAPTER 27

So THEY BEGAN—Louis Washkansky's five wonderful days of life. Each one blended into the other, and if they were separated at all, it was by a growing strength and awareness that it could never end.

SATURDAY–WEDNESDAY, *December 9–13: Sixth–Tenth Days*

The first morning was dramatic. To the surprise of everyone, Washkansky awakened full of life and good humor. The man who had lost his spirit, asking only to be left alone, now insisted upon joining the world. He spoke to Sister Papendieck about it from beneath his plastic oxygen tent.

"When are you going to take away this candy wrapping?"

"Soon—why? Is there something sweet under it?"

"No, just me," he said, with a grin.

Then he pointed to one remaining intravenous needle in his left arm, used for the isoprenaline drip.

"You can take this out, too," he said. "I'm fine now. I can eat anything—even hospital food."

"All right," she said, laughing. "As soon as the Professor comes, we'll tell him about it."

When I arrived, Louis told me himself—explaining it further.

"Looking at the nurses through this plastic, you don't see much of anything," he said.

"Is there something to see, Louis?"

"I think so, but I won't know until you let me have a good look."

"There's not much to see, Louis. These girls are all wrapped up."

"Doesn't matter," he said. "If I'm going to look, there's no reason for it to be all blurred—is there?"

"No, you're right."

His heart was behaving nicely, between 88 and 100. Everything else had also improved. So we removed the tent and took out the last drip line. Except for the ECG electrodes, which had been moved to the chest wall, no other links bound him to the bedside.

He was given a gas-sterilized radio and immediately turned on the news, hearing about himself for the first time: Louis Washkansky was now entering his seventh day—a day of crisis that would determine whether or not he would reject the heart of Denise Darvall.

"Did you hear that?" he asked Sister Georgie Hall, who had relieved Sister Papendieck.

"Yes."

"If he thinks I'm giving up this heart, he's *mishugah*."

"He's what?" asked Georgie.

"*Mishugah*—nuts," said Louis. "I never felt better in my life . . . or happier."

Happier . . .

That was it, one word which revealed he had reached a plateau of life—limitless and immeasurable as happiness itself. One minute of it was as much as a hundred minutes, or a hundred days, or a hundred years. It could never be measured or placed against its multiple because it could not be multiplied, any more than a laugh could be used as a multiple or as a basic unit of time. It was both the beginning and the end—a state of being once owned and once more regained, assumed as a child walks without looking back, or a bird takes wing without looking down. It was a happening within the fold of nature, yet also beyond it—making its own internal laws as it developed.

Washkansky obeyed its impulses with a natural ease, accepting every aspect of it as he had accepted the insertion of a female heart.

"Do you think," he asked Georgie Hall, "that I might develop busts like a woman?"

"You?—never!" laughed Georgie.

"Or become chicken-hearted?"

"Oh, no."

"You're right," he said. "She was a brave girl. I know she was a brave girl."

After that, he rolled over to look at the girl's heart beating on the monitor, following its steady progress across the screen as it made close to nine beats—a good pulse rate of eighty-nine to ninety.

Watching him do this, I wondered if he thought of it as the girl's heart—or his own. Did he feel it was lodged temporarily in his own being, a foreign body over which he had no control, a partner he could never completely trust to remain with him?

A day or so later, I asked him to tell me his first thoughts after the operation.

"I woke up and it was all different and I wondered why it was different," he said. "Then I realized that I was breathing. I could breathe again. I was not gasping for air. I could breathe because my heart had been fixed up."

That was it—*my heart*. He did not say "her heart" or "our heart." At the moment it began to pump for him, it became his own, part of his own being, as indistinguishable as a cornea or a skin graft, fused with his own blood, its dying cells replaced by others washing in from his own system—beach waves leveling a child's sandcastle. In this way, it was his from the beginning, from the moment of its first beat, accepted without question yet not without one assumption: *She was a brave girl.*

So it was in the five days of life on the plateau—days also marked by visits from different members of his family who came to witness the miracle of rebirth.

Anne Taibel, a Sister

"When I came into the room, he said, 'Hello, Annie' and smiled like only Louis could smile—like all the lights were turned on. Before the operation, when he was fighting for breath, he couldn't smile like that. I mean it couldn't last long because he was trying to stay alive. Now it was there again, and I knew it was the same old Louis.

"Then he said: 'Tell me, Annie, tell me about the day the ice took the bridge away.'

"I said: 'Why Louis, whatever made you think about that?'

" 'I'm lying here the whole bloody day thinking about a lot of things,' he said.

"In the old days, when Louis was a little boy in Lithuania, we used to tell him stories. This was in Slabodka, the Jewish half of Kovna. Our father had already come to South Africa and our mother was working in her little store until late. So we used to take care of Louis—we were two brothers and two sisters and he was the youngest—until she came home.

"We would wait before the white-tiled oven and Louis would ask us to tell him stories. Often the *Bubba,* our granny, would come and she would tell stories about the village. Some of them were about young people who got married without ever knowing each other until they met under the *chuppah,* the marriage tent. You see, the parents arranged the marriage and sometimes a matchmaker helped them. A boy and girl would dream about each other and sometimes the dream did not come true under the *chuppah.* All sorts of surprises like that.

"Then one year the ice was so thick on the river that it broke up, and took away the bridge—the bridge separating Slabodka from Kovna. Louis never got tired of asking how people got across to the other side. 'I'd have built a boat,' he used to say.

"Long before the winter began and the rivers were frozen and everything was white, he used to start making a sledge. You could hear him going knock-knock, preparing for the winter, and when the snows came he would ride down the hills with it.

"You couldn't get hold of him. You know, we had a brewery in Slabodka and instead of going to school, sometimes he would go onto the beer wagons. He would take his books and his lunch and my mother thought he was going to school. But instead he was waiting for the men on the wagons. When they didn't want to take him, he would put a stone under the wagon wheel, so the man would shout at his horses to pull, but the cart wouldn't go.

"When my mother found out about his skipping onto the beer wagons, she wanted to punish him—even though he was very bright and never failed at school. But she could never catch him, until he came to bed. Then it was hard for her to do anything.

"She would say: 'How can a little boy in bed look like a devil?'

"Sometimes my sister Leah and I used to tease him and he would start fighting with us. He never cried, no matter how much you hit him, and it made us even more angry. He used to cry when he saw blood, because he thought he was going to die. But otherwise, you could hit him as much as you wanted and he'd never cry.

"I think maybe he stopped crying when he was a baby. He was only three when the First World War began and the Russians came into Slabodka, saying the Jewish people were spies for the Germans. So we had to leave. They walked from house to house, giving us twenty-four hours notice to leave. Now in twenty-four hours what can you take?

"We took a few things like cushions and clothes and they put us on a train, in cattle cars. We were pushed in, about fifty or sixty to a car. It was like in *Doctor Zhivago*, where the people are lying on the railway line, and when the train comes along, they all tried to push in.

"They said we were being sent to Russia—we didn't know where—but we had relatives in Poland and thought we could get off and find a home there. But the Russians wouldn't even let us look through the boards of the cattle car.

"We traveled for seven days and seven nights and eventually got to Meletrople in the Crimea, next to the Black Sea. There were so many people from Lithuania that there was no place for us. They put us in colleges, one family in a corner, another there, just spread out. And the richest Jewish people used to come and cook for us.

"As soon as we found our feet there, my mother started looking for a little house. Then she took a store in the market, selling men's socks, shoelaces, children's stockings. From that she made a living for us, and we never heard from my Dad during all those four years.

"Then the government started changing and there was a lot of trouble. Every few days we used to have a new government. The White Russians would come and kill the others, then the Communists came and killed the White Russians, and all of them used to raid our shops, so that none of us were safe. We used to hide under the beds and we were afraid.

"Then one day my uncle, Elia Kemagov, came to say they had decided to go back home to Slabodka. He said to my mother: 'We're not going to leave you here with four children, you must come back, you had a home in Slabodka.'

"It took us two months to get home, riding the cattle cars. There were hundreds of people at the train stations trying to go home. They said to us, 'Please help us . . . we've been here for weeks, they promised to give us trains to go back to our places . . . the winter will soon be setting in and we'll still be here.'

"My uncle managed for us. You see, he took with him a lot of scarce articles like flour, candles, and soap. He would give something to the station master and that's how we traveled. So we arrived in Kovna and our house was empty with the roof broken. But we were home again and my mother began to work for us, bringing in poultry and eggs.

"Louis was seven then and for four years he had known nothing but cattle cars and wandering around in exile. I think it was during those years that he finished with tears and learned to look out for himself.

"So I said: 'Louis, why was that bridge always so important to you?'

"He said: 'I don't know. Maybe because it went somewhere.'

"I said: 'Like where?'

"And he said: 'From where we were—where else?'

"He smiled again and I thought maybe he had a new heart—if they tell me so, I'll believe them. But it looked to me more like the old one had been fixed up. Because there was the same old smile—like before, only more so."

Anne Taibel was not alone. Those who had known Louis Washkansky before the operation were amazed at what they saw upon entering the room. It seemed a miracle to them. A dying man had been transformed into one charged with life.

Clinically, it was quite dramatic. As the heart took over, it repaired damage caused by lack of strength in the old one. It did this mainly through the kidneys and liver, which were once more able to draw on a supply of fresh blood, enabling them to not only function but also to effect long-needed repairs in an ailing body.

Among these was the festering wound in Washkansky's left calf—irradicable focus of the special hell he had suffered before the operation, stemming from five days and nights when he had sat upright in a chair with needles draining from his legs into a basin, the liquid rising around his cold, blue feet.

Perhaps even more surprising, the renewal of Washkansky's body brought about a renewal of his identity in the minds of all those who came to see whether or not a foreign heart had turned him into a stranger. Nor did it stop there. For as the family came to identify Louis Washkansky, so he looked back at them to establish his own awareness of himself.

This was evident in what he said and the way in which he met the members of his family, each one reflecting some precious part of his past that once more invested his life with meaning. Perhaps these bits of the past had even more meaning now, causing him to race back half a century to scenes from his childhood.

Nor was he alone. For if the present—that is, the new life—was invested with meaning taken from the past, so was his renewed identity determined in much the same way. Those who came to see him—hands upraised and eyes wide with wonder, as in a fresco depicting the miracle of a medieval saint—measured the rebirth against what they had known and loved in him before he was stricken by a failing heart.

His sister Anne discovered that his smile was once more capable of enduring beyond a gasped breath. His brother-in-law, Solly, looked else-where—seeing the rebirth more clearly expressed in his leg.

Solly Sklar, Brother-in-Law

"I came with his son, Michael, and Louis thought we were very funny in our hospital gowns. I went in first and he said: 'Well, if it isn't Santa Claus.'

"Then he saw Michael and said: 'That makes two of them. This is going to be some Christmas.'

"After a bit, he said Professor Barnard thought he might be home by Christmas, and he was sure he could make it.

" 'Solly,' he said, 'you'd better get ready for that party you promised, because I'm really getting out of here.'

" 'Louis,' I said, 'when you come home, we'll have a party that'll blow the town apart.'

" 'Good,' he said.

" 'How's the leg?' I asked.

" 'One hundred per cent,' he said.

" 'Would you like to see it?' the nurse asked, and pulled back the covers.

"It was a miracle. I had seen him Saturday afternoon before the opera-tion, sitting on the bed with his feet resting on a chair. The left leg was very swollen with the infected sore and the foot was blue. I touched it and it had no life. But now it was perfect, the edema was down, the blueness gone, the legs were nice and perfect.

"When I saw that, I knew he had made it. I told myself, this Louis is going to be home by Christmas. And I told him so!

" 'Louis, if I hadn't seen this I'd never believe it. It's like it was.'

" 'You ought to know, Solly—you knew the old Washkansky.'

"He was right about that. I met him at the gym, before the war. He was about twenty-eight then and keen on weight-lifting and a bit of wrestling. We got to be friends, which was strange because we were both born near each other in Lithuania and we came to the Cape when we were kids, but we never met until we began lifting weights at the gym.

"Louis—we called him Washy then—could handle himself, no matter what. Put him down in the middle of the desert without a drop of water and he'd come out of it riding a camel loaded with beer.

"During the war in Italy—we joined the South African Engineers to-gether—he built a contraption to make his own brew out of orange skins and raisins. It had pipes and tubes like a chemistry department and after five days, it would start bubbling up and dripping greenish liquid into a can.

"He traded it off for fresh eggs, which we all ate. Then he found a flour depot left by the Germans and he traded this off for some live oxen so the whole company could have fresh meat instead of canned bully beef. Louis knew the MPs would take it for themselves if they found out. So he loaded the oxen up on a truck at dawn and when it left the farmyard, he ran behind the truck with a broom, sweeping away its tracks—out the gate and down the road for half a mile.

" 'If anybody asks where these oxen came from,' he said, 'we'll say they just showed up in the morning roll call.'

"Everyone loved the guy. At Sonderwater there was a Senior NCO who was a nasty piece of work. I think only a mother could love a chap like that. The company was due off at twelve-thirty, and we had only half an hour to catch the train, but he refused to let us off earlier. One of the chaps, whose wife had come up to see him, said: 'The sonofabitch could at least give us a few extra minutes.' The NCO heard this and asked who said it, but no one came forward. 'All right,' he said, 'you can all stand here until tomorrow morning.' To save the chap with his wife, Louis stepped forward saying, 'I said it—so what?'

"That's the type of fellow he was—with a heart of gold, and always a bit of a rebel. He refused to wear army shoes and carried a medical certificate claiming they hurt his big toe. Instead, he wore knee-high boots—beautiful ones he got in the Abyssinian campaign. Nobody could get him out of them, not even the MPs. You'd see a parade, everyone with the same uniform and shoes, and then Washy with his black boots. He wore them right through the war, for five and a half years. When he was discharged, he claimed payment for his own shoe leather and received a lump sum for the whole time of his service.

" 'I got the last laugh on the army,' he said and threw a big party for all his friends. After that, he began to see a bit of my sister and six months later they got married. Nobody could have asked for a greater friend or brother-in-law.

"I went to see him twice in the hospital. When I came the second time, on the tenth day, he was doing exercises with the help of a lady physiotherapist, lifting arms and legs and breathing.

" 'Louis,' I said, 'I'll tell the boys at the gym to get the weights ready for you.'

" 'Yeah,' he said, 'the one-pound ones.'

"The stitches hurt when he moved and he was still very weak, but you could see he was steadily picking up strength. They had removed the wires from his chest to the heart monitor, and he was much freer to move around.

"After the exercises, he sat on the edge of the bed and Dr. Bosman came in.

" 'It's your wife on the phone,' he said. 'She wants to know if she can send the Rabbi to see you tomorrow.'

" 'The Rabbi?' said Louis. 'Do I look like I'm dying?'

" 'I hope not.'

" 'So why should I have a Rabbi?'

" 'Louis,' I said, 'you're a famous man now. So the Rabbi wants to come and shake your hand.'

" 'Naah, tell her I'm not ready for any Rabbi.'

"Dr. Bosman went out and came back, laughing.

" 'She says you've got to see him. He's head of the community and you have to be polite to him.'

"Louis sighed. 'So,' he said, 'the mountain comes to Mohammed.'

" 'She's sending him tomorrow with your brother. She still has a sore throat so she won't be with them.'

" 'Poor girl,' said Louis. 'Just when I'm getting back in shape, she can't come to see me.'

"They allowed a photographer into the room and he took some pictures until Louis said he had enough. When he was gone, Louis shook his head.

" 'It's like a fishbowl,' he said. 'I can't wait to get out of here. We'll go back to Italy, you and I, and see all the old places together.'

"Then he said: 'Do you think any of the bridges we put up are still there?'

" 'Maybe,' I said, 'in the little places.'

" 'Israel,' he said. 'We have to go there, too. All of us together.'

" 'Yes, Louis.'

" 'Solly,' he said, 'It's been wonderful. Even if we never get there.'

" 'What do you mean?'

" 'Just to live again, man, to lie here and breathe again and talk about old times with you. Just to have this is enough. You know what I mean?'

" 'You feel better all the time?'

" 'Better and hungrier. I get so hungry that I have pains in my stomach, like now. If they give me some milk or soup, it goes away.'

"I thought that was sort of odd, but I didn't say anything about it and shortly after that I left—and I never saw him like that again."

CHAPTER 28

THE DESCENT FROM the plateau was at first gradual—almost imperceptible. There were some indications that it had begun, but we did not notice them because no one believed it was possible. Only Louis Washkansky seemed aware of what was happening—as though he alone had the courage to look back and discover the green plateau was already above us and we were, indeed, on the way back to the jungle of his death.

THURSDAY, *December 14: Eleventh Day*

The night that led into this day was broken three times by the patient's awakening with strong abdominal pain accompanied by his asking for food. At eleven-thirty he had an omelette and two slices of bread. Again at two-thirty the pain returned, and he took a slice of toast with a glass of milk. Then milk again at four-thirty.

Aware that steroids can induce an ulcer, we had continually neutralized acid secretions of his stomach with alkalines. On the ninth day, when the pain first appeared, this was intensified. The next day the pain had decreased, but now it was back again in greater force. Eating brought relief, and in between his snacks Washkansky slept peacefully.

Despite this, he awoke at six o'clock—tired and irritable. After breakfast, however, he felt better and began to think about the day before him, confiding his anxieties to Sister Papendieck.

"Everybody in town is coming here today. The Mayor and that Rabbi and also Dr. Bosman said there were some television people. Who are they?"

"I don't know," said Sister Papendieck. "Americans, I think."

"I like Americans," he said. "They're like South Africans."

"Are they?"

"Yah—no bloody nonsense. They make no bones about it."

Then he said: "You know what? I'll shave myself today. If you give me a razor and some water, I can do it myself."

He sat up in bed with a bowl of water and a mirror propped up on a bed trolley. It was a big event, and Sister Papendieck watched with open delight.

"I'll tell you," he said, "when a man can't shave himself, it's a terrible thing—like you're a nobody."

He twisted his mouth around to get it into position squinting into the little mirror.

"That Gene Ferry isn't a bad type. We used to swim together in the old Woodstock Bath."

"Mayor Ferry?"

"Umm. Too bad we don't have any traffic tickets to give him. That would be great fun. Do you have any?"

"No."

"Maybe Professor Barnard does. But he doesn't need help like that. Not him. Not that man. He can do anything—right?"

"Right, Mr. Washkansky."

"You know, I'll never have words to say what I think of him."

When he had finished, he looked at himself in the mirror and smiled happily.

"Who would've thought that a shave could be such a big thing? I used to do it with my eyes closed, so I didn't have to look at myself and ask who's that ugly fool."

"You're not ugly," said Sister Papendieck.

"Nah . . ."

Then he said: "Say, will you come to my party when I get out?"

"Of course."

"We can have a dance, maybe."

"Lots of them," she said.

"That's the kind of medicine I like," he said.

Sister Papendieck's paper mask moved with her smile. She had dark eyes, and they blinked gaily at Louis Washkansky.

The influx of visitors came later in the day, beginning with Washkansky's brother, Tevia, and the Rabbi who stood by the door and said he would never forget the day he married Louis and Ann under the *chuppah* twenty-one years ago.

"Why don't you Rabbis tell us what we're getting into before we do such things?" said Louis.

Rabbi Israel Abraham laughed. "I never saw two people more in love than you and Ann."

"You know, it's still that way. We must be crazy. Who'd have thought two old people can still feel like that?"

"You're not so old Louis—not any more."

"Wait a minute," said Louis. "You got it wrong—they only transplanted a heart."

Both Georgie Hall and the Rabbi laughed.

"No," said Louis, "I was lucky to get Ann."

"You were, Louis. But you're all right yourself, even though you don't come to the synagogue like you should."

"Umm."

"Doesn't matter, Louis," he said. "We're proud of you."

The Mayor came next, and after talking about the old days in the Woodstock swimming pool, he asked what to tell the people of Cape Town.

Louis said to tell them Merry Christmas and a Happy New Year. This pleased everybody and after that there appeared the ponderous elements of the American television team.

Washkansky's sister-in-law, Gracie Sklar, arrived at about the same time with two other members of the family. Louis Washkansky loved her in a special way. And to her came the first dramatic sign that the man whom she also loved was not what he had appeared to be.

Gracie Sklar, Sister-in-Law

"I was with Louis' son, Michael, and his niece, Chavia Taibel. We were sitting on the bench outside when one of the doctors came out and said, 'I know you are Mr. Washkansky's family, would you mind very much if the television people filmed you as you walked in to see him?'

"It really upset me, but I could do nothing about it. So we waited while they set up their cameras and this took about an hour. We had dreamed about this moment for so long and when it came we had to wait for strangers to fix their lights and speak to Louis before us. Finally, we got dressed in hospital gowns and suddenly I was afraid to go in. I said to Michael: 'You go first, you've already seen your father, you know what to do.'

"So he went first and I came after him. There were three or four arc lights so strong I couldn't see Louis at first. But when I saw him, I forgot all about the TV people with their cameras and went up to the bed and said, 'How are you, Louis?' and he said, 'How's everybody?' and I said, 'Everybody who hasn't been able to come sends their fondest love and best wishes . . . how wonderful you look.' I said a lot of other things but I can't remember word for word. Then Dr. Bosman said, 'That's enough,' and turned around to the TV people and said: 'Well, you couldn't have asked for anything better than that, could you?'

"They were finished and went away. Louis was sitting on the edge of the bed and I stood against the wall. We were talking a little bit and then he asked Chavia about her father: 'How is Daniel?'

" 'Daddy is upstairs,' she said and looked at me.

"Louis loved Daniel like a brother, more than a brother. When they got together, it was already a party. They used to sit on a Sunday morning, it was their morning, and drink some Jewish schnapps and eat Jewish polony with Daniel's bagels. Daniel used to bake bagels better than any baker. He had a sheet metal works, but in Russia his mother used to bake and he helped her. You've never tasted such bagels in your life. They were like eating cake. Every Sunday he would bake them and bring them around to Louis, hot and fresh in a bag.

"Then the trouble began. Louis had his first heart attack and Daniel got cancer in the gum and they both suffered. The cancer was cut out and Daniel was all right for about five years. Then it got worse and he had cancer all over his face and he was dying. They said there was one chance if they cut off his face, the bottom half, and he came to say good-bye to Louis one night when the room was full of visitors. As we were leaving, I happened to turn around and see those two saying good-bye to each other. Daniel was going the next day to Johannesburg to have his face cut off and they held each other's hands. I'll never forget the look of compassion on Louis's face as he held Daniel's hand.

"Louis was still in the cardiac unit and everyone said he was going to die. Daniel came back wearing a plastic mask and he sat on the bed with Louis. He couldn't talk any more so he made signs or wrote out his words on little pieces of paper. It went like that each day until Louis was going to be operated on. On that day, Daniel came to see him, and he didn't write anything. He just stood there, wearing his mask, with his fist clenched and the thumb sticking up—telling Louis he had to live. That was their sign.

" 'How's Daniel?' Louis asked me.

" 'Like Chavia says, Louis, he's upstairs in bed but he's holding on, you know.'

"He was dying in the bed on the second floor. He could no longer get up and each day he was worse. Louis must have understood this because right out of the blue he had a very sad expression on his face, and suddenly the tears came to his eyes.

"In all the years of my association with Louis I had never seen him like that, and it left a terrible impression on me. I was at a loss for words. I didn't know what to say to him. I tried to force myself to make conversation but I couldn't.

"Then he turned round and, looking at the wall, he said: 'You know, I feel a little bit tired today, Gracie, would you mind going?'

"So I said: 'Not at all, Louis, we will go if you want to have a rest.'

"As I went out I saw them putting him back into bed and that was the only time I saw him."

Before we entered the team meeting that evening, Dr. Bosman showed me the last blood report from Dr. Reuben Mibashan, head of the hospital's hematology department. The white cell count had been mounting steadily for the past four days, going from 15,900 to 29,860. We had considered this to be the result of heavy doses of steroids, which were now being reduced.

Dr. Mibashan had appended a note, however, which suggested something else: "There are toxic changes in the white cells, probably due to immunosuppression, but they could also come from an infection . . ."

I shuddered and looked at Bossie.

"What do you think?"

"I don't know where he could have an infection," said Bossie, "unless it is a pancreatitis. But the stomach pains seem to be better. He's irritable though, and this afternoon, when his family came to see him, he cried. He's never done that before."

At the meeting, we discussed the rise in white cell count and decided it was probably due to the steroids. Similarly, any toxic change could also be due to this. There was a sudden change in the LDH enzyme level—from 368 to 752—which could indicate the heart was breaking down with rejection. But Dr. Potgieter believed this came from something else—a breakdown of red cells whose life span had been reduced through injury from the heart-lung machine.

"Their normal life is 120 days, but here we can expect a breakdown any time after ten days, which would release these enzymes."

Professor Eales found a strange increase of coproporphyrin in the urine.

"Yesterday we found it and again today," he said, "meaning there is a general trend starting."

"Going where?" I asked.

"I cannot answer that. I can say there are many causes for this porphyrin change. They include heart failure, liver trouble, hemolytic anemia, or a vast variety of toxins."

"It could also be caused by the Imuran we are giving?"

"Yes."

That left us nowhere and we went on.

The chest X ray was clear. The stools and urine showed no infection. The urine osmolarity was good, the serum amylase not abnormal. The electrocardiograph voltage had come up again, as had the creatinine clearance. So I was not worried about infection either in the pancreas or elsewhere.

That night Washkansky slept well, although he awakened three times complaining of stomach pain, which was again relieved by milk and toast, together with antacid pills.

FRIDAY, *December 15: Twelfth Day*

This day followed the pattern of the one before it, yet with greater intensity—as though the descent was becoming more rapid.

The tormented night lead once more to an irritable morning, bringing something new: pain in the left shoulder. We ordered an X ray but did not consider it to be serious. Everything else indicated that the patient was improving remarkably well. Val Schrire confirmed the heart was better than ever. The stomach pains seemed under control, and there was even a drop in the puzzling white cell count.

Despite this, Washkansky was grumpy and complained of being tired— just when he should have more energy. This worried me and I tried to determine its cause. A patient's behavior can often signal trouble before it shows up on a report.

One possible explanation was too many visitors and interviews. Too much was being asked of this man. We had agreed that today he could be seen by a cabinet minister, his wife, and family, as well as being photographed by *Stern,* interviewed by the BBC, and televised by CBS. I decided to honor these but restrict their time and allow no more until he felt better.

Washkansky enjoyed his visit with Minister Carel de Wet, and he looked forward to seeing his wife for the first time in five days after her recovery from a cold and sore throat. Before this occurred, however, he had an unpleasant interview with the BBC.

The telephone company arranged for a sterilized phone to be placed in the room, and at 3 P.M. the call came through from BBC in London, congratulating him on being famous. He gave his usual reply: He wasn't famous—it was the doctors. This led to a few other remarks, and suddenly they threw him a difficult question:

"Mr. Washkansky, as a man, how does it feel to have a female heart?"

"Oh, that doesn't bother me, as long as it's a good heart."

"Do you think it is?"

"Oh, yes, I think so."

"And how do you, as a Jew, feel about having a Gentile's heart?"

"How do I what?"

"As a Jew, what is your feeling about having the heart of a non-Jew, a Gentile?"

"Well, I never thought of it that way, I don't know . . ."

"Cut the line!" cried Dr. Bosman.

At their sound controls outside the room, the BBC team apologized, saying the questions originated in London.

"Well I've got one for you," said Dr. Bosman. "How do you, as men, feel about working for a company that asks a stupid question like that?" He followed this by another question equally impossible of reply: "Everybody's been so kind and good, why couldn't we leave it like that?"

The CBS crew followed, shooting through the door from a porch outside the room. On the seventh day we had moved Washkansky from the recovery room into another one, allowing for greater sterility. It was connected by a porch to a second room where we could scrub up—going from there onto the porch and then into Washkansky's room, without opening the door onto the hospital corridor. This also allowed for greater control of visitors and incidentally provided a way of photographing the patient without entering his room.

After the television crew left, Ann Washkansky stayed behind to be with her husband for a few minutes. Georgie Hall helped him stretch out, and his wife adjusted his pillow.

"Louis," she said, "I think you're getting a cold."

"Naah. I'm just tired from all these people. And I have a pain in the shoulder."

Ann turned to Georgie Hall.

"Georgie," she said, "he's got a cold."

"No, Mrs. Washkansky, never."

Louis waved a dismissal at his wife.

"Ah," he said. "She's at me already. I've got a cold. I don't happen to have one, but if it makes her happy I've got one."

"Listen to him," said Ann. "And he's not even home yet. What'll I do when he comes home, how will I be able to control him?"

"You'll have to tie him down," said Georgie.

"Georgie," said Louis, "I thought you were my friend."

"And your wife isn't your friend?"

Louis Washkansky looked at Ann standing by the bedside. Then he stretched out his hand and she took it.

"The greatest friend I've ever had," he said.

For a moment they continued to hold onto one another. They had touched hands today, for the first time and for the benefit of the American television audience. Now they had done it again without thinking of the rules of sterility.

"You don't have to cry about it," he said.

"I'm sorry, Louis, I can't help it."

"Well you don't have to cry. I told you I had it in the bag."

"All right," she said, "if you tell me so, I'll believe it."

"Do me a favor, Ann. Believe it."

"Yes, Louis, I believe it."

She left shortly after that. On the way out they spoke for the last time, and now it was Louis Washkansky who was worried about his wife.

"You'll come tomorrow?"

"Yes, I'll be here."

"Take it easy, kid, don't get another cold."

"No, I promise . . . good-bye."

"Good-bye."

Nothing important was decided at the team meeting that evening. We noted the blood pressure had fallen slightly, and the venous pressure was now normal. The enzymes had dropped, as had the white cell count. Everything pointed to general improvement, though the patient did not seem as good as he should.

Dr. Forder reported finding more of the dangerous klebsiella bacteria in the patient's mouth and nostrils—a sober warning of the ever-present threat of infection. We ordered a more stringent control of oral hygiene, and the meeting ended.

Shortly after that, the phone rang and it was Val Schrire.

"Chris? Your next candidate has arrived."

"Dr. Blaiberg?"

"That's right. He had a crisis yesterday, and his doctors brought him in. His condition is worse than we first pictured it to you. There is further damage to the myocardium, and he's a bit cyanotic. But I believe he can hold out until you've got Washkansky further along."

I thanked him and went down to D-1 Ward where I found Dr. Blaiberg dozing in bed. He looked like Santa Claus, with a tubby belly, red cheeks, blue ears, and a big mouth—except this was no laughing Santa. His mouth was open and gasping for air.

I nudged him slightly, and he looked at me with elfish eyes.

"Dr. Blaiberg? I've come to introduce myself—or do you know who I am?"

"No, I don't."

"I'm Professor Barnard."

"I'm sorry, Professor . . ."

He gasped for air and continued.

"I should have recognized you . . . I've seen your pictures often . . . but we've never met."

"Well, I've come to say hello and see how you are."

"You can see . . . I'm not well."

In a way, he was worse off than Washkansky had been—especially, in the struggle for air.

"Do you know there's a possibility we can help you by doing a heart transplant on you?"

"Yes, I know."

"How do you feel about that?"

"The sooner, the better . . . I'll co-op . . . cooperate in every way."

I looked into his eyes to see if there was fear. There was none. This was not a fighter like Louis Washkansky. He was not a loner. He was a company man—one of many. But he was without fear, and he believed that we could do it.

"Good," I said. "I'll come again soon."

"Thank you, Professor . . ."

He began to cough and I waited for him to finish.

"The sooner . . . the better," he said.

I returned to my office in the medical school. There was the usual crowd of waiting correspondents and photographers. After speaking to them, I tried to work, but it was impossible. The telephone rang with calls from magazines, newspapers, and other doctors. My secretary came in continually, unable to stem the flood.

Finally Bossie called, suggesting I stop by the ward on my way home.

"What is it?"

"Something you might want to look at in Washkansky's X ray."

"What is it?"

"There's a part I don't understand."

"What do you mean? Speak clearly, man."

"A shadow. In the lung."

I felt suddenly sick—as if I had dreamed it would happen. Then I told myself it was not possible. Also, Bossie did not sound too sure of it.

"It's very tiny," he said. "Maybe it's nothing. But I thought you'd like to look at it."

"Yes," I said and hung up.

On the way out, I was again engulfed by waiting reporters and began to feel irritated. I needed the freedom to be alone and think of my patient. Jumping into the car, I drove to the hospital and quickly ran up the two flights to Ward C-2. Bossie came out of Washkansky's room with the X ray in hand, and together we went into the Doctors' Office.

"Where is it?" I said.

"There," he said.

He pointed to a miniscule shadow in the left lobe of the lung—overlooked by everyone until that moment. Our attention had been focused primarily on monitoring the heart shadow for signs of rejection.

"What do you see?" I asked, holding the X ray against the light.

"I don't know. What do you make of it?"

"Looks to me like a vascular shadow—where's the previous X ray?"

We compared the picture with an earlier one, but there was not enough difference to give a clear reading. Bossie remained worried.

"Besides this, he's running a slight temperature, 98.6. Also he isn't feeling well."

"He's seeing too many people," I said.

"I was going to a party at Marius'," said Bossie, "but maybe I'd better stay."

"No, go to the party. But could you check him again at ten and call me?"

"Okay."

When he called, the temperature was unchanged, but there was pain in the shoulder and chest. I told Bossie it was probably a postpericardiotomy syndrome. Yet I was not convinced of it. Something told me that I was being misled by the feeling that nothing could seriously be wrong with this man.

SATURDAY, *December 16: Thirteenth Day*

The early morning call to Coert Venter was brief.

"How is he?"

"Not too well. There's tubular breathing, especially on the left side."

"You think there's lung consolidation?"

"I'm afraid so."

We were in trouble. The lungs were being invaded—but by what?

"How's the heart?"

"Fine—nothing there."

"What else?"

"He still has a temperature, pain in the left shoulder and chest, and he's not very chirpy."

"We'd better get the team in this morning. Call them for a ten o'clock meeting. Have you ordered X rays?"

"Yes, Professor."

When I entered the room, Washkansky was reclined on a partially raised bed, dark-rimmed glasses up on his forehead, and a discarded book by his side—*Die Rich, Die Happy*.

"Hello, Louis, how are you?"

"Terrible."

His voice was hoarse, there were dark rings under his eyes, and he seemed to be breathing more rapidly. The chart confirmed it: respiration rate increase from 20 to 24. Pulse up to 100. Blood pressure down from 115 to 105. Temperature rising: 101.6.

"What's the trouble, Louis?"

"I'm worn out and there's pain here," he said, placing his hand on the left side of his chest.

"Also there," he said, indicating his shoulder and root of the left side of his neck.

"Maybe you threw it out of place grabbing that telephone yesterday," I said, trying to hide my sense of alarm.

We were in trouble and you could hear it with the stethoscope on his left chest wall: high-pitched sounds, as of air being forced through a tube—tubular breathing caused by consolidation in the lungs.

"So?" he said.

"Sounds like you caught a slight cold," I said.

It was more than that, and he knew it. Avoiding his eyes, I turned quickly to Coert Venter.

"Is he coughing?"

"Yes, a little."

"Any sputum?"

"Nothing yet."

"All right," I said, with a wink to Louis. "We'll have to keep you quiet for a while. No more television shows."

He nodded but said nothing—watching me closely for some clue to the truth. I left the room, and shortly after that we received X rays confirming my worst fears: bronchopneumonic patches in the left lung, plus some consolidation in the lower right lung with other soft patches above it.

The small shadow of the previous day had magnified a hundred times and was spreading from the left to the right lung. It was a pulmonary invasion of remarkable speed, and it required immediate treatment—but of what sort? This was the problem. For until we knew what was causing the trouble, we could not treat it.

Washkansky could be getting pneumonia. He had the normal symptoms of pulmonary infection. Yet he was not a normal patient and his trouble could also come from something else. A blood clot could have broken away from the suture line in the right atrium where the old heart had been folded back to make the anastomosis—going from there into the lungs and causing a pulmonary embolus. This would have resulted in an infarct—death of lung area due to obstructed circulation. If there was one clot, there could be two or more of them—causing multiple areas of infarction and explaining the shadows in both lungs.

Treatment differed for these two complications. An infarct required heparin to prevent further clotting. Pneumonia called for one or another antibiotic, or drug, specific to the virus, bacteria, or fungus causing it. Until we knew this, we could not treat for infection. And we would only know this when we had something we could study, such as sputum, since it was not possible to examine a piece of the lung. At the same time, it was dangerous to wait. We were in the position of having to fight an approaching enemy, without knowing its identity or the weapons at its command.

Most of the team arrived. It was a public holiday and a few were missing—including Val Schrire who had gone to the airport to meet a visiting relative. We gathered in the doctors' office, and I began by reporting on the rapidly deteriorating condition of the patient, indicating either pulmonary infection of an unknown origin or multiple pulmonary infarcts. Since we had no sputum or other evidence confirming pneumonia, I was inclined to believe it was an infarct—what did the team believe?

Dr. Werbeloff held the X rays against the light, pointing to the round shadows.

"I must say that radiologically the evidence fits an infection better than an infarct. This doesn't look like an infarct as I usually see them."

Dr. Thatcher was equally puzzled.

"It looks like a lobar pneumonia of some unusual source—but what? A fungus or virus infection doesn't usually look like this. If it is bacterial, why aren't we getting any bacteria?"

Everyone looked at Dr. Forder as though expecting him to produce some germs from the pocket of his white coat.

"I regret to say we have had no sputum and therefore no specimen to monitor," he said.

Dr. Forder paused, hand over mouth, as though acutely aware of germs in the air and thus unwilling either to add to them or receive any more than necessary. He was a slight, balding man of precise manner and dress—and a brilliant bacteriologist.

"You'll recall," he said, "we have found klebsiella in his nostril, mouth, and rectum—but that doesn't mean he has a klebsiella pneumonia."

Klebsiella was a particularly dangerous bacterium. Normally it infected the nose and accessory sinuses and only seldom—when the body defenses were lowered—did it gain entry to the lungs. Once there, however, it was frightening and difficult to control without massive doses of the proper antibiotic. Viral and fungal pneumonias were equally lethal unless caught immediately. On the other hand, pneumococcal bacteria were easily controlled by penicillin. If Washkansky had pneumonia, it was infinitely better that it be the pneumococcal type, which could be knocked out in twenty-four hours.

"Maybe the patient has pneumococcal pneumonia," said Thatcher.

"Maybe," I said. "But if he has an infarct and we treat him only for pneumonia, we may lose him."

"Not only that," said Dr. Forder. "If he does not have a pneumococcal infection and we administer large doses of penicillin, we are going to unnecessarily upset his normal defense mechanism. We will knock out all the protective bacteria and leave him even further open to invasion by klebsiella or anything else that's hanging around."

We all knew this, but it sounded so ominous that for a moment no one said anything. Finally, I decided we had only one course open to us: Treat for an infarct, pending a sample of the sputum or any other evidence proving this was a lung infection. There was general agreement and we decided to give 25,000 units of heparin over twenty-four hours as an anticoagulant. At the same time, we would continue the daily forty milligrams of gentamycin to help ward off other dangerous organisms, such as klebsiella.

We started treatment and shortly after 1 P.M. Val Schrire arrived—entering the room as Washkansky began coughing up his first sputum. Bossie phoned me at my office, and I came immediately, meeting Val as he returned to the corridor.

"He has pneumonia, Chris."

"How do you arrive at that?"

"His sputum is rusty, and he looks pneumonic. He has all the indications of it—what else do you think he has?"

"It could be a pulmonary infarct."

"From what?"

"A clot formed in one of the veins of his leg, or on the anastomotic side in the right atrium."

Val shook his head.

"No, sir. This is old-fashioned rusty pneumonia. It's a pneumococcal type, and penicillin will wipe it out with no trouble."

"Perhaps you're right."

"I know I'm right. You'll see as soon as they report on the sputum."

Dr. Forder came and quickly took a sample to his laboratory, made a Gram-smear and immediately called Bossie.

"I've got masses of pneumococci," he said, with unusual excitement. "I think you can start the penicillin immediately."

"Anything else?"

"I can't tell yet. As soon as we have a culture, I'll inform you."

We began treatment—20-million units of penicillin, to be given without stopping the heparin. It seemed to be just in time, for Washkansky had deteriorated further. His temperature was up to 102.2, his breathing 26, pulse 110. His coughing left him exhausted, and as we introduced a second intravenous lead for the penicillin, I tried to cheer him up.

"You'll soon feel better, Louis," I said.

He said nothing.

"It's like we said. You have a bad cold. Tomorrow it should be better."

"Did you tell Ann?"

"She called," said Bossie. "But I said you needed rest and suggested she stay away for a day."

"Thanks," he said and began to cough again.

Bossie followed me out to the scrub room.

"I think we caught it just in time," I said.

"I hope so," he said, without enthusiasm.

The team met again that evening. We reported the diagnosis of pneumococcal infection, based on sputum findings, and everyone agreed on the treatment. Dr. Werbeloff, examining new X rays, found further evidence to confirm we were on the right track.

There was little more to discuss, and the meeting ended with the feeling that we finally had the crisis under control.

I returned that evening to check on Washkansky and found Sister Papendieck in the scrub room. She was to have taken two nights off—her first since the operation two weeks ago—but she had returned after only one night.

"What are you doing here, Sister?"

She did not answer me.

"Hey?"

She shook her head and went back into the room. I entered to find Washkansky asleep—still showing evidence of pneumonia. He was breathing heavily with a temperature of 103.8. His pulse was better, having fallen to 106, and the temperature would also drop as the penicillin took effect. But he was a different man from the one Sister Papendieck had left thirty-six hours ago.

"Where's Dr. Venter?"

"Looking at the patient in 273."

"What made you come back?"

She looked down at Louis and put her gloved hand on his bedside. Then without lifting her eyes, she shook her head.

"Thank you, Sister Papendieck . . . thank you."

SUNDAY, *December 17: Fourteenth Day*

I slept that night on the other side of the bed away from the phone—but it rang anyway. The press had learned of our trouble, and they called at any hour and from anywhere in the world. At 4 A.M. I decided to leave the phone off the hook in order to get three hours of unbroken sleep, and I called Dr. Venter to let him know it.

"How's the patient?"

"Not good," he said, "he's passed urine twice in bed, his respiration is up, and the temperature is 103.5."

"What's the respiration?"

"Thirty-two. Also, he refuses to eat or drink. He won't do anything, and refuses to cooperate."

"What else—how's the heart?"

"It's all right. The pulse is up to 106 and the blood pressure is 115, but I think that can be expected with what we have."

"What *do* we have?" I asked.

"Pneumococcal pneumonia—no?"

"I'm beginning to wonder. He should be responding better to the penicillin. Is he still coughing?"

"A little less—maybe."

"All right, if he continues to wet the bed, slip on a Paul's tube. Make sure it's sterilized. And as for the oral intake, let's see how he reacts in the morning. I'll be in early."

"Okay—good night, Professor."

"Good night, Coert."

After that, I could not leave the phone off the hook. Fortunately, no more calls came. I awakened at seven and went straight in, without phoning. If there was going to be more bad news, I wanted to see it.

When I arrived, Sister Papendieck was giving the patient a tepid sponge bath. They had connected a Paul's tube to his penis, allowing the urine to drain into a bottle, and while this was momentarily exposed Washkansky lay with his eyes closed. When the sheet was back in place, he opened his eyes and shook his head.

"Hello, Louis, how are you feeling?"

He shook his head again.

"Come on, man, Dr. Venter says you're improving."

"It hurts when I breathe," he said. "And it hurts in the rear."

"Where?"

"He has an excoriation of the scrotum," said Coert.

"Did you send a swab to Dr. Forder?"

"Yes."

Breakfast arrived, but Washkansky refused it.

"Louis, you have to eat."

He shook his head and looked at me as though I had betrayed him.

"Louis—"

"No, Doc—I can't do it."

Sister Papendieck offered him a spoonful of cereal.

"Please, Mr. Washkansky—just a little bit."

He closed his eyes.

"If you don't do it," she said, "I won't keep my dance date with you."

That did it. He took the spoon himself and began to eat. He could not control his urine. He had trouble breathing. But he could feed himself, and he still believed he was going to get out of bed and dance with a pretty nurse.

"What's this dance date?" I asked.

"Something very private," said Marie Papendieck, with a smile for Louis.

I left the room feeling better. He was eating again and probably was at the point of passing his crisis. After all, we had given the penicillin for only sixteen hours. The morning X ray would probably show that the lungs were clearing.

When the picture came, however, it showed no improvement—at least that I could see. The heart was fine. Its size remained unchanged. There was no sign of rejection there. But dark shadows still clung to the lungs, indicating the penicillin was having no effect. Perhaps something besides pneumococcal bacteria was invading Washkansky's lungs.

The team gathered and Dr. Werbeloff led off with his reading of the X rays. Surprisingly, he was optimistic.

"My impression is that the lesions are less dense than the intensive pattern of last night. It looks as though they are clearing slightly."

Dr. Forder also suggested that the penicillin might be having an effect.

"The sputum we reviewed this morning contained only small traces of pneumococci. We are culturing it, of course, and will know much more tomorrow. But I think it's safe to assume we have just about obliterated the pneumococci that were there. I must add, however, that from yesterday's sputum we have obtained a scanty growth of klebsiella. And for the first time, we have found some pseudomonas—but these unpleasant pathogens were not seen in sufficient amount to suggest that they were anywhere other than in the oral cavity."

Dr. Potgieter said he did not like the slow drop in the white cell count—from 27,390 to 24,600.

"Since we are tapering off the steroids, this points strongly to an over-whelming infection somewhere and specifically to the lungs. But if you're getting nothing from them, I don't know what to say other than continue the therapy for a while longer."

Dr. Thatcher felt we should broaden our defense against the more dangerous bacteria especially since we had now discovered pseudomonas—an uncommon but dangerous organism of the antibiotic era. Dr. Forder said cephaloridine was indicated against the specimen he had cultured—and we decided to administer one gram every eight hours.

We adjourned, expecting to find further improvement when we met that evening. Instead, we encountered an even more confusing situation. Another X ray revealed denser lung lesions with indications that new ones were forming. To confuse matters more, Dr. Forder reported no more pneumococci and only scanty pus cells, suggesting this specific infection was under control.

It could mean that Washkansky had another type of pneumonia—perhaps caused by a fungus or virus we had not yet discovered. If so, we had slight chance of saving him. Yet this was not at all certain. He might have multiple emboli—our first assumption—caused by multiple blood clots breaking away from the heart. Or he might still be fighting off pneumococcal pneumonia. Finally, there was the possibility that these lung shadows were immunologically induced as a response to a foreign heart—a condition known as transplant lung, and reported in some kidney transplants. If this was so, the correct treatment would be to increase the steroid drugs rather than reduce them. On the other hand, this would be completely incorrect if it was an infection.

After discussing all these possibilities—and lacking any evidence to support a change—we agreed to continue the therapy of heparin and penicillin until the next morning. This would give the drug an optimum time to take effect, and allow us to consider what next if Washkansky did not rally.

Almost immediately it was clear that there was going to be no rally. Struggling for air, he finally refused to take any more food—constraining us to insert a gastric tube through the nose. Besides this, a pathogenic fungus was grown from the scrotal swab, requiring his scrotum be painted with gentian violet every four hours. After that, an even more distressing symptom appeared: He began passing feces in bed and developed diarrhea, so that his linens were constantly dirty.

In this way, he deteriorated hour by hour, suffering more and more as he entered the night. The pain in his chest spread to his arms and legs, so that he refused to be moved, preferring to lie in his own feces rather than suffer the agony of movement.

It was heart-breaking to see this happen. I especially did not like it because Washkansky was a man of dignity—proud of being able once more to take care of himself. Yet now he had lost control, not only of what went into his mouth, but whatever emerged from him. He was in pain and somewhat numb with drugs, but he was also aware of what was happening to him. I worried that this might crush his spirit and cause him to give up.

So I came to see him shortly after midnight. He was awake and his arms were folded across his chest, with intravenous lines running in each arm, fastened with white adhesive tape. The gastric tube was in his nose, and he was breathing through his mouth.

"Hello, Louis—how goes it?"

He shook his head. On the bed table, the radio was softly playing "Good Night, Irene."

"I'll never get home by Christmas," he said.

"You might, Louis. There's a chance."

"No, not now."

He lifted his arms to indicate the intravenous lines. Once again he was bound to his bed.

"I'm losing every round," he said.

"You lost a few today, Louis, but we're still ahead. We can still make it."

"You think so?" he said.

"Yes, I'm sure of it."

He looked at me and I suddenly had the feeling that he was measuring me to see if I had the strength to tackle what lay ahead. I had come to give him courage and found him ready to give it back to me. It was buried in his reply.

"No," he said. "They haven't got either one of us yet—not by a long shot."

I touched his arm and he took my hand.

"I believe you," he said.

"Thank you, Louis," I said and left before he could see anything else in my eyes.

MONDAY, *December 18: Fifteenth Day*

Very quickly this became a dramatic morning. Upon reaching the ward, I found Washkansky had deteriorated still further. When I entered his room, he gave me a weak thumbs-up sign to say that he was in there, doing all he could to hold onto life and the belief that I would save him.

But it was a desperate gesture. He was now gasping for air in increasingly shallow drafts. His respiration rate had gone up to thirty-two, and with a stethoscope you could hear crepitation in the lungs, a sound resembling fine salt being thrown into a fire—tragic indicator of air urgently seeking entrance to millions of alveoli, or air sacs, now clogged or blocked by fluid.

The pulse was 110. The heart was doing what it could to meet the grave crisis in the lungs. At the same time, peripheral circulation was failing: The feet and hands were cold. Clearly, this man was going to die unless something was done to stop his decline. I went into the office with Bossie, and

when the morning X ray arrived, it confirmed the disease had spread further in the lungs, with mottled areas beginning to touch one another. At
this rate, the lungs would soon become sealed up and Washkansky would
die of asphyxiation.

I was scheduled to do an operation that morning, but with this before me
I had to cancel it. Then Eddie Steinhardt of CBS phoned to say he had set
the date for my appearance on "Face the Nation" in Washington. I told
him I could no longer go and when he persisted, I hung up—realizing this
was another mistake since it, in effect, told the press that we were in full
crisis.

"Damn it, Bossie, this man is going to die unless we do something.
We've got to find out what's going on in that lung."

"Professor, the change in this man in the last thirty-six hours is far too
fulminating. We are fighting something very big."

He'd been on night duty and looked like he had been fighting something
big. Solemn and haggard, he slumped into a chair and lit a cigarette.

Dr. "M. C." Botha, the pathologist in charge of tissue typing, arrived
early for the regular morning meeting. He took one look at us and did not
even bother to ask the condition of the patient.

"What next?" he said.

"I don't know," I said, "let's review this and see where we are. We
treated for a bacterial infection and knocked out the bacteria we found. So
far we've found nothing else, meaning we have no proof this is a bacterial
pneumonia. We have treated for embolism and this has had no effect. So it
is either not that, or it is so advanced that we can do nothing about it.
Next, it could be a virus infection. If it is, there is nothing we can do about
that, either, because at this stage he would be beyond recovery. That leaves
the possibility of an immunological pneumonia—an immunological attack
on the lungs."

"You mentioned that yesterday," said "M. C." "I've never seen it—have
you?"

"No, but Dr. Hume has described it in kidney transplants—a side effect
of the rejection process. The lungs develop a condition as though they had
been transplanted. It is called transplant lung."

The team members began to arrive and soon the office was crowded.
This was a showdown day and everyone came, excepting Val Schrire. I
reviewed our position again and said I felt the only possible course was to
treat the patient for transplant lung, with heavy doses of steroids—unless
someone else had a better diagnosis.

Dr. Werbeloff confirmed that the radiological picture showed progressive
decline, but there was no indication of what was causing it. It could be an
infection but it could also stem from an unknown immunological complication.

Dr. Mibashan said the blood analysis indicated infection.

"There continue to be toxic changes in the white cells. Besides granules, there are also vacuoles in the cells. If you take any of these slides and send them to ten of the world's top hematologists, I'd be surprised if less than nine would not agree that this is a grave bacterial infection."

This put us back to where we were three days ago—indicating a bacterial pneumonia but with no bacteria to prove it.

Dr. Forder quickly made clear that he had found none.

"Today's specimen of sputum showed numerous pus cells. The lung pathology is becoming quite marked—but we found no pathogenic bacteria."

"And you've grown no more klebsiella and pseudomonas from yesterday's samples?" asked Dr. Thatcher.

"None," said Dr. Forder.

"Strange," said Dr. Thatcher.

"Even more strange," said Professor Eales, "is something we found— Delta aminolevulinic acid. I've never seen it in urine in my life. I can only assume that some particular enzyme has been knocked out completely, but I can't say which one."

"What does it mean?" I asked.

"I don't know," he said with a frown.

"Certainly the enzymes indicate serious trouble," said Dr. Potgieter. "They've doubled in the last twenty-four hours. Even the SGOT has gone up from seventeen to thirty-six."

"What's the meaning of that?"

"It could mean infection of course," he said.

"I think Chris is on the right track," said "M. C." "This is a case of a transplant lung."

"I can't argue with that," said Dr. Thatcher, "I've never seen one."

"Nor can I," said Dr. Forder.

"For me," said "M. C.," "it's a matter of treating the patient for rejection."

The discussion continued for some time, but it never got beyond that point. Some members felt we were dealing with an infection but did not know what it was. Others were ready to accept the diagnosis of a transplant lung—if I was sure of it.

I was not sure, however, and after the meeting went back to my office to study David Hume's report.

"M. C." Botha came along, and together we compared Hume's case study with our knowledge of Washkansky's illness. It seemed to fit in every detail.

"Maybe this is it," I said.

"I'll back you on it," said "M. C."

"Thank you, but I'm not sure. I want to consider it some more."

I returned to the ward to find Georgie Hall again changing the bed linen—more diarrhea. There were also signs of mottling on his legs: spotty patches indicating circulatory failure. His feet had become colder and his breathing more difficult. He looked at me and only his eyes spoke: Is there still a chance?

"Yes, Louis," I said. "We're now going to start a new treatment."

Bossie had refused to go home, and, together with Coert Venter, we went into the office. I called Dr. Forder and asked if he had any further evidence of bacterial infection—or of virus or fungus. He had none.

I hung up and turned to Bossie and Coert.

"All right, let's start treatment for rejection."

I outlined the therapy—hydrocortisone, 100 milligrams and actinomycin C, 200 micrograms intravenously. We would also raise the Imuran to 250 milligrams and prednisone to 200 milligrams in divided doses over the next twenty-four hours. This was heavy immunosuppression, but it was needed at this stage to be effective.

Having made this decision, I was convinced this was right, and it was only a matter of time before there would be improvement. When I phoned in later, Coert would have good news. He would say: "You know, Professor, there's been a dramatic change in his condition. The temperature is normal, and he's breathing much easier." That was how it would be.

A blood report arrived. Bossie took it and passed it to me.

"Looks as though he'll have to go back into the oxygen tent."

He was right. The oxygen PO_2 level—a measurement of the oxygen-carrying capacity of the blood—had fallen from 100 to 70. We were going steadily downhill.

"All right," I said. "Also we'd better connect him to the monitor for a constant check on his heart action."

"The poor guy," said Bossie. "He was so happy when we took the tent away."

"It doesn't have to be for long," I said. "It'll help him, then we can remove it."

Bossie's blue eyes blinked slowly in disbelief. It irritated me.

"Don't be so pessimistic, man. Part of the cure is a belief in your own ability and in your treatment. The patient can sense this—especially if you don't have it."

Bossie nodded—but still said nothing.

I returned home and with reluctance began to dress for an official dinner. Deirdre told me my wild fig tree was dying, and I went out on the lawn to see if it was true.

I had planted it on the shore of the lake, near the docking shed, hoping it would be strong enough to withstand the burning heat of the southeast wind. At first it had done well and put out little green leaves, but now, in the twilight by the lake, the leaves were black from the heat and wind.

Deirdre followed me out, and together we felt the leaves and their brittle limbs.

"You're right," I said. "This tree is going to die."

"How sad," she said. "All it needs is a few little leaves, and this has been taken away. Such a little thing—and so much."

"The edge between life and death is just that—a few little leaves, a little patch of lung."

Before leaving, I phoned the ward. Coert Venter said Washkansky was sleeping and responding well to steroids. He was breathing easily under the tent and seemed to be better off.

"You can tell he's better," said Venter. "He's protesting again.

"What about?"

"The tent—he didn't want it and he asked for you."

"What did you say?"

"I said you'd be around as soon as you could, but it didn't stop him. Even after we had the tent up he kept asking for you."

There it was again: *He asked for you.* But it was not the same this time. It did not mean the same thing. Louis Washkansky was going to live. He would not die.

After the dinner, I drove back to the hospital and found him asleep. His chart indicated he was holding his own. I waited for a while, then decided to leave.

"When he awakes," I said to Coert Venter, "Tell him I came by. If he asks for me again, tell him I'll be here early in the morning."

On the way home, I told myself again that it was only a chance phrase. It had no meaning other than that.

TUESDAY, *December 19: Sixteenth Day*

This was a morning of two frightening episodes. It began with Washkansky awakening in a mentally confused state, and incapable of coherent speech. Coert Venter quickly discovered it was hypoglycemia—too little sugar in the blood—and corrected it by giving him glucose through the nasal tube.

The second drama began with an urgent call from the hematology laboratory. Analyzing blood taken that morning at 6 A.M. showed Washkansky's white cell count had fallen from 22,200 to 5,640—an incredible drop, placing him in real danger. This was something far more serious than insufficient sugar in the blood. Without white cells, which destroy bacteria and dead cells, he was stripped of the means of defending himself from injury or infection.

The team met hurriedly—the crisis evident in their haste of arrival and manner of speaking to one another. We immediately discussed the white cell drop.

Dr. Potgieter noted that the destruction was mainly of neutrophils—a type of white cell.

"Since this occurs immediately after a change in therapy, it might be caused by the actinomycin C—though this doesn't rule out a toxemia of infection, or even both."

Most everyone agreed to this: It was either caused by actinomycin or else the white cells were being destroyed as they moved into an area of overwhelming infection. We decided to eliminate the actinomycin and also the Imuran—while raising the amount of the other antirejection drug, prednisone, from 200 to 400 milligrams.

It was also decided to give the patient a transfusion of white cells to help build up his supply, as well as some ordinary blood since his hemoglobin had dropped.

After the meeting, "M. C." Botha hastened back to his laboratory and put in a call to the Western Province Blood Transfusion Service, which keeps a panel of donors on stand-by for such emergencies. From the blood of four donors, he skimmed off the leukocytes and suspended them in a plasma solution. The first transfusion was given to Washkansky in the early afternoon. There was a rise in the white cell count, but it quickly fell off from 4,600 to 4,000. At 7 P.M., after the second transfusion, the count rose once more, but then fell to 4,600—with no donor neutrophils to be seen. It was like pouring water onto sand—even as we gave the injection, it kept falling.

We discussed this at the meeting that evening, and there seemed little we could do—other than hope that our decision to halt the two most powerful antirejection drugs would allow a return of the white cell count. As protection against further infection, we increased the cephaloridine to two grams every eight hours. To help regulate the heart through the crisis, we again put up an isoprenaline drip at twenty drops a minute.

Yet despite all our efforts Louis Washkansky's lungs continued to close in on him. He turned blue from lack of oxygen, and it finally became necessary to put him back on artificial respiration. It was sad to come to this point for it meant cutting off all speech between us, and was like saying good-bye to part of him.

I came to tell him about it. Under the tent, he was fighting for air with a respiratory rate of thirty-two. His oxygen PO_2 was down to seventy. He was blue and haggard.

"Louis, we're going to have to put in an endotracheal tube again to help you breathe."

He shook his head.

"No, Doc."

"Yes, Louis."

He shook his head and with both hands grabbed the sides of the plastic tent to prevent us from lifting it up.

"Louis, there is little we can do other than this right now. We have to get some oxygen into you so that you can fight off your lung trouble. By tomorrow there should be some improvement."

He looked at me through the plastic cover and still said nothing.

"Louis, you said you believed me, remember? Well now you have to believe me on this."

He nodded that he understood but said no more. Dr. Ozinsky came in to insert the tube through the nose. When it was in place and attached to the Bird respirator, Louis closed his eyes and rolled away. I left the room for my office.

A call came from Mrs. Washkansky, and I took it.

"Professor, the newspaper people keep calling. They say that Louis is dying."

"They are lying to you, Mrs. Washkansky."

"Thank God."

"Don't listen to them. Don't answer the phone."

"All right, if you say so. But then how will I know when you are calling me?"

"Then get someone to answer it for you."

"I've done that. My sister-in-law, Mrs. Sklar, is here with me. But then she doesn't know what to say when they ask about Louis."

"Tell them to call the hospital."

"How is he today—better?"

She said it with her voice rising, and I imagined her face, the eyes unblinking, waiting for an answer.

"He's . . . holding his own, Mrs. Washkansky. We think we've isolated his trouble and there will be some improvement."

"Oh, thank God . . ."

"We will let you know—all right?"

"Yes, God bless you, Professor."

WEDNESDAY–THURSDAY, *December 20–21:*
Seventeenth and Eighteenth Days

This day began as had all the others in the week before it—without any sign of how we could turn back from the path now plunging us into the unseen valley. The morning was passed with intermittent visits to Washkansky's bedside and in the usual team huddle—collective witness of our inability to halt the rapid decline of the patient.

Shortly after one o'clock, Bossie phoned me at my office in the medical school.

"Professor, I think you'd better come over right away. Forder just called. He's grown klebsiella and pseudomonas from yesterday's sputum samples."

"Where's he now?"

"On his way up."

"I'm coming."

When I arrived, Dr. Forder was in the office with Bossie who handed me the bacterial report:

. . . from the sputum specimen of Dec. 19, heavy growths of klebsiella and pseudomonas have been obtained. This indicates the patient is suffering from extensive bilateral pneumonia due to these organisms . . .

"My God," I said. "We should have known. It was there all along."

"Only it wasn't," said Bossie. "It was there, and then it disappeared."

"It was there," said Dr. Forder, "in the oral cavity and then worked down into the lungs. Probably after we treated for pneumococci, it walked in and took over."

The penicillin had wiped out one organism, but it had also exposed Washkansky's defenseless body to further infection. Two other organisms had entered and not reappeared until after seizing almost all of the lungs. This reduced the margin of recovery to hours, even minutes. We had to move immediately.

"Carbenicillen is particularly directed against both these bugs, especially the pseudomonas," said Dr. Forder. "They are also sensitive to cephaloridine and gentamycin."

We decided to use all three—one gram of carbenicillen per hour through the intravenous drip, plus 80 milligrams of gentomycin and two grams of cephaloridine over eight-hour intervals.

Scrubbing quickly, we entered the room. Washkansky was asleep as Bossie put up the cephaloridine drip, but he began to awaken when we moved him to inject into his thigh the remaining antibiotics. At that moment, I was feeling his lower legs for peripheral circulation, and I shook one foot to help him wake up.

"Louis, listen to me . . ."

His eyes opened.

"Louis, we've got the answer. Do you hear me? We've found the way to correct your trouble."

He raised an arm with two intravenous lines—wiping his eyes as though unable to see clearly.

"Louis, it's me—Professor Barnard. We have isolated the trouble in your lungs and have begun to treat it."

His open mouth closed once, and reopened—no sound. The vocal cords were paralyzed by the endotracheal tube. Again the mouth closed once, then twice. What was he trying to tell me? What words were formed by lips closing once, then twice?

Tell me. Tell me more.

"Listen, Louis, it's a matter of time. You have to hold on, just keep holding, and we can make it. Do you understand me?"

Again he tried to speak, and again the hand was raised. I realized then it was a gesture of despair at his inability to make himself understood.

"Louis, I understand . . . I see you, I know what you are saying."

The unspoken words were not important. We had understood that we shared a diminishing margin of time. Within it he would find his life—if we had time enough to eliminate multiplying millions of germs within his lungs.

It was a question of whether or not the drugs could act against the bacteria before they sealed off those remaining air pockets capable of putting oxygen into the blood. This still-functioning area of the lung was Louis Washkansky's beachhead onto life. If he could hold onto it long enough for the drugs to turn back the klebsiella and pseudomonas, he would be able to slowly regain more and more of his lungs until they were able once more to accept all the air needed for life. If he could not hold onto this beachhead, death would follow from asphyxiation.

So I shook his foot, as one blowing a bugle to awaken a camp. It was vital that he use every effort within him to retain whatever he had left. The more he was convinced of this, the better were his chances. Indeed, he had to be encouraged to believe it. I spoke to Dr. Venter, and we agreed to call his wife.

Ann Washkansky arrived with her brother and brother-in-law. She wore a bright green suit, and she had been crying. Her face, which seemed made to hold a smile, bore the violation of a trampled garden.

I described the situation and how important it was for Louis to keep struggling.

"He has a chance, a fighting chance," I said. "It's not a large one, but it's there and he must be made to know it."

"Professor, I'll do everything I can. Tell me what it is to do."

"Go and talk to him. Make him realize the importance of not giving up now."

"Me alone?" she asked, looking at those with her.

"Yes, you alone. They can come afterward."

She scrubbed and put on the gown, mask, boots, and gloves and entered the room—going straight to his bedside.

Five days ago she had stood there with her husband, holding his hand and smiling before the television cameras, while they talked about being home by Christmas. Now he lay on his back, the bed slightly raised to help his breathing, tubes in both nostrils, intravenous leads into both arms, and electrode lines from his chest to the heart monitor. Eyes that had reflected love for his wife now were closed. And the voice that had risen to the memory of love was now muted by a tube in the windpipe.

"Louis, here I am. They let me come to see you."

He opened his eyes and made an effort to nod, but his wife was not sure he recognized her.

"Louis, can you hear me? It's me—Ann."

He nodded again.

"Speak to me, Louis."

Sister Hall explained he could not speak.

"He has a tube down his throat," she said.

"Where?" asked Ann, seeing only tubes in his nose.

"It goes into the throat, to help him breathe."

This caused her to move closer to the bedside—as though she might hear something, anyway. She stood next to the bed and put her gloved hand on the pillow.

"Louis, Professor Barnard says you must fight. You must keep on fighting. He says you can make it if you don't give up. Louis . . . are you listening to me?"

She straightened his sheet fold.

"Please, Louis, please do it for us. You told me, 'Ann, it's in the bag, you must believe it's in the bag,' so I'm still believing it's in the bag. You said so yourself, and I'm believing it now. I'm not believing anything else."

His eyes closed slowly.

"Louis, please don't . . ."

He opened them and moved an arm toward her. She took his hand, holding it as though he had given her an enormous gift.

"Thank you," she said, pressing his hand into hers.

When she looked up again, he was smiling, too.

"You'll get well," she said, "and it'll be like old times. You'll say, 'Let's go to Durban,' and we'll get in the car and go there—just like that . . . like the last time when you found that native woman singing in the street. The big fat one with the two kids, you remember? We went around Durban for two hours, listening to her sing in front of hotels. Only she was singing mostly for you, because you couldn't stop giving her things. She must have thought it was her birthday. I remember telling you 'For God's sake, it's night already'—but no, you wanted to hear one more song. So I said to myself, 'That's my Louis. If he wasn't that way it wouldn't be Louis and anyway I couldn't love anybody but him . . .' "

She could speak no more, and those who were in the room left them alone.

After that, the other members of the family paid brief visits, and then went home—everyone hoping and praying that Louis would be able to hold onto his small beachhead of life.

We helped where we could, rushing in support when he fell back in one or another sector. Two pints of blood raised the oxygen-bearing hemoglobin from 11 to 13. A subsequent fall in blood pressure was corrected with adrenalin. The heart rate rose to 120 and to help it through the varying demands, we raised the isoprenaline from 15 to 25 drops per minute. The enzymes stabilized, though remaining quite high, and the urine output held without serious change. His respiration rate, fixed by the machine at 20, was raised to 23.

At first he did seem to hold his own. Then he began to lose in some areas. The white cell count fell further—to 2,790—a very dangerous level, leaving him without the ability to fight infection. At the same time, we witnessed something even more serious. The lungs were returning blood to the arteries without the proper amount of oxygen—turning the patient blue. The beachhead was being seized.

We needed Dr. Ozinsky immediately but did not have to call him. He showed up at that moment, walking in with his usual smile and a self-conscious disclaimer: "May I come in? They say this is the best place in town to hide from the newspaper reporters."

Within a few minutes, he rapidly secured our position. The automatic Bird respirator, working on normal atmosphere, was capable of delivering only 40 per cent oxygen. To increase the percentage and pressure, Ozzie connected the endotracheal tube to a Boyle's anesthetic machine. This allowed him to ventilate the lungs by manually pumping the bag and gave him the ability to deliver any level of oxygen up to 100 per cent.

It had the double effect of lifting not only Washkansky's oxygen PO_2 level, but also our spirits. We felt that nothing could touch us now. Ozzie stood by the bed pumping the bag at twenty-three times a minute and even he seemed to believe that we could hold to this last line of defense—forcing oxygen into the last remaining area of Washkansky's lungs.

"I'm not even giving 100 per cent oxygen," he said. "We still have a margin to play around with."

I left for my office and found Solly Sklar, the brother-in-law, waiting in the corridor.

"Hello, Doctor. So what's new?"

"There's been a slight improvement."

"You mean he's better?"

"Yes—we took him off the respirator and we're forcing oxygen into him. So there's a slight improvement. We may have a chance."

"Dr. Barnard, may I phone my sister and tell her?"

"Tell her exactly what I said—don't elaborate."

He phoned from the office. When he had his sister on the line, he looked at me to make sure he got it right.

"Ann? Now don't get excited. I can only tell you there's been a slight improvement . . . no, don't elaborate . . . just that—a slight improvement. I got it from Professor Barnard himself. There may be a chance. Yes, you can tell all the family."

We had fallen back to our last line of defense—from oxygen tent, to automatic respirator, to hand pump with pure oxygen. If we could hold at this point there was a chance—for immediately with the rise in the oxygen level Washkansky began to improve. It was simply a matter of putting oxygen in his blood. If we could keep the PO_2 above sixty, the chance would become a reality.

At the bedside, Ozzie sought to save as much ammunition as possible—regulating the oxygen to support the patient, yet never giving more than needed. Slowly, however, a flow of 40 per cent oxygen with the respirator became 70 per cent—with only 30 per cent reserve. And as we approached midnight, it became necessary to fall back on this reserve, pumping 80 per cent pure oxygen, then 90—and finally 100.

We had reached the limit. With all reserves in the line, we had to hold onto what remained—or lose the battle. This was Washkansky's final chance and for a short while—between midnight and 1 A.M.—he seemed to be making it.

Ozzie was superb. Besides pumping without rest, he was the standard bearer of our morale.

"I'm getting improvement, definite improvement," he said, repeating it whenever there was the slightest reason to do so.

He also spoke to Washkansky, making small talk as though they were sitting together in a clubroom.

"You do feel better, don't you?" he asked, getting an occasional nod in return.

When this did not come, he would accept a motion of the eye or a moving hand as a reasonable reply and plunge on to some other subject. Occasionally, he brought Sister Papendieck into the game.

"What's all this talk about you and Mr. Washkansky having a dance date when he gets out of here?"

So it was that Ozzie sought to conjoin his own indomitable spirit with the last reserve of oxygen—much as a regimental flag would be grabbed from the hands of a falling bearer and carried forward yet a few feet more.

It fell, of course. Slowly the PO_2 level went down to sixty—then to fifty and to forty. Washkansky registered the fall before we obtained readings from the blood. His body became cyanosed, or blue, as the arterial blood lost its oxygen.

It was the beginning of the end. We refused to admit it, however, and desperately struggled on, doing what little we could. Ozzie increased the rate of respiration, and we raised the isoprenaline drip to 30—but with little effect. Slowly, irrevocably, the last open area of the lungs was being overrun by invading *pseudomonas aeruginosa*.

Louis Washkansky was now condemned to die for lack of oxygen. And we were condemned to watch it happen—spectators to a drowning. A human being who had been near death and then returned to life was once more approaching that divide with no hope of turning back again. He was taking with him a heart which had also made this same trip once before—going even beyond it into the realm of death—yet returning to live for eighteen days with a stranger who was now carrying it back again, this time to be more securely fixed in the chamber of its death.

On the monitor, the heart beat on in beautiful rhythm, crossing the screen with twelve beats—a pulse of 120—as though it had not learned what lay ahead, or perhaps felt that it could escape once more.

For it would die within the chest of Louis Washkansky as it had died within Denise Darvall—suffocated by lack of oxygen. It would be subjected to the same cycle of blood returning to it without the means of life. Once again, it would obediently pump the impure blood up to the lungs for cleansing, only to have it returned uncleansed and heavy with carbon dioxide. So it would go, on and on, until the heart would begin to beat wildly for support that would never come—fluttering like a bird trying to rise, falling finally onto its plain of death, never to rise again.

On the monitor, it beat on, oblivious to what lay ahead.

Beep . . . beep . . . beep.

There were going to be two deaths here—a man and a heart. Two deaths at the same time, within a double beep.

Beep . . . beep . . . beep-beep.

I couldn't bear to look at the screen. There was such beauty in the line as it went into each of its phases—the soaring ventricles sweeping down for an instant onto the valley of the intersystole, followed by a slight rise from the receiving atria, then rolling into another flight of the great pumping muscles—flight and descent, followed by rest and roll, flight-descent, rest-roll . . .

So it went, like a bird turning forever in fixed arcs, constant as the sweep of day into night, fixed as the stars, permanent as the tides. If life was a miracle, this was its epicenter—and the termination of life in this way was the destruction of a miracle.

It was too much to witness, and I turned away to look at Louis Washkansky—only to find his eyes, covered now with a slight glaze, speaking for the muted lips.

You asked me to believe. Is this the end of belief?

I don't know, Louis. I don't know . . .

It's like drowning in a child's pool in three feet of water. I can see everyone on the lawn around me.

We're trying to reach you, Louis.

But you do nothing except touch my hands and feet. It's going higher. It's reaching for the liver, and after that the heart—and then what?

I don't know, Louis.

I'll tell you—a glacier on top of a jumping frog.

sliss-SSSH!

It was Ozzie adjusting a connection to the oxygen lead, while Coert Venter continued pumping the bag.

"We've got to do something more," I said. "We've got to give him more time."

Ozzie looked up from the Boyle's pump—gray-blue eyes questioning mine, as though in pumping oxygen into Washkansky he had also fused something of himself and so became invested with the same question: How will you do it?

"We can do it with the heart-lung machine."

"What?"

"We can put him back on the oxygenator. It will clean his blood and give us the time we need to fight the infection."

Ozzie looked at Washkansky as though he wanted to ask him what he thought of it.

"How much time do you think that will give you?" he said.

"Twelve, maybe twenty-four hours."

"But we've never had a man on bypass for longer than five hours."

"That doesn't mean it can't be longer. And even five hours might be all we need."

Ozzie shook his head and took the bag from Coert Venter.

"I'll pump," he said. "You try talking to him."

"How will you do it?" asked Coert.

"A thoracotomy—we don't have to open the sternum or touch the heart."

"I mean, where will you do it?"

"In the theater, or here in the ward."

Ozzie moaned.

"If you bring everything from the theater up here," he said, "there won't be room for anybody to breathe—even the patient."

"In the theater, then."

"But are you sure it will work?" asked Coert.

"No, I'm not sure of anything—except that we have to do something. Don't you see it?"

"I agree, Prof, but I don't see . . ."

"Then don't *see* it—just *feel* it. We can't let this man die. We can't!"

I left the room to call Val Schrire. The phone rang on and on with no reply. It was almost 3 A.M. Finally, his wife answered.

"Ruth, can you get Val, please?"

"What is it?"

"I must speak to him."

Val came on, a little sleepy.

"What is it, Chris?"

"Val, we can't ventilate Washkansky any further and I'm considering putting him back on the oxygenator."

"On the what?"

"On the heart-lung machine. It'll give us more time . . ."

"More time for what?"

"To control his infection. We're treating the real thing now, and if we can just carry him a short while more perhaps we can overcome it, because there's no doubt, as soon as he gets oxygen he improves rapidly. So all we need is time."

"Chris, you have no more time. It was up yesterday or maybe even the day before. It's all over."

"My God, how can you say that?"

"Listen, Chris, Washkansky is clinically lost. Everybody knows it except you . . ."

"Everybody doesn't know it. We had a chance until tonight, and we still have a chance. I mean we don't know that we haven't a chance—not until we try everything."

"All right, try everything. That's what makes you a surgeon. You have to do something. I'm not saying you should stop doing everything possible to save him and also extend his life. But to put him back on the pump is madness. You'll increase his agony, and torment everybody else."

I did not know how to reply. Was I really proposing to increase his agony for no end—other than to delay the recognition of my own failure? Was I subjecting him to further pain merely because I refused to give up? How much of this was now myself—and how much Washkansky? If there was a chance, then anything was worth trying, and it was all for Washkansky. If there was none, then it was all for myself, and the heart-lung machine was madness.

"Chris, are you there?"

"Yes, so you think there is no chance left?"

"No—I'm sorry to have to say it."

"All right—good-bye."

I hung up and I went back to the room.

"Coert," I said, "you'd better call his family and tell them."

Ann Washkansky, the Wife

"Dr. Venter called me again and I went there with my brother-in-law, my brother, and my son, telling myself it was not possible. I had a wonderful life with him, and I just didn't want him to die.

"So I told myself something would happen—another miracle, maybe, like the transplant. Professor Barnard would do something.

"But when we got there, he came out of the room, throwing his hands up in the air.

" 'We've done everything, everything,' he said. 'I don't know what to do any more.'

"I had never seen him like that. He looked like somebody demented."

" 'It's too much,' he said. 'The heart, it keeps on going. It's a perfect heart. There is nothing wrong with it.'

" 'And Louis?' I asked.

" 'Louis?' he said. 'Your husband kept his word. I'm ashamed that we couldn't keep ours.'

"This frightened me and I said: 'Is he dead?'

" 'No, not that,' he said and left me.

"I was so upset when I put on the sterilized clothes that I forgot my gloves and mask. When I came into the room, I saw Dr. Venter in the corner and Sister Papendieck by the bed—and Louis there, lying on his back. He looked dark, sort of blue, and when I came up to him I saw his eyes were open but he did not see me.

"I called him by his name. I said: 'Louis, Louis—it's me. I've come to be with you.'

"It was no use. His eyes were glazed and I don't think he heard me. But I wasn't sure of that. He couldn't speak, but I thought maybe he could hear. Maybe he wanted me to say something to him.

"So I said: 'Louis, can I do something? Tell me, Louis, what I can do.'

"He didn't even move, but his eyes were open, and I thought maybe he wanted to look at me. So I moved him to look at me. His hands were cold but his face was warm and then I realized I didn't have any gloves on and no mask, and it was the first time I had touched my husband this way since before the operation because they were always worried about my infecting him.

"I thought if he was going to die, it no longer made any difference. So I held him a little bit and I talked to him about how wonderful our life had been.

"Like I told you, maybe he could hear me. Maybe he wanted to know. Maybe he wanted someone to hold him. At least I could do that, because he must have been so lonely there with no one touching him.

"So I said: 'Louis, you don't have to say anything because I'm not going anywhere. I'm staying with you now. I'm not going away.'

"Then I saw Sister Papendieck, sitting in a chair on the other side of the bed, and in her lap was the black bag they use to pump him. She was pumping and crying. Her mask was wet from the tears streaming down her face.

"And I said: 'Sister Papendieck, let me help—let me help you pump a little bit.'"

One by one, the members of his family came to see him and shortly after 4:30 A.M. we had to ask them to leave the room. His stomach had begun to distend, and it became necessary to suction off some of the liquids.

"I think you'd better go home now," I said.

"I don't want to go," his wife said. "I don't want to leave him."

"All right," I said, "you can sit in the office."

She had been very brave, but now she began to cry, and her brother put his arm around her.

"Annie, there's nothing more we can do waiting here. It's better we go home like the Professor says. They have important things to do."

"I can help," she said. "I can help Sister Papendieck."

"Michael needs your help more," the brother said.

"He might need me," she said. "He might ask for me, and I have to be here."

"Ann, Michael needs you more. He's closed himself up in the car and is all broken up."

"What's happened to Michael?"

"He asked for the keys to the car and I said what do you want them for? Never mind, he said, give them to me. And now he's down there in the car, weeping all alone. I think we'd better take him home."

So they left, the two men and the woman, and from the porch you could see them come out and go across to the car below the palm tree where I had parked my car. The boy had locked himself in Louis' red Zephyr and would not open it until Ann spoke to him.

"Michael, we have to talk to you—open the door."

Yet what could they say to him? Nothing. He didn't need them now. He needed only to be alone so that he could see his father once more and perhaps hear his words—as I had heard my father speak to me on a cliff above the sea. When he had found the image of his father in him, no one could take it away—not even death. And when people asked him about it, he could tell them.

My father was a man, a real man. He was so big I thought he would never die.

He didn't die, Michael. As long as you see his image and hear his words, he will never die.

Sometimes I see him, especially the way he laughed and how he used to put his hand on my shoulder.

He loved you and he was proud of you.

He used to say, "Kid, you're going to be bigger than your old man. I'm going to look at you and say 'That's my boy, that's him all right—did you ever see anything like him?' " I was always so little, and I hoped I would not disappoint him.

You won't disappoint him.

Never.

Then your father will never die, Michael.

The car motor started, breaking the night silence. Slowly it pulled out and started down the hill, taking into the city all that was left of Louis Washkansky's family.

It was shortly before dawn and from the porch you could see the lights of Cape Flats starting to go out. Behind me in the room, I could hear the steady beep of his heart and the oxygen being pumped into him. Once I heard Ozzie say that there was an improvement.

"He looks a little better to me," he said.

"No, he's still deteriorating," said Coert Venter.

Dr. Venter was a cool clinician. He could see it coming, and he was not going to turn away. Ozzie looked elsewhere to find fresh hope amid the wreckage of eighteen days of hope. Occasionally, Ozzie or Coert said something to Sister Papendieck who worked in silence. And when Ozzie needed a rest, she pumped for him, or sometimes Dr. Venter took over.

Shortly after 5 A.M., there was a rapid deterioration. The circulation fell off, and we gave intravenous calcium—but it did not help. The lungs began to return an increasing volume of venous blood and he turned dark blue, almost black.

Despite this, the heart beat on in regular rhythm—once again refusing to die, as it had with Denise Darvall. I was to witness the same struggle, only now it was much closer. At the first one, we had been spectators to the death of a stranger's heart. This one was a member of the family. It had been carried in our hands, we had assisted in its rebirth and nursed it into life.

The first cry of help came at 6:30 A.M.—the symmetrical green line breaking its pattern with extrasystoles shooting up wildly against a load that had become unbearable. The child was going under, the immortal bird was floundering, the miracle was fading.

Beep . . . beep . . . beep-beep . . . BEEP . . . BEEP-BEEP!

I closed my eyes against the erratic green line and turned away, going out again onto the porch.

Dawn was coming and only the far mountains continued to cling to the shapes of night. There was something about this hour—the slow exchange of night for day, the soundless creation of a new canopy of light—which caused life to fall back, mute and naked, at its lowest ebb. Most people die at dawn, as though night was a temporary death to be perpetually defeated at 20,000 dawns—until one of them came too late.

This was to be his last one and the last one for that incredible heart—

two deaths at dawn. Living, they were together. Dying, they became two. It was this division that ended it all, taking with it one life and something of myself. For my life was also under this dawn. From birth, it had built toward one moment in an operating theater when a blue heart turned red with life, and a man was reborn. At that moment, two lives had been fused into one. My life had found its meaning there, nowhere else, and now the dying of this one life was my death, too.

Inside the room, they continued to watch the rise and fall of the heart on the monitor and finally it was Coert Venter who told me.

"Professor, it's gone into fibrillation."

I returned to the room to find the line rolling slowly—like an ocean settling after a storm. And then suddenly, it shot across the screen: one flat green line.

Sister Papendieck began to cry. She was a wonderful woman, and I think it was this which made it more than I could bear. I thanked each one of them, and then I went out into the doctor's tearoom and just stood there for a while.

CHAPTER 29

I WANTED TO LEAVE, to go away somewhere—but Bossie arrived to remind me this was not possible.

"Have you arranged for a postmortem?"

"No."

"I'll phone Professor Thomson and Dr. Forder."

"All right."

We had to do the postmortem immediately, while the tissues were fresh for study. Inevitably, this would come as a shock to Ann Washkansky. For Orthodox Jews, the body is the temple where *Ruah,* the spirit of God, dwells on the earth. After death, it is to be treated with extreme respect, and postmortem mutilation is not allowed. Yet this was essential for future transplants, and we had to do it.

"Have you obtained permission?"

"Mrs. Washkansky's coming now," said Bossie.

I started to leave.

"Where are you going, Prof?"

"I don't know."

"Will you be in your office?"

"I don't know."

"I'll call you there."

I walked out of the hospital and my car was there, but I did not take it. It was better to walk, just walk, and I started down the hill with the sun in my eyes—not caring about anything, except to get away.

Eventually I came to the bottom road next to the cemetery. Its gravestones were gray and ugly and tilted in every direction—inevitably the dead were abandoned. I turned away, going down a narrow lane that ran between the animal house and the laboratory where we had done the dog transplants. Behind it was the postmortem theater, which would soon receive Washkansky for examination. A door connected them both, so that you could walk from one to the other—eighteen steps from a dog to a corpse. That was how far we had come: eighteen steps. The flight toward immortality—amid a chorus of barking dogs, squealing pigs, screaming baboons, and one man saying *I had a dream*—had ended on a cold marble slab.

Further down the lane, I came to my office in the medical school. At that hour—it was shortly after 7:30 A.M.—there was no one. The corridor had been filled with journalists for eighteen days, but now it was empty. The phone in my secretary's office, which had rung with calls from around the world, was silent. Next to it lay a copy of *Time,* my picture on the cover stained with the brown halo of a coffee cup.

Did I look like that? The right ear was higher than the left, the jaw was lopsided, and the lips and mouth were edematous—as though I was dead. Only the eyes were alive and they looked like my father's, making it even more unreal. I was dead, and all that remained were my father's eyes. The artist's concept of a human heart dangled over my head, like a tropical fruit with red and blue roots stripped of their dark loam, seeking to insert themselves into my left shoulder where rode a black-lettered epaulet: Dr. Christiaan Barnard.

I shuddered and went into my office. Even this seemed unreal—as if it belonged to someone else. Sitting down at my desk made no difference. Nothing altered the sudden sense of being a ghost—a face on last week's magazine with the eyes of my father and the mouth of a dead man.

I glanced at the urgent file on my desk: telegrams, letters, invitations to appear at universities, civic groups, and medical gatherings. They came from all over the world—Japan, Australia, France, Canada, the United States. Among them was a letter from CBS, saying all arrangements had been made for me to appear on their nationwide news show, "Face the Nation."

. . . we are pleased to advise you that both Dr. Michael E. DeBakey and Dr. Adrian Kantrowitz have accepted to appear on the panel with you. It has been scheduled for December 24 in our Washington studios . . .

My secretary had put a red line under "December 24" with a note in the margin: "Didn't you tell me you canceled this? It's only four days away!?!?"

I had canceled it. I had told Eddie Steinhardt that I was not going. He had done nothing about it, or else this letter had been sent before receiving his message. Either way, I was now in an awkward position. How could you reply to such a letter, and what would CBS tell DeBakey and Kantrowitz?

Professor Barnard cannot come. His patient is dead.

Was that it? Or was it something else?

Professor Barnard cannot come because his patient died and he has lost confidence in himself . . .

That was more like it.

Professor Barnard came in for a crash-landing at dawn, December 21, in Ward C-2 of the Groote Schuur Hospital His co-pilot, Mr. Louis Washkansky, was killed instantly. Professor Barnard walked away from the crash, visibly shaken. Preparations have been made for another take-off with Dr. Philip Blaiberg, as soon as they have found a donor heart—provided Professor Barnard hasn't lost his nerve . . .

There was a knock at the door, and Dr. Jacques Roux came in.

"I thought you'd be here," he said.

"How'd you know?"

"We heard it on the radio. I'm damn sorry, Chris."

He had heard it on the radio and had come, knowing I would be alone and lost. That was Jacques. Our friendship had begun when we were rival registrars and Jacques had the grace to congratulate me on my victory with the gall bladder operation. It had continued through the years, even though we worked in different hospitals and did not often see each other. And now he had heard of my defeat and had come to be with me.

"I was in the shower," he said, "and my children came to tell me."

That was how it would be all over the city—children running to their parents, crying out: "Washy's dead!" And all over the world people would hear the news and look at one another: Louis Washkansky, the first man to live with a transplanted human heart, died this morning at the Groote Schuur Hospital in Cape Town. He lived eighteen days with the heart of a twenty-five-year-old girl . . .

"I crash-landed, Jacques."

"Yes," he said, "but you flew. You flew for eighteen days—nothing can take that away from you."

"Except that we crashed and the patient is dead."

"No—not even his death can cancel what you've done. If he had died on the operating table, or lived only a few hours, it might be different. But this man lived long enough to begin a new life. He opened the way for others. He is a hero everywhere, and you are part of it. Don't think otherwise."

"No, Jacques, we crashed because of my mistakes. I should not have used cobalt treatment. I gave too many antirejection drugs. He got an infection because we lowered his resistance too much. And we didn't correctly diagnose that, until too late."

"Chris, who hasn't lost patients from mistakes? You were working with the unknown, feeling your way. You were in the dark. How can you blame yourself if you felt around for the door and ran into the wall? Now you know better. Now you have something to work with, and it'll be different next time."

"I don't know if there'll be a next time, Jacques. Even with what we know now, it'll still be working in the dark and I've lost my nerve. I'm afraid, Jacques. I'm afraid of the dark."

"After a death, we all feel that way, Chris. But then your confidence comes back as you start to work. That's why you have to do another transplant. You've no other choice."

I shook my head and for a while we said nothing—until the phone rang. It was Bossie, saying the postmortem was ready.

"You've got permission?"

"Yes—from Mrs. Washkansky. I explained it was necessary to help us with other transplants. She said, 'If Mr. Darvall said yes, how can we say no?'—and then she signed it."

I could imagine the permission form on the backside of the pink folder holding Washkansky's papers: I, Mrs. Ann Washkansky, hereby give consent for an autopsy to be performed on my husband, Louis Washkansky . . . 21 December 1967. And then Ann signing it, tears falling onto the paper.

"Are you coming, Prof?"

"Yes."

"They're gathering there now."

Jacques walked with me up the lane to the postmortem theater. Louis Washkansky was already there when we arrived—stripped of his clothes, naked and very white on the marble table, his head resting on a dark wooden block. An hour and a half ago, he was still alive, a man whose life was precious to us, touched only by hands with sterile gloves, seen only by those wearing masks. And now his dead body was of great worth to those gathered to witness its dismemberment—some twenty pathologists, physicians, and members of our team, standing in a group around the table.

I tried not to look at him—especially at his eyes. There was a side table where they would eventually put the separate organs—beginning with the heart and lungs—and I looked at that empty table, telling myself it would be easier that way. If I saw only the heart, and the lungs, I would not see the man.

Yet when the autopsy began, I watched it anyway. It was impossible to do otherwise. Professor James G. Thomson, head of the university pathology department, began it with a stroke of the knife, cutting from throat to abdomen and then snipping open the rib cage. After that, he severed the tongue and pulled it out with the esophagus—allowing for removal of the heart and lungs.

The lungs were grossly diseased, filled with blue-green pneumonia, leaving them almost solid with no air space. I thought of Ozzie forcing oxygen into those few small areas, speckled with reddish foci, and how he had desperately looked for some sign of improvement. Nothing would have helped this. It was a disaster, and Val had been right. The heart-lung machine would have been useless.

Professor Thomson made occasional comments as he sliced through tissue and organ: "Clearly, we have confirmation of lobar pneumonia. . . . There is considerable edema, as you can see. . . . Some of the arteries show acute arteritis but this is probably part of the pneumonia and not a rejection process. Now to the heart . . ."

He opened the pericardial sac, and I saw it again—the heart I had held in my hands and sewn into place, the heart that had leaped back into life, red and strong with the miracle of its rhythms. Now it lay there, blue and dead and around it were my suture lines, as I had made then, each one as I had left it—clear and regular, without any evidence of clotting or rejection.

I could take no more and hurriedly left the room, going out the rear door into the animal laboratory and through this to the little alcove where they keep the rabbits. Finally alone, I could no longer contain my overwhelming sadness and began to weep at the terrible tragedy of that little heart, so young and strong and ready to live—killed by two lungs filled with pus.

Where was God when all this happened? It was not fair. We didn't ask for any special favor. We had asked only for a fair shake, an even chance. But what sort of chance was this—to kill that heart before it could begin to live with the man who bore it? If there was a reason for this, what was it?

I opened my eyes to find a rabbit staring at me from a few inches away in a cage—two blue eyes looking into mine, a pink nose twinkling back and forth, all of it throbbing from a little heart beating fast and hard with excitement, all of it asking one question: What's happening?

Jacques Roux came to find me and we stood there without speaking, just looking at the rabbits. All of them wanted to know what was happening. Gentle little creatures, they wanted only to live, and while they were alive, they asked a fair question—the same one I was asking as I wept next to their cages.

There had to be an answer, somewhere, and we would find it if we went on long enough. I spoke to Jacques.

"I think we'd better go back to the postmortem now."

When we entered, Professor Thomson had cut along the aorta into the left ventricle, exposing the valves and also the suture lines. As I came up, he stopped work to look at me—as did everyone else.

"Chris," he said. "These suture lines are perfect—there's not an error or a clot anywhere. It's beautiful."

I looked from him to the other faces around the table. Each one nodded, or in some way said to me: "Well done, Chris."

At that moment I had my answer and I began to build again. I had not failed. I had succeeded. The first attempt, with all its pain and sorrow, had been made for the second. To now turn back would be to deny the first—to turn away from Louis Washkansky's dream.

Leaving the postmortem with Jacques, I said I was going to do another transplant.

"What's more," I said. "I'm going to America and appear on 'Face the Nation.' I'm going to face the world—and then come back and do a transplant on Dr. Blaiberg."

"Provided Dr. Blaiberg is still willing," said Jacques.

"Yes," I said. "And I'd better find that out right now."

When I reached the ward Dr. Blaiberg was awake, and his wife, Eileen, was sitting with him. I had never met her, and he introduced us. After that she began to leave.

"Where are you going?" he asked.

"I'll wait outside," she said.

I knew then that Eileen Blaiberg had not yet told her husband. She knew but she had not told him.

"Don't go, Mrs. Blaiberg. I want to talk to both of you."

"All right," she said, with a sigh.

She stood by the bed and you could tell from the way she looked at her husband that she was worried about what this would do to him.

"Dr. Blaiberg, do you know that Mr. Washkansky died this morning?"

"No, I didn't know it."

"I didn't tell him," said his wife. "I didn't know how to tell him."

"I expected it," he said. "I've been listening to the radio . . . I knew how ill he was."

"I've come to tell you why he died and what we found on examining him."

Dr. Blaiberg nodded and his wife held his hand.

"He died of pneumonia, and there was no evidence, as far as we could see, of a failure of the transplanted heart. But the transplant was a failure anyway, because we kept him alive for only eighteen days. So if you don't want to have your operation, you don't have to go through with it. It's for you to decide."

"Professor . . ."

He stopped to glance at his wife, then continued.

"I want to be a well man, and if I'm not well, I'd rather be dead. How soon can you do the next transplant?"

"Thank you."

"How soon can you do it?"

"I have to go overseas for about ten days, but we'll do it as soon as possible after I come back. In the meantime, I'll have you transferred to my ward."

"More than ever," he said, "I want this to be a success—not only for my sake, but also for you and the other doctors."

"You can help us by doing one thing."

"Yes—what is it?"

"Stay alive until I get back."

"Don't worry," he said. "You'll find me here—waiting."

INDEX

INDEX